KIWIS DO FLY

NEW ZEALANDERS IN RAF BOMBER COMMAND

PJ Wheeler

Foreword by:

JL Munro CNZM, DSO, QSO, DFC, JP
Squadron Leader (retired) 617 Squadron

Published By:

New Zealand Bomber Command Association Inc.
PO Box 180202, Luckens Point, Auckland, New Zealand 0663

2010

All rights reserved: No part of this publication may be reproduced, stored in a retrieval system,
or transmitted in any form or by any means without the prior permission of the copyright holder.

Cover Art By: Leaf Design

Layout and Print By: Longley Printing Co. Ltd

Cover Illustrations:
Front Cover: Clockwise – RAF Memorial Flight Lancaster over Rutland Water 2001 (J. Pote), Mark 8 Flying Goggles, Robin Craw's crew, 7 Squadron Oakington 1944. Mark 1 Navigators Computor. Pilots notes (Air Ministry Official)

Back Cover: Anticlockwise – 109 PFF Squadron VE Day 1945. Raid over Tobruk 1941.
Roy Montrowe's (692 Squadron) Log Book. Lancaster VN-T of 50 Squadron, Skellingthorpe 1944 (H. Cammish).
Flight Lieutenant Les Munro (617 Squadron) is presented to King George VI, May 1943 (L. Munro).

ISBN: 978-0-473-15014-3

Foreword

It has been an unfortunate fact of life since the end of the 1939–45 War that of the just under 4000 Kiwi's that served on Bomber Command and survived the war, very few have told their story of their experiences during their service, particularly during the post-war years.

One reason, and one common to a large number of those who returned, can be attributed to a reluctance to talk of their service years, particularly those involving actual operations of a dangerous nature, and seeing other planes shot down.

A second and perhaps equally important reason was that most of us were far too busy creating a life in civvy street, getting married and bringing up a young family to worry about writing and recording life on operations in Bomber Command and, for that matter, other branches of the service.

In many cases recalling near misses, being injured, badly damaged aircraft, surviving crashes caused emotional and unwelcome distress. However with the healing of time many veterans, with the encouragement of interviewers, have been able to talk of their experiences of some sixty odd years ago. So in the compilation of 'Kiwis Do Fly' the Author has managed to extract from the many contributors recollections of not only the dangerous aspects of their service but also the lighter moments experienced during their service careers. He is to be congratulated for that.

JL Munro CNZM, DSO, QSO, DFC JP.
(Squadron Leader (Retired), 617 Squadron)

Prologue

The time will come, when thou shalt lift thine eyes

To watch a long-drawn battle in the skies;

While aged peasants, too amazed for words,

Stare at the flying fleets of wond'rous birds.

England, so long the mistress of the sea,

Where winds and waves confess her sovereignty,

Her ancient triumphs yet on high shall bear,

And reign, the sovereign of the conquered air

Translated from Gray's Luna Habitabilis, Cambridge 1737

Contents

Foreword JL Munro CNZM, DSO, QSO, DFC, JP (Squadron Leader 617 Squadron Rtd) 3

Prologue 4

Author's Note 10

Introduction 11

Acknowledgements 14

Memories 15

Map 17

Chapter 1 – Why Me!

Introduction		18
I wanted to be a Bomber Pilot	Ted Kepplewhite	19
From Gunner to Fighter Pilot	Jim Sheddan	20
A Zero Op Dam Buster	Arthur Joplin	21

Chapter 2 – The Early Days

Introduction		22
Down in Flames	Jack Shorthouse	23
A Grain of Sand	Roy Montrowe	26
From Vincents to Stirlings	Dick Broadbent	32
Back to the Taxation Office	Jim Dermody	34
Into the Fray at OTU	Jim Dermody	35
Kiwi Mates in Training	Bill Simpson	37

Chapter 3 – Excuse Me I'm On My Way

Introduction		39
From OTU to SOE	Phil Small	40
In the Wrong	Alan Wiltshire	42
Goodbye Rommel, What's Next	Roy Montrowe	44
To Europe from the Blue Pacific	George Hitchcock	46
Potato Peeler to Pathfinder	Jack 't Hart	48
Singapore Sling	Keith Boles	50
Where's the War	Bob Barron	51
A Goldfish First	Harry Saunders	52

Chapter 4 – What a Beauty

Introduction		54
A Slightly Worn MkIII	John Tarbuck	55
A Safe Lancaster	Harry Widdup	56
Good Kites	Jack 't Hart	57
One to Remember	Arthur Joplin	58
Press on Stirlings	Bunny Burrows	59
A Delight	George Hitchcock	59
Mossie for Me	Bill Simpson	60
Nothing Like a Mossie	Ted Kepplewhite	61
Ode to a Mosquito	Anon	62
Vote for Stirlings	Laurie McKenna	63
And What About the Ground Crew	Joe Tomlin	64

Chapter 5 – A Line

Introduction		65
My Friend George	John Tarbuck	66
Long Legs are Advantageous	Ivor Marsh	67
What Ju88	Bill Simpson	67
Ghost of a Whitley	Bill Simpson	68
What's on my Tail	Harry Furner	69
Turn the Lights Out When You Leave	George Hitchcock	69
Mpg	Des Hall	70
Lancaster Vs Mossie	Bill Simpson	70
A Gong for Poker	Peter Booth	70
Welcome Home Once More	Des Hall	71
Praise the Lord	Vic Viggers	73

Chapter 6 – A Dodgy Do

Introduction		74
A Bad Prang	Arthur Joplin	75
Dam Buster	Les Munro	76
Shot Up	Harry Furner	77
Nuremberg	Harry Furner	79
A Skipper at 21	Laurie McKenna	81
Nuremberg 1943 and 1944	Bunny Burrows	82
I Took to My Scrapers	Harry Cammish	82
Court Martial and a DFM Award	Jim Dermody	83
156 (Pathfinder) Squadron	Jack 't Hart	85
A Shaky Start	Des Andrewes	87

Chapter 7 – Time out, On Leave, Watering Holes, In the Mess, OTU

Introduction – On Leave		88
Watering Holes	Various	89

The Service Police	Plonk	90
What Petrol Ration	Harry Furner	91
In the Mess	Bill Simpson	92
Travel Permitted	Doug Taylor	93
Nude Statues	Doug Taylor	93
Nice for Some	John Buckley	94
A Welsh Cousin	Stan Davies	94
Survived the Chop	Des Andrewes	94
Off Duty at the Red Lion	Various	95
Brighton	The Boys Remember	96
Bikes	Anon	97
Is it a Mine	Jim Dermody	98
Becoming a Cardinal	The Boys Remember	99
Where has Everyone Gone	Harry Furner	99

Chapter 8 – Near Misses all in a Days Work

Introduction		100
Follow the Leader	Bill Simpson	101
Not my Funeral	Des Hall	102
Bumps	Ted Kepplewhite	103
That's Not Fair	Roy Montrowe	104
Cookie on My Toe	Bill Simpson	105
Hole in One	Roy Montrowe	106
Oops!	John Buckley	107
Flying's Not Dangerous	Stan Davies	108

Chapter 9 – Gunners Lament

Introduction		109
What Fighter	Harry Furner	110
I'm Going Backwards	Tom Whyte	112
The Air Gunner	NZBCA Newsletter	114
A Fighter Pilot Remembers	Jim Sheddan	115
Recollections of a Rear Gunner	Winkie Kirk	116

Chapter 10 – A Wizard Show

Introduction		117
PFF	Bill Simpson	118
Gestapo HQ	John Buckley	120
Daylight and 30,000 feet	Bill Simpson	122
D-Day and The Invasion	Robin Craw	123
Hitler's Lair	George Hitchcock	124
Dropping Big Ones	Arthur Joplin	126
Flying in Oblongs, Operation Taxable	Les Munro	131
Daylight Raid	Neville Selwood	133

Chapter 11 – Welcome to the Caterpillar Club

Introduction		135
Into the Frying Pan	Stan Davies	136
Bail Out	Winkie Kirk	141
Home via The Pyrenees	Harry Cammish	153

Chapter 12 – Remember This

Introduction		158
NOTAM		159
Form 700		159
Aircrew Alphabet		160

Chapter 13 – Gallery

161

Chapter 14 – Special People

Introduction		177
Brothers in Arms	The Shorthouse Family	178
Born to Lead	Stephen Watts	183
An Exceptional Young Man	John Thomson	189

Chapter 15 – Keeping Lucky

Introduction		193
What Oxygen	Keith Boles	194
Low Flying is Fun	Les Munro	195
A Stuff-up is Always Fun	Harry Widdup	196
To Berlin in a Big Wind	Des Andrewes	197
Our Last Op	Jack Owen	199
Diversions	Bunny Burrows	202
Altimeter Check	Robin Craw	204
It's all Over	Colin Emslie	205

Chapter 16 – The Other Half

Introduction		206
Canada Oh Canada	Mary Shorthouse	207
Arrested	Jopie 't Hart	209
Sister Sunshine	Bill Simpson	210
Blitz Nurse – Once a Kiwi	Jim Dermody	211
War Bride	Des Andrewes	213

Chapter 17 – Long Service

Introduction		214
In Command: Wingco	Jack Shorthouse	215
One Year Two Tours	Robin Craw	218

Two Tours	Laurie McKenna	220
Pathfinder	Keith Boles	221
617 Squadron	Les Munro	224

Chapter 18 – Thanks for Coming

Introduction		226
Goodbye		227
What's Next		228
Around the World	Keith Boles	229
An Early End	Jim Dermody	230
Welcome Home	The Andes Boys	231

Chapter 19 – Back Into The Blue

Introduction		232
Back Wearing Blue	John Buckley	233
Pacific Blue	Jack Shorthouse	235
Again	John Buckley	236
Nuclear Deterrent	Dick Broadbent	237
Op Number 15 with a 60 Year Gap	Harry Furner	239

Chapter 20 – Casualties of War

Awareness		240
Counting the Butchers Bill		241

Chapter 21 – A Memorial … 243

Epilogue
AVM D. Bennett … 244

Afterword
Sir Winston Churchill … 245

Appendix

1. RNZAF Flying Badges	246
2. The RNZAF at War: Europe and the Pacific	247
3. RNZAF Aircrew Training Scheme	251
4. NX665 New Zealands Lancaster – A Brief History	254

Maps … 257

Bibliography … 259

Glossary … 260

Index … 264

Authors Note

After the publication of 'Wednesday Bomber Boys' in 2005 many members of the New Zealand Bomber Command Association felt there was more to tell, not just of the big events but of the many incidents that occurred during wartime. Today those times are remembered by the veterans as 'the best years of all'.

Old albums have been opened, log books hunted out and memories refreshed. Although now in their eighties, these veteran aircrew can still vividly recall the events of sixty years ago.

This book is not intended to be a definitive history but a collection of memories, most written by the veterans themselves. They give a very personal insight to the days when the 'Chop' could be that night. As veterans numbers continue to fall, this collection will be one of the last compiled from those with first hand experience of those years. A number of contributions are from English aircrew who served with New Zealanders and emigrated here post-war.

Humour and mateship were essential to cope with the stress of operations and the veterans have gladly shared their special outlook on life with me. Thank you, and to the friends, families and researchers who have made diaries, letters and scrapbooks available.

Special thanks for the support and advice given by the late John Barton (Navigator 101 Squadron) NZBCA historical mentor, and to Wing Commander Bill Simpson QSO, DFC (RAF Retired) President of the NZ Bomber Command Association, for the contribution of Squadron Leader Jonathan Pote MBE (RAF Retired) for producing the glossary and index; and finally to Karola Wheeler, Gena Hansen and Carol Longley for the hours of computer work.

My thanks to you all.

The support of the Lion Foundation and the NZ Lotteries Grants Board are acknowledged with thanks.

PJ Wheeler
Auckland, 2010

Photographs

The majority of photographs are from contributors collections, many undoubtably taken by the stations official photographer on Air Ministry equipment and paper and 'purchased' by the crew member. The original source has been noted where known. If copyright has been unintentionally breached we apologise. Please advise the publisher for correction in the next edition. If the reader can add any additional information about any photograph it would be most welcome.
Special thanks to the RAF Museum for permission to reproduce some images and to J. Pote MBE for the use of his RAF Memorial Flight Lancaster photographs.

Accuracy

The text, captions and photographs have been checked for accuracy and detail by both technical proof readers and amateurs. I know some errors will have crept through and new research will add to the detail. Any errors are mine. Veterans memories have been recorded basically as they were told with a minimum of 'scripting' in order to preserve the essential authenticity of the narrative.

Archives

The New Zealand Bomber Command Association welcomes additions to its archives and displays. Records, logbooks and diaries are particularly valuable for research as are 'souvenirs'. Association contact details are on page 2.

Introduction

"Fighters will not stop bombers. Nothing will stop determined bombers. Nothing. Not guns, not balloons, not interceptors or anything else. I have never heard of a formation of bombers turning back even when the odds were against them. I should be a fool to pretend that bombers will have an easy time in the next war. They will not. They will have to fly through hell and back, but they will get there. And that is the point."
 Capt. W.E. Johns, January 1939 – Editor of Popular Flying and author of the Biggles series.

On September 7th 1940 Hitler's Luftwaffe raided London for the first time, killing 437 people. It has been said that over the next five years the population of Greater London faced enemy action every thirty six hours. This was truly the Home Front.

Cities throughout England were 'repeatedly and heavily bombed'. After 'D-Day' 1944, the southern cities and London particularly faced another blitz this time from V1 and the unopposed supersonic V2 rockets.

In Churchill's famous speech about 'The Few' he continued on to recognise that RAF Bomber Command provided the only available offensive weapon against the Nazis until an invasion of Europe. He said:

"Never in the field of human conflict was so much owed by so many to so few <u>but we must never forget</u> that all the time night after night, month after month our bomber squadrons travel far into Germany .... and inflict shattering blows upon the whole of the structure of Nazi Power."

On the outbreak of war in 1939 the RAF could muster 118,000 personnel and 9,343 aircraft (of which just 1911 were considered first rate). The 1911 included several hundred single engine Fairey Battles that were already outdated.

By the end of World War II in May 1945, the Royal Air Force had grown to 1,079,000 personnel, 540 Squadrons and 55,469 aircraft.

During WWII New Zealand (with a population of just 1.6 million), committed troops, aircrew and naval forces to European battlefronts, while maintaining large forces in the Pacific to face a Japanese threat which was much closer to home. The effects of such a huge commitment on such a small Country became so dire by 1944 a manpower shortage forced the Army to become farmers and harvest the country's grain crops.

In 1940 the RNZAF rapidly established aircrew training schools within New Zealand to meet its commitments to the European war while later to man the seven bomber, fourteen fighter and two attack Squadrons in the South Pacific. In addition, two flying boat squadrons were tasked with a patrol area of over five million square miles of the South Pacific ocean. Ultimately the Royal New Zealand Air Force underwent expansion to become 44 times its peacetime size.

New Zealand's commitment to the War effort was huge – by1943 half of the country's total income was being spent on the war, while almost every able adult male was either in uniform or in essential war industries. The country's determination to defend England and New Zealand, and to defeat its Axis enemies, the Germans and Japanese, was total and losses were large.

New Zealand lost 12,050 servicemen killed in action during WWII which represented 0.75% of the entire population. In today's terms, with a population of four million, the equivalent would be 30,000 and in todays political climate such losses would be unacceptable.

Young Kiwis were keen to volunteer for overseas service and many were concerned that it might be all over before they had had a 'crack'. Uniforms, weapons and travel all added to their excitement. The RNZAF was alone in accepting 18 year olds as volunteers, the Army minimum age was 20. The aircrew trainees joining were just teenagers, not entitled to vote nor legally allowed to drink!

By 1942 these trainees could expect to fight the Japanese in the Pacific, the Germans in Europe or be retained to man the increasing number of Air Training Schools and growing RNZAF structure.

From 1939 to 1945 over 6,000 Kiwi volunteers were to serve with RAF Bomber Command. A third of them were killed in action, the official count being 1852. Including losses during service at training establishments, on leave, and in transit the revised total is 2,152, a death rate of 35.8%. By war's end New Zealanders had served on half of all RAF Bomber Command Squadrons.

Kiwis Do Fly

RAF Bomber Commands casualties are well recorded, 55,358 aircrew losing their lives during WWII. In the period September 1943 to September 1944, there was a loss rate of 1,578 every month and 40% of these casualties were volunteers from the Commonwealth. Pilots were at particular risk with almost 50% of all Commonwealth pilots being killed.

Historical debate on the success of the RAF bombing campaign will continue just like the Gallipoli and the Crimea campaigns before it. However the sacrifice made during 1939 – 45 did end in victory. There was no other option.

Albert Speer (in charge of all German War Production) simply stated "the irreparable damage to industrial plants by bombing meant that Germany lost the greatest battle of all."

And what of the effects on those 18 – 25 year olds who flew on operations? David Stafford was the Medical Officer on a Bomber Command station. He observed that:

"For each man there was a constant awareness of danger, danger from the enemy, from sudden blinding convergence of searchlights accompanied by heavy accurate and torrential flak, from packs of night fighters seeking unceasingly to find and penetrate the bomber stream, of danger from collision, from ice in the cloud, from becoming lost or isolated, from a chance hit in a petrol tank leading to loss of fuel and a forced descent into the sea on the way back if nothing worse."

"There was no single moment of security from take-off to touch-down but often the sight of other aircraft hit by flak and exploding in the air or plummeting down blazing to strike the ground an incandescent wreck."

"The chances of any particular individual surviving his thirty trips alive, unwounded, and without having been taken prisoner were generally accepted by the air crew themselves as being one in five."

"Their attitude to losses and death of friends was particularly striking. It was one of supreme realism, or matter of fact acceptance of what everyone knew perfectly well was inevitable. They did not plunge into outspoken expression of their feelings nor did they display any compromise with conventional reticence about the fact of violent death."

They said "Too bad.......sorry about old so-and-so....rotten luck." Their regret was deep and sincere but not much displayed or long endured. They were apt and able to talk of dead and missing friends before mentioning their fate just as they talked of anyone else or of themselves. It took the loss of particular friends or leaders, flight commanders or squadron commanders to produce a marked reaction amongst a squadron. Then they might feel collectively distressed, have a few drinks because of that, go to a party and feel better."

"But they made no effort to escape the reality of the situation nor was there any of the drinking to forget referred to in accounts of flying in the first War. They were young, they were resilient, they lived until they died."

And behind these vunerable aircrews were families; parents, brothers and sisters, uncles, aunts and cousins at home, all very aware of the message that a telegram could bring.

Yet closer to the Bomber Boys daily lives were the hundreds of ground crew and operations staff, essential parts of every bomber station. Without the aircraft riggers, engine fitters, armourers, wireless and gunnery specialists, the radar and radio WAAFS and the planning staff, there could be no raid or continuing offensive. In all, perhaps a team of two thousand supported two dozen crews at a bomber station. All contributed and all felt the loss of a missing crew, some very keenly. Those girlfriends, sweethearts and new wives also just had to bare it.

"You had to be a fatalist. Always the other chap got the chop, never me – until it's my turn. In the meantime let's have a bit of fun!"

It has been an honour to share their memories both good and bad and for a brief moment experience those times.

P.J. Wheeler
Auckland

LEFT: October 2008 and Association members meet to promote a permanent memorial to those lost in RAF Bomber Command service

Left to Right: Des Andrewes (622 Sqn), Roy Montrowe DFC (148, 692 Sqn), Bob Barron (576 Sqn), John Tarbuck LdeH (626 Sqn), Phil Small (148, 624 Sqn), Doug Taylor (57 Sqn), George Hiam (10 OTU), Rt. Hon Bob Tizard (75 Sqn)

ABOVE: March 2009, The NZBCA annual country luncheon – Left to Right:

Standing: Harry Furner (51, 578, 35 Sqn), Tom Whyte (101 Sqn), George Hiam, Frank Prebble (75 Sqn), Phil Small, Des Andrewes, Doug Taylor, Bob Barron, Keith Boles DFC (109 Sqn), Roy Montrowe, Wally Halliwell (Aircraftsman), Des Hall (463, 61 Sqn), Rev Jack Ward (75 Sqn)
Seated: Peter Wheeler, Bunny Burrows (VP), Bill Simpson DFC, President (109 Sqn)

Kiwis Do Fly

Acknowledgements

A special thanks to all of the ex aircrew, their friends and family for providing the material in this book, and for their support.

New Zealanders in RAF Bomber Command – 'Kiwis Do Fly' is dedicated to them and the many who did not survive.

Name	Rank	Squadron	Role	Pages
Andrewes, DY	W/O	622 Squadron	Navigator	87, 94, 197, 205
Barron, RJ	Sgt	576	Navigator	51
Barton, CJW	P/O	101	Navigator	165, 167
Boles, KM DFC	S/L	109	Pilot	50, 194, 221
Booth, P (RAAF)	F/O	202	Pilot	70
Broadbent, R DFC, MID	S/L	40, 75	Pilot	32, 109, 237
Buckley, JW DFC	F/L	627	Pilot	94, 107, 120, 233, 236
Burrows, HN	F/L	15, 487, 622	Navigator	59, 82, 202
Cammish, HS	Sgt	50	Flight Engineer	82, 153
Craw, RK DFC	F/L	199, 7	Pilot	123, 204, 218
Davies, GS DFC	F/L	75	Pilot	94, 108, 136
Dermody, JM	F/L	99, 75	Navigator	34, 35, 83, 98, 211, 230
Emslie, CC	F/O	75	Navigator	205
Furner, HJ	Sgt	51, 578, 35	Air Gunner	69, 77, 79, 91, 110, 239
Hall, WD	F/Sgt	463, 61	Flight Engineer	70, 71, 102
't Hart, J DFC*, FC (Neth)	S/L	103, 156	Pilot	48, 57, 85, 209 (Mrs)
Hitchcock, GC DFC, MiD	S/L	6 (RNZAF), 635	Pilot	46, 69, 124
Joplin, AW	F/O	617	Pilot	22, 58, 75, 126
Kepplewhite, E	W/O	90, 487	Pilot	19, 61, 103
Kirk, ACF	W/O	75	Air Gunner	116, 141
Marsh, I	F/O	298	Pilot	67
McKenna, LD DFC	S/L	101, 75	Pilot	63, 81, 220
Montrowe, RJ DFC	F/L	148, 692	Pilot	26, 44, 104, 106
Munro, JL DSO, DFC	S/L	97, 617	Pilot	76, 131, 195, 224, 229
Owen, J (RCAF)	W/O	7	Flight Engineer	199
Saunders, HW	Sgt	202, 356	Flight Engineer	52
Selwood, FN	F/O	75	Navigator	133
Sheddan, CJ DFC	S/L	485, 486	Pilot	20, 115
Shorthouse, JS DFC, MiD	W/C	12, 44, 189	Pilot	23, 178, 207 (Mrs), 215, 235
Simpson, WJ DFC	F/L	109	Pilot	37, 60, 67, 68, 70, 92, 101, 105, 118, 122, 210
Small, PH	F/O	624, 148	W/Op, Dispatcher	40
Tarbuck, JP CdeG	F/O	626	Pilot	55, 66
Taylor, DP	F/O	57	Air Gunner	93
Thomson, JF DFC*	F/L	12, 156, 627	Pilot	189
Tomlin, RN	Sgt	75	Engine A/C Fitter	64
Viggers, VC DFC	F/O	98, 101	W/Op, Gunner	73
Watts, SD DSO, DFC, MiD	Wg/Cdr	77, 692	Pilot	183
Widdup, H DFM	Sgt	100	Flight Engineer	56, 196
Wiltshire, AS	Sgt	75, 550, 207	Navigator	42
Whyte, TB	P/O	101	Air Gunner	112

NB. Wartime Rank and awards.

Memories

From an Aircrew Veteran

Those days of sixty years ago are not so long ago now.

*The memories of our best years still vivid, and even now
bring a lump to my throat and a tear to my eye.*

*So many lost friends, a squadron of ghosts,
we were closer than any married couple could ever be.*

Shared hopes, fears and terror, I relied upon you all for my life.

We braved the sorrow of seeing them chopped down but remember them still.

We who returned are less every year but not old or infirm, we are still in our prime.

I remember it all so clearly, yet not the events of last week.

I may just go back there and stay a while this time.

"I never thought what it meant to my parents when I volunteered nor their worry when I went overseas."

"I never thought what my daily letters meant to mother, nor what the casualty lists the papers published every day meant to the neighbours."

"I never thought my time was up, the others always copped it, but not me."

"A war bride, a son, the end of the war, I never thought it could be me."

"But I think now, a half century and ten later –"

"I never thought I'd be here while my ghostly mates await."

"One day I'll think again of the times we were invulnerable."

J T M 2000

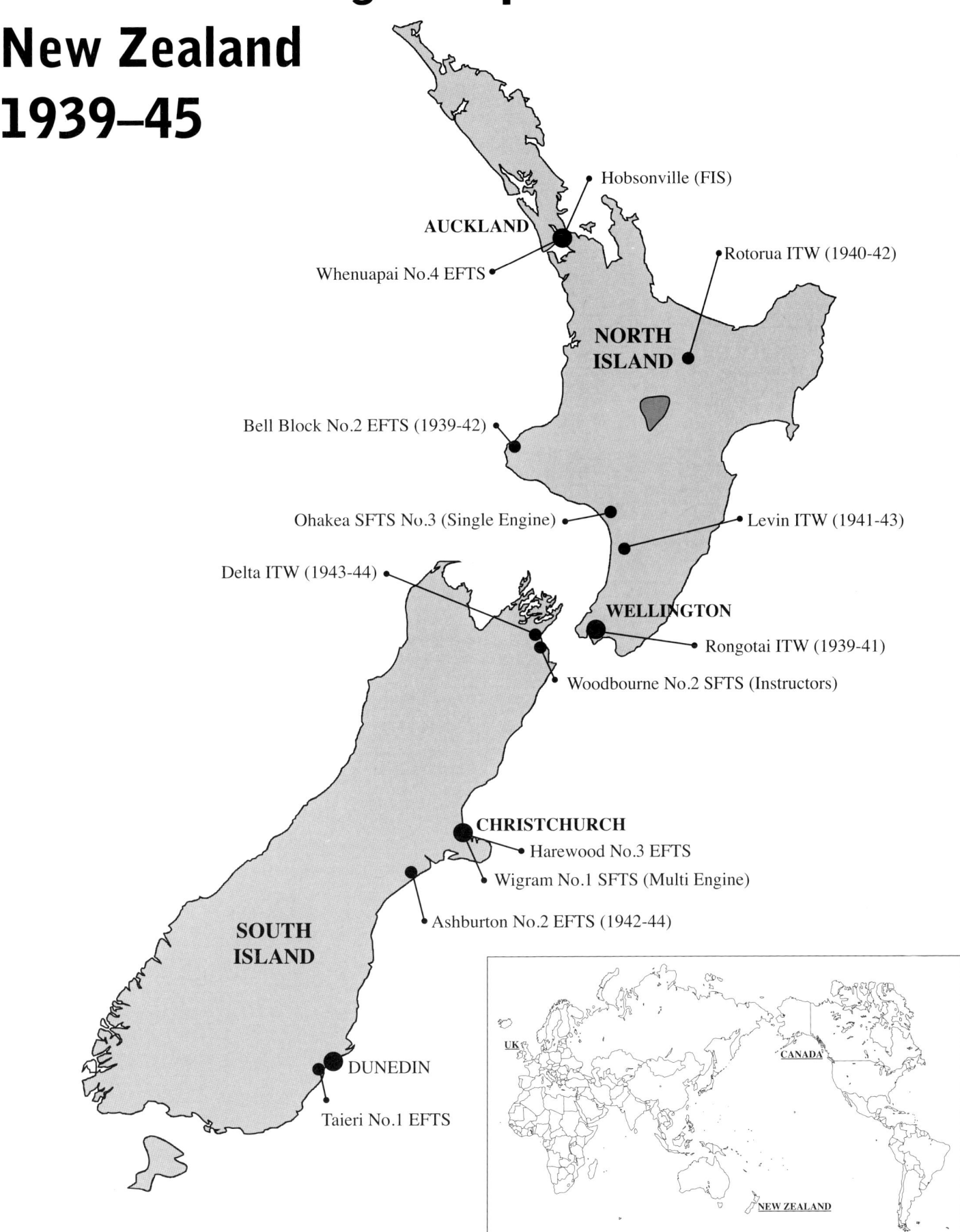

Chapter 1

Why Me!

During WWII the apparently simple task of 'joining up' wasn't at all simple. While the RNZAF accepted eighteen year old volunteers, the Army required men to be twenty while the Navy had their own selection processes including boy entrants at fourteen.

Having been accepted into the RNZAF, early War Courses were overwhelmed and many successful entrants were often sent back to their civilian duties to await call up.

With the sudden entry of Japan into the war, New Zealands own security was at risk. With the majority of our professional forces overseas, those already enlisted in Army, Navy or Air Force were quickly remustered to defend the country's shores often without any weapons.

Eventually those progressing through the RNZAF entrant scheme were screened for aircrew, technical, trade and general duties. In retrospect it seems that the screening was heavily influenced by the needs of the time. "Need more pilots yes," "but I enlisted as a driver," "bad luck, there's a war on don't you know!" So expert mathematicians became riggers, not navigators, gunners became pilots and yachtsmen became flying boat captains.

The posting may at times have been surprising but the need was urgent.

Chapter 1 – Why Me!

I Wanted to be a Bomber Pilot

"After joining up in 1939 I went through the normal flying training scheme and ended up as a junior flying instructor at RNZAF Wigram. We had some of the early Harvards supplied by the US and eventually I learnt safe aerobatics."

Keen to get into the real war, Ted applied for a posting to England. He was duly accepted and shipped via Capetown to England for further training.

"I finally arrived on 90 Squadron and their Stirlings during 1943. The Squadron was based at Wratting Common at the time and our crew settled into Station life pretty well. By the time I'd flown nine operations, my confidence was growing but I was pulled off Ops and posted to 12 AFU then on to 1536 Beam Approach Training Unit (BATU) at Spitalgate."

"With BAT we were expected to be 100% accurate and know where we were at all times. My instructor (a South African named Fred Snout) said during one flight "you know where you are, don't you," and threw the navigation map out the window. "Now find your own way home." I did, but with a bit of a sweat up. It's the Pathfinders for me I thought, but I didn't allow for the RAF's sometimes mysterious ways. I was in fact posted not to the PFF but to the Night Fighter Flight at Harlaxton on Blenheims and Beauforts. The models we flew on familiarisation were crudely modified old bombers so I still felt a return to Bomber Command was likely."

"Later it occurred to me that my liking for aerobatics and with the Stirling quite nippy, perhaps one of my flying exhibitions convinced my 90 Squadron Commander that I was better off in fighters."

"Finally with a posting to Twinwoods and Beaufighter experience I fell firmly into Fighter Command territory."

– Ted Kepplewhite

LEFT: Ted Kepplewhite 2006

BELOW: Flying instructors, student pilots and crew, Wigram 1942. Ted sitting on the ground

19

Kiwis Do Fly

From Gunner to Fighter Pilot

LEFT: Following service with 485 (NZ) Squadron, remustering to an aircraft delivery unit, P/O Jim Sheddan took to the Hawker Typhoon and was posted to 486 (NZ) Squadron.
On 2nd October 1943, his aircraft SA-J (JP676) was hit by flak and he successfully ditched in the English Channel.
He was rescued the following day by an ASR Walrus.
(R. Fulstow, J. Sheddan collection)

Jim Sheddan (later Squadron Leader and Commanding Officer of 486 Squadron) was a fighter pilot and today is a beer brewer of great repute. His tally of seven and a half kills confirmed, makes him an ace. "I nearly became a Bomber Boy, but in Fighter Command we didn't see a lot of them, even on leave they tended to stick together. Pretty quiet actually. I suppose it was due to the nature of the trade they were in."

"On Second Tactical Air Force operations often we'd be providing top cover for returning daylight raids and to see the poor buggers just ploughing along through flak and all, they just kept going. Not for me. It must have taken a special sort to do that."

Jim would suffer the loss of his only brother in RAF Bomber Command. "Our Alex, a Flight Sergeant in 166 Squadron, was killed on 20 December 1943 (in Lancaster R5552 P2-I)) and like so many, was on his first operation."

"At the time I'd been in England on Spitfires since 1942 and knew of the high losses, but it still came as a shock. Mother never really got over it."

But Jim very nearly also became 'a special sort.'

"Like everyone else, I volunteered for the RNZAF to be a pilot but missed the cut and was remustered into Air Gunnery and was certainly destined for Canada and then Bomber Command. I had a good eye and could hit most things with a rifle or shotgun but a lack of schooling left me shy of the arithmetic side of things. So I thought bugger this. If I'm to be a gunner, I'll be the best." Many in his class also lacked secondary education so Jim formed an after hours theory course to help them all. The result was he topped the gunnery course with perfect results and was quickly remustered back into the Pilot's Section. That regrading by a now-forgotten RNZAF officer would cost the Germans seven and a half aircraft and nearly a dozen V1 missiles shot down.

In April 1945, patrolling the Denmark-Norwegian Strait, Jim and his wingman spotted a flying boat. Suspecting it was part of the reinforcement of the planned final redoubt in Norway (the Luftwaffe were at the time transferring many of their latest weapons including Arado 232 jet bombers, high ranking officers, SS infantry and loot), Jim's Tempest easily caught up and opened fire with its four 20mm cannon. Eventually his magazines were empty. Other than a motor or two out the Blohm und Voss Bv222 just carried along. Jim called in his Wingman who likewise emptied his cannons into it.

Very gracefully this large aircraft landed, the crew and passengers took to the life rafts and finally to Jim's relief the flying boat sank.

"The Second Tactical Air Force wouldn't credit me with it though, officially it was logged – destroyed by sinking!"

– Jim Sheddan

Chapter 1 – Why Me!

A Zero–Op Dam Buster

After arriving in the UK in September 1943, Arthur Joplin was rapidly processed through continuation training (on Airspeed Oxfords), 17 OTU Silverstone on Wellingtons (where fellow Kiwi Loftus Hebbard joined as his bomb aimer) then on to 1660 HCU Swinderby (Stirlings) and finally No. 5 Lancaster Finishing School. On August 13 1944, Arthur's crew were posted to RAF Woodhall Spa and a surprise awaited:- 617 Squadron – the famous Dam Busters.

"To say we were non-plussed is an understatement. This squadron drew its members from volunteer second-tour bods or exceptional mid-tour crews, not us sprogs. Apparently 5 Group's Chief, AVM Cochrane felt an experiment with fresh blood was worth trying and we were certainly fresh!"

Arthur Joplin's bomb aimer recalls that it was the following day before he found out that he was on 617 Squadron.

"For the first few days, I kept thinking so here we were in Bomber Command's most famous Squadron with no Ops up on the board. I didn't drink or smoke so finding a mess mate was difficult. We just had to play catch up on so many of the things everyone else took for granted."

"On August 18 1944 I flew as second dicky to American Lieutenant USAAF Nick Knilans (DSO, DFC) on a daylight raid to U Boat pens at La Pallice, carrying a 12,000 lb Tallboy bomb. Nick was an American who joined the RCAF in October 1941 and completed 53 operations with 617. On August 27 we completed our first real Op to Brest carrying twelve 500 pounders."

Welcome to the Dam Busters!

– Arthur Joplin

RIGHT RNZAF: Ashburton 1943. Pilot Training Course No 35, Arthur Joplin bottom left. The white cap flash indicates aircrew status. Arthur underwent two CFI check flights before going solo after nine hours dual

BELOW: RNZAF Wigram 1943. Flying Training: Arthur (left) and his instructor F/O Ebbett after multi-engine training

Chapter 2

The Early Days

From July 1937 until the outbreak of war in September 1939 the RAF held selection courses for pilots in New Zealand.

The few successful volunteers (many thousands applied) were trained to pilot standard either by the RNZAF or by contracted provincial flying clubs.

On completion of these courses, pilots were offered short service commissions in the RAF and left for England and service flying training.

Almost 350 New Zealanders were trained under the War Course scheme and became amongst the first to carry out early Bomber Command raids against Germany.

Along with the pilots posted to RAF Fighter Command these New Zealanders were soon committed to the Battle of France and then the Battle of Britain.

Of these pre-war volunteers, half lost their lives on active service.

Chapter 2 – The Early Days

Down in Flames

When Jack took the Wanganui Aero Club Moth ZK-AAX on his first solo on May 4 1939 he never dreamed he would be bombing German tanks in France just a year later.

Holding a pre-war RAF Short Service Commission, Jack arrived in England in early 1940 and was immediately posted to 207 Squadron at Benson for continuation training on Fairey Battles. With the Battle of France in full swing, Jack transferred to 12 Squadron at Echimines during May. Leaflet drops became bombing raids in June and the Squadrons casualties were horrific.

On June 11, Jack, with rear gunner LAC Copley and navigator/bomb aimer Sergeant Cotterill, took their fully laden Battle (L5324 PH-A) to the front lines in an attempt to cut bridges and thus slow the German advance.

Messerschmitt 109s soon found them and the large slow Battles had no chance. Three 109s took a particular liking to Jack's A-Apple and stern attacks soon killed LAC Copley, smashed the instrument panel and set the Merlin engine ablaze. "I opened the canopy but that sucked the flames into the cockpit so I shut it again but it got terribly hot so I got off my seat mighty quick and stood on the wing. I watched open mouthed as a line of bullet holes marched along the wing past me and up over the engine cowling, all in slow motion. The appearance of each hole seemed to fascinate me. I turned around to see Cotterill still in the aircraft so I climbed back into the cockpit and crouched on the seat, pulled the pole back but the flames were spreading quickly.

ABOVE: Jack Shorthouse at home 2006

BELOW: Fairey Battle L5324 PH-A of 12 Sqn in flames as Jack bails out in the dusk of 11 June 1940
(John Crisp, Jack Shorthouse collection)

23

Kiwis Do Fly

Finally I couldn't hold the Battle any longer, my fingers and chest were getting pretty burnt so over the side I went. The 'chute' opened fine and I landed quite safely. There wasn't a sign or sound of life, no birds, no cows or dogs, nothing. It was quite eerie."

"At that stage my burns weren't troubling me; I was more concerned about the Germans and the French so I hid in a hedge. Some time later (maybe the next day) my hands were giving me hell and when I spotted a van with Air Force roundels on the door, I yelled and waved. It was a Belgian Air Force ambulance. Like everyone else they were headed for the west coast."

"The roads quickly became blocked with refugees. Some tried to take the ambulance, and at times they became quite menacing. We eventually came across a nunnery and thought we would see if there was anybody that could dress my wounds. The nuns were very helpful but very drastic with their treatment. They dipped my hands into what felt like raw lysol. Whatever it was, it caused me great pain."

"By the third day or so, our fuel was getting short and the driver showed me on a map where we were. Fortunately, with a minor deviation, we were able to locate the airfield near Echimines where I had taken off from on June 13. We were very lucky to find some aviation petrol left by the departing engineers. Our Belgian AF ambulance ran on aviation fuel well enough to carry us a long distance."

"I was becoming delirious by the time we reached St. Nazaire two days later but my luck still held. In the organised chaos at the port we were able to find the Royal Navy boarding officer for evacuees. I was put on to a stretcher then carried aboard a destroyer. We set off for the 'Lancastria' which was moored in the harbour. En route the destroyer fouled a mooring buoy and we came to a halt. The Luftwaffe arrived and started bombing the port, eventually sinking the Lancastria. After discussion, it was decided to move me and other wounded personnel to a nearby P & O liner. We were taken on board and headed for Plymouth."

"Once in hospital, other than saying who I was, I was totally unable to prove it as my uniform had been burnt off me. I was badly burnt, but after some garbled

ABOVE: 12 Squadron Battles lined up at Echimines 1940

BELOW: Log book entry recording Jack's downing and his return to flying ten weeks later

Chapter 2 – The Early Days

conversation with the local RAF Doctor I remembered my Aunt's address in Portsmouth (which also happened to be my birth place). Within a day she and my cousin arrived to identify me."

After a considerable time in hospital, Jack was posted to Heston PRU on Sept 1 1940 and began flying Spitfires on photographic reconnaissance.

Unfortunately, the high altitude flying at that time (35,000 ft) didn't suit Jack. "I was very lonely, flying an aircraft with no guns, no radio, not pressurized, only a supercharged engine, extra fuel and camera, and no crew. Basically a high-powered camera bag. It was decided that because of my health that I could no longer carry on and I was posted to 32 SFTS Ternhill. Shortly after, the entire station was posted to Moose Jaw, Canada (32 SFTS was one of three RAF run flying schools relocated to Canada)."

– Jack Shorthouse

POSTCRIPT
The Belgian driver who had picked up Jack was given a note of commendation by the RAF boarding officer. The 'driver' turned out to be Baron Allard. The final part to this story came in 1965 when Jack was flying Air NZ DC 8's to Hong Kong and finally met his 'driver' for the first time in 25 years.
Sergeant Cotterill became a POW. He escaped and returned to England and went back in Ops only to be shot down again.

ABOVE: Squadron log for 13 June 1940 showing the loss of L5324, L5580 and L5531. Take-off was recorded at 1730, L5324 eventually crashed near St Barthel

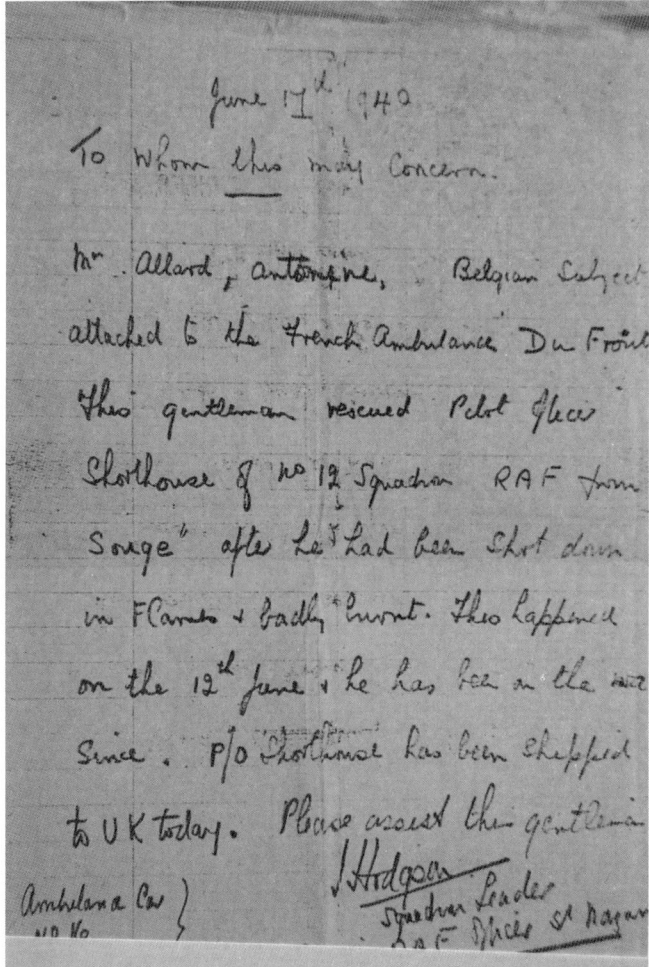

ABOVE: The written request by Sqn Ldr Hodgom to assist Baron Allard, Jack Shorthouse's rescuer

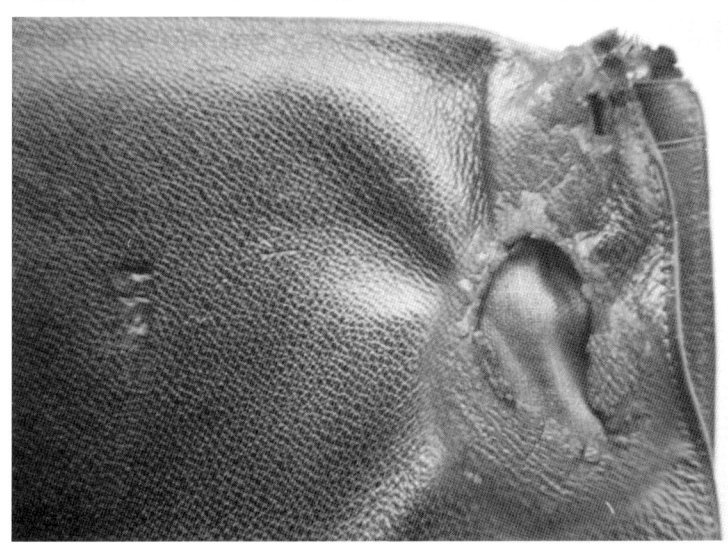

LEFT: The wallet carried the day he was shot down, still showing the burn marks

Kiwis Do Fly

A Grain of Sand

For New Zealanders, the Desert War in North Africa was in everyone's mind as it involved thousands of New Zealand soldiers of Freyberg's '2nd Div. boys' fighting Rommel. Similarly the naval battles in the Mediterranean and the defence of Malta were well known back home, yet little was heard of the desert air war, especially the operations of 205 Group RAF.

Flying 'clapped out' machines and fighting a constant battle with the dust, sand and flies meant aircraft maintenance and Squadron life was carried out in appalling conditions and it required a huge effort to maintain nightly bombing raids against Rommel's supply ports.

The following extracts from Sergeant Roy Montrowe's diary are an insight to a largely forgotten part of this campaign. These unedited notes give some idea of the problems the ground and air crews faced every day.

The operational hazards, night fighters, flak and searchlights are commented on in a very laconic manner, without dramatics.

"We met, crewed up and trained on a Wellington Ic at 11 OTU, Harwell, in April and May of 1942. Our crew consisted of myself, (Captain), Stan (Co-Pilot), Guy Soulsby (an English Nav/BA), Johnnie Reekie (Canadian Wireless Operator), Eddie Cooney (Canadian front gunner) and Les Mears (English rear gunner). We were all Sergeants with the exception of Guy whose Commission came through while we were at OTU. On completion of our training on May 18th, we were posted to a Ferry Flight in preparation to flying out to

ABOVE: 16 June 1942, HX440 (Jukebox) RAF Harwell before departure to Egypt via Malta. This Wellington Ic was nicknamed "Jukebox" as the Canadian Front Gunner Eddie Cooney had a gramophone player that went everywhere with him, including on the aircraft.

ABOVE: Airfield Beat Up by Roy Montrowe at LG106 on 14th November 1942 flying 'Z'
NB: The cyclist wasn't blown over, but the CO was not impressed!

ABOVE: On leave. P/O Roy Montrowe at Helwan, (Egypt) showing the effects of a Desert diet and gyppo tum

Chapter 2 – The Early Days

the Middle East and so missed being rostered on the first 1,000 Bomber Raid. Our OTU instructor, with a new trainee crew, did not return from that raid."

"On June 18th 1942, after coping with several test flights, aircraft unserviceability and awaiting suitable weather, we finally departed from Portreath in Cornwall along with several other aircraft bound for the Middle East. We took off in the dark flying a heavily-laden Wellington Ic (HX 440) packed with spare engines, aircraft parts, stores, baggage and what have you. We landed at Gibraltar after a 7 hour 45 minute flight."

"Next day (19th June), we departed Gibraltar at noon for Malta, flying off the north coast of Africa. We had been warned and were very aware of the Italian and Vichy French fighter squadrons based in Algeria and Tunisia. Approaching Cape Bon (in Tunisia), our final turning point for Malta, we encountered severe thunder storms, lightning, very heavy rain and nearly missed the turn due to the poor visibility. Because of the bad weather we were vectored into Malta on QDMs (headings from the ground direction finders) and landed at night after an 8 hour 35 minute flight."

"We had less than an hour on the ground for refuelling but no servicing as Malta was under constant threat and attack from the Luftwaffe."

To quote 'Wellingtons in Malta' (published by George Cross Island Association), "Refuelling aircraft at Luqa, especially Wellingtons, was a very primitive operation. The fuel came in hundreds of four gallon tins, mostly brought in by submarines. One man stood on the wing with a metal dustbin converted into a funnel stuck into the tank being filled. Another was below with a fire axe with which he knocked an air hole in the top of the tin. The metal cap was levered off, the can was carried up a stepladder for the man on the wing to pour into the dustbin. The petrol load of the Wellington was about 450 gallons. A lot of four gallon tins. The empties were filled with sand and used to make new aircraft pens." Surely primitive days.

"At the last moment we loaded two extra passengers and luggage, an extra 500 lbs on an already

RIGHT: Ju88s dive bombing Luqa Aerodrome in Malta 1942

LEFT: 148 Squadron Al Fresco dining. The Sergeants mess store at LG 237 40 km from Cairo.

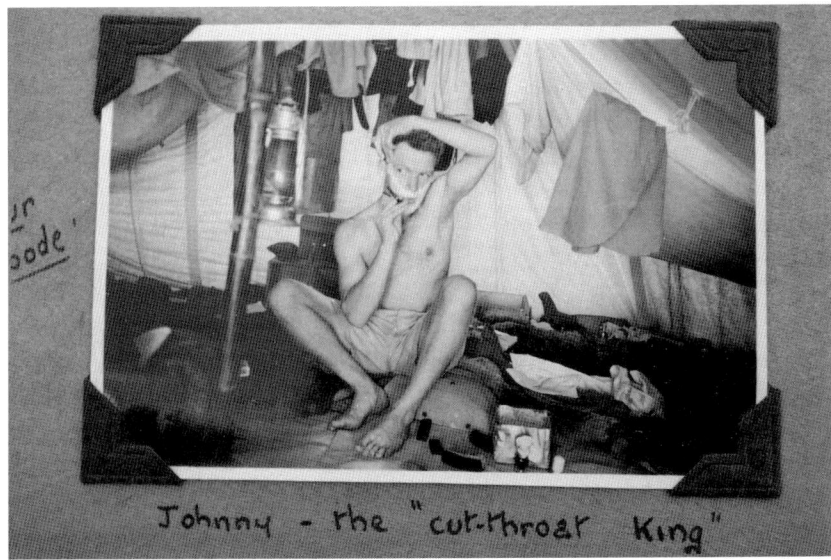

LEFT: Ablutions – A shave in a mug inside their tented home Oct 1942 LG 237

Kiwis Do Fly

overloaded Wimpey! The take-off in bad weather with reduced runway lighting was difficult especially when most of the instrument panel lights failed during take-off. We just made it! Rough flying conditions for the first hour then things settled down, for the 8 hr 35 minute night flight to LG 224, near Cairo."

At this stage Roy and his crew were fresh from OTU without any operational experience.

"We had flown an overloaded Wimpey in difficult conditions for over 25 hours in less than two days, no auto-pilot on those aircraft. We were one of only three crews and aircraft that made the trip within the planned time span out of the twelve despatched from Portreath. Others suffered from various mishaps, unserviceability and two crash-landed after running out of fuel."

"At the dispersal on LG 224, we waited for two hours before we were transported to de-briefing and then on to a small hotel in Cairo. Our Wireless Operator told me that his kit bag and the aircrafts survival kit had gone 'missing' during re-fuelling at Malta. Within two hours of our arrival at the Hotel, my wallet had been stolen. Welcome to the Middle East!"

28 June 1942

The crew as a whole was posted to 148 Squadron at Kabrit, close to the Suez Canal. The airfield was very crowded with several Wellington squadrons (over 54 aircraft) based there. Most were equipped with Wellington Ic's with air cooled Bristol Pegasus radial engines, but 104 Squadron with its Wellington II aircraft, were fitted with Merlin engines. Being liquid cooled these had continuing serviceability problems.

"On the day of our arrival I carried out my first 'Op' under the supervision of Sergeant Porter. He was near the end of his Operational tour, and he flew with us on our first few trips. On this first Op we bombed enemy concentrations south west of Mersa Matruh."

30 June 1942

"Our second 'Op' was a long haul to Crete. Due to very bad weather we overshot the target, encountered a night fighter, had to jettison the bomb load and return to Kabrit, an 8 hr 10 minute trip. Of twelve aircraft despatched only three found the target, others landed in Palestine, and two or three crash landed after running out of fuel. A bad night for the Squadron. As there were no navigational aids every trip had to be by dead reckoning."

Early July 1942

"The Axis was still advancing on Cairo and our kit was sent to Palestine as we were expecting to move there in retreat. Awful food, we were surviving just on bully beef, hard tack biscuits and dodgy water."

5 July 1942

"There were several night fighters over the target at El Daba. Kelly's aircraft was shot up, Wireless Operator killed by a cannon shell and the badly damaged aircraft crash landed at base. On 12 July, New Zealander Bob Coddington joined our crew as co-pilot."

14 July 1942

"Our first 'Op' with me as Skipper. Off to Tobruk in an old clapped out aircraft. (Sprog crews often got

ABOVE: Inside one of 148 Squadrons overworked Wellingtons at LG 237

ABOVE: A good wheels up desert landing, (not mine says Roy)

Chapter 2 – The Early Days

LEFT: Sgt Roy Montrowe's Crew July 1942. 148 Squadron Wellington HX393 in the background.

Left to Right: Les Mears (Rear Gunner) Eddie Cooney (Front Gunner), Guy Soulsby (Nav/BA), Roy Montrowe (Pilot). Bob Coddington (2nd Pilot), Johnny Reekie (W/Op) took the photo

BELOW: Air Raid over Tobruk 1942

the worst aircraft). It struggled for two hours to reach 10,000 feet and cruised at only 105mph. The motors used almost as much oil as petrol with one crew member constantly pumping oil from the reserve tank to the motors. Tobruk was obscured by low cloud so we bombed Sollum. A nine hour trip. The aircraft was then grounded."

15 July 1942

"A 104 Squadron aircraft returning from an aborted trip with a faulty motor, swung on landing and collected the Chance light and the motor pool before catching fire. One aircraft, one Chance Light, five lorries, one car and several runway lights all destroyed."

16 July 1942

"Another Tobruk trip, we were coned by searchlights over the target and held for ten minutes in their beam, a great target for the flak. We finally managed to evade the attention but were caught again by a searchlight on leaving the target. This took us 8 hours 40 minutes."

18 July 1942

"Tobruk, yet again. Over the target the starboard engine lost oil pressure, with high temps and fluctuating revs. We bombed the target. There was increasing and more accurate flak. (Blown gaskets apparently caused our engine trouble)."

21 July 1942

"An aborted trip to Tobruk due to a faulty port engine. We returned to Kabrit direct instead of via the safe corridor and thus set off air raid alarms at Port Suez, although we did have IFF (Identification Friend and Foe) on, and also all navigation lights. I had big strips torn off me by the Group Captain Commanding Kabrit, the Squadron Commanding Officer and finally our Flight Commander. There wasn't much skin left!"

24 July 1942

"A bad day for Kabrit. While loading a 40 lb anti-personnel bomb on a 108 Squadron Wellington, the armourer dropped it and it exploded. Four men killed, three aircraft burnt out. Other bombs exploded, plenty of shrapnel and bomb pieces flying everywhere. One nose-cap landed just 12 feet in front of me and I was some distance from the explosion!"

25 –26 July 1942

"All of our gear is packed, all tents down and folded ready to move out on one hours notice. I suspect an enemy break through at Alamein. Spent a most miserable night among packed gear. Heavy dew, all soaked, and no food!"

25 July 1942

"104 Squadron went to Tobruk, nine went out, two returned and two crash landed in our territory, others missing. A really unlucky Squadron with a lot of engine unserviceability."

26 July 1942

"Target el Daba area. Stooging along at 6,000 feet we suffered almost a direct hit from flak, and holed in several places. This really gave us a shake up."

28 July 1942

"On the way home from Tobruk we were plotted and straddled by several ack-ack shells, bursting just beneath us. The aircraft went into a steep diving turn – 360mph registered on the clock before we were able to pull it out, lots of fabric torn from the fuselage. Trip 8 hours 35 minutes. Spent 45 minutes over target."

30 July 1942

"Another long Tobruk trip. Coned by searchlights over the target and had heaps of flak thrown at us. Lots more searchlights and flak defences now at Tobruk as it now is the main supply port for Rommel. There's a particularly large and accurate battery at top end of the harbour we know as 'Fat Eric.' Ops are getting tougher and night fighters are now also present over Tobruk. 148 Squadron carried out 333 Ops in July of which 'B' Flight (ours) carried out 186."

Kiwis Do Fly

Early August 1942

"We've had several more Tobruk trips and various encounters with flak and searchlights."

3 August 1942

"I was roped in to act as pall-bearer for a crew member drowned when a Wimpey crashed into the lake following a motor failure just after take-off. He had been in the water for a few days and the stench was awful. As I saw the dung beetles scurrying over the coffin in the grave I could not but think, what a terrible way to go."

12 August 1942

"My tent-mate and closest friend was badly injured when another Wimpey of the same Squadron crashed into the same lake following an engine failure just after take-off. He survived, but two other crew members drowned. While the lakes were good navigation aids, if you lose an engine on take-off it is into the drink as the takeoff was over Great Bitter Lake."

19 August 1942

"Moved up to LG 237: just a sand landing strip with no messes, no ablution blocks, no buildings. We are crowded into a low-level tent, terrible living conditions with no fittings of any sort, we are sleeping on the dirt floor. No wonder we were allowed to bring only half of our personal gear. No rest for us as off to Tobruk the same night! Lots of ships in the harbour, had a good bombing run."

24 August 1942

"Another Tobruk trip. Heavy flak over the target again, we landed at 3 am to a breakfast of a cheese sandwich and cold tea!"

25 August 1942

"Told to pack up ready to move in an hour. We sat in the heat and flies all day then slept amongst our packed gear at night. A most miserable day with no food."

26 August 1942

"Repitched tents and unpacked gear. Another Tobruk trip."

1 September 1942

"We bombed enemy concentrations in the battle area but more engine trouble. A 104 Squadron aircraft had crash landed on the runway, so I landed on the sand and gravel parallel with the runway."

3 September 1942

"At 2,000 feet after take-off the port motor cut, and kept on cutting with boost dropping right off. Had to jettison bombs as we were losing altitude and returned to base with a low 600 feet ceiling. A rather hairy experience."

8 September 1942

"Op to Tobruk again, lots of flak and searchlights with new batteries of ack-ack guns. Starboard engine trouble with low oil pressure but it was kept going by continually pumping oil to the motor. We had a 500 lb bomb hang-up and couldn't get it to jettison. It dropped off on landing and tore through the bomb doors, bounced off the runway, back aboard, tore a big hole in geodetics, rebounded off the runway again and took away part of the tailplane. We were a very shaken crew and had a badly damaged aircraft. The engine fitters told me the next day that the starboard propeller was about to fly off or seize due to lack of oil. Our lucky night."

"A few nights later another Wimpey landed on a strip with a 500 lb bomb hang-up which dropped off on touch down, exploded, and completely demolished the aircraft killing all the crew. When I visited the site a few hours later a native employee was shovelling sand on to a still smouldering corpse. What a terrible smell of burnt human flesh."

"During September we had odd Ops to Tobruk but a shortage of serviceable aircraft and lack of bombs meant we were stood down on various days. We often hitched rides on trucks to Cairo, 40 kilometres away, to buy a decent meal and have a shower."

21 Sept 1942

"We lost the generator, all radios,

ABOVE: November 1942 at LG 109, Johnny and Bob Coddington on a German tank

IFF and the aircraft communication system but carried out the raid successfully."

30 Sept 1942

"To Tobruk, on the long way home the starboard engine packed up, no oil pressure, unable to land at fogged in LG 237. Finally after an eight hour trip, I got in at Abu Sueir with little fuel left. The fog rolled in just after we landed. We were lucky."

5 October 1942.

"The Squadrons 'B' Flight lost two aircraft out of four sent on Ops last night. Both had new Captains."

11 October 1942

"Tobruk. Bombed defences south of the harbour. It was a rare good trip but a 250 lb bomb hung-up, then dropped through our bomb doors badly damaging them. Two other aircraft also had hang-ups."

13 October 1942

"Wellington "M" crash landed on the airfield and burned out. 'Z' landed with a bomb hang-up which fell off and badly damaged the aircraft. Kelly of 108 Squadron got badly shot up along with two others. We weren't on Ops that night."

15 October 1942

"To Tobruk. Got caught in

Chapter 2 – The Early Days

LEFT: Before our last Op (November 10 1942) carrying 250 pounders and flares LG 237

searchlights but managed to get free of them. Bad weather with thunder storms, lightning etc. Only a few aircraft found the target."

16 & 17 October 1942

"Off on a short leave to Cairo, big sandstorm blew up and was followed by heavy rain. Bob and Guy had a breakdown in their truck and spent the night as guests in a native police station, wet and uncomfortable. On return to LG 237 we found that many tents had blown down and all of our gear was saturated. What a night, what a place, what a war!"

24 October 1942

"Big push by the Allies at Alamein. Our targets in the battle area on enemy concentrations etc."

8 November 1942

"Bombing Hellfire Pass from 3–4,000 feet. We had flares dropped above us and were targeted by the light ack-ack."

10 November 1942

"Bombed enemy convoys along Tobruk – Ghazal Road and saw aircraft shot down over Tobruk. 'K' from our Squadron failed to return. We had four rodded 250 lb bombs hang-up which we were unable to dislodge."

"We discussed roping the bombs to the floor geodetics but finally dislodged them by force after chopping through the flooring!"

13 November 1942

"We moved up to LG 106 near Duba. Two Squadron aircraft pranged on take-off for Benghazi and another pranged on landing. Six Wellington Squadrons on the airfield makes it very crowded. There's little food and lousy conditions. Heavy rain on 16th, everything flooded and tent wet through again."

15 November 1942

"Another move this time to LG 109 somewhere south of Fuka."

21 November 1942

"The Squadron was down for Ops to Crete but we were suddenly told we had finished our tour. My log book shows 42 Ops; we had done the most Tobruk trips (22). Apparently we had officially completed our tour a few trips previously but had been kept back to bomb and harass the fleeing Axis."

"I was posted back to Helwan on 24th November enduring a 16 hour trip on the back of a lorry. At that stage, I and the rest of the crew and the Squadron I guess had not had a shower or a proper wash for five weeks – Ye Gods!! Later, at Helwan, I was informed that my commission had come through two months earlier, I had not been advised due to lack of communication in the desert."

"My memories of life on the Squadron are of the awful living conditions, unbelievably poor food, difficult flying conditions and the rather poor operational performance of the Wellington Ic. The desert conditions resulted in a lot of failures of aircraft engines and components. There was an almost complete lack of navigational aids or radio communications. Most of us suffered from various medical problems, I myself had long bouts of 'gyppo gut' and lost over 25 lbs in weight whilst out in the Middle East."

"Considering the cramped living conditions, lack of messes and amenities and any recreational facilities I think that as a crew we got along fairly well. We had quite a number of very 'shaky' do's including the take-off from Malta and I personally feel that we were rather lucky to get through the tour relatively unscathed."

– Roy Montrowe

ABOVE: Desert Life, Roy pictured outside his 'quarters' complete with NZ Army Lemon Squeezer and, most importantly, a rare beer issue

Kiwis Do Fly

From Vincents to Stirlings via Wellingtons

Dick Broadbent was one of the early War Course Pilot trainees qualifying as a service pilot on RNZAF Vincents on 28 June 1940. With Japan not yet in the war, trained pilots were posted directly to UK and six months after flying the elderly RNZAF Vincent's, Sergeant Broadbent was captain of Wellington T2515 in 40 Squadrons 'A' flight based at Wyton.

On May 27 1941 Dick joined the search for the German battleship Bismark flying with two other Wellingtons from 40 Squadron. They patrolled at maximum endurance over the Bay of Biscay but sighted nothing.

ABOVE: Sergeant Pilot Dick Broadbent 1941

"Operational flying was much less organised than later in the war, we plotted our own courses, flew individual sorties. There was no such thing as bomber streams or concentrated targets." However Dick was destined to be in Bomber Command for the long haul. He finished his 33rd Op on 16 July 1941 (in T2986) against Hamburg. "I still had only 506 hours up and just 135 at night but RAF rules meant a Commission. So off to 12 OTU I went and put in another 1,000 hours, learning to fly better myself, while teaching others."

In mid-1942 the Operational Training Units were combed to provide enough experienced crews to mount three 1,000 bomber raids. The first was to Cologne on May 30th, Dick's Wellington taking two 500 pounders plus incendiaries, then two nights later in T2809 a raid on Essen ended in a DNCO (duty not carried out) when the wireless fuses all blew out. Finally, came the delayed raid on Bremen in X9605 on June 23.

ABOVE: Vickers Vincent, NZ316 (ex K4746) Pilot Training 1940

Chapter 2 – The Early Days

After nine months at 12 OTU and an MiD for his efforts there, Dick converted on to Stirlings at 1657 HCU Stradishall. "I had some excitement on my solos with the old Stirlings, 'O' had a port inner fail during a circuit while 'A' caught fire on landing. We all got out but the aircraft was damaged badly enough to be struck off." After this course he was posted to 75 (NZ) Squadron at that time based at Newmarket racecourse. "The Stirling III's 75 (NZ) Squadron flew were lovely aircraft despite what others said and certainly it was a big step up from the underpowered Ic Wellingtons I'd flown for the past eighteen months."

"The Stirling was highly manoeuvrable although rolls were not approved neither were loops. Its comfort and accommodation was top notch, the pilots seats were just superb. Only at altitude did it suffer from its 100 foot wingspan, we topped out at 15,000 feet in summer and 18,000 feet in winter (I never had a chance to compare it with the Lancaster until after the war had ended)."

Dick was allocated BK778 and began life in 75 (NZ) Squadron. The Squadron was unusual in that 'A' and 'B' flights were coded 'AA' under New Zealand officers while 'C' flight was coded 'JN' and commanded by an RAF Squadron Leader. Geoff Rothwell, ('The Man with Nine Lives'), was 'C' flight commander at the time.

However RNZAF Headquarters were insistent that all 75 (NZ) Squadron flight commanders were to be New Zealanders and by mid April 1943 this had come about with Wing Commander Roy Max (75 (NZ) Squadron Commanding Officer), and Squadron Leaders Jack Joll 'A' Flight, Frank Andrews 'B' flight, and Dick Broadbent 'C' flight Commanders.

"75 (NZ) Squadron did have a 'press on' reputation. I believe the Squadron dropped more bombs than any other in Bomber Command but certainly many crews got the chop early!"

Even in 1945, 75 (NZ) Squadron losses were comparatively high, losing three crews on a raid on Munster on 21st March but these were to be the last of 75(NZ) Squadrons many casualties.

June 1943 was a busy time for Dick Broadbent and his crew. On the 11th in his regular BK778 (JN-U) "we bombed the red markers but were coned by searchlights. The Stirling performed well in these situations, I dived it very sharply and the Flight Engineer, McIvor, burst his ear drums. We came out at 1,500 feet on three engines." On the 25th (again in BK778) Stan Jones the rear gunner shot down a night fighter during a raid on Gelsen, when high level Wanganui target marking flares were used for the first time to achieve a greater concentration of explosive.

Dick completed his second tour with his 65th Operation on 16 September 1943 and was screened from operations and posted to RAF Bomber Command HQ.

"I enjoyed some very interesting postings before being repatriated including, a staff course and spending some time attached to the Third Division HQ of the USAAF Eighth Air Force at Honington."

– Dick Broadbent

27 April 1943, Dick's Stirling is loaded with mines before his crews first solo operation. "Gardening, six veges planted" Dick recorded in his log

Kiwis Do Fly

Back to the Taxation Office

Irish born but New Zealand raised, Jim Dermody was amongst the first Kiwis to be accepted for training.

"With the establishment of the RNZAF on April 1 1937, the RAF decreed that twelve pilots were to be trained at their cost for permanent commissions in the RAF. Twenty two hundred applied and so the RAF allowed another two dozen to be accepted (No 2 Course). As the only RNZAF base (at Wigram) could accommodate just the first dozen, we were allocated around various aero clubs. I went to Rongotai airfield and Wellington Aero Club. By the time we had completed initial instruction, sufficient bunk rooms had been built at Wigram and so back we went in late 1937."

"We were treated like gentlemen, the tone being set by the RNZAF's founder Group Captain Cochrane. The Honourable Sir Ralph Cochrane, later AOC 5 Group RAF, quite a toff. Our uniforms and even our shirts were hand tailored. I was lucky in having Erik Moen as an instructor. He was a peppery Dane but a great guy. On my course was Len Trent, the VC winner. He had a real problem with his instructors."

"The Avro 626 being used for initial training was a delight and I solo'ed happily on it. But the Vildebeest was another story. A beast it was and my instructor didn't help."

"I was confined to bed with a tooth abscess and my instructor couldn't accept this and it all got a bit heated. As a result I was invited to resign and so back to the Tax office I went."

— *Jim Dermody*

RIGHT: Dressed like WWI veterans, War Course Two, pilots in hand-tailored lambskin flying gear, Wigram 1937
Left to Right: Dave Rankin (killed 1940, over France) Les Ransom and Jim Dermody

ABOVE: "A delight to fly, the Avro 626." Only four served with the RNZAF (NZ 201–204). NZ 203 (centre) survived and became ZK-APC. It is now back at RNZAF Wigram museum as NZ 203

Vickers Vildebeestes. From 1939 and after Japan's entry into the war these venerable beasts patrolled New Zealand's coastline and were the RNZAF's only strike force

Chapter 2 – The Early Days

Into The Fray at OTU

ABOVE: Storm mid Atlantic on the Tamaroa, only the masts of the leading ship are visible. The previous convoy had been badly hit by U Boats and this convoy took seven weeks to cross the Atlantic, stopping at Iceland

BELOW: Legendary NZ High Commissioner Bill Jordan at OTU Bassingbourne, December 1940. Note the blackboard order
Left to Right: Ivan Hendrickson, High Commissioner, Jim Catell, Jim Dermody

After Jim's fall from Air Force grace in 1937, he re-volunteered in April 1940 and the Recruiting Officer, noting his file, suggested he apply as an observer.

Following training in gunnery, wireless and navigation (as was the prescribed course then) Jim shipped to England aboard the Tamaroa.

"Being one of the early birds in the OTU system it meant lots of training and VIP visits, probably used as PR exercises to show a Commonwealth united against the common foe."

After crewing up, Jim was posted onto 99 Squadron's Wellingtons at Newmarket. The poor weather was a major problem during early 1941 and Jim's log book shows:

7/4	Target Kiel – Left target at 200'
9/4	Controls iced up
15/4	Ditched bomb load
17/4	10/10 cloud DNCO
20/4	Frozen bomb releases, hang up
12/5	Icing, forced to return
17/5	Abandoned Operation, motor problems
25/5	Target not identified, brought load back

Kiwis Do Fly

The crew's original Wellington LN-B was finally replaced with the reliable X9700 and Jim completed a difficult tour on 17 July, unloading 1,500 lb on Cologne. The effort, difficulties and danger faced in these early days of RAF Bomber Command were in stark contrast to three years later when Mosquitos of the Light Night Striking Force were delivering 4,000 pounders all over enemy territory every night with just a two man crew and a very low casualty rate.

"Once my tour was complete I was posted to 12 OTU as a Navigator instructor but like many experienced airmen 'on rest' I was called in for the 1,000 bomber raids of 1942, Cologne on May 30, Essen on June 1, and the delayed raid on Bremen on the 23rd June."

"While the recall to operations came as a bit of a surprise, we just had to accept it. The nastiest job at OTU was being mustered on to a funeral party, and there were quite a few, OTU fatalities were depressingly common. The worst was when a just-married Wireless Op copped a shell in his back over Germany. The skipper landed at the nearest airfield to get him attention as he was shrieking with pain. Back at base I was detailed with a scratch crew to fly his new wife down to be with him, but he had died by the time we got there, it was an awful thing. My job was to recover the navigation gear, which I did, it was all soaked in Dick's blood."

– *Jim Dermody*

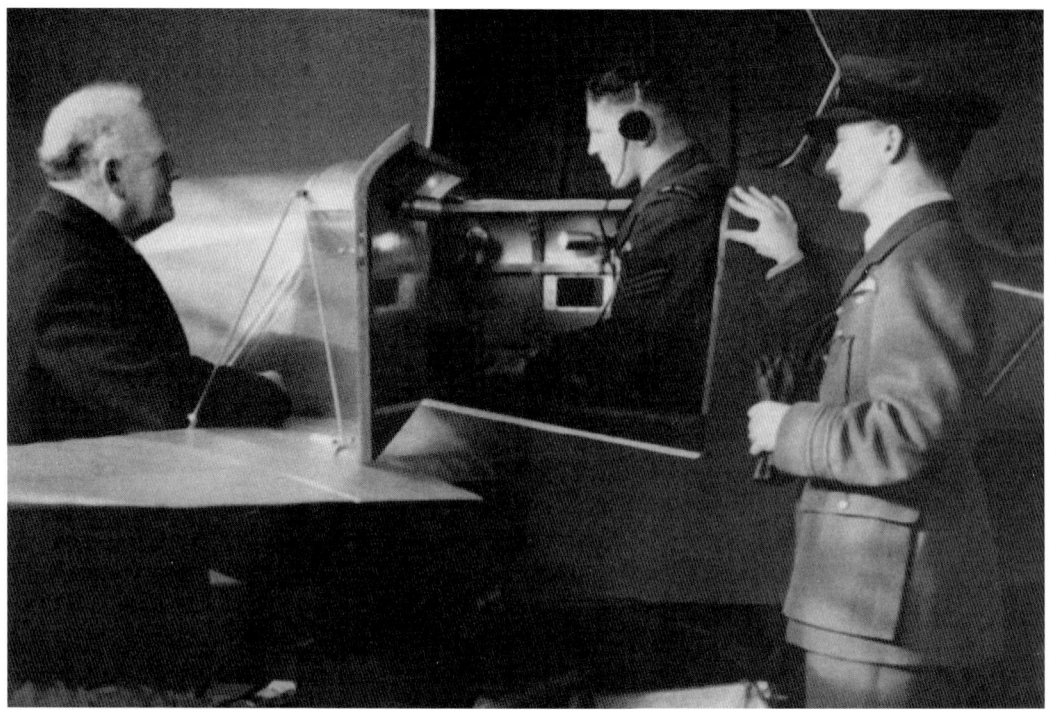

ABOVE & BELOW: Another two of the series taken during the High Commissioner's visit. Link training and inspecting a downed Ju88 at Bassingbourne's satellite airfield. The High Commissioner spent much of his war visiting New Zealanders in all services and was never backward in dealing with red tape or perceived wrong doings by authorities in HM forces

Chapter 2 – The Early Days

Kiwi Mates in Training

In 1941 a new course of would be pilots arrived at the Levin Initial Training wing. Here they discarded civilian clothes for the next five years and were taught how to keep their uniforms clean and tidy with buttons being polished every day. They were housed two to a tent with a boarded floor and were required to keep them tidy with the bedding folded just right.

"My tent mate was Johnny Rothwell from Whangarei and our next neighbours were David 'Wattie' Young from Milford and Pere Morgan from down south, our one Maori on the course. Going through the grind of drill, lectures and study brought us very close together. After six weeks of this we were posted to Elementary Flying Schools to see if we could learn to fly the Tiger Moth. Half of us went to RNZAF Whenuapai near Auckland, the others to Taieri in Otago."

"This was it then. We had to shape up or ship out, and a fair percentage failed to cope or to go solo on the Tiger Moth. They were sent off to retrain as navigators. Our instructors were from pre-war flying clubs and were very hard on us, screaming and shouting into the headphones through a Gosport tube – no radio. I had one instructor briefly who smoked in the air and puffed his smoke into his tube and straight into my helmet, not nice at all."

"After six weeks at Whenuapai, attending lectures and marching everywhere, we were posted to Service Flying Training School, Ohakea to start on Airspeed Oxfords for multi-engine training and Hawker Hinds for the few who planned to be fighter aces."

"During the next six weeks getting to know the Oxford we, the Gang of Four, stuck together all the time, with the same pairs flying together. Once solo in the Oxford, one would fly as pilot and his mate acted as navigator. We had no time off except one weekend between the two six week segments of training, such was the urgent need for pilots. Finally after four months as airmen we were awarded our wings and spent the last six weeks on advanced flying (cross countries, bomb training, and night flying). On went our Sergeant stripes and off on final leave, before going overseas."

"The training was not all simple stuff and many accidents happened. One trainee was killed in a silly Tiger Moth accident and one Hawker Hind in our flight lost his engine and crash landed in the bush. He managed to walk out uninjured and went on to fly Spitfires in England. One Oxford disappeared totally on an exercise and the aircraft and bodies were not found for eighteen months."

"We four mates sailed off for Europe about three weeks later with 35 others on the S.S. President Grant which left Wellington on the 20th January 1942 for Los Angeles. Our first adventurous OE. From Halifax Nova Scotia, we sailed as part of a 56 ship convoy across the Atlantic with just one corvette as escort. Apart from odd U boat alarms (false fortunately) we reached Glasgow after twelve long days. The ship was crammed, the food was awful, many were seasick and all had to do stints at the ships stern on depth charge watch. Later others faced heavy attacks by U boats in the Atlantic crossing."

The initial challenge for would-be pilots was the de Havilland Tiger Moth. De Havilland (New Zealand) produced 350 for the RNZAF from a factory at Rongotai airport, NZ 780 shown

"We saw nothing of Glasgow as we disembarked that night and were put straight onto a train and stepped off it in Bournemouth twelve hours later. We were fed only dry bread and cheese followed by lukewarm cups of tea."

"Once billeted in now empty blocks of holiday flats, we were issued with tin hats and gas masks and were officially at war. We paraded twice a day to learn whether we had been posted. This went on for a week but we were able to have a little fun at night at the dance halls. One night we were in Bobbie's restaurant on top of a largish block and had to rush out because of an air raid. A few nights later Bobbie's ceased to exist when a German mine dropped on it!"

"We were given our first leave of one week and naturally most headed for London. Our first stop was the NZ Forces Club in Charing Cross Road near Leicester Square for information on what to see and to meet or hear about old mates. The NZ Army Base PO was nearby and we would check there for mail or parcels. We mostly stayed in the nearby Strand Palace Hotel as it was reasonable at 12 shillings per night for a twin bed room plus breakfast."

"Back in Bournemouth we paraded again and I was posted (without a by-your-leave) to become a flying instructor. I was still only 18 and was wanting to get into the war but they told me I'd be able to do that in less than a year. So with two other Kiwis, older than I, off to RAF Church Lawford near Rugby. We were the first Kiwis to be selected for this posting. More followed, including the other three of my mates."

"Six weeks later I was a fully fledged instructor and sent to an Advanced Flying Unit at Ossington near Newark. Pilots who had been trained elsewhere, usually overseas, eg. New Zealand or Canada plus American volunteers, were given a month or more on Airspeed Oxfords to learn more advanced procedures and to become accustomed to flying around Britain and its thick fog or mist. Navigation was by map reading, this was not easy and many became lost and landed at other airfields. Night flying was also difficult with the country blacked out and with only a 2-letter coded flashing beacon to identify individual airfields. During my time at Ossington I found I was on night flying instruction for a period of a month."

"Night flying duty held its own excitement and dangers at Ossington. I had just landed when a German aircraft, who must have followed me in, dropped two bombs. One landed in a field short of the runway, killed two cows and the other hit the runway not far behind me. The blast smashed into my Oxford turning it onto its side. My back was hurt badly but I managed to get out safely with help from my pupil. Afterwards I picked up a fragment of the German bomb, a rather thick jagged piece of metal and this is now in the Bomber Command display cabinets at MOTAT in Auckland."

"Soon after we were startled by a Halifax bomber crash landing on our flare path which stopped flying for the night. It was a terrible mess and two of the crew were dead. It was a wake up call on the dangers we faced, but we all knew that it wouldn't be us!"

"My old mate Pere Morgan from ITW days also ended up as an instructor. We sometimes flew together when no pupils were around and one New Year we managed to get away with the station Avro Anson and fly up to Dallachy in Scotland to spend a night with David Young. The other one of the foursome, Johnny Rothwell was based in the Midlands and I only visited once before he was sadly killed by a single engine Miles Master which flew into the back of him. They both went down."

"After a year of instructing I was posted to South Cerney in Gloucestershire where I faced six months more instructing on a Beam Approach Training flight. Finally after two years in the UK I went to war on a Pathfinder Squadron, No 109 flying Oboe equipped Mosquitos on marking operations."

Later, both David Young and Pere Morgan were to fly Mosquitos on what was known as the Light Night Striking Force. Pere was killed when his engines failed and while he baled out, his parachute failed to open. David continued and was credited as the last to drop a bomb on Germany in late April 1945.

"I'm now the sole survivor of the Famous Four (for a time)."

– *WJ Simpson*

**ABOVE: Initial Training Wing, Levin 1942.
Back row: Dave Young 7th from left, Bill Simpson, 8th
Front row: Pere Morgan 3rd from left, Johny Rothwell 7th**

RNZAF Ohakea 1942, with Service Flying School Airspeed Oxfords and Hawker Hinds on the apron

Chapter 3

Excuse Me, Wait for Me, I'm On My Way

In the 1940s New Zealand's young men grew feverish trying to get into the real war. Danger wasn't in their minds, but overseas travel and adventure was. Even if it meant being in a highly explosive aluminium tube flying at 20,000 feet with thousands of enemy shells being fired at them and Luftwaffe night fighters stalking their bombers from the time they left base. These young men thought of themselves as invunerable; "Just let me at the buggers!"

In those desperate times young airmen could find themselves in a front line Squadron with less than 100 hours flying experience and many often added only a few extra before the chop came and finished their war.

Yet others lingered in OTU's or aircrew centres for weeks. Brighton was a familiar home to many New Zealanders waiting to go up the line. The concern wasn't getting the chop but that it would be all over before they had a go!

And for others their posting onto a frontline Squadron in Bomber Command was some time away and their journey was often interrupted.

Kiwis Do Fly

From OTU to SOE

Once released from coastal defence duty Phil Small was one of the stream of RNZAF aircrew volunteers in 1943 following the well worn path to No11 OTU Westcott, via Wireless School in Manitoba, Canada.

At HCU prior to the inevitable posting to a Bomber Command Squadron Phil's skipper applied for an overseas posting. To their surprise they were allocated a Stirling IV to take to Morocco and then on to India.

"Once we'd arrived in Rabat in Morocco, there was no way the Air Group Commander was going to let us leave for India. We were virtually kidnapped and posted into 624 SOE Squadron and Halifaxes." The Middle East Air Force had a reputation stretching back to the Malta days of 'filtering' the flow of aircraft and aircrews bound for India. Phil was one of many who were caught.

Destined never to be the wireless operator he trained for, Phil became a qualified dispatcher. Having survived a four jump course he swapped the Observer badge for a Winged Parachute.

As a trained dispatcher, Phil was transferred onto 148 SOE Squadron. His job was "pushing odd sized bundles into the night plus the occasional Joe (agent). I always made sure I was hooked on as the odd dispatcher had gone out with his load or been pulled out by the agent."

Unlike regular Bomber Command crews, Phil's role saw him on Ops over Southern France, Yugoslavia and Greece flying with most of the Squadron's crews. "As a dispatcher I was mobile going from crew to crew as needed. In fact I flew with sixteen different pilots."

ABOVE: Phil Small's crew at Chedburgh 1653 Heavy Conversion Unit
Left to Right: Jerry Shephard (NZ Nav), Doug Clements (Pilot), Taffy Mathews (F/E), George Sherman (NZ M/UG), Frank Parrott (RG), Phil Small (NZ W/Op), G. Sarsky (B/A) 1944 with Short Stirling BS-E

ABOVE: The main gate at Blida, Algeria, warning those found on the airfield without a pass will be shot, February 1944

Chapter 3 – Excuse Me, Wait for Me, I'm On My Way

"Warrant Officer Jock Hall had done trips to Warsaw in August 1944 and survived (he received the Polish VC) and it was his crew I really became part of, but I was always on call for the other runs."

"Our last Op was on April 2 1945 in (Halifax LL290, FS-N) to Yugoslavia. Jock Halls second tour was finished so the crew was transferred."

"Because of the secret nature of 148's work, my log book was handed in and even at the last reunion we were reminded of the Official Secrets Act. Strange after 50 years."

"Before demobbing, my final post was as an Educational Vocational Officer in Rome so three years after I was posted to Bomber Command I still hadn't dropped a bomb or done an Op over Europe."

— *Phil Small*

ABOVE: On leave at the Hotel Timeo in Sicily 1944

BELOW: Phil with his 'home' crew by LL290 at Brindisi 1945
Left to Right: J. Hall (Pilot), J. Leeming (F/E), G. Ward (B/A), H. Wild (Nav), V. Murphy (RG)
Front: T. Nicholas (W/Op) and Phil Small (right)

ABOVE: The only way to earn a Dispatchers Badge was to do four jumps at Parachute School. Phil on his last jump

ABOVE: Dispatchers badge

Kiwis Do Fly

In the Wrong

When Alan Wiltshire joined up as an 18 year old in May 1942 he certainly didn't expect a three year delay before getting into action.

Although accepted as an RNZAF volunteer, the immediate Japanese threat to New Zealand was so serious that all the available manpower was drafted onto coastal defence.

Alan's job was with an Aerodrome Defence Unit at Milton. In 1943 with American troops now in New Zealand and the Pacific battle at least stabilized, Alan was released. Further delays were caused by Initial Training Wing courses being transferred from Bell Block in Taranaki to Rotorua. In both camps the landing ground and racecourse shared premises and "it seems that HQ felt that new cadets and horses required similar training and housing."

With his initial training and Navigator/Observer training started, Alan was shipped to Canada in July 1943 to complete the course.

By January 1944 (after eighteen months in the pipeline), and now in England, Alan was finally posted on to Flying Unit at Llandwrog, North Wales, then onto 11 OTU Westcott. Heavy Conversion Unit and Lancaster Finishing School (LFS) followed. Now suitably trained after eight months in the UK, Alan was posted to 75 (NZ) Squadron based at Mepal in Cambridgeshire. This Squadron was the RNZAF 'glamour' bomber Squadron, its original Wellington aircraft and crews being 'gifted' to England at the outbreak of war in 1939. "It was a gungho group full of press-on types, and they consequently suffered great casualties."

"I had to fit into this pressure cooker Squadron and our first Op was to Emmerich on the Rhine on October 7, followed by Duisberg on

ABOVE: Cadets 'manpowered,' digging potatoes on Booths Farm, Carterton 1942

BELOW: HCU Stirling BS-N 1651 Conversion Unit Wratting Common 1944. The nose art depicts a witch on a broom

the 14th. On the night of 15th October our Lancaster was in the take-off queue. There was a pranged Liberator just off the perimeter track and in swinging round it, one Lanc ahead of us hit another. There were delays while the wrecks were cleared away but our third Op wasn't destined to be finished. After further delays and much shouting by the Station Commander at last we hurtled down the runway. Our pilot put one wheel into the grass and started a classic ground loop. 400 yards from the boundary he retracted the undercarriage and pancaked us into the dirt. We all got out safely but the pilot copped the Commanding Officer's frustration and he went back to LFS."

The pilotless crew was then sent on to RAF Ganston

Chapter 3 – Excuse Me, Wait for Me, I'm On My Way

to pick up a new skipper, "as I'd run foul of 75's Wingco a day or two earlier, they had to look for a new navigator as well! In the end I was attached to the flight commander's crew lead by Squadron Leader Martindale."

"So far I'd accomplished two Ops and a crash landing and the score didn't improve as Martindale was taken off operations to run a Court Martial."

"The rest of us were sent to help out in the Squadron Records Office; what a mess. It's a miracle that people we posted actually ever appeared again. Just before lunch one day I was told to clean up a crew room by the Orderly Officer. As it was a good half-mile from the mess

ABOVE: 75 (NZ) Squadron, Mepal 1944, under AA-A with its Foaming Tankard nose art
**Left to Right: Jim 'E', Our pilot before going back to LFS,
Alan Wiltshire (Nav),
Ken Futter (F/E), Jim McKenzie (B/A),
Peter Dean (W/Op),
John Valander (RG),
Gordon Burberry (M/UG)**

I told him I'd do it after lunch. So on a charge I went, six months loss of seniority (I was a Flight Sergeant) and a month at the Norton 'rehab' camp. Norton was a discipline camp, square bashing 6am – 9pm and the barbed wire standards faced inwards! However there was a hole in the fence which I'd duck through to go out for a pint at the local pub. One night walking back I was yarning to a Flight Lieutenant, assuming he was an inmate like me and also used the hole. But he wasn't and didn't use the hole but went marching up to the front gate. Next morning I was on a charge and the Flight Lieutenant I'd been yarning to turned out to be the Senior Camp Officer. He gave me another week in rehab."

"Finally in 1945 I was back at the remustering unit alone as my crew had long gone onto Ops with Martindale. I was picked up by an Aussie Skipper Flying Officer Bothy and the remains of his crew and posted in March 1945 to 550 Squadron at North Killinghome."

"Our first Op was to Hamburg and we did another six including Nordhausen in late April. So in three years I'd fitted in nine and a half Ops. We did a couple of manna drops in Holland, brought POWs back from Brussels and did the Bari run bringing Eighth Army troops back from Italy. Those boys had a great swap market going, Army issue blankets for liquor. The poor UK Customs didn't cope at all well with these hard men."

"After VE day we really just messed around waiting to go home. I was posted first to 207 Squadron (Tiger Force) with Flying Officer Roberts then to Spilsby in October. Finally I got the call and left for home in January 1946."

"All in all, I seemed to have spent three and a half years for about 36 hours on Ops."

– *Alan Wiltshire*

ABOVE: The same crew, Alan on the left, showing off the size of a Lancaster's bomb bay

Kiwis Do Fly

Goodbye Rommel, What's Next

Having been 'lifted' from 11 OTU at Harwell in May 1942 and posted to a Ferry Flight, Roy and his crew were presented with a new Wellington Ic and told to take it to Cairo in Egypt and bomb Rommel's Africa Corps.

Six months and 42 operations later, Roy, tour expired, returned to Cairo on a unique journey back to the UK.

"After a sixteen hour truck ride, and full of dust and sand, I arrived at the Air Force transit camp at Helwan in West Cairo. I was told that my commission to Pilot Officer had come through back dated three months to September 16. Communications had been so bad my recall and promotion just never got through. After a bit of leave I thought that a spell at Cairo West OTU instructing on Wellingtons would be likely. But no, the RAF had decided that I was needed back in the UK, and I wouldn't be travelling by troopship."

"I was quickly turned into a civilian, complete with clothes and a passport and on December 22 boarded a Belgian Sabena Airlines Ju52 on a trek across Africa."

"Just after midday on December 22 our Junkers 52 (00-UAG) left Almaza airfield bound for Lagos. Now an officer I was put in charge of a Sergeant and a couple of soldiers who where also enjoying the luxury of air travel."

"The Junkers was very slow with a speed of about 120 mph. We flew low over deserts, scrubland and jungle in bumpy, hot conditions. The three crew members wore pith helmets in the cockpit."

"First stop was Wadi Halfa in British Sudan, a four and a half hour flight. The next day we took off at dawn, refuelled at Khartoum, refuelled again at Malakal (also in the British Sudan) and finally to Juba."

"On Christmas Eve we left before dawn for Entebbe and landed at Stanleyville in the Belgian Congo after six and a half hours flying. Being Christmas Eve we took the chance to see the Stanley Falls. It was strange to be enjoying Christmas in such a foreign place."

"Christmas Day and we were off again to Bangui in French Equatorial Africa to drop off some passengers then onto Lebange in the Belgium Congo for Christmas. This stop was in the heart of the Belgian Congo with only ten Europeans in the place, all worked for Sabena. However we had a great Christmas lunch with a spectacular menu."

"Finally on 26 December we arrived at Lagos after an amazing trip across a continent."

"Two days later (on the 28th) the British Overseas Airways service departed for Lisbon. Myself and a few other 'civilians' and the odd military type boarded the Boeing Clipper G-AGBZ for an eleven hour flight to Bathurst (British Gambia). Refuelled, it took another four and a quarter hours to arrive in Lisbon. The Clipper was comfortable and very spacious, just as well considering the fifteen hour flight. The Clipper was obviously flying to its maximum range as weight restrictions meant that my kit bag with battledress and flying boots was off loaded. Surprisingly the kit bag was delivered to my home address in Canterbury in the middle of 1946, three and a half years later."

"The passport issued to me in Egypt had only one page valid for my stop over in Portugal. I was looked after very well, my 'billet' being the Estoril resort hotel about fifteen miles up the coast. When the departure flight for the UK was delayed three times and took the chance to have a good look around. What was obvious was that the

ABOVE: Christmas Day with the children at Le Bange in the Belgian Congo

BELOW: On the way back to England. Roy's journey on a Sabena Ju52 from Cairo. Photographed at Bangui, French Equatorial Africa, December 26 1943

Chapter 3 – Excuse Me, Wait for Me, I'm On My Way

ABOVE: Christmas Eve 1943 at Stanleyville

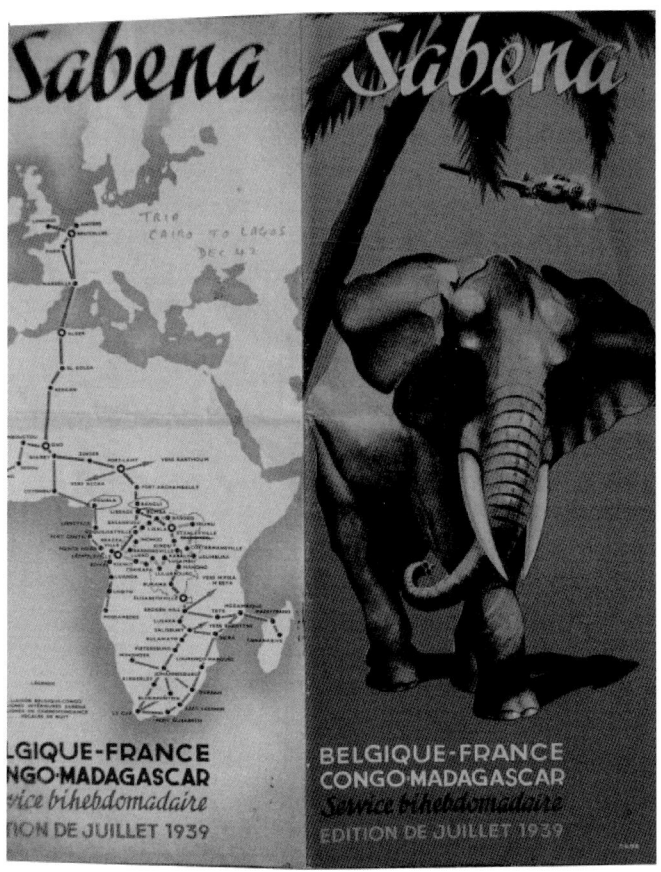

LEFT: Sabena route Map

British Embassy where I reported to, shared the same street as the German Embassy and they kept a close watch on the visitors each other had. More alarming for us was the great view the Germans had of the harbour and the Empire flying boat waiting to take us back to England."

"Then on January 2 1943 we left Lisbon on a Short Type G flying boat, the Golden Hind (G-AFCE). We left at night and flew well out into the Bay of Biscay before heading north to avoid the Ju88's. A few months earlier a similar aircraft had been shot down, killing all aboard, including actor Leslie Howard."

"The Golden Hind landed at Foynes in Ireland after seven hours, was refuelled by the neutrals then flew another two hours to Poole in Dorset."

"Finally after 68 flying hours and having visited eight countries in thirteen days I was back in Britain. The cost to fly me and a dozen other anonymous civilians back to the UK must have been enormous. Just six months previously I had flown a Wellington from the UK to Cairo in 24 hours 55 minutes."

"I am not sure why I got this special treatment but two days later I was posted to 15 OTU as an instructor."

– Roy Montrowe

Kiwis Do Fly

To Europe from the Blue Pacific via Singapore, the Japanese and the US Navy

On April 25 1945, Squadron Leader George Hitchcock was a flight commander in 635 Squadron flying Lancaster PB922 (FU –U) as Deputy Master Bomber on a massed raid to Bertchesgarten, one of RAF Bomber Command's last raids of World War Two.

Sixteen months prior to this George was a Flying Officer heading Crew 8 of the RNZAF's number 6 Squadron. 6 Squadron was equipped with PBY Catalinas flying search and rescue 'Dumbo' missions from Solomon and New Hebrides island bases.

G C Hitchcock (NZ412006) volunteered for RNZAF service in March 1941. Following a pilots course on Tiger Moths and Oxfords he was commissioned and posted to Singapore in October 1941.

"My 19th birthday (on December 7) was spent watching the Japanese Army aircraft bomb us. I had been posted to the RAF's 100 Squadron but never got to fly their Vildebeestes as almost all were shot down on their first daylight Op against Jap ships."

"With the rapid Japanese advance down the Malayan Peninsula, aircrew with no planes to fly were considered too valuable to leave behind. Some left by ship but I was lucky enough in January 1942 to be evacuated by flying boat back to Australia. It was intended to reform the Squadron on Beauforts but that idea was abandoned. By April 1942 I was back where I started back in New Zealand with just 200 hours up and no combat experience."

"I was finally posted to Fiji and a RNZAF general reconnaissance flight based at Nadi. We had ex civilian de Havilland 89 Dominie but I found myself allocated an unarmed (DH82A) Tiger Moth. In July I moved across Viti Levu to Suva and No 5 GR Squadron equipped with rather elderly Singapore flying boats. I was to spend the next two years on 'boats.'"

"There I was, trained to fly the latest all-metal high speed heavy bombers but I had a 1936 model 'Gentle Annie' to fly about the Pacific looking for submarines. The four push-pull Rolls Royce Kestrels gave us a 75 knot take-off speed and an 80 knot cruise. Our search altitude was limited to 800 feet!"

After the Pearl Harbour raid in 1942 and the USA now in the war, re-equipment of the RNZAF became a priority and a complete range of fighters, bombers, sea planes and trainers began being supplied under Lend Lease.

In October 1942 George Hitchcock was posted to the US Navy to undergo a conversion course onto PBY Catalinas. For combat experience he was posted to Patrol Squadron VP 11. The Squadron was based in the New Hebrides around the 10,000 ton flying boat tender USS Curtiss which was moored in Espiritu Santo's harbour.

"I spent five months operating with the US Navy and at times it was quite exciting. Initially we flew twelve hour missions north looking for Jap forces heading south! Little radar, all eyeball, but rather than the old Singapore's 800 feet, we cruised at 6,000 feet."

"In the middle of November we were on patrol in our usual PBY-6 2391 when we located a ditched B-17 crew who had been hit by flak over Kahili. This base was about 500 miles behind the Japanese lines but held an airfield and a camp of about 1,000 troops. We landed about a mile from the camp and loaded the B-17 crew. We eventually landed to refuel at the just liberated island

LEFT: Detailed with the delivery of new Catalinas from the Consolidated factory in San Diego California, the ferry route via Honolulu took 43 hours flying over the Pacific without any navigational aids. Pictured is JX233 (NZ4005) mid Pacific taken from Georges 08373 (NZ4004) Fiji bound on June 1943

Chapter 3 – Excuse Me, Wait for Me, I'm On My Way

ABOVE: Log book entry while flying with the US Navy VP8 Dumbo patrol, picking up a downed SBD Dauntless pilot and a day later a 10 hour 55 minute mission to rescue a B-17 crew

of Tulagi in the Solomons, after a 13 hour flight. Funnily enough, the B-17 captain was named Colonel Saunders but he was no chicken!"

After 15 patrols with VP11, George was posted to VP98 at Halavo and flew another 22 patrols on Catalinas but this time with a fighter escort. "We regularly flew behind the front lines and provided a freight service, delivering machine guns, rifles and other gear for the coast watchers. On one trip we were very surprised to be presented with a Jap pilot trussed up on a pole like a pig. I bet he thought he was going to become native tucker."

"My last patrol took us mid-Pacific to the small phosphate island of Nauru then held by the Japs. To our great surprise we were attacked by a Jap medium bomber with a 30mm cannon in its tail. His speed was much greater than ours and as we headed back south, the bomber kept presenting his rear end to us and pumping out a few shells. The number of holes in our hull proved his accuracy. Finally he went away."

By the end of February 1943 George was back in Suva and again on Singapore flying boats. These tired sea planes needed replacement and George as a qualified Catalina Captain (with 600 hours) was one of the first group of pilots selected to ferry new PBY aircraft for the RNZAF from the factory in San Diego to Fiji.

On the 12th and 21st May George flew as second pilot from San Diego to Suva.

"It was 18 hours from San Diego to Honolulu, then 8 to Palmyra or 15 to Canton and another 10 to Suva. Our trip back to California was courtesy of US Air Transport Command and their Liberators or the much preferred Pan Am's Clipper flying boat. Life in San Diego was great, no rationing, a spending allowance and very nice home comforts."

George flew six trans-Pacific deliveries. One highlight was meeting up with another RNZAF Catalina (also being delivered) mid-Pacific 'with crack navigation.' George also captained an eighteen hour direct flight from Honolulu to Suva. "It was a bit of a strain on the fuel tanks but we needed to pick up a bit of time to get back for a do." One low moment was having a storm of St. Elmos fire around the aircraft for 12 hours of a 17 hour flight.

For the rest of 1943 George flew PBY patrols around the South Pacific but he managed to log several VIP flights, including taking US General Puttick to Tonga, Samoa and back to Auckland and a trip with the Governor of Fiji around 'his' islands.

George was posted back to the SW Pacific front in October 1943 flying with No 6 Squadron (RNZAF) out of Espiritu Santo and Halavo (Tulagi) in the Solomons. By February the Squadron had moved up to Bougainville in the Treasury Islands based on the tender USS Coos Bay. The Squadron was tasked with giving Dumbo cover for the air attack on the Japanese held 'fortress' at Rabaul.

"Open sea landings were always hazardous and we lost a few boats doing this. On February 18 we managed to save two of the crew from a B-25 off Buka Island and two days later both pilot and gunner from a USMC SBD Dauntless. Skipper Bill Mackley held the record though, after doing a tour on Whitley's in Europe he came back to New Zealand joined 6 Squadron as a boat captain, and on January 26 1944 pulled ten crewmen from a ditched USAAF Liberator. With his own crew of eleven, NZ4013 must have been full."

George finished his second tour in the Pacific and as a 'rest' flew another PBY back from San Diego before returning to New Zealand.

"I wanted to get into the real war in Europe; I had over 1,000 hours in my log. My friend Jim Hendry (also a PBY Captain) felt the same and with the help of a friendly Group Captain at RNZAF Headquarters we were posted to the NZ Sunderland Squadron in West Africa (No 490 Squadron). Luckily for us the posting was via England."

"After eight days in the Brighton aircrew transit area we had a change of heart, so off to Pathfinder HQ we went, gained entry and showed an Air Commodore our log books." "We can use you two!" "I'm sure it was our long distance flying over the Pacific with virtually no navigational aids that got us the job."

The resulting immediate posting to the PFF training unit at Warboys really upset the Wingco at Brighton as some aircrew seemed to sit there for months.

"Jim and I were off. No West Africa for us! We'd had enough of the tropics."

"So Germany was going finally to be added to my log book after three years of war service and over 1,800 of flying hours."

FOOTNOTE: George's friend Jim Hendry was shot down on a raid to Hanover but survived as a POW.

– George Hitchcock

Kiwis Do Fly

Potato Peeler to Pathfinder

The path from civilian to pilot was often lengthy as Jack 't Hart was to find out. Jack was perhaps fortunate that on the outbreak of war in 1939 he had just joined Cambridge University as an undergraduate. Unable to return home following the German invasion of Holland, Jack volunteered for the RAF.

"I didn't get very far as I was an 'alien' and would have to wait until the Dutch Government in exile re-established their own armed forces."

Finally called up in October 1940 Jack found that he had been posted to the Dutch Army Irene Brigade in Wales.

"Playing soldier wasn't my cup of tea! Their main activity was playing soccer against other Allied teams."

Every so often volunteers for RAF service were called for but Jack kept missing out. "In September 1941 (after eleven months as a Khaki wonder) our Brigade was based at Wolverhampton camp and a Captain Berdenis van Berlekom arrived and started interviewing aircrew volunteers in a room adjacent to the kitchen.

"I was busy peeling potatoes when I spied ten to fifteen hopefuls so with Cooks permission I joined the queue. When it was my turn the Captain was packing his bag. I wasn't on the list but I got an interview anyway. On admitting I was actually the potato peeler he laughed and sent me off to the RAF Air Crew Reception Centre in St Johns Wood. Using ones initiative must have carried some weight!"

I had to sign a service contract that wouldn't expire until three years after the wars end. "That's a bit tough, I said, but I want to fly."

Ironically Initial Training Wing courses were held at Jack's old Trinity College in Cambridge. "We had fifteen Dutch, a few French, two Poles and two English. When a 10pm curfew was imposed we suddenly lost our understanding of English."

"By 22 April 1942 when the ITW Course finished I'd been a soldier for eleven months and an airman for four months and yet to see an aeroplane. Little did I realise that another nineteen months would pass before I'd finally get into action." Yet those months were busy, twelve hours EFTS training in Tiger Moths established that Jack was fit enough to fly and in June he joined many others being sent to Canada for flying training.

BELOW: Conversion course on Halifax Ia, 1656 HCU Lindholme 1943

Chapter 3 – Excuse Me, Wait for Me, I'm On My Way

It was just as well Jack had patience, on arrival they waited in Moncton, New Brunswick for two weeks. Then followed an eighty seven hour train ride to 31 EFTS at De Winton. "It was my 21st Birthday."

"Initial flying training was on the roomy and very sturdy Boeing Stearmans and I completed my course on 25 September 1942 after 79 hours tuition. As future bomber pilots, our group moved onto Medicine Hat (about 300km SE of Calgary). There we had half day flying and half day classroom instruction. It kept us all busy. My first instructor was a Pole, typical of the English they put two foreigners together. The Pole was a nice guy but spoke appalling English with a very heavy accent. I simply couldn't understand the man. After a chat with the CFI, I was assigned an English instructor and things moved on apace. The wooden Oxfords we flew weren't that easy to fly for us trainees but we later found that they gave us a great grounding for flying bombers."

"We had a fair bit of fun, the barracks were heated with coal, the burners were automatically fed, in the middle of the night. Ironically right below us were the great oilfields Canada was to discover post-war. Alberta was dry – no alcohol. So on leave we crossed the border into the United States. Enormous hospitality, great beer and we simply weren't allowed to pay for any of it. In Butte, Montana, we were interviewed on radio about our experiences escaping from the Nazis. When it came to my turn the other two called out – "he swam the English Channel!" When it came time to go back to Moose Jaw, the local State Highway Patrol simply drove us back to base."

New Zealander Jack Shorthouse was instructing at Moose Jaw during this time having transferred with 31 EFTS.

"Finally on 19 February 1943 we were presented with our wings and made Sergeants. Our papers for commissions had been sent to the Dutch AF HQ in London."

Jack paid his second visit to New York without stopping and the RMS Queen Elizabeth brought him back to England. Now firmly in the 'system' Jack progressed through Advanced Flying Unit training at South Cerney (where New Zealander Bill Simpson was instructing) then on to OTU at Hixon.

Like many others before him Jack found the crewing up system unusual. "The English had a peculiar way of forming crews. About 100 of us gathered up in a hangar and the Wing Commander said a few words finishing with – "now sort yourselves out." The idea was to pick a likely looking navigator and after a few quick words as a pair chose the rest of the crew just as quickly. When I think back now, it comes across as a bit of a dangerous lottery as you had no idea at all how they would behave when things got serious."

"But the system must have worked I had picked a colossus of a Navigator, Pilot Officer Dudley Charles Jones, and a wonderful and courageous crew. We served and relaxed together over two tours of operations."

"Finally two years and two months after signing up I was posted with my crew to 103 Squadron Elsham Wolds, a Pilot Officer with 420 hours up."

Jack completed his tour with 103, then finished another with 156 (PFF) Squadron based at Upwood.

ABOVE: Jack undergoing pilot training in an Airspeed Oxford

LEFT: Formation flying at 31 EFTS Moose Jaw, Canada 1942

– Jack 't Hart

Kiwis Do Fly

Singapore Sling

Like George Hitchcock, Keith Boles was one of the early graduates from the RNZAF War Mobilisation scheme and as a fresh Pilot Officer was posted to Singapore 34 Squadron and in December 1941 Keith celebrated his 21st birthday while George his 19th on the same day but by then 34 Squadron's Blenheims had ceased to exist.

"During January 1942 a Squadron of Lockheed Hudsons arrived at RAF Tengah and were promptly bombed by the Japanese. An informer was caught and was tried as a traitor. He was shot summarily and his corpse was thrown into the harbour. They were desperate times."

"More disasters followed, some Hawker Hurricanes arrived and a special Operation was laid on for them as they were the only modern aircraft left in Singapore. Catastrophe! The gun access panels were left open overnight and the nightly tropical storm put an end to the Hurricanes serviceability. The Station Adjutant roped me in to collect and parcel up the Station Commanding Officer's, personal gear, and to unload his revolver with one shot fired. The Commanding Officer had taken responsibility personally and had committed suicide."

"Without aircraft to fly, we just messed about until I learnt that as a pilot I should have been evacuated already. It was really a shambles. Twice I attempted to board a transport ship only to be turned back at Godown 62. Finally on February 9, 1942 I boarded the twenty passenger, 1,900 ton SS Darvel. There were about 450 aboard including 140 of the New Zealand Aerodrome Construction Unit. We left the dock to moor in the harbour only to return. We all had to disembark and were transported back to the base at Seletar. We finally reboarded at 5pm to sail for Batavia, and there was complete chaos. Our ship waited for a naval escort only to be bombed by the Jap's who succeeded in wrecking all the wooden lifeboats killing two and injuring thirty others. The skipper gave up waiting for the Navy pretty smartly."

"At Batavia in the Dutch East Indies we were moved onto the liner Orcades, one of four cruise liners engaged in trooping. So with 5,000 Aussie troops, 700 women evacuees and a similar number of Air Force bods we left the Dutch Indies. Surprisingly we first sailed northwards to Colombo (Ceylon) to let the troops off, then back across the Indian Ocean, deep below Western Australia and finally northwards. We eventually docked in Adelaide, South Australia, in April 1942. I'd been away nearly five months and never flew one hour."

Posted back to the RNZAF Levin training camp, Keith finally got his wish for overseas service when he volunteered to lead a draft of other aircrew trades to Canada.

"I duly delivered my 99 bods to Edmonton. Forty four of them wouldn't survive the war. I went on to Ottawa and best of all, seven days leave in New York."

"The Atlantic crossing went by with little drama but a lot of overcrowding and I soon completed the standard familiarisation courses in UK. Ready for war I thought, but others thought otherwise, and like a good number of other RNZAF pilots I was posted to grading schools giving would-be pilot entrants a taste of flying Tiger Moths. After three months of this it was into the warmth of an Airspeed Oxford cockpit – but for a year! I finally was given a Beam Approach instructors course for seven days and promptly spent another two months on a BATF. Here I was a trained pilot who had never seen action after two years service and kept being told;" – "We are short of instructors." "I played my Ace – I'm a volunteer!"

"Ah well, then off to Bomber Command you go."

– Keith Boles

LEFT: Amongst the few vintage aircraft defending New Zealand in 1941 were ex RAF Fairey Gordons, Forty nine served with the RNZAF coded NZ601–649. Shown are K4005 and K4009 before repainting in RNZAF colours

Chapter 3 – Excuse Me, Wait for Me, I'm On My Way

Where's the War

Bob Barron shipped out of New Zealand in February 1944 on the SS Mariposa and became one of the last aircrew to be trained in Canada. With training complete Bob was sent by ship to England and by late 1944 was posted to the Brighton Crew Centre to wait. "At that stage of the war there was apparently a surplus of pilots and navigators and here we were all ready to have a crack at the Germans but instead our whole group was posted to a camp near Carnarvon in Wales to wait for nearly four months."

"Finally I was called into 11 OTU at Wescott and completed the course on May 8 1945, just one day prior to VE Day."

"But the system kept working and I was duly posted to HCU at Woolfox Lodge, then to 576 Squadron (1 Group) at Fiskerton. Once there, the Squadron didn't have much on and the one 'Op' we were down for (to collect troops from Bari in Italy), we had one engine go u/s and back to Woolfox Lodge we went. So there I was, overtrained, under raced and due for demobbing after considerable expense."

– *Bob Barron*

RIGHT: Navigator training on RCAF Avro Ansons taking turns and also doing basic wireless work, February 1943

ABOVE: The final test for navigators, this records D. Andrewes (later on 622 Squadron) passing with 66%

ABOVE: The well built camp huts that needed to withstand the Canadian winters

ABOVE: Crewing up at 11 OTU Westcott, Bob Barron on the far right

51

Kiwis Do Fly

A Goldfish First

RAF trained Flight Mechanic (Engines) Harry Saunders served on 600 (City of London) Squadron's Spitfires in 1941 and decided flying duties were for him. He was accepted for a Flight Engineer's course and posted to St. Athan in Wales. "Part of this course was stooging around in the turret of a Boulton Paul Defiant flown by a crazy Pole."

"I passed the gunnery course (compulsory for all crew, except pilots) and got a surprise posting to a Coastal Command OTU up in Alness on the Solway. All of our flying was done on Catalinas and training went well until very early one morning, about 5am (16 March 1943) our skipper touched down a bit out of level. The starboard float dug in and we water looped. The swing was so violent it ripped the starboard engine free and it crashed into the fuselage. The navigator received quite a nasty blow as well as a hell of a fright. We all got out basically undamaged although we were in chest deep freezing water by then."

"We clambered into the inflated dinghies and paddled out of harms way. The Catalina sank. Because of this our skipper was sent away and the crew was split up. However we did receive Goldfish badges, having ditched in the sea on 'operations'."

"Coastal Command kept me on and I was transferred to 202 Squadron based in Gibraltar. A Coastal Command tour was 24 trips (240 hours) and we spent it looking for U boats in the Atlantic. We never sighted one. I expect they saw us and submerged, or simply sailed around the perimeter of our patrol area."

"With the end of the tour I was re-mustered as a Bomber Boy and shipped out to India to catch up with 356 Squadron (SEAC). The Squadron was based at Salbani, east of Calcutta (the airfield is still visible today). Our early Ops with the Liberators were standard bombing runs into Burma with Rangoon being the favourite!"

"Our best strike occurred on 15 June 1945, when we were diverted from our planned target onto a big Jap tanker spotted in the Siam Gulf. Three of us basically dive bombed the 10,000 tonner, we came out at 300mph, quite a thing to do. The ship was destroyed."

"By July 1945, our Liberators had been stripped of armour plate and secretly deployed to the Cocos Islands. "From here we could do 12–14 hours supply trips to Sumatra and Malaya with food and personnel. Even after the end of the war and the Jap's surrender, we still carried out drops of food to POW camps and leaflets for the Japs, who still shot back. During a run down Kuala Lumpar's main runway days after the cease fire, Jap machine gunners made things pretty lively for us and we were probably the last British bomber to suffer flak damage in WWII."

356 Squadron finally left the

RIGHT:
202 Squadron Gibraltar 1943
Left to Right:
Top: 2nd Pilot Brownie, Sgt Osborne.
Middle: F/S Cadd (Nav), Sgt Rudkin (W/Op), Sgt Munro (W/Op), Sgt McTaggert.
Front: Harry Saunders (F/E), F/O Hackman (Skipper), Frank Bithell (W/Op Mechanic)

BELOW:
A PBY Catalina as flown by Harry Saunders from Gibraltar. This example is a PB2B-1 used by 5 Squadron RNZAF in the SW Pacific theatre

Chapter 3 – Excuse Me, Wait for Me, I'm On My Way

Cocos Islands in November 1945, this 'quiet' area of the war had cost the squadron 18 aircraft over one years operation.

"The thing I remember about briefing was that, unlike Europe or the Med, the Indian Ocean had no diversionary airfields and any problem ended up with the crew being in the drink. Probably half the Squadron's losses were from ditching. Once a Goldfish was enough for me."

— *Harry Saunders*

ABOVE: Liberator KN752, Cocos Islands, showing the black and white tail markings of

RIGHT: Notices dropped onto POW camps along with supplies

TO ALL ALLIED PRISONERS OF WAR

THE JAPANESE FORCES HAVE SURRENDERED UNCONDITIONALLY AND THE WAR IS OVER

WE will get supplies to you as soon as is humanly possible and will make arrangements to get you out but, owing to the distances involved, it may be some time before we can achieve this.

YOU will help us and yourselves if you act as follows:—

(1) Stay in your camp until you get further orders from us.
(2) Start preparing nominal rolls of personnel, giving fullest particulars.
(3) List your most urgent necessities.
(4) If you have been starved or underfed for long periods DO NOT eat large quantities of solid food, fruit or vegetables at first. It is dangerous for you to do so. Small quantities at frequent intervals are much safer and will strengthen you far more quickly. For those who are really ill or very weak, fluids such as broth and soup, making use of the water in which rice and other foods have been boiled, are much the best. Gifts of food from the local population should be cooked. We want to get you back home quickly, safe and sound, and we do not want to risk your chances from diarrhoea, dysentry and cholera at this last stage.
(5) Local authorities and/or Allied officers will take charge of your affairs in a very short time. Be guided by their advice.

LEFT: VJ Day Cocos Island, August 1945

ABOVE: Flight Engineers Log book for a 4 hour 50 minute patrol in a Catalina

Chapter 4

What a Beauty

All crews and particularly pilots had their own favourite aircraft from perhaps the Tiger Moth that carried them on their first ever solo or a navigator's dream of the warm and comfortable table in a Stirling. Probably only with the Mosquito did the pilot agree with his crew member. Although the nav/radar operator had little room, his chance of survival was much greater than in a four engine heavy.

Even within a squadron particular aircraft were known to perform better or have their own peculiar vices but once a crew had settled on their 'lucky' one they were loathe to swap it. They also were very superstitious about what flying gear they wore (a lucky sock perhaps) to having a last pee on the tail wheel. Be it the comfort of a Stirling or the speed of a Mosquito, all aircrew have memories of a special aircraft – she was a beauty.

Chapter 4 – What a Beauty

A Slightly Worn Mk III

A few air crews were lucky enough to sail through a tour without mishap. In RAF Bomber Command that was rare especially until the end of 1944. Even then losses on daylight raids were high.

Yet John Tarbuck captained his 626 Squadron Lancaster III through a full tour without mishap. "Perhaps it was because we only visited the Ruhr once, which was enough, but we did a lot of low level Ops around D-Day when Mother 2 (UM–M2 ME830) became our allocated aircraft. It was a good plane, looked after very well by a great ground crew. We brought it back untouched Op after Op except on a daylight run to Caen on July 7 1944, when shrapnel from flak punched a hole through the astrodome. After 30 Ops I could sign off the Form 700 for a slightly worn Mk III Lancaster. So many others didn't quite match this."

John's ME830 later served with Ad AEE at Bascombe Down in February 1945 and eventually struck off charge 12 March 1948.

– John Tarbuck

ABOVE: John Tarbuck's 'Slightly Worn' office

Kiwis Do Fly

A Safe Lancaster

Flight Engineer Harry Widdup joined his crew at 1656 HCU at Lindholme in November 1943. His skipper (Sergeant Terry Cook) and the crew were to complete 24 Ops together mostly in Mark III JB603 HW-E, with 100 Squadron. But first they had to endure their first four Ops, all to Berlin within a week. "We thought, this is pretty tough, how the hell are we going to do another 26." In the event Harry and JB603 never went back to Berlin on their tour. On 25 February we had to return early with a sick crew member and needed to dump fuel.

Despite all Harry's efforts the shear pin on the dump valve trunking wouldn't break and he was concerned that the recommended remedy of lowering undercarriage and flaps would simply suck the vapour back around the engines. "I felt that a number of aircraft losses were due to similar problems and had been caused by the petrol vapour igniting, the aircraft then simply blowing apart." By using the hand pump Harry pressurised the system until at over 100 psi, the pin finally gave.

On 27 April 1944 JB603 was on her final run into Freidrickshaven when a 30 lb incendiary thumped into their starboard wing punching through a fuel tank. "Someone's timing was out, either we were late or those high level squadrons were early. Mind you it could have been from one of those bods who always kept above the stream out of harms way, keen to get in and get out."

The rear gunner reported that 'Easy' was making a vapour trail, not of condensation, but of 100 octane petrol. With a quarter of their remaining fuel gone the captain and crew had a choice of Switzerland or home.

RIGHT: Crew Left to Right: Terry Cook (Pilot), John Pawsey (M/UG), Harry Widdup (F/E), Jack Wookey (R/G), Eric Norman (B/A) Canada, Harry Peachey (W/Op), With JB603

BELOW RIGHT: Welcome to 100 Squadron, an opener to Brunswick on 2 January 1944, then on to Berlin on 20th, 21st, 27th, 28th and 30th January. DCO denotes 'Duty Carried Out' as against the dreaded DNCO, the 'N' standing for 'Not'

LEFT: Pilot, Sgt Terry Cook, and Harry Widdup on the morning after their trip on 27 April to Freidrichhaven in HW-E (JB603). Having completed 45 Ops it was about to go for rebuild

RIGHT: April 27 1944, Harry's log showing the crew's 16th Op. A marathon 8 hour 25 minute trip with a punctured fuel tank and a DFM to acknowledge a crew's bravery

"With careful fuel management we got back to Grimsby." The real surprise was Harry's DFM and four DFC's for the crew.

Grateful to be returning home rather than becoming a Swiss internee, his ever faithful JB603 was repaired and returned to 100 Squadron. JB603 had been to Berlin eight times in its career. It was hit six times, finally crashing on the night of 5/6 January 1945 near Haarbroek with all the crew being killed. Delivered to 100 Squadron in November 1943 this aircraft was on its 113th Op when its service ended but it had looked after Harry and his crew mates.

– Harry Widdup

Good Kites

"Our crew were posted to 103 Squadron at Elsham Wolds on November 23, 1943 and were allocated a brand new Lancaster III JB746 code 'B'. The Wingco believed that if we had our own plane we'd take pride in it. Along with the new Lanc came a terrific ground crew of five mechanics."

"JB746 flew faultlessly, carried us safely through twenty-two Ops and always got us home. This particular Lancaster had a ton of power which kept us out of trouble, even on the notorious Nuremburg raid in 1944. We climbed to 24,000 feet and never saw a night fighter, but below was a bloody shambles."

(On the Nuremberg raid 95 of the 779 Lancasters were shot down with 745 air crew either killed, taken POW or wounded. The number of RAF Bomber Command crew who lost their lives on that one night was more than the whole of Fighter Command losses during the Battle of Britain).

"A month or so after our last Op with 103 Squadron, we had been posted to 156 Squadron PFF and were returning damaged from a raid on Hassalt (in ND342). I elected to put down on the big emergency strip at Woodbridge in Suffolk. The next morning we were wandering around the perimeter track looking at around a hundred wrecks that littered the airfield. There to our amazement was JB746. There wasn't a lot left of it and it wouldn't fly again but once more it had brought its crew home. You couldn't ask any more of a plane." (JB746 did return to service but was lost over Le Havre on 31 July 1944).

– Jack 't Hart

The key to a good aircraft: a great ground crew. Elsham Wolds 1943

Flt Lt Jack 't Hart in the office of JB746 PM–B showing 27 operations completed. The apparent nose art isn't, but is actually wear and tear

RIGHT: Jack 't Harts crew boarding JB746 at an Elsham Wolds dispersal 1943

Left to Right:
Jack (Pilot),
Dudley Jones (Nav),
Jim Kilminster F/E,
Bill Dalgleish (B/A),
Alan Bridges (W/Op),
S. Seldon (RG),
P. Langston (M/UG)

Kiwis Do Fly

One to Remember

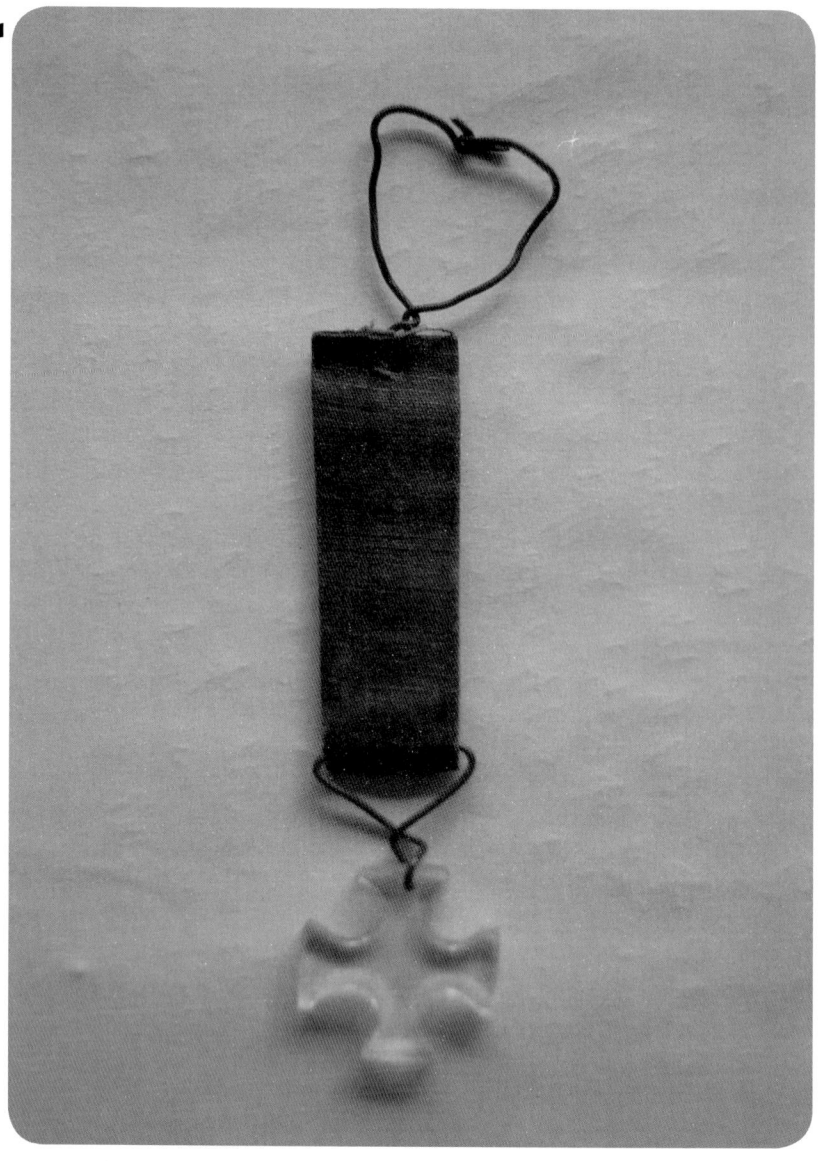

After a surprise posting to the famous 617 Squadron at Woodhill Spa, Arthur Joplin's crew as the new boys were initially put on continuation training. "As we hadn't completed our first Op yet the OC Flying felt we would benefit from a little more experience. He was right. We would do air tests with some cross country exercises."

As well as the current squadron aircraft (617's being constantly modified), there were always a few spare Lancasters available.

"The strange thing was that many of the surviving Dams Raid aircraft remained on the airfield. For our first fighter affiliation exercise we were allocated AJ-S, ED912. Probably we'd been picked to test fly it as we were a new crew and were quite expendable as 'Sugar' hadn't flown for a while."

"This Lancaster had been skippered by Les Knight on the Dams raid in 1943 and it was his bouncing bomb that breached the Eder dam. Sugar hadn't been converted since the raid and the bomb bay was still fitted with the rotational drive gear. I recall it being very fast, as it had a lot of weight stripped out to carry Barnes Wallis's Upkeep bomb."

"Anyway we duly completed our F/A exercise and once we had landed the ground crew put on quite a show. They assembled and awarded me a perspex cross as a Dam Buster. They were certainly taking the mickey out of this new Kiwi skipper, but it also showed the great pride the ground crews had in their aircraft and the Squadron's achievement. I accepted the gong with due ceremony and secretly was pleased I'd passed their scrutiny."

"This was mid October 1944 and the Dam Buster Lancasters were still at Woodhall Spa when I left the Squadron in 1945."

NB: Wing commander Guy Gibsons Dams Raid Lancaster ED 932; AJ-G remained at Woodhall Spa after VE Day and was scrapped in 1947

– Arthur Joplin

ABOVE: The EPC (Emery Paper Perspex Cross) awarded to Arthur Joplin following a Fighter Affiliation exercise in the ex Dam Buster Lancaster ED912, AJ-S

RIGHT: Fighter Affiliation Exercise, this time with a Spitfire at low level seen from a Lancaster's astrodome. If the bomber captain didn't corkscrew or respond to his gunners call "break" the dreaded rat tat tat would come over his earphones from the fighter pilot (J. Pote)

Chapter 4 – What a Beauty

Press On Stirlings

"As a Navigator on 15 Squadron's Stirlings, I soon discovered that they had bags of room and very comfortable seats. They were so much better than the the OTU Wellingtons that we had graduated from. The Wellingtons were invariably worn out, cold, draughty and noisy. Even the Lanc wasn't my favourite, it was too hot and unstable, but the Mossie was streets ahead of any of them.

The Mossies were very quick, getting to the target and home again in less than half the time a Stirling would. Post-war I was reminded of just how quick they were when we ferried a new T3 from Bankstown (Australia) to Ohakea in April 47 (our fourth by the way). The skipper, Squadron Leader Johnny Checketts, an ex fighter boy, did the trip in five hours dead. For 1,500 miles that wasn't bad and a great show for all, especially when the civil Shorts flying boats were taking eight to ten hours."

"Anyway back to Stirlings, the night of 23 August 1943 wasn't that flash. On 15 Squadron we generally flew the same aircraft and ours was an old Stirling, BK818 / EF-O. It was our 15th Op and over Berlin we got shot up, the rear gunner being killed."

"Our skipper, Squadron Leader McGinson, was 'B' Flight Commanding Officer and decided despite the damage and no gunner we would finish the run to the target and bomb. He felt that we'd come too far to waste a 7 hour 40 minute Op with a DNCO in our log books. The skipper picked up an immediate DFC and was marked up as a 'press on' type, the gunner was replaced and old BK818 retired, probably to an OTU for some poor sod to train on."

– Bunny Burrows

A Delight

"Despite what many non-pilots have said, the Stirlings we flew at HCU were beautifully built and finished. They were smooth to fly and so roomy compared to a Lancaster. The pilot's seat was a delight. As I didn't use the auto pilot 'George' that often, I found the Stirling light on the controls and therefore not tiring. It was stable and had good performance even with a full load."

"We always had a stand-in crew member trained to take over from the pilot in emergencies (including Elsan breaks). On 101 Squadron the wireless Op stood in as often we were carrying two. One Wireless Op would be carrying normal duties reporting position, times, weather and so on, and while the other concentrated on the Squadrons Specialist duties jamming enemy frequencies by either amplified engine noise or holding the Morse key down. At times we carried a German speaking crewman who gave false orders. When I moved onto 75 (NZ) Squadron it was standard practice for the flight engineer to become my second pilot, at least to keep straight and level. Mind you, it didn't take much to keep one on course. But really the Stirling was my pick."

– George Hitchcock

Kiwis Do Fly

Mossie for Me

"The Mossie was always my favourite type; even later in the 1950's and 60's when flying jets the memory of how good the Mossie was has never left me. On 109 (PFF) Squadron I had some great moments in them. On March 2 1945 (in MM295, Bar Peter the famous Grim Reaper with at least 120 Ops) I marked for 858 Bomber Command aircraft over Cologne and ten days later again marked for 1008 heavy bombers over Dortmund (in MM114/G). Both were incredibly heavy raids and an amazing sight as something like eight million pounds of high explosive was dropped on a single target. It was unbelievable that anything could survive such destruction, but it did."

"Post-war in the CSE (Central Signals Establishment), I was flying out of Watton on radar development and was taking a Mossie up to 58,000 feet over Buchan. It took a while to get there and she wasn't happy, just mushing along but what an aircraft. It gave the GCI radar boys who were tracking us something to think on, as 60,000 feet was at the limit of most of the RAF's jet fighters of the time."

– Bill Simpson

ABOVE: Meeting an Old Friend 2 April 2009 at Ardmore Airfield, New Zealand. Three pilots with over 130 operations on Mosquitos in the Pathfinder Force
Left to Right: Keith Boles DFC, Squadron Leader 109 Sqn OBOE Squadron PFF
Bill Simpson DFC, Flight Lieutenant 109 Sqn OBAE Squadron PFF, **Roy Montrowe DFC**, Flight Lieutenant 692 Sqn LNSF Squadron PFF, with a Mark 26 (KA114) being restored to fly by Av Specs Ltd

RIGHT: Mosquito BXVI P2-P of 692 Squadron, LNSF, Graveley, January 1945 flown by F/L Roy Montrowe

Chapter 4 – What a Beauty

Nothing Like a Mossie

"I first flew a Mossie at 51 OTU and later with 25 Squadron at Castle Camps and finally on 488 (NZ) Squadron until wars end when we were based at Gilze in Holland."

"I'd always enjoyed aerobatics since my Harvard days at Wigram. A transfer to an OTU put me into the driver's seat of the beautiful Mosquito. Even the well used models we had there were a delight to fly, quick, great visibility and very aerobatic!"

"After the course I was posted to 25 Squadron at Castle Camps in 1944, where we flew intruder missions over Germany giving some protection to the bomber stream. I'd hang back out of the stream sitting at maybe 30,000 feet and try to pick up the exhaust glow of the German night fighters."

"When the buzz bomb raids on London started after June 1944, we were put onto night defence of the Capital."

"By the end of my tour the log book score stood at seven damaged as I was never keen to follow the flamers down to see them crash. I knew they were goners. I was better off staying up in the action looking for another."

"For a break from operations I pulled drogues around for hapless gunners and pilots. I wasn't in a Mossie then of course, but found it more dangerous than being behind the bomber stream over Germany."

"I joined 488 (NZ) Squadron in 1945, this time on Mk XXXs. Again they were great to fly and I spent a lot of time in the maintenance hanger. The engineering and mechanical side of things held a great fascination especially the beautifully made Merlin engines. It certainly helped when I raced motorbikes after the war."

– *Ted Kepplewhite*

TOP: OTU Mosquito line up 1944

MIDDLE: Big nosed NF Mk XXX 488 Squadron

BELOW: Ted Kepplewhite's interest in the mechanics of Mosquito's saw him spend a lot of spare time in the maintenance hangar

ABOVE: 488 (NZ) Squadron about to leave for Europe 1945

BELOW: Awaiting servicing at OTU

Kiwis Do Fly

Ode to a Mosquito

Her name was Joan
She was one of the best
But that was the night
I gave her the test

I looked on her with joy and delight
She was all mine, just for the night
She looked so pretty, so sweet, so trim
The night was dark the light was dim

I'd seen her stripped, I'd seen her bare
I felt around her everywhere
But this was the night I loved her the best
Listen to me and I'll tell you the rest

I got inside her; she screamed with joy
It was her first night out with a boy
I got up high as quick as I could
But I handled her gently – Boy was she good!

I turned her over on her side
Then on her back as well I tried
It was one great thrill, she is the best in the land
The twin-engined Bomber of Coastal Command!!

– *Anon*

ABOVE: Ted Kepplewhite's copper Mosquito. Made by fitters on 488 Squadron on 'spare' sheet

Vote for Stirlings and One for Lancs

"Stirlings were a superb pilot's aircraft and much bigger than anything we'd previously flown. Perhaps limited in bomb load and altitude compared with the later heavies (Halifax and Lancaster), but what a step up from the Wellingtons we had flown. Even the poor old Whitley boys whose hog nosed, head down flight attitude we scoffed at, could at least put a few thousand feet on us Wellington boys. But the Stirling was a step up again."

"Later when I was posted onto my second tour I flew Lancasters with 101 Squadron (Ludford Magna). They were very powerful machines. My crew was mainly RAF types, and unfortunately I had to get rid of the only other Kiwi from my crew. We had a couple of Londoners, and Paddy Butler was obviously Irish and loved a few pints. He was always broke and somehow he had been overpaid for a year or so. When the RAF pay section woke up they stopped his pay until it had been re-earned and the books balanced. Also on our crew was Bill Brown, a Flying Officer, and our rear gunner. He was bloody good with amazing eyesight. He gave our crew a real life saving advantage by seeing everything. Funnily enough he's now in London in the banking game complete with bowler and brolly. I often wonder does he ever think of the times I was up front going for the horizon when he's watching where we've been."

– *Laurie McKenna*

ABOVE: 101 Squadron Lancaster at dispersal Ludford Magna 1945, SR-W² has had its ABC aerials removed by the censor

And What about the Ground Crew

RIGHT: Engine fitters work on a 627 Squadron Mosquito at Woodhall Spa, September 1944

"The ground crews rarely get a mention because there were so few New Zealand tradesmen involved in Europe. But the ground crews were not invisible, they worked very hard and we depended on them so much to provide us safe aircraft to fly."

The RAF had organised a large flight engineers and mechanics school based at St Athan in Wales, but as the RAF expanded satellite schools operated throughout the UK to the same very high standards.

Joe Tomlin remembers 1944. "I was an RAF instrument repairer at Mepal, the home of 75 (NZ) Squadron of Lancasters. I had been trained to service the 'auto pilot' known as 'George' and at morning briefing I was told that 'George' in one aircraft was not working correctly, could it be fixed."

"The crew of this aircraft was skippered by a mad Aussie pilot named Popsy. They were most concerned as they only had two Ops to go to finish their tour and felt that a change to a new aircraft might change their luck. Popsy asked if there was any way their regular mount could be made serviceable. I suggested we do a flight test."

"The aircraft took off with the crew in their seats, all harnessed-in except me. I had an inkling what would happen, sure enough, when the auto pilot was engaged, the control column moved forward faster and faster until we were in a steep dive. I floated off the floor until the pilot was able to reach the autopilot disengage lever, and regain manual control."

"When I told the pilot it was a "stuck elevator valve," he said "what can you do?" I told him that the correct procedure was to remove the whole elevator gyro unit and return it to base maintenance for repair and testing on a gyro table. The pilot was a bit stubborn and said "no way, it might upset our luck. Can you do something?" I said I could try sitting on the floor of the bomb aimers compartment where the unit is situated, pull the elevator valve to pieces, clean it, reassemble it, air test it using the aircraft as a gyro table and re-level the unit. The pilot said "okay, do it, we still have time."

"I had a can of anti-freeze oil and a few tools and did as requested, doing the levelling procedure and pronouncing 'George' serviceable. On landing I signed off the aircraft as serviceable and the ground crew Flight Sergeant signed it out. I only stated the 'George' was okay on the Form 700, not how it was done. The crew did carry out the bombing trip that night and returned safely."

"My diary of 13 June 1944 reads; "went up to the White Horse for a loaf of bread and a few drinks and met Popsy, the mad Aussie. He and his crew had just finished their tour of Ops and when they saw me, they stood me several beers saying I was responsible for getting them home several times and did so much by getting 'George' spot on. It was nice to be appreciated."

– Joe Tomlin

Chapter 5

A Line

Shooting a line was a favourite RAF past time. Bomber Command 'lines' were perhaps less flamboyant than the Fighter Boys and perhaps closer to the truth. While the standard fighter line was always upside down at zero feet and a gaggle of Huns on their tail, Bomber boys were content with a more subtle line often developed with great care during the many hours during stand down from operations. Like today's best urban myths a good 'line' could take a life of its own, include local variations and adapt to the latest news.

The best lines travelled from station to station. The closer the line was to fact, the better. Some were undoubtedly based on the truth, and then suitably updated to take in later targets and aircraft.

Kiwis Do Fly

My Friend 'George'

"I found 'George' (the autopilot) always a great airman, in many ways better than me. On 626 Squadron (Wickenby) we had a great instrument basher who tuned 'George' on our Lanc UM-K2 every day. In September 1944 we were on our return leg from an Op to Stettin. For once 'George' didn't want to settle on 18,000 feet and kept wanting to put an extra 1,000 feet or so. After fiddling around a bit and finding nothing wrong I let George have his own way (perhaps her way and George was in fact Georgina!) Anyway, we settled at around 19,200 feet."

"Just before crossing the French Coast a hell of a barrage erupted below us. Our rear gunner commented that some poor bugger was copping it. Little did we know that poor bugger was meant to be us. Back at Wickenby, Spy (The Intelligence Officer) checked to see if we'd been caught in the new radar controlled flak trap. The Germans had laid this one especially for returning bombers who'd started their let down a bit early. "oh no" we replied, we had an inkling about this and kept well up. After that George (or Georgina) did a lot more flying and a little more commanding."

– *John Tarbuck*

ABOVE: The automatic pilot (George) control was mounted on the cockpit wall to the left of the pilot's knee. It can be seen in the lower left of the photo. George had three positions – Off, Jink and On

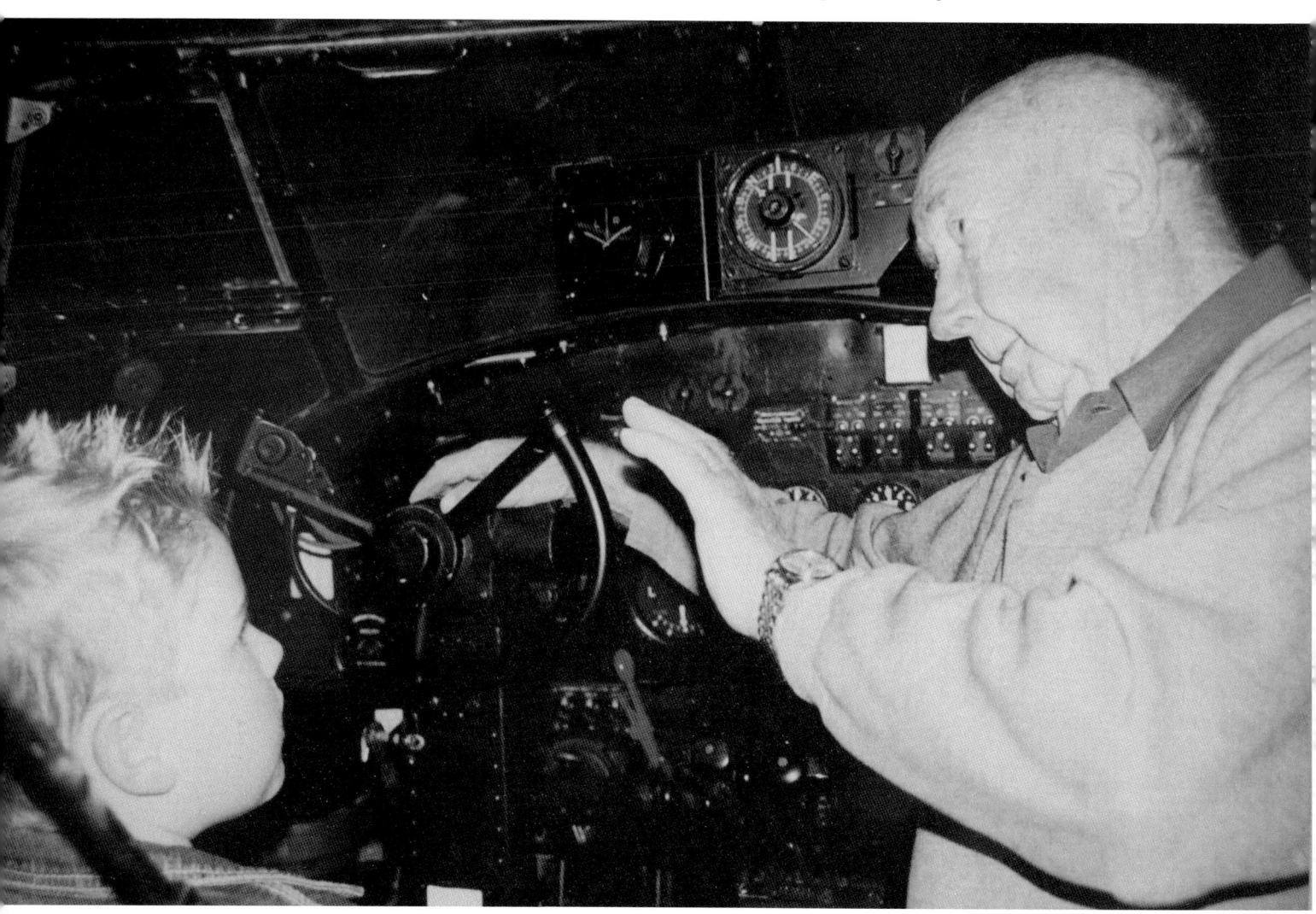

ABOVE: Age shall not weary them; John Tarbuck back in the office after 60 years, this time with a seven year old trainee. Anzac Day 2005

Long Legs are Advantageous

The SOE support operations into occupied Europe are only now being reluctantly revealed. The nefarious wanderings of Stirlings and Halifaxes of 298 Squadron (Tarrant Rushton) and the Halifaxes of 148 Squadron (Bari) even today are often restricted reading. Flying Officer Ivor Marsh (298 Squadron) recalls flying the Stirling with reservation although other pilots didn't seem to worry, "its need for a level of muscular strength by the pilot, was beyond me, so onto Ablemarles I went. However one night a 298 Squadron Stirling flown by a Canadian (Campbell by name) had a bit of a dust up with a German night fighter and by the time Tarrant Rushton was in sight the cockpit was full of smoke. By releasing the canopy hatch above his head Campbell stood up on his seat and put his head out into the slip stream. The landing was successful and a marvellous piece of airmanship. An immediate DFC was awarded but he could only have done it by being very strong, and having his Flight Engineer handle the throttles and flaps. With the Stirling having such long undercarriage legs, Campbell must have felt like standing on a pile of chairs at a circus when he came into land."

"Ablemarles weren't anyone's favourite aircraft but if you treated them like the cars of the time, underpowered, slow to go, slow to stop and steering vaguely in the right direction, you would be okay. Their nose wheel undercarriages caught a lot of pilots out and I'm sure post-war transport Squadrons were relieved that so many were written off during war time."

– Ivor Marsh

What Ju88

"In 1943 I was with a pupil in an Oxford on a night flying exercise out of South Cerney and had just flown over Cheltenham when bright flak filled the sky all around us. A bit shocked, I grabbed the controls and made a sharp turning dive but the flak seemed to follow. Back at base I made a call to the Anti Aircraft outfit in Cheltenham and spoke to a Captain complaining about them firing at me on a simple training flight, "Not to worry old boy he said, we were shooting at the German Ju88 on your tail. I offered to buy him a beer some time."

– Bill Simpson

Ghost of a Whitley

A twin engined Whitley was crossing the North Sea heading towards German occupied Europe when the pilot heard a voice in his headphones saying, "Be careful tonight – things could get a little difficult." This annoyed him and he shouted into the intercom "Who the hell was that?" But all crew members denied saying a word so it was left at that.

Indeed, they did have a rough time being shot up by a night fighter heading over Holland. The flying controls were damaged and one engine was misfiring badly as they approached England. The pilot finally reached the coast but was not happy about continuing towards his home airfield so decided it best to abandon the aircraft. He ordered his crew out and turned the aircraft back towards the nearby coast so it might fall into the sea rather than on some innocent civilians below. He clambered to his escape hatch and as he was later to tell his rescuers, he felt two hands give him a helping push out.

Later a coastal radar station reported a lone aircraft circling just off the coast and a fighter was sent up to investigate. He reported that it was a Whitley and identified the numbers which were later established as the abandoned aircraft. Yet it was still flying and the fighter was ordered to shoot it down as it was a menace to returning aircraft. He did so and the Whitley crashed into the sea.

On landing the fighter pilot reported his successful sortie then added that the Whitley rear gun turret fired at him. He was ridiculed for this but then said, "Come and have a look at the starboard wing and the bullet holes."

AND THEN AGAIN ...
In 1941 on one of Bomber Command's early raids a 9 Squadron Whitley was damaged over Germany and the captain found it very hard to control to the extent that he decided it would be better to abandon it over France. He ordered the crew to bale out and soon followed.

However the rear gunner did not hear the order to abandon ship and remained where he was. The aircraft somehow stabilised and ambled slowly down to a rather rough belly landing in a field. The rear gunner rather shaken and peeved when he clambered out of his turret and went to give his skipper a piece of his mind. He was staggered to find there were no other crew members in the aircraft!

– Bill Simpson

What's on my Tail

"Around D-Day 1944, a lot of 35 Squadrons Ops were over France targeting the transport networks and fighter bases. As Mid Upper Gunner I had a great view of proceedings. Rennes Airfield on 09 June in TL-H (ND 693) was notable for being at low level and gave we gunners the chance to "shoot the place up." It was good to see the ground troops running for cover, the light ack ack was a pretty sight and it was the first time we'd encountered 'flaming onions.' As we went down the airfield Neville took on one side and me the other and we let them have it."

"The airfield was never used again by the Germans; it had been an important target as the Germans were to use it as an advanced fighter field for strafing the beach heads." "As we'd gone in at low level we had to gain height for the trip back to base. I was watching to see when we crossed the coast and I heard Bobby (the Bomb Aimer) in the nose call out that we had crossed the coast. I wondered what he was on about and I said that I could still see the ground below but was told by Reg (the Navigator) that on this part of the coast (Saint-Malo) the sea water went out as much as three miles and that we had crossed at low tide. They built a power station on it after the war to use the tide to generate electricity."

"On the way back we had to go around the Channel Islands before making a track towards Exeter, I remember it was a beautiful moonlit night and the four dots of the main islands were a lovely sight along with the moonlight on the water. We got word that there were fighters waiting for us overhead near the English coast so Geoff (the Skipper) said that we would head for the deck so that any fighter trying to attack us from above would find it difficult diving down on us. We were nearing the coast and I'll always remember hearing a little voice over the intercom saying "Skipper, can we pull up, my bloody feet are in the water." It was Neville calling from the rear turret!"

– Harry Furner

Turn the Lights Out when you Leave

"On 635 (PFF) Squadron I was lucky enough to pick up a very experienced crew of odd bods, all of whom were on second or third tours."

"At the beginning of 1945 a raid on Magdeburg was scheduled for January 16 and we were to act as 'Visual Centre' and carried F/S Dunkely as an extra radar operator. Our Lancaster was loaded with six Green Target Indicator flares, one 4,000 lb and eight x 500 lb high explosive bombs."

"There was moderately heavy flak and searchlights over the target but once we'd done our marking run the bomb aimer found the 4,000 pounder hadn't released. He could see this through a small round perspex window at the front of the bomb bay. We did another two runs trying to get rid of the wretched thing but eventually the team got a bit grumpy about staying over the target as when it wouldn't release I would take us around again. Mid-January at 18,000 feet was decidedly chilly, maybe fifty below zero and gear did freeze up."

"An intercom 'discussion' suggested we run home at a lower altitude that would maybe unfreeze the release mechanism. It made us a bit more vulnerable to searchlights and flak and we were eventually picked out by a very persistent searchlight, one of the dreaded blues which were radar controlled."

"Bugger this we thought, the navigator got a fix on the site and we did a bomb run over them. The 4,000 lb fell away just fine and the searchlight vanished. I bet that German crew got a hell of a fright and any survivors would tell others to take care as the RAF were now targeting searchlights with 4,000 pounders!"

– George Hitchcock

Mpg

"In the private world that flight engineers and navigators occupy, a line shoot had to be accompanied by enough technical gen to be convincing (especially to other Flight Engineers and Navs). Not good enough to fly in 11/10 cloud for four hours and only be twenty yards adrift from the target, "LINE, LINE" would be the derisory call. However in our group of flight engineers on 463 Squadron there was a bit of a competition about air miles flown per gallon of petrol and being RAAF, a few bets were laid."

"No matter how hard I tried, a bit over 1 mpg was as good as I could get. Juggling with the throttles, mixture and boost to no avail. Zero point nine or one air miles per gallon or worse."

"The Skipper was let into the problem, "no trouble at all" was the reply, so on a trip back from Harburg in March 45 the skipper cut the outboards and began a long descent from 20,000 feet back to Waddington. "We'd done it, achieving a rare (and highly suspicious) 1.3 mpg. The Squadron Engineer knew there had been some dirty work involved but it could never be proven. The record stood for quite sometime. Being an Aussie, the Skipper would have had a few bob on it with the other pilots and, yes, I got my dividend as well."

– Des Hall

Lancaster Vs Mosquito: Unfair Competition

"Post-war I was flying a CSE Mosquito on calibration work just off the English Southern Coast when my Radar/Wireless Op said "Skip there's a Lanc coming up behind us." Cheeky bugger I thought and opened the throttles a tad, enough to keep a Lanc at bay. "He's still gaining," shouted the nav, so up went the boost with absolutely no effect. This Lanc then cruised past with both inners feathered! Our mouths hung open. Worse still, their crew giving us various rude signs."

"This was in the early 1950's a time of many strange test beds and conversions. We had just been passed by a jet engine powered Lincoln (probably RA716). What a line shoot the Lincoln Captain would have – streaked past that Mossie old boy with both inners feathered, can't beat a Lanc you know!"

– Bill Simpson

A Gong for Poker

In 1943 the U Boat threat to the Trans Atlantic convoys was critical. The flow of munitions, personnel and oil was essential to continue the war against Germany and losses were large. The threat was sufficiently dire for some Bomber Command main force Squadrons to be diverted to Coastal Command. After two-thirds of a Bomber Command Tour, Peter Booth's Squadron was posted to Coastal Command to fly over the Bay of Biscay on anti U-Boat patrols. The crisis passed and after almost 23 of the normal 24 Ops for a Coastal tour, the Squadron was sent back to Bomber Command. They converted on to Halifaxes at Elvington. Before Peter could carry out his first operation a leave pass came by. On returning he was told "your war is over and off to Stanton Harcourt OTU you go from Elvington."

At the OTU one foggy morning, he was playing poker in the flight office waiting for the weather to clear. In came the Commanding Officer, a Group Captain. He chatted a while as the game carried on. Then he said, "Booth, you're improperly dressed." "How's that sir?" Booth replied, "You're not wearing your gong." "I haven't got one." No more was said, but a month later he was Gazetted for an AFC. Now Peter can truthfully claim he is the only officer recommended for a gong while playing poker.

– Peter Booth

Chapter 5 – A Line

Welcome Home Once More

The station admin officer was clearly in a state of some tension and frustration, as he paced back and forth across the yawning doors of No 3 hangar. Just within its doorway the Group Captain had parked his Humber wagon, and from its misty interior a steady drift of tobacco smoke curled into the wintry early morning air. Clearly feeling equally uneasy and turning occasionally to peer into the pre-dawn south eastern skies, a small group of air force and news media photographers and reporters had gathered a few yards away.

The admin officer suddenly stopped in his pacing, ground out his State Express 333 butt and walked over to the Group Captain's vehicle. He had come to a big decision. "Sir" he said. "I don't think we're going to get anybody out now – not without some persuasion. Do I have permission to…"

There was a distinct pause as the Group Captain struggled with the weight of the decision bearing down on him. "I think we can give them a few more minutes" he said. "What's the ETA for the crews now?"

The admin officer consulted his watch. "The latest I have, sir, is 0430, about another half hour. They'll have to be down soon after that or they'll be landing all over Lincoln and Suffolk. Or the North Sea," he added meaningly.

"Couldn't we try that suggestion of getting the ground crews out to meet them – you know, a few WAAFs and some of the old men, fatherly types and all that, and just do without the school children and babies?"

"Isn't going to work sir" the admin officer said. "We chewed it over last week as a sort of reserve exercise but it's no good. Nobody's got any civvy clothes now and they weren't going to look too happy about being rousted out at 0400 anyway. They're miserable enough at 0600" he added in a vague attempt at humour.

"I don't see why the Air Ministry has picked on us for this nonsense" the Group Captain grumbled. "Our lads did two long trips back to back last week. Munich and Gdynia. I mean, they were totally stuffed after that lot and they were supposed to be climbing out all laughing and cheerful with people hanging round their necks and crying and all that stuff. Eh?"

"We managed to get some of the local villagers to help us out before that sir, a couple of weeks before you were posted here. They were all right for one or two trips. They did the 'welcome home heroes' stuff on cue, but by the time the cameras and reporters had demanded some re-runs they were getting distinctly chokka and they've refused to turn out again. All except a couple" he added.

"So what happened to them?"

"It seems a couple of bomb aimers were still feeling quite fresh, got in a bit of kip on the way home and all that and were tackled rather too warmly by some village maidens. Never got back as far as debriefing, in fact we didn't see them at all for another two days. Big trouble there sir" the admin officer added. "Court martial questions from Group HQ, very untidy. When they got back on squadron we had to bring in the Ministry of Works to clean up after the Mess party."

"And what happened to the village, er maidens, involved?"

"They wrote in and said they'd be happy to oblige any time but could the aircrew bring their own rations and

71

liquor supplies?"

"Hm, so it seems we've tried everything tonight except getting their own families here to greet them. Or has that been tried?"

"It was tried months ago sir, but it didn't work for long. All sorts of funny stuff came to light. There were pregnant girlfriends who'd been looking for young airmen all over England, there were Mums giving young fellas hell for not writing home, there were two or three girlfriends turning up to have a snog with the same air gunner. Actually sir it got, well, one station had to call in the SPs."

"Colonials, I suppose?," the Group Captain muttered.

"A bit of all sorts actually sir. Between you and me my own brother-in-law."

"Yes well we've all got one of those in the family somewhere." He was interrupted by a sergeant who came running from a hangar office with a piece of paper. He held it out to the Group Captain through the car window. "For you sir, the tower has just phoned it through to me. Fog's coming in fast from the North Sea, all our aircraft have been diverted to Colerne. Down south sir" he added.

"I know where the damn place is."

"Sorry sir, I didn't mean, that is, what shall I tell them out there, the press and news people? They're going to be a bit sort of annoyed like. I mean no crying wives and mothers and carry on…"

"Oh tell them what the hell you like" the Group Captain snapped. "Tell them nobody's coming home, all our planes were shot down over, over where was it?" He turned to the admin officer.

"Not sure sir, they're so busy these days it's hard to keep track." The admin officer turned to the sergeant. "Tell them it was a top secret target and we're not allowed to name it." The sergeant gazed back at him, baffled.

"With respect sir, the bloke – the Germans – will know where it was."

"For Gods sake," the Group Captain exploded, "will you just get those cameras and reporters off my Base. You," he turned to the admin officer, "here jump in. I'm off before this circus turns into a real shambles. Damnd reunions, damnd greetings, damnd tears and stuff, damned war."

As the Group Captain's vehicle turned down the peri track toward the Station HQ, the admin officer said "I've had a thought sir."

"Well what is it?"

"In one way it might be a good thing. I mean look at it in fifty years time. This war isn't going to last forever."

"So?"

"Well sir, we might just look like a lot of big soft jessies to people in the future when they see pictures of our men coming back from a raid being smothered in kisses and hugs and tears and all that, and cameras and kids and…"

"Y'know" said the Group Captain, "you might be right at that. Best we forget the whole silly game eh. If I were operating I'd rather have my egg for breakfast than waterfalls of weeping rellies three times a week."

"Me too sir" said the admin officer. "I'll draft you a memo for Bomber Command HQ."

Behind them the first tiny sliver of daylight slid into the eastern sky and the last of the station's, battered bombers and crews homed in thankfully on their diversionary base.

– Des Hall

Long after the last Op has been flown, are airfields like this still busy with spirit crews and ghost aircraft looking for a final place to land and rest?

Praise the Lord

"On 101 Sqadron the Commanding Officer wanted to put in an operation so he elected to fly with our Lancaster crew on what was felt to be an easy target. At the time easy ones counted as one-third of a 'real' Op. Some Air Ministry bright spark must have thought not enough of us were getting the chop on the pre D-Day daylight raids and so cut them to count as half a 'normal' Then they made them a third. Three to France equalled one to Germany. The boys were most teed off. Eventually the chop rate must have gone up as these part Ops were cancelled and reinstated counting as one again. Anyway our target on 3 May 1944 was Mailley Le Camp, a short 5 hour 40 minute jaunt... or so we thought. We arrived over the target to the brightest and noisiest reception I'd ever seen. The Rear Gunner (a God fearing gent who rarely swore) was on this 58th op. and was calling for continuously as the night fighter activity was also rather disconcerting. He called the skipper (F/L DH Todd DFC from Palmerston North) and said, "Toddy the bastards are everywhere" whereupon the guest Group Captain cut in and said, "Don't worry rear gunner, the Lord is with us" and back came the reply "he may be up your end but there's no sign of the bugger down here."

43 Lancs were lost on that raid, 11.6% of the force, including four from 101 Squadron. It is recalled by all crews that it was a 'bloody dodgy do'.

Vic Viggers completed a full tour plus one (31 ops), eleven to Berlin with fellow New Zealander F/O D. Todd as his skipper. Their aircraft DV302 (ST-H) was to complete 127 operations and was struck off charge in January 1947.

It was rare that a W/Op was decorated, Vic recalls.

"Our navigator Bill Fraser had a couple of bad ops and 101 Squadron O/C Flying, W/C Alexander, insinuated a lack of moral fibre. Our skipper was furious and demanded that Bill be looked at by a proper doctor – not the station's M/O. They found that Bill had TB."

"We became press on types and set something of a squadron standard for the best target photos, reliability and for bringing 'Harry' back even when it had 220 holes in it." At the end of the tour we all received DFCs and our Scottish Flight Engineer, the DFM.

– Vic Viggers

ABOVE: February 2006, Vic Viggers with film maker Peter Jackson during research for the new Dam Busters production

Chapter 6

A Dodgy Do

Perhaps it was their pioneering background but New Zealand aircrews rarely spoke out about operations that were incredibly dangerous or plain terrifying. Enough to say, "that was a bit close."

Most were keenly aware that just thirty years earlier the country had suffered thousands upon thousands of deaths in the horror of trench warfare. Most would have had relations killed in that war and seen the lingering deaths of the gassed.

Even in this war, there was a feeling they as aircrew were somehow lucky and certainly better off than other Kiwis in the Army fighting on the ground in the Desert or Italy. "At least we had a clean bed and reasonable food every night if we got home!"

So near misses, the loss of crew members or Squadron mates were remembered as 'a bit of a dodgy do!'

Chapter 6 – A Dodgy Do

A Bad Prang

During December 1944, 617 Squadron and their Tallboy bombs were in great demand. Arthur Joplin and his crew flew operations on the 8th, 11th, 15th and 21st.

The raid on the 21st targeted the Politz hydrogenation plant which produced synthetic petrol, a ten hour round trip. Arthur and his faithful ME561 took off at 1654 and bombed successfully. The original plan had the Squadron returning to Scotland but increasing fog ruled this out. Woodhall Spa, 617 Squadrons home base, was fogged in and Ludford Magna's FIDO system was unlit. Arthur's fuel situation was becoming of real concern when Ludford's FIDO was finally lit. "On joining the circuit a collision occurred, knocking out an engine, and down we went. We crashed just before three in the morning and came down with a hell of a bang. The rear turret was torn off, my legs were caught under the instrument panel and I was in a pretty bad way. The only reason I'm still here was that my Navigator, Basil Fish pulled me out (along with a couple of others)."

"The Bomb Aimer, Flying Officer Arthur Walker DFC, and Flying Officer Sergeant R B Yates (Rear Gunner) died in the crash. The most tragic part was that Arthur Walker had already completed his tour but had stood in for our regular bomb aimer so we could do the Op. He had been of great help to us and was one of the few real friends I had on the Squadron."

"Even though Basil was badly shaken, he set off through the fog and found a farmer's house. No home phones in these days! But the farmer guided him to a public phone box to report the crash. Finally the crash crew got to us. I had suffered two broken legs and back injuries so they took me off to hospital."

"When I had eventually recovered enough I returned to 617 (after VE day) but never flew again. A red log book endorsement was my reward, but poor Basil (who deserved a medal) got a red blot as well. The powers relented later and Basil was finally promoted and eventually commissioned."

"I arrived home (on the S.S. Maltan) on December 20th 1945 and got on with life, but the legacy of the injuries suffered all those years ago is with me today. It wasn't until 41 years later we had a bit of a 617 reunion in New Zealand, something I'd tried to avoid. Since then I've grown to enjoy being with the other Boys at our do's."

NB. Details of the accident investigation and Arthur Joplin's subsequent appalling treatment can be found in BARNES WALLIS, BOMBS, (Stephen Flower).

The FIDO system used controlled petrol fires in pipes along each side of the runway to disperse fog. An added bonus was the glow it created above the airfield acting as a beacon. However the thermals formed by thousands of gallons of petrol made for rough conditions but at least there was a clear pathway down to the runway threshold. lights. However, that night the duty staff at Group Headquarters had been reluctant to order Ludford's system lit and this delay had tragic consequences for Arthur Joplin and his crew.

– Arthur Joplin

ABOVE RIGHT: Arthur Joplin at home 21st March 2007

MIDDLE RIGHT: The crash site in 2001. ME561 (AJ-T) was a write off two days short of a year's service with 617 Squadron

ABOVE: The phone box at Tealby (Lincolnshire) where Arthur Joplin's Navigator, Basil Fish, phoned Ludford Magna for help

RIGHT: 617 Squadron mini-reunion in New Zealand, 1986
Left to right: Arthur Joplin, Frank Cardwell (Navigator), Leonard Cheshire VC, Lofty Hebbard (Arthur's B/A) and Les Munro (who flew on the Dam Busters raid in 1943)

Kiwis Do Fly

Dam Buster

"After crewing up at 29 OTU and having flown one operation (to Dusseldorf) in a Wellington we converted onto Lancasters and were posted to 97 Squadron at Woodhall Spa. Like everyone else, I felt that luck was on my side and just accepted the dangers. I was always too busy concentrating on flying to feel more than a twinge of fear. Not that I was fearless, but during a raid to Berlin in March 1943 we arrived over the target and the city was a mass of fires. Searchlights were waving with lots of bursting flak and exploding bombs. As we were completing our run, Percy Pigeon (my Wireless Operator) decided to leave his radio and come up to have a look. "Jesus Christ," he said, "have we come through that?" and promptly went back to his station. Obviously what you can't see you don't worry about."

"In mid March the Squadron received a circular from 5 Group HQ calling for volunteers to join a new Squadron for a Special Operation. Within a couple of days our crew along with F/Lt Dave Maltby and F/Lt Joe McCarthy had been posted to Scampton and 617 Squadron."

"We trained for the still secret special target until early May 1943, when modified Lancasters were delivered and over the 11,12 and 13th we began dropping inert Upkeep bombs at Chesil Beach. I was then detailed by Wing Commander Gibson to be part of the Northern Group scheduled to drop our 'Upkeeps' in the Sorpe Dam."

"This was a concrete cored earth dam and unlike the others we planned to attack by dropping the Upkeep midway along the crest. The bombs weren't to be spun like the others, so they sank down the inside wall and exploded at 35 feet. Barnes Wallis hoped that the successive concussions and shock wave of several bombs would crack the inner concrete core and seepage would gradually create a breach."

"The raid itself is well documented. In my case we were hit by flak crossing the coast which took out our intercom system, and were forced to return. I had perhaps the dubious distinction of being the first to land with an armed Upkeep on board. Cyril Anderson's crew became the second."

"I was disappointed that my part in the operation had been aborted and felt quite uncomfortable in joining the celebrations by the surviving crews. But perhaps considering the Squadron's losses that night, maybe Lady Luck had played another card for me."

This famous raid was notable in representing a huge advance on precision flying and special ordnance not repeated until the advent of GPS controlled smart weapons.

Eight of the nineteen Lancasters taking part in Operation Chastise were lost and fifty three airmen killed, but the skill and bravery of the crews and the audacity of Wallis's bouncing bomb remain a remarkable achievement.

– *Les Munro*

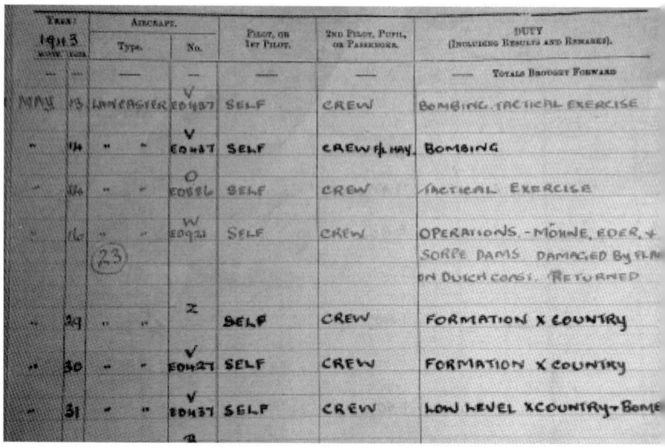

ABOVE: ED 921 AJ-W Les Munro's allocated Dam Buster modified Lancaster

ABOVE: Les Munro's log book entry for the Dams raid, 16 May 1943

LEFT: RAF Lossiemouth 2003, Les poses with an Upkeep dropped during practice in May 1943 at Chesil Beach. It was recovered and rebuilt

ABOVE: Les Munro, 617 'B' flight commander, Woodhall Spa 1944

Chapter 6 – A Dodgy Do

Shot Up

"On 23 June 1944 the Op scheduled that night was to Coubronne, France and we were allocated Lancaster 'TL-F (ND 916).' I was mid-upper gunner as usual. It was the first time we'd flown an 'F' for Freddy."

"After bombing the target (V1 buzz bomb sites), we crossed the French Coast on the way home, but near the Pas de Calais area, we were attacked from the starboard quarter by a Ju88. I couldn't see him initially because of the Lanc's tail plane. We'd been hit, so I returned fire by hosing shots over the end of the aircraft to where I estimated the fighter was." Further attacks by the Ju88 resulted in both gunners being wounded. "Most of the perspex in my turret was shattered, hydraulic pipes punctured and I was blinded in both eyes by the perspex, I also received various shrapnel wounds to my arms and legs, in all a bit of a mess."

"As well as the rear and mid-upper turrets being put out of action in the attack, the Lancaster's port inner petrol tank was holed, a booster pump was shot away, the H2S dome shattered, bomb doors and fuselage damaged. With the holed fuel tank on fire our Skipper, Geoff Marsden, put the aircraft in to a dive in an effort to put out the flames and we flew into cloud. No further attacks were made. The Ju88 pilot probably assumed that we were bound to explode or crash. Our steep dive put out the flames, but it took all of Geoff Marsden's and Charlie's (our Flight Engineer) strength to pull the aircraft out of the dive. Charlie had his back against the instrument panel pushing the control column

ABOVE: Now a Sergeant, Harry Furner, Mid Upper Gunner 35 Squadron, Graveley 1944

RIGHT: Perspex gone, the mid upper turret of ND916

77

Kiwis Do Fly

while Geoff was pulling. Once they'd got the Lancaster straightened up and level we headed back for base."

"Due to my wounds I was put on the rest bed and patched up as best as possible but I refused any morphine. I also asked Harry Rolls to take my boots off as I always wanted to die with my boots off but he refused as it was so cold. Our rear gunner, Neville Farley, had been extracted from his turret and laid on the rear spar. We eventually landed back at Graveley. My flying days were over, three days before my 20th birthday."

"I was then transferred to the RAF hospital at Ely, where I spent time in the convalescent ward. My wounds had been treated, and I started to adjust to life with only one eye."

– Harry Furner

ABOVE: The Rear Gunner also suffered from the attack

RIGHT: TL-F's starboard wing showing cannon shell damage

Chapter 6 – A Dodgy Do

Nuremburg

Nuremburg before (1945) and after (2006)

"Our Nuremburg trip was down for 30/31 March 1944. When the operations staff opened the curtain in the briefing, we saw that the route was pretty much a long straight line running into the target. We couldn't believe it. There were cries of disbelief all round the room."

"We found out after the raid that 96 aircraft had been lost that night, I saw five aircraft go down in flames on the way to the target but we didn't fire a shot. There wasn't a shadow to be seen:- it was a quiet night for us."

"We knew some had bombed Stuttgart and Schweinfurt, whether it was because of diversionary fires I don't know. They used to make the dummy fires in England to put the German bombers off and use fake target indicators to try and draw bombs away from the real target. Sometimes others would drop their bombs when they saw one aircraft let them go, I don't know if it was panic. If they'd have followed the rules then the bombing by mistake of the other cities wouldn't have happened. We bombed the target successfully. We always had a joke with the bomb aimer, Bobby, we'd go left, left ... steady ... left, left ... steady ... then back a bit!!!!!"

"Our Pilot and Bomb Aimer always did well as a team and we had pretty good bombing results. That's the reason, I think, why we were 'volunteered' for Pathfinders."

"On the Nuremberg raid we found the target and bombed successfully but on the return leg we got off track somehow and the Skipper needed a position, I don't know if it was because of the winds we encountered but the Navigator guessed we were west of Paris, so on we flew. Eventually I spotted an English airfield the occult light signalling JK (Johnny King) and our Wireless Operator Harry Rolls found JK was Northolt (just out of London). He switched on the IFF smartly as we'd had one warning shot already from the ground defences. Eventually we had to divert to Elvington due to an aircraft having crashed on the runway intersection at Burn."

"There was a fair amount of ground fog over Elvington and 'Charlie,' as we called Carl (the Flight Engineer), was starting to panic about our fuel state to which Geoff said "pour the bloody coffee in." We called up Elvington but got no reply so as the fuel was now getting critical Geoff decided to go straight in. We got down and had just turned off the runway when the engines spluttered. "If we'd had gone round again, we'd have had it."

"Elvington was home to a Free French Halifax Squadron but they showed no hospitality and we had to fend for ourselves. To thank them for their hospitality we took their piano apart before we left!"

Nuremburg attracted many raids, partly because of the city being a traditional home to the Nazi party where the huge rallies were staged

ABOVE: St Lorenz Church 1945, below 2006

79

Kiwis Do Fly

pre-war. USAAF target records show the city supported four motorcycle works, a ball bearing plant, a machine tool plant, and was a major railway hub. City records list nineteen raids between August 1942 and 21 February 1945, the largest raid being carried out by RAF Bomber Command on 2/3 January 1945 when 1573 tons of HE and 479 tons of incendiaries were dropped.

Yet despite nineteen raids, much of the stadium was undamaged and today this huge building is part of the city's park.

– Harry Furner

ABOVE: The Meriden Grand Hotel.
Left 1945, right 2006

BELOW LEFT: The Medieval City Gate 1945

BELOW RIGHT: The City 1945

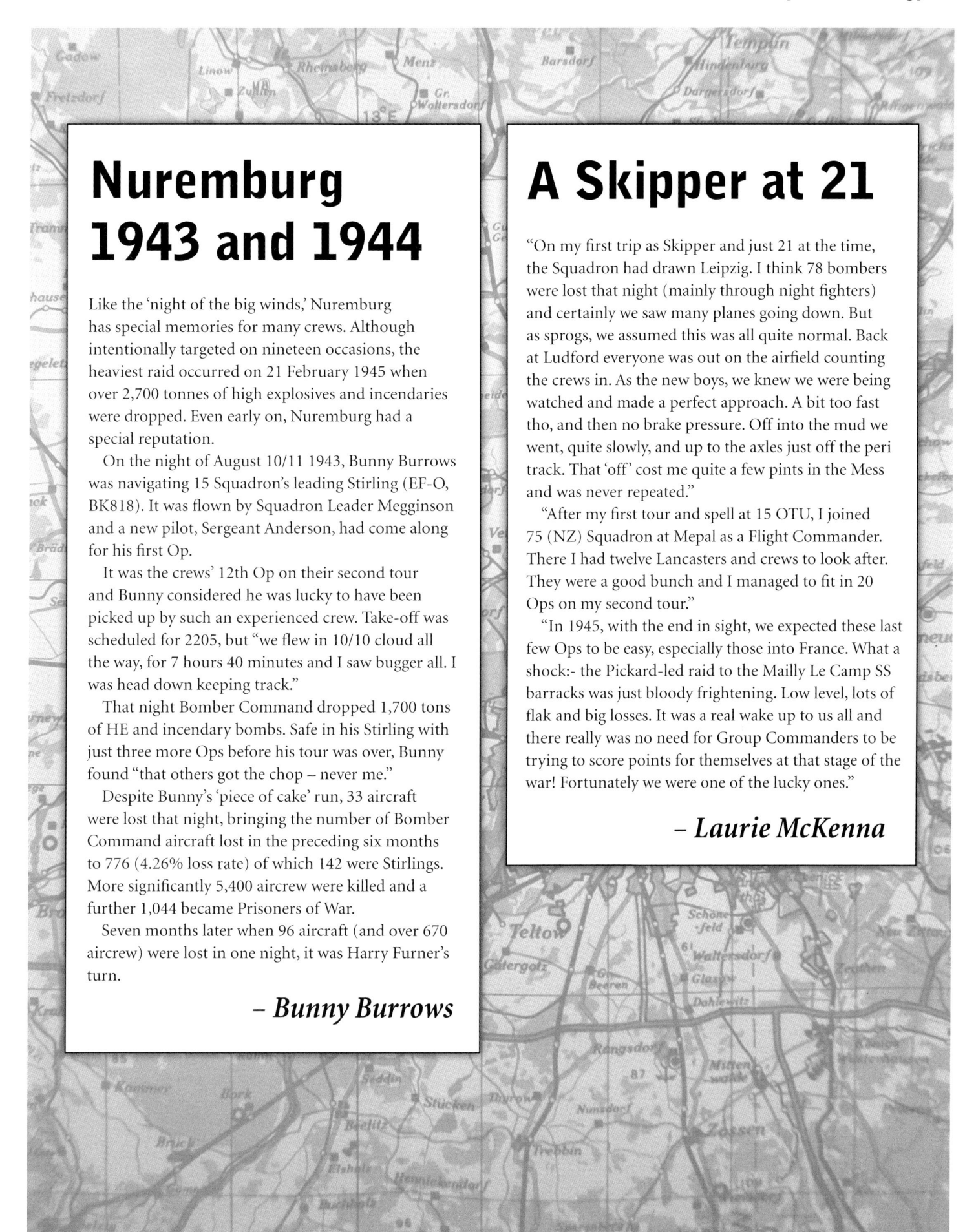

Nuremburg 1943 and 1944

Like the 'night of the big winds,' Nuremburg has special memories for many crews. Although intentionally targeted on nineteen occasions, the heaviest raid occurred on 21 February 1945 when over 2,700 tonnes of high explosives and incendiaries were dropped. Even early on, Nuremburg had a special reputation.

On the night of August 10/11 1943, Bunny Burrows was navigating 15 Squadron's leading Stirling (EF-O, BK818). It was flown by Squadron Leader Megginson and a new pilot, Sergeant Anderson, had come along for his first Op.

It was the crews' 12th Op on their second tour and Bunny considered he was lucky to have been picked up by such an experienced crew. Take-off was scheduled for 2205, but "we flew in 10/10 cloud all the way, for 7 hours 40 minutes and I saw bugger all. I was head down keeping track."

That night Bomber Command dropped 1,700 tons of HE and incendary bombs. Safe in his Stirling with just three more Ops before his tour was over, Bunny found "that others got the chop – never me."

Despite Bunny's 'piece of cake' run, 33 aircraft were lost that night, bringing the number of Bomber Command aircraft lost in the preceding six months to 776 (4.26% loss rate) of which 142 were Stirlings. More significantly 5,400 aircrew were killed and a further 1,044 became Prisoners of War.

Seven months later when 96 aircraft (and over 670 aircrew) were lost in one night, it was Harry Furner's turn.

– Bunny Burrows

A Skipper at 21

"On my first trip as Skipper and just 21 at the time, the Squadron had drawn Leipzig. I think 78 bombers were lost that night (mainly through night fighters) and certainly we saw many planes going down. But as sprogs, we assumed this was all quite normal. Back at Ludford everyone was out on the airfield counting the crews in. As the new boys, we knew we were being watched and made a perfect approach. A bit too fast tho, and then no brake pressure. Off into the mud we went, quite slowly, and up to the axles just off the peri track. That 'off' cost me quite a few pints in the Mess and was never repeated."

"After my first tour and spell at 15 OTU, I joined 75 (NZ) Squadron at Mepal as a Flight Commander. There I had twelve Lancasters and crews to look after. They were a good bunch and I managed to fit in 20 Ops on my second tour."

"In 1945, with the end in sight, we expected these last few Ops to be easy, especially those into France. What a shock:- the Pickard-led raid to the Mailly Le Camp SS barracks was just bloody frightening. Low level, lots of flak and big losses. It was a real wake up to us all and there really was no need for Group Commanders to be trying to score points for themselves at that stage of the war! Fortunately we were one of the lucky ones."

– Laurie McKenna

Kiwis Do Fly

I Took to my 'Scrapers'

With his St. Athan's Flight Engineers course complete, Sergeant Harry Cammish joined 50 Squadron at Skellingthorpe with the crew he met up with at 1660 HCU. As Flight Engineer, Harry was the last to join the crew, the others having teamed up at OTU.

"Our first Op was to Hamburg on 7th July 1943 and it certainly was an eye opener. No matter how much you had pumped the Squadrons few old hands for gen on, "What's it really like?" Nothing prepares you for the reality. Noise, lights, bangs, whoomps, thumps. I felt it best to keep busy filling in the log sheet calculating petrol consumption, and not looking out."

"Lancasters, with all props rotating anti clockwise, had a reputation of swinging to port on take-off. On July 12th we were ready for take-off on our third Op. Our pilot, like the rest of us, was new on the job. We lined up on the runway, the pilot pushed the throttles forward, with me following (as a good flight engineer should) and off we went, swinging well to port. Our skipper struggled and struggled against the swing until at 90 knots our Lanc became uncontrollable and left the runway, bounding across the grass toward the nearest hangar. We were still going at a fair clip when the port wing hit the hangar corner, which ripped it clean off. The Lanc went into a ground loop. The rear fuselage broke away, carrying the rear gunner with it, all blazing with hydraulic liquid from the ruptured lines."

"As soon as we'd stopped I was out and just ran, on through bushes, hedges and right off the airfield. I went into a small cottage and called out "there's a crashed Lanc over there and its about to blow." Which it did! Much later!"

"The cottage owner went and got the local bobby to check on me. He cycled back to the police station, phoned the base then came back to check if I was the missing flight engineer. He went back to the station and confirmed that he had the missing flight engineer. Finally I was picked up. I wasn't in good shape and my battledress was torn to pieces after running through the hedges. The rear gunner had been badly burnt and the others all injured. After a few days in hospital, off I went on seven day survivor's leave. But the Commanding Officer made me take a test flight before I went on leave, obviously to restore my nerve."

"When I reported back to Skellingthorpe, my crew were either still in hospital or dispersed. The Commanding Officer kept me on the Squadron as a spare flight engineer. Usually in these cases I would have been sent back to crew up again at HCU. So for the next fourteen Ops I was a fill in for sick flight engineers and rarely flew with the same crew and rarely even knew their names. That was to be a problem later on."

– Harry Cammish

ABOVE: Lancaster VN-T of 50 Squadron at Skellingthorpe 1944

Chapter 6 – A Dodgy Do

Court Martial and a DFM Award

In early 1941, after OTU training and with just 16 hours of night flying logged (twilight was also counted as night in those days), Jim Dermody joined 99 Squadron at Newmarket flying Wellingtons. "I was the navigator and the only Kiwi, Stan Holloway was our Skipper and a Pom like the rest of the crew."

"Our first Op in LN – B (T2984) was meant to be Boulogne but we got off to a DNCD (did not complete duty) when our motors cut and our bomb load was jettisoned off the coast."

"Two nights later, on 9th April, in a now cleared LN – B, we went to Berlin with three 500 pounders and six lots of incediaries. Our navigational briefing was to turn 29 miles north of the target and begin our run-in to the South when the river and lakes in Berlin should show up clearly in the moonlight. In those days the Squadron tried to stick together but getting a little off course was still acceptable. So our crew agreed to vary the track a little. (to miss the worst of the flak)."

"My navigation that night was spot on, there was the river and Berlin's Zee lakes were clear to see. The puzzle was no lights, no flak – oh dear, we must be the first ones here!"

"There was a lot of haze over the target and our bomb aimer (and second pilot), Bob Holden, couldn't get a clear view. So over Berlin we back-tracked, swung around, over we went again and again, no luck. The German ack ack boys must have wondered what this idiot was doing tracking over their Capital. On the third run there was a terrific whoof, whoof, whoof. I'd just come up from the nose when this flak took out the bomb sight and selector panel, letting in a terrific gale. Another whoof removed the top wire from the control column. The balance spring in the control now took over the elevator and down we went from 13,000 feet to about 300. I wasn't watching the altimeter but did have to look up to see a small chapel on the hill drift past."

"Stan used all his strength (with Bob's help) to overcome the dive

BELOW: Jim Dermody's crew on 99 Squadron alongside their Wellington LN-B (T2984)

Left to Right: Lionel Knight (observer), Bob Holden (2nd Pilot B/A), Percy Rankin (W/Op), Stan Holloway (Captain) Jim (Nav) and Bob Butler (RG)

Kiwis Do Fly

and the Wellington struggled back to 1,000 feet. We were safe from any more heavy flak as it sailed over the top."

"The motors continued to run well so we carried on. The crew earlier had agreed not to bale out unless there was a fire. To help our Pilot Stan, we ripped cordage from the emergency dinghy and tied the column back on to the forward frames. We finally made it back to Newmarket."

"Later in the mess our red faces weren't about returning a badly damaged aircraft but of being charged with wilful damage to H.M. property by hacking the dinghy about. Eventually nothing was said."

"Stan then decided that our leave periods would be much better served with a motor car and proceeded to buy an old wooden-bodied Standard. Petrol was scarce but could be 'obtained.' One of our ground-crew corporals asked Stan for a loan of the car for an important date prior to going on leave. Stan said sure and the next day he returned the little Standard and parked it under some trees near the Flight Office."

"The temptation to our resident SPs was too great and they decided to check the petrol. Of course it was the wrong colour, and of course it was 100 octane aviation petrol. "You are on a charge of stealing H.M. petrol!'"

"Stan being the car's owner was court martialled and the officer acting as the prisoner's friend at the hearing asked us, as Stan's crew, to support his appeal. I stated the events of April 9th and concluded that Stan undoubtedly saved the crews lives and brought a badly damaged aircraft back to base. That day, the car-borrowing Corporal returned from leave and owned up to using aviation gas. The Court Martial was abandoned.

"We thought that was the end of it, but back at RAF Records Office, receiving the Court Martial details, they asked why Stan had not been accorded a decoration for bravery."

"A DFM was immediately awarded."

Jim finished his tour and began another before returning to New Zealand, but the remainder of LN-B crew were all killed during subsequent service.

– Jim Dermody

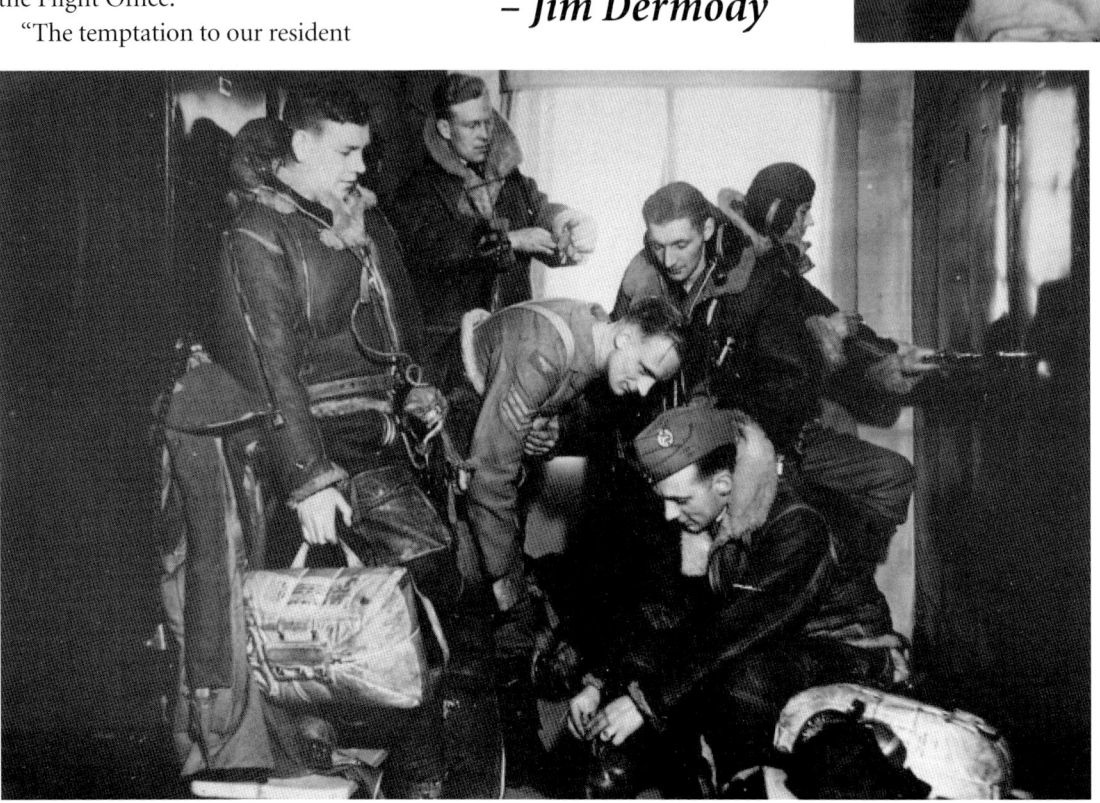

ABOVE: An Infrared photograph of Bob Holden in Wellington T2984, taken by Jim down in the Bomb Aimers compartment

LEFT: An experiment in Infrared photography in near total darkness, June 1942. Jim Dermody's crew gearing up.
Left to Right: Lionel Knight, Percy Hawkins, Bob Butler, Stan Holloway (seated, lacing up his boot). Bob Holden, Jim Dermody (at the locker)

156 (Pathfinder) Squadron

"Before we were transferred to 156 Squadron, we completed a Pathfinder course at Warboys to upgrade the skills of navigators and bomb aimers. On 28 April 1944 we moved to Upwood, where both 156 Squadron and 139 (Pathfinder, Mosquito) Squadrons were stationed."

Upwood was a pre-war airfield with permanent buildings. It had hangars, central heating and a comfortable officers' mess. This was in some contrast with Elsham Wolds!

"Our first operation with 156 Squadron was to Hasselt (in Belgium) on 11 May 1944. The Master Bomber radioed instructions as to the exact location for the markers and every- thing possible was done to limit casualties to the Belgian population. En route from Brussels to Hasselt, we were told that Hasselt was shrouded in thick fog, and so the mission was aborted. As we turned around we were attacked by a German fighter and quickly were on fire."

"In the fuselage the hydraulic oil in the Mid Upper Turret was burning, one engine was hit and on fire. Fortunately the crew extinguished the fire in the fuselage, but we weren't able to control the fire in the wing. I had thrown the aircraft into a spiralling dive to get rid of the nightfighter and the fire in the wing only went out after a steep dive to 2,000 feet. In addition to the dud engine, we had other problems. We still had the bombs on board, no electrics at all and the bomb release mechanism was out of commission, but luckily we had shaken off the nightfighter. He must have thought that the dive as well as the burning wing was an indication that our end was close. Through a little hole in the bomb bay we were eventually able to release all twelve bombs one by one by pressing them with a screwdriver. One relief was the flight engineer reported that the fuel tanks hadn't suffered damage."

"Given that I wasn't able to communicate with the gunners, I sent the flight engineer back to see what was going on. He was back pretty fast with the news that both of them had jumped. Who can blame them? ... a steep dive, on fire, unable to communicate with the rest of the crew they decided to take the safe way out. They were both taken prisoner of war."

"Meanwhile with the bomb load gone our lighter Lancaster could start to climb despite one silent engine. Our onboard searchlight (Aldis lamp) wasn't working either and so we had no idea what the damage to the wings would be. We had no navigation lights, and maybe no brakes!"

"I decided to set a course to Woodbridge (near Ipswich) which was an emergency landing area with three parallel runways of 2,000 metres (6,000 feet) – in those

ABOVE: Left to Right – Jack's crew:
Sgt Kilminster, F/O Dalgleish and F/Sgt Jones ready for ops. All were to be decorated for their actions on 11 May 1944

Kiwis Do Fly

days an enormous stretch!"

The airfield was easy to find. Three searchlights intersecting at one point were visible from far out in the North Sea. Two runways had the usual white and yellow lights. The third was lit in green.

"We had no communication with the control tower and had to bear in mind that there was a possibility of wing damage. We had also discovered a one square metre hole in the fuselage and had no idea if the landing gear would hold but decided on the green runway anyway and the crew took up crash positions."

"I did two circuits of the airfield while we tried to get the landing gear down and because of the damage to the wings and the large hole in the fuselage I made the approach at 20 to 25 miles an hour faster than normal to make a careful landing with the tail up. The landing gear held but the brakes were ineffective and needed the full length of the long runway and finally came to a halt on the grass."

"A few seconds later a fireman climbed through the non-existent back door – as the gunners had, on departure, failed to close it behind them!!!"

"A loud voice said; "Anybody hurt?"... We shouted "No." Then the reply, "Well then, have a whisky.""

Meanwhile our plane was pulled off the runway to keep the green strip clear.

"After debriefing by the station intelligence officer and a traditional meal of bacon and eggs, it was off to bed. It was hard to get to sleep!"

"We assumed that the Woodbridge control tower would be in contact with our base in Upwood. They didn't and Upwood had no idea what had happened to us. By the afternoon we had heard nothing and sent our own message. Until that moment we had been registered as missing and the adjutant had even gathered up all our belongings."

"That morning we wandered around Woodbridge. A couple of hundred wrecks were scattered around the place, lots of American Flying Fortresses and Liberators as well as English Lancasters, Stirlings, Halifaxes and fighters."

"Naturally we were very interested in our aircraft. The damage was considerable, and there were indeed several holes in the wings and the fuselage. The bomb aimer had been lucky; where he had been in the nose several bullets must have shaved him. We felt as if we had won first prize in the lottery."

"What I remember most was the stink of the burning rubber and electric wires. The smell hung around in my nose for days."

"In the afternoon we were picked up by an Upwood Lancaster and had to be interviewed by the Squadron's Commanding Officer, Wing Commander Bingham Hall."

ABOVE: Jack's ND342 (GT-H) at Upwood prior to their first operation with 156 Squadron

"Two days later I was summoned by him. He congratulated me and informed me that I had been awarded an immediate Distinguished Flying Cross. A fortnight later the Officers in the crew were also awarded the DFC, and Sergeants the DFM (Distinguished flying Medal)."

"Under normal circumstances I would have been summoned to London where King George VI would have presented me with the DFC but this was not procedure for Allied Military personnel who still had family in Occupied areas. So they held a ceremony at Upwood. All off-duty air and ground staff made up a parade. I was called forward and had the DFC pinned to my chest by Air Vice Marshall Bennett."

"That night in the mess there was a real party!"

Jack and his crew completed their tour nine months later and in November he was posted to Upavon CFS for instructor training.

– Jack 't Hart

ABOVE: Jack's log book records Sgt Seldon and Sgt Asquith (rear and mid upper gunners) as baled out, and the award of a DFC to Jack, to Sgt Kilminster a DFM, F/O Dalgleish a DFC, F/Sgt Jones a DFC and Sgt Bridges the DFM.

Chapter 6 – A Dodgy Do

A Shaky Start

As a sprog crew, Des Andrewe's first Op with 622 Squadron was to Stuttgart on 15 March 1944. Early in the trip they lost their port inner engine, and with that height. "At 14,000 feet and over the target we copped a couple of incendiaries through the starboard wing. We were too low and well below the main force at 18,000 feet. However we bombed and on the return track W4248 attracted a night fighter. Fortunately the planned corkscrew manouvre worked and we finally headed home for Mildenhall but with parachutes strapped firmly on."

"Our Skipper was pretty concerned that the incendiaries may have wrecked the starboard undercarriage wheel, so he let down very gently on the port side. As soon as the starboard touched, its burst tyre sent us into an almighty ground loop. Boy, were we glad to get back. We all thought – this is just the first of 30 trips, how do we do it! We did of course but never again had to face anything like that first Op!"

– Des Andrewes

TOP RIGHT: March 15th. In W4246 (GI-J) Des Andrewes has his first experience of an operation. Later W4158 served with No 3LFS and was SOC 5/12/45

RIGHT: Sixty years later, at the Nav station in MOTAT's NX665

BELOW: Des Andrewe's crew, who completed a full tour 'undamaged' in W4158

Left to right: Les Hillford (B/A), Bill Joy (RG), Denis Swilt (M/UG), Burt Dawkins (F/E), Des (Nav), Chook Struthers (Pilot), and Peter Brook (W/Op) – Their final Op 18th July 1944

Chapter 7

Time Out, On Leave, In the Mess, Back to OTU

While an individual's rank didn't figure in New Zealand airmen's social events and pub crawls, RAF crews found it quite different.

Des Hall (Flight Engineer 463 Squadron) and Harry Furner (Mid Upper Gunner 35 PFF Squadron) both of whom later migrated to New Zealand, remember the distinct class barriers between non-commissioned crew, and Officers. "The carry-ons of RNZAF and RAAF crews on leave all together opened our eyes. We flew as a crew but lived as strangers. In my total service of one and a half tours (39 Ops) we only got together twice, and one of those was the Skippers birthday. We didn't bunk together, mess together or have leave together. We were a flying team and that was it! No wonder most crews liked to have a sprinkling of Kiwis or Aussies as they just ignored conventions. Perhaps that's why I ended up in New Zealand after the war."

The stream of volunteers who signed up for wartime service with the New Zealand Forces were independent spirits and may have lacked the social skills of their English comrades but they also lacked any pretensions to class. They treated Officers, NCOs and ACs equally and expected the same courtesy in return. Often they were stunned to witness the offhand manner and lack of respect shown by some 'Non Kiwi' officers to their men.

Many found that the further from the front line, the thicker the bullshit and the importance of looking after Number One, and there was little mateship even in the ranks.

A famous quote attributed to New Zealand General Freyberg VC was that on hearing a British officer complaining about the lack of saluting by New Zealand troops, Freyberg suggested he tried waving instead.

Coming from what was in 1940 a sparsely populated country, without many services, it was expected that people just got along together and helped where possible, regardless of 'station' or wealth, just like at home. It came as a shock to many that many of the English weren't like that at all.

So the New Zealanders on leave sought out their own countrymen or the other Colonials in a crew and all went on the town together.

Chapter 7 – Time Out, On Leave, In the Mess, Back to OTU

Watering Holes

Kiwi crews invariably headed to London on their leave. With no families to go home to, the whole crew would take off for the bright lights.

The NZ Forces Club in Charing Cross Road was always the first stop for aircrew to check on mail from home, meet up with mates and have a feed of sausages and mash for one shilling and sixpence. Then off to the nearby pub – the famous Sussex. The pub was run by a Mr Cakehead. Always a friend to the Kiwis he was happy to lend them a quid if they were hard up. He had spent time pre-war in Gisborne (on New Zealand's East Coast) and had a soft spot for Kiwis. Come the afternoon and closing time at 2.30, the crew's next stop was across the road at the Two Greeks Restaurant.

Overseen by 'Ma,' great steaks could be had for just three shillings and for meat-loving Kiwis, the temptation of a tasty big steak overcame any thought of its origin. Horse or no horse, it still tasted great.

"Under the Sussex was the 'Tartan Bar,' a bit of a dive, but we found it good fun until an invasion by Canadians. There were a few stouches and that took the shine off. Many moved allegiance to Covent Gardens and the White Swan (aka 'The Dirty Duck') and by 1944 it was the place to check for a mate. There was always mostly good natured competition between the Aussies and Kiwis whenever they met. On leave the Kiwis acted like they belonged there, the Aussies like they owned it."

To those returning in recent years the Suffolk remains, a little sprucer but unchanged. The 'Duck' had fallen on bad times and was swallowed up in the redevelopment of the Covent Garden area.

TOP LEFT: Wing Commander Stephen Watts (centre) at the New Zealand Forces Club, London

LEFT: Today's Sussex in Charing Cross
(P. Barrowman)

BOTTOM LEFT: New Zealand aircrew about to go on leave complete with gas mask bags (no mask but loot), greatcoats and pipes. In this case it was pre-embarkation leave.

BELOW: NZ Forces Club ex Italian Embassy, is now the Westminster Library

Kiwis Do Fly

The Service Police

These important people are known as the 'SPs' or 'Snoops.' They were a sort of race apart and aircrew sergeants were always a popular target for the SPs.

"If I'm about to leave camp Snoops is on duty at the gate and will inspect me as rigorously as if I was suspected of being about to carry leprosy into the outside world."

"When I return and wish to enter the camp – (not that I ever do wish, but I have to enter) – they examine my pass and documents with as much suspicion as if I was a forger just out of gaol."

"Their game is 'ask to see my pass.' If it is not in order, ghoulish grins of glee spread over their faces and they get busy slapping me on the fizzer."

"I've often felt that being a Service Policeman is not a trade, it's a disease."

"Incorrect dress, out of uniform, leave pass or travel warrant lost, too early reporting or too late back on base. Gas mask bag check for contraband. Not saluting or not saying 'Sir.' All were traps eagerly set by the SPs."

"They were a very hard lot and only sympathetic to us when they were well out numbered. The only time I saw a patrol of them speechless when they stopped a member of our Squadron who happened to be a member of the aristocracy and he insisted they addressed him as 'My Lord'.

– *Anon*

RIGHT: Watch out for the SPs
Tom Whyte (R/G) 101 Squadron still posing as the remainder of his crew exit left. Sorrento, May 1945. "The overnight runs to Bari were great, good food, hotels and sunshine. Plus plenty of wine made these trips spectacularly good fun. With the black market bulging with rationed goods, the trips could also be very profitable provided the SPs and H.M. Customs could be avoided."

ABOVE: Lancasters lined up at Bari ready to take Eighth Army veterans home along with contraband, always of great interest to the SPs.

What Petrol Ration

"Whilst at Burn, Geoff, a crew mate of mine, wanted to visit his sister. She was a WRNS Officer and was on leave at their home in Yorkshire. He hadn't seen her for some time and wanted to catch up. Geoff managed to get permission to go but couldn't get any petrol for his motorbike."

"The only source of petrol available was in a huge concrete mixer next to our billet. The mixer had two tanks on top, one for water, the other for the petrol. You could stand on the framework to access the bottom of the petrol tank which had a wing nut type arrangement with a nipple inside so when the nut was loosened it allowed the petrol to stream out. We used an old pint bottle to collect the petrol needed. It was the job of one of the workmen to check the level of the petrol tank by banging on the side of it with a hammer. It used to wake us up in the morning! So after putting the petrol in the motorbike and getting Geoff on his way, a couple of us peed in the pint bottle and poured the contents back into the tank. The next morning, after the workman was satisfied the tank level was Okay, he started up the engine which, after a short time it began to splutter. He quickly checked, the cause was found and from our billet we could hear him using a great selection of adjectives to describe our parentage!"

Aviation fuel not surprisingly found its way into many of the weird and varied range of cars and motorbikes favoured by aircrew. At wars-end ex-mid upper gunner and now Flight Lieutenant Douglas Taylor was posted to the crash strip at RAF Woodbridge in Suffolk as OC. The aerodrome was equipped with a fog dispersal system known as FIDO. A mix of fuels was pumped into pipes along each side of the runway and set alight.

Amongst his problems post VE day was a missing 500,000 gallons of mixed fuel kept in enormous storage tanks to supply the FIDO system. "I'd signed for it and was told by the rapidly departing previous Commanding Officer, "just lose it old boy." By the time I left, the awol petrol tally was down to 150,000 gallons. A good practical introduction to very creative accounting."

– Harry Furner

BELOW: What petrol Ration?

Flight Lieutenant J Thompson (627 Squadron) swaps his Mosquito for a Morris. Note the stylish paintwork on the guards. Another trusty steed appears in the background. Woodhall Spa 1945

Kiwis Do Fly

In the Mess

"At Westcott OTU, we had dining-in nights at the Officers Mess perhaps once a month. There was a strict protocol and of course wearing your number one uniform was obligatory."

"At times the speeches would go on and on, and of course most of us had already had our fill of beer before dinner. It was the done thing to ask the Mess President's permission to leave but it wasn't good form to leave just for a leak. So you'd have these chaps on hands and knees quietly crawling around the side of the room heading for the door and relief. Funnily enough, the Mess President must have had very poor peripheral vision or was blind to the event as he never hauled up one of the crawlers."

"Of course at Wescott NCO instructors didn't do dining-in. We preferred boozing out but we'd have the odd dance night. At Mildenhall, even though it was a beautifully built pre-war station, the Sergeants' mess was upstairs and not really well supported. But we did have a few social dos up there. Serving at the Station Headquarters was a really attractive WAAF but those who got 'friendly' with her all seemed to end up getting the chop. Fact or superstition, call it what you will, it got so bad that one night a mess regular, a Canadian rear gunner who was well into his rum quota and further into singing 'Balls to Mr Bennington' when he spotted one of the sprogs getting cosy with this WAAF, he pulled the guy away saying quite drunkenly, "No, No you mustn't – she's the 'Chop WAAF'.""

"With the aircrew no longer interested, this WAAF turned to the ground crew for company. Funnily enough, her special erk backed away into the propeller of an engine being run up on test. I don't know what happened to the poor girl after that."

"As a crew with an Aussie skipper we went off the base for a few, nearly always beer and lots of it but once whisky. That one bottle was enough for a lifetime."

The officer's messes delighted in playing games, crossing the room without touching the floor, picking up rolled newspaper with only one's teeth or a solid game of mess rugby all added to the fun and eventually to the mess bill for furniture repairs.

The Officers Mess Secretary and the Sergeants Mess Catering officers and their cooks were often in the firing line, although the boys were continually hungry and simply ate what ever came along.

Phil Small's memory is of an over supply of canned salmon which took the stations catering supply by surprise for us it took a solid weeks eating to clear the backlog, "I still don't like salmon."

– John Tarbuck, Bill Simpson, Des Andrewes

ABOVE: Free French and RAF aircrew in the Mess at Mepal *(R Broadbent)*

Chapter 7 – Time Out, On Leave, In the Mess, Back to OTU

Travel Permitted

A leave pass usually involved travelling by train, as petrol was scarce, but there was a special concession for aircrew who owned cars and they would be given petrol coupons for just enough fuel to reach destination and return.

Trains were fewer than in peacetime and with limited track maintenance they travelled at lower speeds and were invariably late. On occasions they could be running 24 hours behind schedule and one would catch Tuesday's train at about its scheduled time on a Wednesday!

"Invariably they were overcrowded and I well remember on one occasion managing to climb in through a window and was passed over their heads by those standing in the corridor until there was a small space where I was able to be dropped, fortunately feet first, and there I stood for the next few hours."

"After dark all blinds in carriages had to be drawn so they wouldn't draw the unwelcome attention of any enemy aircraft which happened to be overhead and that, combined with the overcrowding, made them very stuffy and, dare I say it, rather smelly."

It made little difference if your rail warrant was for first or third class as all were equally overcrowded. An officer was supplied with a first class warrant and those fortunate enough to get a seat in a compartment for six would be compressed as all the armrests were pushed back and there would be four, and even five, a side. Not the acme of comfort but better than standing in a corridor, or in a compartment, for hours.

"I don't remember how it was done, but we must have been supplied with a few ration coupons for our leaves, as just about everything edible was rationed in addition to petrol and clothing."

"Whilst the army chaps (referred to as 'pongos') could be overseas and away from home for years on end, and naval fellows the same, most Bomber Command aircrew operated from U.K. bases and were given seven days leave every six weeks which was the envy of the other services. It was, I assume, to try to compensate for the high 'chop rate' Once 'on leave,' local city travel was commonly on trams."

"What did you do on your leave in Newcastle upon Tyne, your nearest home town? The 'in' thing was to go to Fenwick's Tea Room for a cup of coffee at about 11 am and anyone who was on leave would be there so you could meet up with friends. If circumstances didn't permit getting to the Tea Room the next gathering place was at noon in 'the sink' which was the cocktail lounge of the Eldon Grill. Then plans could be made for the evening which usually involved a few drinks, somewhere or other, of the weak wartime brews."

"The seven days would pass very quickly and before you knew it father and mother would be seeing you off onto another equally late and crowded train heading back to Station and discipline."

– Doug Taylor

Nude Statues

"We often were issued forty-eight hour passes when the weather clamped in and no flying was possible, so off to town we'd go. Travelling by tram I'd hold out my penny or tuppenny fare and usually the clippy wouldn't see it and would walk past. On her return I'd hold it out again and again, she wouldn't see it and would walk past. As an 'erk' on three shillings a day, the saving of a tram fare, only a penny or tuppence was a factor to be considered. Mind you beer was a shilling a pint, and cigarettes when obtainable, were eleven pence half-penny for a twenty pack."

"There were concessionary rates at cinemas for servicemen in uniform and in London you could buy a 'red, white and blue' which gave unlimited travel for that day on all of London's transport system, tube trains, trams and buses."

"While in London we'd join the queues outside the Windmill Theatre near Piccadilly Circus. The Lord Chamberlain permitted 'nude statues' on stage provided they didn't move. Some unkindly 'gentlemen' would sneak in a peashooter and aim at the unfortunate young ladies in an effort to produce at least a wobble!"

"The Windmill Theatre proudly boasted that, "We never close," and they didn't through the London Blitz."

"Occasionally I would head west to stay with friends I'd made. They had a farm where there would be plenty of butter and bacon, and the meat ration could always be supplemented with rabbits."

"On one occasion returning to base an attractive young lady I knew saw me off at the station and on the walk back to the exit she passed a packed troop train. Although not a Windmill girl she attracted great attention. A train load of troops giving wolf whistles is something to witness and I think my friend may have secretly enjoyed it."

– Doug Taylor

Nice for Some

During John Buckley's time at Beam Approach Training Flight (BATF) at Little Rissington he got to know an Army Colonel who was the local district commander. "He was always suggesting I apply for a commission as things were better for officers. Anyhow he introduced me to Captain Spencer Churchill who had been badly wounded in WWI and he invited me to visit the estate at Northwood. He instantly made me feel at ease and of course I was treated very well. He had staff; we ate well, went rabbit shooting on the estate and swam in the lake. Churchill always had interesting weekend guests. Admiral Evans was one and even with my rank of Pilot Officer he had the ability to make me one of them. As time went by I often took other BATF mates to Northwood on leave as we had an open invitation to stay."

"Spencer Churchill was from the monied side of the family and didn't seem to be too fussed with day to day things. At Northwood was a splendid 60 foot long room, an art gallery really. Churchill commented to me one day that that particular picture (and the one he was pointing at wasn't that big) had been chased by an American buyer offering £60,000. To me it was a huge amount especially in those days. But he just commented it wasn't worth it as it would leave an unsightly gap on the wall!! Nice for some."

– *John Buckley*

A Welsh Cousin

"During OTU I crewed up with fellow Kiwi Claude Greenough and as the only two Kiwis in the crew we spent much of our leave together."

"On an earlier leave I'd been introduced to the Freelance Club in Fleet St, the attraction being the bar which was open between 2 pm and 4 pm when the pubs were shut! So, on our mid-OTU course leave Claude and I went to London and into the Freelance Club. That afternoon we were puzzled by the frequent short air raid alarms. This was mid-June 1944 and the journalists told us that London was being attacked by a new German flying bomb (the V1) but it hadn't yet been publicly announced. Next morning we packed our bags and went to Birmingham."

"I was also lucky in having a cousin living in Wales and the peace and quiet there was just what we needed. During the hectic December 1944 – February 1945 period we flew 25 Ops and had one leave. I think we did nothing but sleep once we had arrived in Wales."

– *Stan Davies*

Survived The Chop and off to OTU (again)

"It was a strange feeling to have done a tour and be back at OTU perhaps just a few months after qualifying from it."

Des Andrewes, by then a Warrant Officer went back to 15 OTU at Westcott, where many New Zealanders were trained. "Although we might only fly once a day there were always trainees log books to check, lectures to give and give help where we could. With trainee navigators, nerves and the pressure on them to get it right first time took its toll but I remember precious few failing. In fact we were under pressure to get the course through on time, bad weather or not."

"One chap was making heavy weather of it, having genuine equipment failures that stopped him navigating. Our course Flight Lieutenant (a raw Scot from Aberdeen) told me, "just give him a bollocking." "Why?" "You're not here to accept excuses, you've done a tour and had to make do. To them you've done a bloody miracle, you survived," and off he went.

"There were always a couple of courses going at a time and on the advanced course I had a formal complaint from a trainee pilot about his Navigator. This pilot had done a tour in the desert as a navigator and had then remustered as a pilot. I flew with them on a check flight and the pilot (named Frazer Jones) kept questioning the navigator and just wouldn't let up or shut up. I told him so," "you are the problem and I'm not about to fail your Nav. If you don't change your ways he will go to another crew and I will fail you." They left Westcott as a crew.

– *Des Andrewes*

Off Duty at the Red Lion

As New Zealand airmen we didn't see much of fellow Kiwis serving in the other forces and so on leave a stop at The NZ Forces Club and NZ House in The Strand was compulsory.

However, those of us serving or training at the AFS South Cerney soon came into contact with a real Kiwi icon, the bushman. He was a combination of lumber jack, log splitter and sawyer.

Early in the war Britain was short of 'foresters' so a group of Kiwi bushmen were enlisted in the NZ Army Engineer Corps. The bushmen were shipped to England nominally as a company in the First Echelon, New Zealand Army. This Division had been rushed to Britain when war had been declared and an invasion seemed imminent. When the New Zealand Division was moved to Greece in 1941 the bushmen stayed behind. Considering that these men had worked the Kauri forests of Northland and the bush in the King Country they were hard men. Remember they were used to dealing with some of the biggest trees ever felled, Kauris in particular having girths of up to 85 feet and height of 150 feet. So tackling the local squire's elms and pines were like dropping 'toothpicks.'

South Cerney's pub, the Red Lion, was the off-duty HQ for those hard case men. As well as cutting timber in the Kings service, they always cut a little extra for their own 'use' and trade was brisk. The Bushmans' Commanding Officer was a British Major and a veteran of WWI. Reports of their wrong doings would send him into a rage but the bushmen would only have him on even more. On one occasion he resented being called by his christian name (normal for Kiwis), and would rage "Don't call me George, I'm Sir," so the bushmen then called him Sir George.

The officers from RAF South Cerney were required to drink in the Red Lion's private bar while other ranks used the public bar with the Bushmen. But these Kiwis were always ready to help out if there was a bit of a scuffle with the call, "can we fill them in now boss?"

"The Red Lion also had a memorable obstacle outside, an old hitching post smack in the middle of the footpath outside the main door. The number of times after a few or sometimes after a lot, this post intercepted me, it seemed to suddenly spring out of the footpath and down you would go."

"Perhaps a few beers did affect my night sight because down at Oakley OTU, I was in the mess holding my pint and didn't spot a rugby tackle coming in. Good tackle it was, gashing my wrist and hand and cost me a few weeks in hospital and my heavy aircraft flight rating. But I got to fly Mosquitos instead which probably saved my life."

Other Kiwis would discover other obstacles and be introduced to hard footpaths, gutters, walls, doors and windows during their off duty hours.

F/Lt Roy Montrowe on light duties flying a Hawker Hurricane on Fighter Affiliation exercises for 11 OTU based at Westcott's satellite airfield RAF Oakley

Kiwis Do Fly

Brighton – The Boys Remember

Far from being a Londoner's seaside resort, Brighton in the early 1940s was a transit camp for Colonials arriving and departing UK shores, a 'holding area' as it was termed.

"When we arrived in 1943, the Kiwis were billeted in the Warwick, The Lion and the Grand and the Aussies in the Metropole. The first surprise on visiting our first pub and being in the seat for the initial shout was the array of maybe six different beers. Mild, bitter, dark and so on. At home under the two brewery system you only got the beer the hotel was under contract to. So it was Lion, Waikato, Standard, or if you were from down south, Speights. The name varied between regions but the beer didn't, but now faced with different brews made by different breweries we adopted the attitude that it would be impolite to refuse any beer offered."

"Anyhow the Brighton Holding Camp was also used to keep any spare bods between postings, I think some stayed there for months, others may never have left. The press-on types were always going up to London to scrounge a posting. After my tour, I went on leave for a while, then a spell at OTU. Then back to Brighton to await shipment home. There was only the odd inspection and the Aussies would tell the Service Police who pulled them up for uniform indiscretions – "Bugger off or we'll have ya!"

They did too, as to delay a serviceman's repatriation on a minor charge just wasn't acceptable. So we filled in time, drew our pay and probably drank too much. Of course there were the stories that some blokes spent all of their war years never moving out of Brighton and collected a DFC on the way."

ABOVE: Life at the Grand, in Brighton, busy doing nothing

Bikes

Almost every photograph of war time airfields shows bicycles in the picture somewhere. With stations covering several hundred acres, the trip from the flights to the mess or canteen necessitated transport. Service issue bikes were recorded on an individual's cards and any loss had to be made up. One bicycle – black, but so long as Bicycle – one – black was handed back in there was no penalty was issued.

So a vigorous black market existed not only in loan bicycles but parts. "Our ground crews always had a bike under construction in their dispersal shed, the parts having been 'acquired.' To buy one from the High Street may be £2/10 shillings for a good Raleigh, or even £8, so you had to keep them chained up. But this meant that you secured only the part chained to the post, the rest could have gone. There must have been thousands in circulation and at demob time I wonder if the RAF got more back than they issued in the first place."

– *Anon*

Aircrew while training at OTU Westcott—Oakley.
Left to Right: Ron Maryan, Air Gunner; unknown; Eddie Robertson, Pilot, N.Z.; Hec Richmond, Bomb Aimer, N.Z.; Tony Herrold, Nav., NZ; Phil Smith, Air Gunner, Frank Tibby, W. Op..

ABOVE: Squadron formation at 11 OTU Westcott, home to many RNZAF aircrew either as learners or instructors

LEFT: Alan Hart (of Hamilton) and his trusty steed. Note the spare machine in the background. Taken at East Kirkby, 57 Squadron's home base

Kiwis Do Fly

Is it a Mine

"The NZ Forces Club, even during the Blitz, was great. Everyone just gathered there, and that's also where I found my wife! Our English crew all went home but our Rear Gunner was a Cockney so I'd tag along with him back to London. During the raids I didn't feel safe stuck down in a basement, I'd rather be up looking, until I saw a parachute. "Oh a Luftwaffe crew man has abandoned his plane I thought," but as it got closer it wasn't a man but a mine. It hit the parapet across the street. The explosion dropped a whole line of flats as clean as a whistle, down they came, wallop."

"I'd always worn my helmet (to protect me from falling shrapnel) but it would have done little good from a mine. We also carried gas mask bags but pyjamas and toothbrush replaced the gas mask itself."

"We drank beer, not spirits; aircrew drank more than most and Kiwis more again especially if Tennant's was on tap, but really anything that looked like beer was always fine by me."

"We would get a six day leave pass every six weeks regardless of being on Ops or at OTU. The pass came with Travel Warrants for the train. Once in London, we would check in for a bed at one of the Forces Clubs (NZ Club not having accommodation) or even the postie's Victoria Leagues Club. We ate everything and anything at the clubs or diners, but the chocolate and cigarettes freely available from the clubs was a real bonus as they were usually strictly rationed."

– Jim Dermody

ABOVE: Beer was well liked, the English cartoonist got the Kiwi expression wrong in describing Jim Dermody as a Hopperhead when the real term was Hophead!

Becoming a Cardinal

"In the Officers Mess at Little Straughton there was a mix of PFF crews, 109 Squadron on Oboe Mosquitos and bods from 582 Squadron on Heavies. The officers often turned to a few light hearted 'amusements' after dinner on dining-in nights."

"We had a harmless little game named Cardinal Puff. Those wishing to become a Cardinal were brought into the mess as a pillion passenger on a motorbike. The assembled Cardinals were all decked out in white sheets and paper hats."

"Seated alone at a table, the aspiring Cardinal needed to pass the Cardinal Puff Test. He sat with a pint of beer and began the patter by picking the pint up and saying, "Here's to the health of Cardinal Puff for the first time." He would take one sip and place the glass down. Then up again, "Here's to the health of Cardinal Puff for the second time," taking two sips and tapping the glass twice on the table. Finally, "Here's to the health of Cardinal Puff for the third and last time," take three sips and on the last empty the pint glass, tapping the glass three times on the table but the last tap was from his upturned glass."

"Many failed at various stages, particularly when having imbibed a few beers prior to dinner and perhaps a wine or two during dinner."

"Commonly the cause of failure was omitting "and last" on the third time and failing to invert the glass."

"The Cardinals would confer, then present the underling with another full pint to try again."

"Amongst those who made dedicated and repeated efforts were some very senior ranking staff members of the Pathfinder's Force who never did become Cardinals despite their dedication to the task at hand."

– the Boys Remember

Where has Everyone Gone – a Diary of a Memorable Leave

"Following the Nuremburg trip on 30 March 1944, we eventually got back to Burn, having diverted into Elvington short of fuel."

"We had to wait at Elvington most of the morning until a fuel bowser arrived to give us enough petrol to get back to Burn. We eventually arrived back at base at around 1300 hours."

"The place was deserted and we couldn't find any food or drink. The guard room didn't want to know us and we ended up being issued 48-hour rail passes. Our Bomb Aimer (Bobby) said he was going home and asked if the crew wanted to join him. We all agreed and headed first to York then on to Glasgow arriving in the early hours of the morning."

"Bobby's father had apparently agreed for us all to stay but couldn't meet us as he had business to attend to. (He was in the scrap metal business and had sold metal to the Germans in the past!) Bobby lived at a place called Cathcart, on the south side of Glasgow. On arriving we were greeted by a lovely old lady who was the house keeper. She showed us to our rooms but everything was blacked out. We eventually found a cord above the beds that turned the light on. We were asleep within a minute."

"The next thing we knew was the phone ringing and after finding the light cord again answered the phone to be told that breakfast would be ready in 15 minutes. We headed downstairs following a lovely smell to the dining room. All the food was on a big platter and we just helped ourselves, the house keeper had even made fresh bread for us, it was the best breakfast I'd ever had! Kippers, bacon, eggs, and porridge! Bobby was engaged to a nurse and she had arranged for another six nurses to meet us after breakfast but first we headed to a local pub named 'His Lordships Parlour'."

"The Skipper went to the bar and ordered seven beers but was given seven whiskies instead. On asking why he had been given whisky instead of beer he was told by the barman that a gentleman sitting in another part of the pub had requested that we drink the same as him. After four whiskies had followed the first, we thought we had better be on our way. We didn't have to pay a penny! We finally met the nurses and went to a restaurant called 'The Blue Room,' very posh it was and we had a nice feed and drinks with Bobby signing for it all. What a lucky crew we were having found a bomb aimer who could bomb but had a healthy bank account as well."

"Our 48 hour pass was nearly up so back to York and then on to Burn. We had absolutely had it by the time we got back and all we wanted to do was sleep, it had been almost as tough as being on an Op!"

– Harry Furner

Kiwis Do Fly

Chapter Eight

Near Misses, all in a Days Work

While operations were always dangerous, OTU duties, flight tests and normal training accidents claimed many airmen. But even more suffered the odd oops! and were lucky to get away with it. Not so much the flak damage on returning with an engine out, it was the times when 'we got away with it.'

Follow the Leader

Late in World War II, some RAF Bomber Command attacks were made in daylight on specialised (and often small) targets.

To improve accuracy, a few operations were carried out by No 109 Squadron with an 'Oboe' Pathfinder Mosquito leading a tight formation of 6 Light Night Strike Force Mosquitos carrying 4,000 lb bombs. They opened their bomb doors when the 'Oboe' leader did and dropped their 'cookies' when the leader did. This resulted in some very accurate raids.

On 23 Dec 1944, a Lancaster of 582 Squadron (which shared RAF Little Staughton with 109 Squadron), was fitted with 'Oboe' gear and was flown by an experienced 109 pilot, Squadron Leader RAM (Bob) Palmer DFC. He led a formation of Lancasters to strike a target near Cologne.

An accurate drop using Oboe required very accurate navigation with no deviation from the slightly curved flight path keeping on the beam until the drop signal sounded firstly then the photo flash image taken 30 seconds later. While at night this straight and level flying was not very dangerous in the dark, daylight raids were a different matter. Unfortunately on this raid, Luftwaffe radar had detected the formation and directed a flight of fighters onto the leading aircraft, so follow the leader in daylight became very hazardous.

The German fighters attacked the formation during the straight and level 'Oboe' run, shooting down one Lancaster and badly damaging Palmer's lead aircraft. Bob nevertheless held to his beam run despite the aircraft being on fire. The formation was able to do its job although Palmer's aircraft was lost immediately afterwards. Bob Palmer was awarded a well-merited posthumous VC, while 109 Squadron reconsidered daylight Oboe raids.

– Bill Simpson

Kiwis Do Fly

Not My Funeral... Just Yet

"Bomber Command stories are usually thought of as; "How I nearly bought it over…." One of my 'nearlies' broke most of the rules. It wasn't at night, it wasn't over enemy territory, it was on my own station during stand down (and broad daylight), and as simple as this."

"Taking my time getting back to the squadron room in No 3 hangar after lunch, I walked in and almost collided with Tex, one of the more popular and competent of the Squadrons pilots and – for Tex – slightly flustered and harassed. The conversation went something like this;

"Ah Engineer Hall, have you seen Mac, (his flight engineer)?"

"He was just finishing lunch when I left the Mess, Sir."

"I've just been detailed to do an urgent air test on Y-Yoke. It's needed by 1600. Are you free to come with me?"

"Yes Sir, I'll just clear it with my Skipper," "and off I went to find my own man, Stan, in the Ops room and tell him of Tex's request. He cleared me on the spot, a sensible thing to do as he would have an excuse to relax until I got back. I went straight to the locker room, hurriedly picked up my tool box, parachute harness and helmet and walked out – just in time to bump into Mac on his way back from the Mess. The conversation carried on."

"There you are. Tex is looking for you."

"What's he want?"

"He's just been told to do an urgent air test on Y-Yoke and he's asked me to be his engineer because he couldn't find you. Do you want to take it or not?"

"That's okay, I'm on my way."

" With that Mac hurriedly got his basic flying gear and left the locker room, donning harness and helmet as he went. I returned my gear to my locker and went back to the Ops room to tell Stan I was free."

"Tex and Mac, their wireless operator, navigator and gunners were clearly in a hurry as it was only a very few minutes later that Y-Yoke's engines fired up and they were taxiing. And that was that, I mean that really was that."

"A few more minutes and one of His Majesty's bombers was a smoking ruin in the middle of neighbouring Skellingthorpe airfield, her crew all dead."

"It was later decided by many that the disaster was probably caused by a smoker in the crew, some of whom were known to smoke in the air. It was established that, in their hurry, the crew had started the motors on the aircrafts internal batteries instead of waiting for a delayed trolley-acc, and it was also realised the batteries would begin charging at a heavy rate as soon as both inboard motors generators were running, and give out clouds of hydrogen gas. Gas which would rapidly seep through the closed fuselage, in which somebody lit a cigarette."

"Well that was the accepted answer at the time and certainly no fault was attributed to the ground crew who had cleared Yoke from the hangar after a major inspection. More important for me were those vital few seconds, that tiny packet of time in a life span, when Mac and I met head-on at the crew room door, and he took my place beside Tex on the flight deck."

"You can hope and pray and light candles and do whatever takes your fancy, but any old flying type will tell you there are some things you just never can plan or train for. All in all I've decided over the intervening decades its just as well."

"On the other hand of course, Murphy does cut it a bit damn close at times….."

– Des Hall

Des Hall had a thing about grounded Avros, this Lincoln (left) of 61 Sq. Cat E at Merignac, France after hydraulic failure while the Lancaster (above) suffered an undercarriage collapse at Lindholme

Chapter 8 – Near Misses, all in a days work

Bumps

ABOVE: A Beaufighter cockpit with its scattering of instruments and levers

Having been posted out of 90 Squadron after nine Ops on Stirlings, Ted arrived at RAF Twinwoods for further training, but on night fighters. "There we picked up Beaufighters. They were certainly ruggedly built, like the Stirling, but had little space. You could tell that it came from the same family as the cramped Beauforts that we had to fly as the initial step on our conversion course."

"The Beaufighter was full of sharp corners and the equipment boxes were just tacked onto the frames at random. I lost a lot of skin getting in and out of the cockpit. However I had my revenge when the hydraulics failed on a daylight run down the coast. The handle for the manual pump was missing so I had to choose whether my navigator and I bailed out and risk getting snagged on those corners or to make a 'forced' landing. For all it's strong build, the port motor came adrift. Definitely a cat 5 prang."

– *Ted Kepplewhite*

Ted's one-engined Beaufighter under recovery. (Ted on the left). Their hands in pockets attitude sums it up "at least we survived". 'Pilot Officer Prune' painted on the nose looks unimpressed.

Kiwis Do Fly

That's Not Fair

"In April 1942 I was posted to the ME Ferry Flight at Harwell, following 15 OTU training."

"The Pegasus engined Wimpys were pretty worn hand-me-downs from operational Squadrons. As part of the course we did lots of cross country runs of eight or more hours to duplicate the duration of a raid over Germany. Anyway on June 6, I'd been allocated this Wellington for a night test. It came off the runway alright but it was a beast to fly."

"The airspeed wouldn't come up and it was very tail heavy to the point of just mushing along. The heavy landing drove the undercarriage up into the wings."

"The aircraft was in a sorry state. We all came through unscathed, but I was put up for a Court Martial – Damage to His Majesty's Aeroplane. I wasn't amused as there had been something bloody dangerously wrong with the aircraft which had been okayed to fly and signed out."

"A technical investigation of the remains found that the airspeed indicator was faulty and when the front turret had been removed no centre of gravity compensation had been made to the airframe. No wonder we staggered up to just fifty feet before coming down. The charges were dropped."

"I don't recall anyone being held to account and ten days later we left for the Middle East."

– Roy Montrowe

BELOW: Roy's Wellington being recovered

Chapter 8 – Near Misses, all in a days work

Cookie on My Toe

"Not long after joining 109 (PFF) Squadron, we had settled in to the routine of dropping 4,000 lb thin cased blast bombs pretty precisely and really without much opposition. One night in January 1945 we again were allotted a 4,000 lb cookie to drop by Oboe, which meant accurate timing all the way in to the target."

"Off we went down Little Staughton's 06 runway within the allocated 30 second take-off time but the BXVI started to swing to the left. All Mossies did this because of prop torque, which you countered by easing the boost on the starboard engine. Anyhow, this swing promised to develop into something much more dramatic so we aborted take-off, ran back toward the taxiway and had another go. Same thing but this time onto the grass."

"The Commanding Officer wanted to know "what the hell." "A quick check showed us the tail wheel had a burst tyre and wouldn't castor. In a flap, Pete my navigator and I were rushed in the Commanding Officer's car to dispersal and the reserve aircraft. But there was no bomb loaded! In the rush we climbed aboard while a 4,000 lb was trolleyed up and hoisted aboard. All clear, and in the ominous quiet we heard the cookie drop 'smack' onto the tarmac, a rumble, while it rolled back under the fuselage and smack into the tail plane. Our ears were certainly pricked. We were so late by now our Op was cancelled, but it needed a few pints to settle us down."

"The 4,000 lb cookies were fairly touchy and being barometrically fused we could never bring one back to base. About a month after that episode we lost an engine and returned to dump our load over the Wash. Down and down it went and then what a blast, you could feel and see the concussion. Pity it wasn't closer inshore as there were undoubtedly enough dead fish to feed the station for a week."

RIGHT: Bill Simpson QSO, DFC with the MOTAT hybrid Mosquito FB VI / T43, NZ 2302

– Bill Simpson

ABOVE: A 4,000 lb bomb and its armourers pose for the camera (RAF Museum)

Kiwis Do Fly

Hole in One

Flight Lieutenant Roy Montrowe loved the Mosquito, especially after 42 operations in the dubious Wellingtons of 205 Group chasing Rommel across the Western Desert. On 692 (Fellowship of the Bellows) Squadron, Roy and his Navigator Harry Hughes enjoyed the 'security' of carting 4,000 pounders across Europe from RAF Graveley. This security was given a jolt when HQ dreamt up an idea of blocking railway tunnels with a 'cookie.' Unluckily a straight release didn't work so the plan was modified to use a toss and run technique."

"Just how we could toss 4,000 pounds of thin walled high explosive at 300 mph into a railway tunnel could be solved by training, the RAF's golden solution!"

"During very low level practice on a Midland Railway tunnel the pilots became exhilarated, the navs weren't and the locals 'disconcerted.' To everyone's relief the plan was called off for our Squadron – just as well as we were told to drop the cookie from just 1,000 feet. The concussion would have been enormous and even at 300 mph the blast wave would have been faster than my Mossie. If we'd got the timing wrong and missed there would have been a bloody big bomb (4,000 lb of high explosive) flying in formation with us. No thank you."

By the time Roy had completed his second tour of fifty operations (all over Germany), he and his navigator had personally delivered 200,000 lb of high explosive (90 tonnes). An impressive total for two men, two engines and wooden airframe.

– Roy Montrowe

BELOW: Roy's 692 Squadron Mosquito B XVI P2-O (PF455) showing its bulged bombing doors. Taken early 1945 at Graveley. 692 Squadron was part of the Light Night Strike Force tasked with placing 4,000 lb bombs across Germany without the losses suffered by the heavies of main force. F/L Roy Montrowe (left) with his navigator Harry Hughes

Chapter 8 – Near Misses, all in a days work

Oops!

"The Mosquito was by far my favourite aircraft, from the earliest mark BXVI I flew to the last PR 35s in the Middle East, although single engine performance gradually suffered. To counter the swing on take-off I always used 19 lb boost on one engine and 12 lb on the other. Once airborne, however, the BXVI was quite okay on one motor. The B35s I later flew post-war on 109 Squadron were fine with one propeller feathered but on the modified PR 35 version single engine operation just wasn't allowed.

In 1948 I was flying PR34s with 540 Squadron out of Benson. September had been a busy month with regular formation flying building up to Battle of Britain Day and then PR exercises over France.

On the 30th, after a run over London and Norfolk I came back to base with one dud engine. I then proceeded to demonstrate a one-engined take off, even though the port motor was out and that fed the hydraulics. Anyway I just couldn't hold it straight, the port prop flew off and we hit the ground, breaking in two. We had no major injuries but when the Station fire truck arrived, their foam system wouldn't work and a small fire was put out with a very minimal amount of water.

It was a humbling moment but soon put right with a few rounds of beer in the mess that night.

John's logbook records 'pranged – cornfield – write off'.

– John Buckley

ABOVE: At home 60 years later, still with a Mosquito

ABOVE: John's PR35 PH-N (RG 311) Cat 5 near Benson, 30 September 1948

107

Flying's Not Dangerous

"During initial training in New Zealand, there were always a few oops at EFTS and SFTS. Quite a few failed the Chief Flying Instructors Chop flight and were remustered as other aircrew. But once we were in England the pressure really came on and quite a few more casualties resulted."

"At Castle Combe (15 AFU) we had witnessed a night landing on our short runway that ended up in the next door farm's haystack. It was quite a blaze and an impressive bang. Our turn was to come."

"On May 3 an Aussie, 'Bluey' Moore and I were doing a night cross country. Being just a month before D-Day, we had been warned about aircraft practicing night towing of gliders. So when we saw two red lights ahead we 'identified' them as the red port wing lights of the tow plane and glider. Wrong. The pair weren't crossing our path so we quickly decided to go under them which we did. As we went 'under' and looked up there were just two red lights. We had just flown between the BBC radio masts at Daventry!"

"The Vickers Wellingtons we had at 12 OTU were pretty well clapped out and many of us suffered engine failures, not fun on an underpowered twin. Of the fifteen pilots, six of us crashed which must have been some record. I have been told that several thousand aircrew were lost in OTU training."

"In mid August 1944 we were on a lengthy night cross country exercise. With a runaway prop on the port engine, I had to overshoot, do a right hand circuit and line up again. At only 200 feet it must have scared the hell out of the village as I went over it. Without enough airspeed to lower the undercarriage and not stall, we belly landed on the grass. No fire, no injuries."

"The last 'oops' before our big one was once we had been posted to 75 (NZ) Squadron and Lancasters. We were put down for the Rheydt raid on 27 December 1944. I'd lost the starboard outer soon after take-off but in the spirit of 75 (NZ) Squadron's 'press-on regardless' attitude, I stupidly carried on. Even with cutting corners on the track into the target we arrived ten minutes after everyone else and at only 11,500 feet (not the usual 18–20,000 feet)."

"We dropped our bomb load, had a hang up, released that, and all alone headed home. A Gunner called that a Fw190 was tracking us and I for what ever reason ordered the wireless Op to fire off a red flare."

"Shortly after the gunners reported "aircraft coming in from the rear" and called "corkscrew" Fortunately for us the aircraft turned out to be USAAF Lightnings and probably responded to our red flare. Were we glad to see them! My first sight was the pair with undercarriages down right off my port wing. I still remember the smile and wave by the pilot. They stayed with us until we were well over Allied territory, waggled their wings and went on their way."

"But that wasn't the end of our day. It was late afternoon in December and Mepal was quite dark with visibility only a mile or two. My first approach was off to the right (the effect of an engine out) so I had to do another circuit. I couldn't get the altitude right and this time I overcorrected and lined up on the left of the runway and only 50 feet above the village, so I decided to land on the grass."

"The occupants of the control caravan ahead of us saw us coming and felt that they would rather be elsewhere and ran like hell through the snow. No worries, I cleared the caravan by a few feet and made a beautiful landing. "Just keep rolling." "How" came the RT, "and don't bog down.""

"Next days briefing was a high point, there on display was our target photo of Rheydt, taken ten minutes after the main attack (and from only 11,500 feet). It was a beaut and we were publicly commended. However, the Senior Intelligence Officer brought me down to earth: "Good show Davies but DON'T do that again.""

LEFT: Stan Davies prize target photograph of Rheydt from 11,500 feet, 27 December 1944

– Stan Davies

Chapter 9

Gunners Lament

Gunners undertook initial training as Air Gunners / Wireless Operators but specialised as Gunners after grading.

The ground gunnery ranges incorporated many ingenious mechanical devices to effectively teach distance perception and deflection shooting at moving targets.

One such range contained an eliptical track on which the target board moved at different speeds. The gunner seated in his mock-up turret needed to traverse, elevate and alter his sights as the target moved through three dimensions.

Later in Anson aircraft the trainee gunners learnt their trade against drogues towed by 'target tug' aircraft and flown by very trusting pilots.

Having picked up a crew at OTU it was at Heavy Conversion Unit the gunners selected their position, mid upper or rear. Often the two would swap until settling in their preferred positions.

On operations the gunners were responsible for the safety of the crew and exceptional night sight by the rear gunner was imperative, if only for his own safety. Sadly rear gunner casualties were frequent, and death common.

It took a special person to sit for perhaps an eight hour operation, constantly searching the black sky for an even darker foe.

Kiwis Do Fly

What Fighter

On 26 April 1943 Harry reported for RAF service at Lords cricket ground. Once duly enlisted he was marched to Regents Park for three weeks square bashing. "I did 'janker's' during the second week for complaining about the big glass mirror panels on the walls falling off every time a bomb dropped nearby. I enjoyed janker's as I 'waited' in the Sergeants Mess where the food was better. We also got served two free pints of beer when we went to the local brewery for supplies for the Mess."

It was here that Harry decided to become an air gunner. "We all wanted to be pilots but they said they needed crews for the bombers. I was given the option of being a Wireless Operator/AG, Flight Engineer or a straight AG. I asked which would get me on Ops the quickest and was told AG."

Harry arrived at Penrhos, Wales and 9 (O) AFU for gunnery training on 19 June 1943.

The first three weeks in Camp were spent learning basic gunnery, including range firing with .303 rifles and Thompson sub-machine guns, but living in boarding houses with only cold water.

The next three weeks were spent in either the classroom or flying in Avro Ansons. Part of the flying segment was to shoot at drogues towed on a cable behind a Lysander. Harry managed to hit and cut the cable attached to the drogue three times and subsequently received a severe bollocking "under threat of death" if it happened again. "My technique was simple; I built up a cone of fire and let the target fly into it. If you shot the drogue down it would cost you five shillings. Putting holes in the Lysander was unforgivable!"

"Back at Bridlington the crew room was the largest we'd seen. The target tugs were flown by Polish pilots who had painted reclining nudes, tastefully done, on the walls, they were huge at least 10 – 12 feet long. The Poles, (mostly Battle of Britain veterans) never spoke to us at all. In the crew room there was a big board with the names of the crew (usually three), pilot and aircraft number along with the flight times. You could do between four and six flights in a day and just met out at the aircraft. The pilot would come out and away you went."

"One Polish pilot in particular always used to urinate mid-flight by means of a funnel and tube system that exited underneath the aircraft. As a practical joke it was decided on one flight that the exit funnel would

BELOW: A Mid-Upper Gunners view in daylight *(J. Pote)*

110

Chapter 9 – Gunners Lament

be turned around to face forward rather than aft. We took off over the cliffs at Penrhos and as usual didn't go very high. During the flight the pilot subsequently urinated and was promptly showered by his effort. Did he get wild! We were out over the Irish Sea with fishing trawlers below us, and he dived straight for them. We could see the crews diving for cover on the decks, he then headed straight for the cliffs and we thought we'd had it but he managed to get the aircraft up and over the top and we finally landed back on the grass strip at Bridlington. He got out of the aircraft and stormed off after slamming the door shut. Thankfully we never got him again after that."

Harry met Sergeant Geoff Marsden, his future pilot and Captain, on 15 September, at the Heavy Conversion Unit where they were to fly Halifax bombers. Harry and the newly formed crew, which included the other AG, Neville Farley, first flew with Geoff as pilot in early October and continued flying training. During the training Neville Farley, then Mid-Upper Gunner, suggested a swap with Harry who was manning the rear turret. As a result each preferred the other gunner's position so they decided to swap permanently. "I much preferred the mid-upper turret especially after flying in the rear turret on Whitleys. Neville and I worked well together and from the mid upper position I could see his turret turn, so if he went to port I'd go to starboard. He could see underneath to the rear and I could see pretty well down either side. I also enjoyed the better view from the mid-upper and if Geoff made a turn I could rotate the turret forward to see where we were heading."

"We really enjoyed fighter affiliation training as we nearly always got the better of the fighters. Our theory was to turn into them and with their fixed guns if they followed they would suffer 'G' whereas we could turn our turrets towards them and shoot them down. We used to practice tight turns during training. The only time a fighter got us was when he approached us from the rear, passed us then made a roll over the top and came down behind us again. It must have been a tight turn for him and a manoeuvre we argued couldn't be done at night!"

The crew were posted to 51 Squadron at Snaith, Yorkshire and on 16 November went on their first Op to Berlin in Halifax 'MH -Y' (JD300). Over France the aircraft developed problems with the magnetos and the decision was made to return to base and logged a DNCO (did not complete operation).

Early February saw 'C' Flight 51 Squadron posted to RAF Burn in North Yorkshire to form the nucleus of the new 578 Squadron. Harry's crew took Halifax 'MH-L' to Burn with them. "Burn had been hastily set up and there was just runways, roads and various huts when they arrived. There were no footpaths but a sea of mud from all the construction. We did thankfully have hot water in the ablutions block for showers."

"Our second Op was to Schweinfurt. We were attacked three times, but we got hits on two of the fighters. Our aircraft was hit and a hole was blown in the fuselage between the exit door and the rear turret which resulted in Neville Farley losing his communications and ammo feed. "Geoff gave the order to prepare to bale out so I made my way to the exit and had my feet dangling out ready to go. I remember seeing the countryside below as it was still light, thinking how beautiful it was and that I wouldn't mind coming back here after the war to live. The order then came over the intercom to return to stations as Geoff had decided to carry on with

RIGHT: Harry Furner on Anzac Day 2006

the bomber stream rather than risk going back alone. On the return leg the condition of the aircraft worsened and we ended up landing at RAF Odiham, a crash drome were the aircraft stayed for several days."

"Ops to Le Mans (twice), Stuttgart and Frankfurt followed. On a second trip to Frankfurt in three days the crew were attacked again. After engaging two fighters the second, an Fw190, flew alongside trailing smoke and the canopy flew off. The pilot stood up and I could see his light brown flying suit, then the fighter nose dived out of sight and that was the last we saw of it. Back at base during the de-brief we both tried to claim it as a kill but the Intelligence Officer said it could only be claimed as a probable as we hadn't seen it crash."

"On one Op we were coming back over the Thames Estuary when we saw an He111 below us, launch a V1 Flying Bomb it was carrying under its wing. The Skipper decided he was going to have a go at the V1 and put the plane in a dive to try and catch it but we had no chance. I think we would have had a good chance taking on the He111 as we had the superior fire power."

"In March 1944 flying LK-K we saw a white light following us and whatever we did it still seemed to follow us. We turned to port, then starboard and even did a corkscrew but it still followed us. It eventually dropped away and we saw it explode below. We were told by the Intelligence Officer at de-briefing that it was a guided missile and that it was probably being launched from an Me110."

"For some reason our crew seemed to have more contact with enemy fighters than others did and we didn't know that more was to follow."

– Harry Furner

Kiwis Do Fly

I'm Going Backwards to Berchestgarten

As recounted in 'Wednesday Bomber Boys' Tom Whyte was re-mustered as a gunner after having a mishap with the CFI's personal Tiger Moth. "I got the chop so back to boot camp, no dashing pilots wings for me!"

After surviving the RNZAF's Camp Delta, Tom was sent to Canada and training at Mount Jole (it was anything but). As an air gunner trainee Tom found he was in competition with a Belgian as Top Gun. "I sure wasn't ready to let him beat me, and he didn't."

On arrival in England and OTU, Tom accepted a rear gunners position. "I found it very difficult during fighter affiliation exercises to call the correct direction for the pilot to dive away. I had to remember I was facing backwards and had to call a turn as if I was the pilot; port and starboard were reversed. After a few times when we turned into the fighters guns rather than away, we'd hear his rat-tat-tat call over the R/T."

"I soon learnt to call turns 'arse about face' and it was so instilled in me that I still have problems with left and right unless I'm facing backwards. I'm not alone in that, as at one reunion all the rear gunners sat with their backs to the stage. Truly!"

– Tom Whyte

(T. Whyte, 101 Squadron)

LEFT: The loneliest post, exposed to extreme cold and cannon shells. Rear gunner casualty rates were always high *(J. Pote)*

Chapter 9 – Gunners Lament

ABOVE: Take-off: 'good bye earth' *(J. Pote)*

ABOVE: Flying backwards at last, where are those fighters? Difficult by day, almost impossible at night *(J. Pote)*

ABOVE: The view an attacking Luftwaffe fighter has of a Lancaster. The Rear Gunner was very vunerable if it was a Ju88 or Bf110 fitted with upward-firing Schrage Musik cannon. Shown is the RAF Memorial Flight. Lancaster PA474 photographed from Dakota ZA947, May 22 2001 *(J. Pote)*

Kiwis Do Fly

The Air Gunner

If I must be a gunner
Then please Lord grant me Grace;
That I may leave this Station
With a smile on my face.

I may have wished to be a pilot,
And you along with me,
But if we all were pilots
Where would the Air Force be?

It takes 'guts' to be a gunner,
To sit out in the tail,
When the Messerschmitts are coming
And the slugs begin to wail.

The pilot's just a chauffeur,
It's his job to fly the plane,
But it's 'We' who do the fighting,
Though we may not get the fame.

But we're here to win a war,
And until this job is done,
Let's forget our personal feelings
And get behind the gun.

If we must all be gunners,
Then let us make this bet,
We'll be the best damn gunners
That have left this Station yet.

– Anon NZBCA Newsletter

40 Squadron Alconbury 1941. Skippered by Dick Broadbent, Wellington Ic BL-U (T2986) took the crew through 30 operations, their tour finished on 16 July 1941. "The two gunners were exceptional and saved our lives many times"

Sergeant Gould (RAF) 'Uncles' rear gunner

Sergeant Whalley 'Uncles' front gunner with Sgts Watson (Nav) right and Smith (W/Op) standing below

A Fighter Pilot Remembers

A four engined bomber is a big target, not very agile and by itself easy to hit. The German fighters had four cannon and a radar screen on which they could see their target on the darkest night. The only defence a bomber had when being attacked from astern was the rear turret which housed four machine guns. These were out ranged and out fought by an attacking fighter with its four cannon. Another advantage of using a cannon was that its loading was in a series of four. First an armour piercing shell followed by another which was semi armour piercing, the next a high explosive and finally an incendiary shell which would set alight anything that was burnable.

"I spent all my war service on fighters and had no personal contact with bombers, but my interest was in three aircrew members who were flying in RAF Bomber Command, one of them being my brother who was killed on his first trip. The other two and myself were cabin mates when I travelled to England, Don Aldridge and Doug Gorden. On arriving in England the three of us were posted to the same holding unit and while there spent a delightful three weeks as guests on a Squire's estate. Don and Doug were posted to bombers and with my posting being to fighters we lost contact. We had promised to keep in touch and after twelve months had passed without a word, I decided to try and make contact."

"I found that Don had joined 115 Squadron and had been killed on his third operation and Doug on his seventh."

"During my search for news of my two mates, I met aircrew from various Bomber Squadrons and realised the tension they were under even when on leave. I got the impression that few expected to reach the thirty trips needed to complete a tour."

"I think the only two other services that were under the same sort of constant stress were the crews of oil tankers and those involved in the Russian convoys."

"I know that Bomber Command losses were huge but when I shot an aircraft down I didn't think of the crew inside, just that they were the enemy. Later when there weren't many Luftwaffe aircraft flying around we took to attacking trains. Again, no thought for the people, just bust the locomotive. I'm sure the Germans thought the same as we really were given a hot reception by their ack ack at times. At least my Tempest was fast and agile, so I don't regret missing out as the air gunner I was originally drafted to be."

Jim Sheddan finished his service as Squadron Leader of 486 (New Zealand) Squadron and was credited with seven kills plus eight V1 Flying Bombs.

– Jim Sheddan

**485 (NZ) Squadron at Volkel, Holland, 1945.
Jim Sheddan second from left**

Recollections of a Rear Gunner

"Being the rear gunner I always saw the target after we had dropped our bombs and never on the run in. Only once when I went with another crew as a mid-upper gunner did I ever see the target before the bombing run. It seemed to me that there was no possible way that we could get through the criss-crossing searchlight beams and the flak from the German ground gunners. As we approached the target a path seemed to open up for us to go through. After that trip I was quite happy being a rear gunner seeing the target, after we passed over it rather than before. I felt sorry for the people below hearing hundreds of bombers flying towards their city, the sound coming from thousands of engines droning above them and hearing the bombs falling must have been frightening. The bombing must have been bad enough but the fires caused by the incendiaries on the ground were of intense heat must have been terrible. I didn't dwell on these thoughts as our own lives were in great danger from flak or enemy fighters."

"We often flew through flak. Some shells set too high would go straight through the aircraft without exploding that would leave a hole the size of the shell. Shells set too low would explode and clatter against the side of the aircraft in small pieces of schrapnel."

"When we trained as gunners we were told not to look at the target because the bright lights would ruin our night vision. But it was most difficult not to look down at the lights. There is no accurate way of describing the scene with all the different colours of flares markers fires bombs exploding and unfortunate aircraft going down on fire. There were hundreds of searchlight beams criss crossing each other. A gunner's vision was lost due to the brightness of the target. If a searchlight passed the aircraft it would light the gun turrets up bright as day. It then took about forty minutes to regain full night vision. If I had time I would close one eye till the light had gone. The eye I shut retained most of its night vision. This gave me a chance of spotting any danger coming in from the darkness."

"Another danger we had to contend with flying together in large numbers was the risk of being shot by another bomber's guns. If a German fighter attacked, the gunners would try and shoot it down or maybe scare it off. All the bullets that the gunners fired had to go somewhere. My rear turret had four Browning 303s and each gun fired 1150 rounds per minute. The lethal range of a 303 round was 400 yards and the maximum about 600 yards. So there was a lot of lead flying around at times."

– Winkie Kirk

ABOVE: Winkie Kirk at home, Christchurch 2003

ABOVE: AA–M (ND756) at dispersal with some of its air crew and ground staff during servicing

Chapter 10

A Wizard Show, A Good Prang

In the RAF a 'Wizard Show' was a great Op, no problems, no interference and best of all, plastering the target. Such comments in log books weren't appreciated by Flight and Squadron Commanders but many survive.

Good raids were also called prangs, but the other sort, 'a bad prang' meant a lost or damaged aircraft with perhaps the crew getting the 'chop.'

Kiwis Do Fly

Pathfinders

"After completing the PFF course at Warboys, my Navigator (Pilot Officer Peter Jones) and I were posted to 109 (PFF) Squadron at Little Staughton. The Squadron was equipped with solid nose Oboe Mosquitos (Mk IX and BMk XVI) and as well as having Gee installed, our aircraft all had the bulged bomb bays to accommodate 4,000 lb blast bombs. The aircraft were well used and even though we were in 'B' flight no individual aircraft was allocated to a crew. It was probably the first time operational aircraft were pooled. Certainly they were in constant use and many clocked up over 100 sorties."

"In early November 1944 we did two consecutive bombing runs to Herford using MM114 on the third and ML989 'L' on the fourth. Funny though, the first trip took 4 hours 20 while the second only 3 hours 20. Either it was a good tailwind or we knew the way!"

"Following our seventh Op we were sent on leave even though as new boys we were always angling for extra Ops."

"Back from leave the operations list had us down for a daylight raid to Duisberg. We were up at 4am (in the dark) and off to the crew room for a check of the Ops list. Two hours before takeoff we underwent briefing. Six aircraft were listed for this daylight run. Ours for the day was MM241 'B' loaded with a 4,000 lb cookie. Going with us were a Primary Marker and four Backers Up who followed in at two to three minute intervals."

"Peter, my Navigator, checked his plot with the Navigation Leader and at the allotted time off we went, on oxygen all the time to improve our vision (and clear any sorry heads). Peter would use Gee to track up to our calling in point where we had to be five minutes before starting a timed run. It took accurate flying and navigation to arrive at this predetermined point at the

ABOVE: January 1945 'B' Flight 109 Sqn Little Staughton in front of the Grim Reaper. Bill Simpson back row 4th from right. His navigator Peter Jones beside him

118

Chapter 10 – A Wizard Show

prescribed 25,000 feet to 30,000 feet. Our MkII Oboe had preset frequencies and was quite reliable. It had to be as we had a window of just 30 seconds to be at the set point when Oboe was switched on. Both Peter and I would hear the beam through the headsets, a dot (a) if we were before the beam or a dash (u) if beyond it. From here on it was critical we maintained height, speed and altitude as the beam curved north/south and was only 50 feet wide (remember that the wing span of a Mosquito is just 53 feet)."

"We had five minutes to locate the beam then work into it weaving between the dots and dashes."

"After two minutes we received the radioed letter 'B' and after a further two minutes the letter 'C'. By then we were expected to be 'on the beam' and at the correct height and speed. Bomb doors open and two minutes more when 'D' was heard. By then we'd better be in the beam and level. Two minutes 30 seconds later five dots were received and Peter with his finger on the bomb release button pressed it on the fifth dot. The bomb release triggered a transmission back to base where the technical lot could immediately determine our accuracy. There was no hiding from them. This straight and level run in took 10 – 12 minutes while we covered 50 miles. It required intense concentration but even then it still wasn't over. We had to stay straight and level for another minute while the camera recorded the drop and finally round we went and back home."

"The radar tech and Intelligence Officers back at the station already knew our result. On the 11th December we had an error of 17 yards but, (over Mannheim on 16 January 1945 in MM 154 'I') we bettered it. After a 3 hour 45 minute Op we came into Little Staughton parked and handed the Mossie back to the ground crew. Then off to wait outside the Intelligence Office for debriefing. There we learnt about our accuracy. That trip to Mannheim was to be our best, zero error. Within 100 yards was accepted but anything outside this too often and the crew was moved on out of PFF."

"The end of this daylight Op was the favourite bacon and eggs flying meal. No herrings in tomato sauce for tea in the mess that day!"

– Bill Simpson

ABOVE: F/O Bill Simpson's official escape photo made to look decidedly European if not dodgy!

Kiwis Do Fly

Gestapo HQ

"Our daylight run on December 30th 1944 was a 'wizard prang.' The weather was brilliant and our target was the Gestapo HQ in Oslo, Norway. The selected crews of 627 Squadron (I wasn't one) practised formation flying for about three weeks prior to the operation, something not normally done. Then on the morning before the Op I was called up, to be told I'd be carrying a cameraman, and to just follow the others as 'Tail End Charlie.' "It will be okay on the day and you will be carrying 4 x 500 lb HE as well."

"I was allocated a Mk XXV Mosquito KB418 along with a cine camera operator named Pilot Officer Heath. He hadn't been on an Op before and certainly never sat in a navigator's seat before, my usual navigator F/Lt Crosbie missed out. Anyway, we took off from Woodhall Spa on the 29th for Peterhead, north of Aberdeen, to refuel and stop overnight. We left early the next morning in brilliant weather and tracked across the Friesian Islands before running towards Oslo at 8,000 feet."

"Approaching the Norwegian coastline we dropped down to 3,000 feet and found the fjord full of flak ships. What a barrage! There was five minutes between flights and as Tail End Charlie of the Squadron I thought no one would get through, especially us. But of the eight Mosquitos only one was hit. I went in to a very steep dive down to 1,000 feet and while my bombs didn't exactly go in the front door, it clobbered the main building a beauty. I was a bit late pulling out and remember seeing ice skaters as we flew across a frozen lake. It was a very dodgy 'do' but I was much too busy beforehand to think about it. I think that the cameraman felt safer than I did. The whole Op took a little over four hours, we landed again at Peterhead before heading back to base. By then I had completed almost one tour and 500 hours."

5 Group used cine camera regularly as many raids were in daylight (unlike 8 Group). Sixty five years after the raid the Imperial War Museum located the film and John Buckley today has his own DVD copy.

– *John Buckley*

ABOVE: 627 Squadron Woodhall Spa 1944. With KB418 prior to the Oslo Operation

Chapter 10 – A Wizard Show

THE SCENE IN OSLO AFTER MOSQUITOES OF R.A.F. BOMBER COMMAND HAD HIT THE GESTAPO HEADQUARTERS. THE ATTACK TOOK PLACE ON NEW YEAR'S EVE, AND WAS THE SECOND RAID ON THAT TARGET.

ABOVE: A job well done: the Gestapo HQ in ruins

ABOVE: A remarkable still from the cine film showing a Flight returning after the attack on the Gestapo HQ

ABOVE: John Buckley's log book with P/O Heath as 'Navigator,' a life changing experience for him!

ABOVE & RIGHT: 627 Squadron BXVI Mosquitos en route to Oslo 30/12/44

121

Kiwis Do Fly

Daylight and 30,000 Feet

"With 109 Squadron (operating from Little Staughton), our Mosquito BMk IXs were all Oboe equipped and operated almost continuously by our crews and 105 Squadron. A pooling arrangement saw many Mossies go back and forth between the Squadrons as the Oboe equipment was serviced and tweaked."

"On December 11th 1944 we drew MM241 'Bar S' and left Little Staughton for Duisberg in company with another Mosquito which we followed into the target area at 30,000 feet, both of us just on the verge of leaving vapour trails."

"We dropped on time (as was expected) with the error not too bad (17 yards). On this clear December day we could see much of France and the Allied battle front. Imagining the turmoil below, here we were, warm, comfortable and nearly at the end of a 3 hour 45 min Op. We couldn't wait for the next one."

"My best memories are marking for the massive raids carried out in early March 1945. To Cologne with 858 main force heavies (in MM 114 'G') and then ten days later to Dortmund with 1108 heavies in MM 295 Bar P – Peter, the famous Grim Reaper."

"Fabulous times with great memories."

– Bill Simpson

ABOVE: Take-off from Little Staughton in MM 241 'S' for marking duties over Duisberg

ABOVE: Formation at 30,000 feet vapour trails just beginning to form beneath

ABOVE: Log book entry for the Duisberg Raid. Four ops in December 44

ABOVE: 109 Squadron's famous 'Grim Reaper' MM295 Bar P – Peter with over 150 ops recorded, New Zealand pilots on 109 in the front

Chapter 10 – A Wizard Show

D-Day and the Invasion

"D-Day was a hectic time for Bomber Command, most of the Pathfinder Force flying twice that day. The last operation we performed was after the bridgehead had been established and when advance had been slowed. Our troops were held up near Caen by masses of German tanks and troops and our mission was to bomb their lines which were only some 600 yards ahead of our front lines. There was very heavy cloud cover over the target, starting hundreds of feet above sea level. Pathfinder Master Bombers were to be used to direct the main stream bomber Squadrons to the target once they had emerged from the cloud."

"On our way out over the channel, we saw dozens of warships, barges with troops and supplies, then masses of material on the beaches – a good deal probably damaged."

"The situation at Caen was assessed by the Army as very serious so the raid had to go ahead. We could hear the Master Bomber calling, "come on down." We emerged over the battle area to see dozens of four engine bombers all heading for the German front line. We were so close to the ground we could feel the concussion of exploding bombs, the sensation was of driving along a heavily corrugated road. The crew had views of rows of tanks being blown up. Being the pilot I had to ensure I didn't hit any other planes and to get the hell out of there. Heavy bombers were rarely used at such low altitudes and we were given quite a thrill the next day as we received a congratulatory message from Field Marshal Montgomery. We had broken their lines and allowed our troops to continue."

John Tarbuck following along in LL959 (UM-A2) of 626 Squadron admired the multi-coloured flak until his crew suggested it was time to bugger off.

Post D-Day raids were just as demanding. On July 2nd during a daylight raid to Oisemont we received eight holes from heavy flak – one hole right through the fuselage where the W/Op's head would have been had he been in his seat. Fortunately Ron was momentarily out of his usual position.

On July 5th, during a short trip we were attacked by a Ju.88 fighter hitting the starboard inner engine which caught on fire. My immediate action was to press the 'grqviner' (fire extinguisher) and feather the engine (which fortunately worked) then taking violent evasive action. Any loose material inside flew around including one parachute which opened adding to the confusion. This fighter persisted for some time but without hitting us again. All I could hear through the intercom was one gun from the two in the mid upper turret – no other guns were firing. I thouht that Ted in the rear turret had been hit – fortunately the reason was a lot simpler. The mid upper turret with two 303 guns is fed by belts and fired electrically by two points located vertically under the guns. These connections were supposed to be wired in. The G forces detatched these plugs and left Bert only firing manually. He never made that mistake again.

The rear turret with four 303 guns was fed by belts channeled along chutes from the ammunition boxes. Their lids were held closed by several strips of parachute elastic – the violent action broke the elastic letting the ammunition belts out, jamming the whole works. I kept the evasive action up for some time as we were virtually defenceless and flew homeward on three engines.

The inner engines are above the housing of the main wheels and I could not tell whether the tyres had been damaged.

Oakington was marginal so I decided to make an emergency landing at Woodbridge. It was designed for emergency landings being situated near the south coast and fitted with FIDO. This lifted the fog enough to permit me to make a successful landing with much jubilation from the crew.

I can still recall the expressions of relief and excitement. The ground crew asked if we'd been looping – open parachute, charts, pencils, thermo flasks everywhere mixed with ammo and one bomb rolling around underneath.

Robin's Rear Gunner Bertie Fox recalls a mixture of fear and excitement, "I wouldn't have missed it for the world" he said. "I don't say I was always happy but every time I got home I kissed the ground."

As for the other moments, "They are just for me to know" he said.

– Robin Craw

ABOVE: Robin Craw and his crew, 7 PFF Squadron, Oakington 1944
Left to Right: Robin Craw (Pilot), Ron Johnson (Nav), Ron Smith (W/Op), Gordon Gibson (B/A), Jack Owen (F/E), Bert Fox (M/UG), Bob Harpur (R/G)

Kiwis Do Fly

Hitler's Lair

"The attack on Berchtesgaten in April 1945 gave Bomber Command a chance perhaps to show off; a daylight raid with little likelihood of fighter opposition and when we took off on the 25th it was a beautiful clear day."

"Flying out of Downham Market I was tasked that day as Deputy Master Bomber flying Lancaster F2-U (PB922). Approaching Germany some of the Master Bombers gear went U/S so we took over. The Alps were a great sight but as we were now head of the team, things were pretty busy. Our H2S equipped Lancasters carried an eighth crewmember to look after some of the electronics."

"Our approach was good, then out of nowhere came heavy and accurate AA fire. We were briefed that the area was being fortified as Hitler's Last Redoubt and many of the German forces were well-trained SS regiments. Well, they certainly knew how to shoot. So much so that after dropping the target indicators I put Uncle into a vertical bank and the target photo taken from 16,600 feet shows just how vertical we were! I believe we missed Hitler's Eagles nest but clobbered the SS barracks and Goering's mansion. Good enough for me."

At the other end of the scale, Pilot Officer Tom Whyte sat as a rear gunner in Skipper Len Hampton's 101 Squadron's Lancaster on just his fourth Op. "Bugger the view, where are these fighters?" – There were none.

– George Hitchcock

ABOVE: George Hitchcock

ABOVE: Downham Market March 1945
Standing: Left to Right: F/L Don Swaffield DFC (Nav), F/S Bill Trowhall (F/E),
Air crew kneeling: Left to Right: F/S John Standing (M/UG), F/O Tom King (Nav 2 set operator for H2s and Gee radars)
F/O Chuck Speacely (B/A), G Hitchcock, F/O Vernon Marks (R/G)

Chapter 10 – A Wizard Show

LEFT: PB922 following servicing on its air test – Note that both port Merlins feathered

BELOW: The target photo taken by Squadron Leader Hitchcock's PB922 in a vertical bank at 16,600 feet

ABOVE: Log book entry for the last few days of the war with the raid on Berchtesgaten prominent

LEFT: The same view taken from the Eagles Nest, this time horizontal

RIGHT: Berchtesgaten photographed from the Eagles Nest 2006

125

Kiwis Do Fly

Dropping Big Ones

When Arthur Joplin and his crew (including fellow New Zealander and Bomb Aimer Loftus Hebbard) joined 'C' Flight of 617 Squadron they would have never thought that they would drop some of the largest bombs ever produced.

Their first operation was to Brest on August 27 carrying 12 x 1,000 lb bombs as a test load. The Squadron claimed a vessel sunk. Following a cross country carrying a 10,000 lb load, Arthur and his crew settled with the specialised task of dropping big ones, 12,000 lb Tallboys.

"On October 7 1944, 617 Squadron and its Tallboys were given the Kembs Barrage, (a type of dam), on the Rhine to remove. Thirteen aircraft took part – six were to attack at 500 – 800 feet with the 12,000 lb Tallboys having 30 minute delayed fuses. The other seven, including myself, were to attack at a higher level with only a 25 second delay on these bombs."

Arthur Joplin was pilot of ME561 (KC-T). "We flew steady at 18,000 feet and locked the mid-upper and rear turrets into their fore and aft position to give maximum stability and to prevent the gunners rotating their turrets and knocking the aircraft askew as the rear turret could act as a rudder if fully rotated. Once the bomb aimer had us lined up on his stabilised SABS bomb sight a red spot light came on in centre of my control panel. I had to keep the spot dead centre, all the while maintaining exactly the right altitude and speed. This needed real concentration. The SABS bomb sight was a very special piece of equipment like a giant mechanical computer and the B/A basically flew the Lancaster by it. Our Squadron was alone in using it as it was an incredible piece of gear receiving electrical, pneumatic and mechanical imputs."

RIGHT: Squadron Operational Records detailing the Tirpitz raid in November 1944

ABOVE: From 617 Squadron's Operations Book for 12th November 1944

RIGHT: Squadron mates meet again 66 years after their raid on the Tirpiz. Arthur Joplin (left) with S/L Tony Iveson, D.F.C. January 2010

ABOVE: Sinking the Tirpitz, picture of S/L Tony Iveson in AJ-F (ME554) coming out from Tromso, with Arthur's AJ-T below. The print is signed by W/C J B Tait and S/L Tony Iveson
(Print 53/550 courtesy of Nicholas Trudgian – A Joplin collection)

126

Chapter 10 – A Wizard Show

"Once the Tallboy was the released the aircraft would rise suddenly in the air but we still had to hold a straight course for the all important target photo."

"That day we had the Polish Mustangs of 306 Squadron with us and they gave us great help by tickling up the flak crews."

"The Morning Post newspaper of the 9th October 1944 published my target photo. I've kept it all these years. 'X' marks our bomb and our bomb aimer, Loftus Hebbard was really quite proud of it and so he should have been. Loftus was a fellow New Zealander and later made detailed comments about the raids."

In October 1944 the German battleship Tirpitz continued to occupy Allied defence minds even though it was moored in a Norwegian fjord. It had been the target of repeated attacks over the years and even 'out of action' required the Royal Navy to maintain a large capital ship fleet on hand in case the Tirpitz 'got out' as the Bismark did in 1942.

Both 617 Squadron and their arch rival No 9 Squadron were given the task to 'Tallboy' the Tirpitz out of the war.

The Lancasters carrying these 'big boys' were progressively stripped to ensure adequate performance.

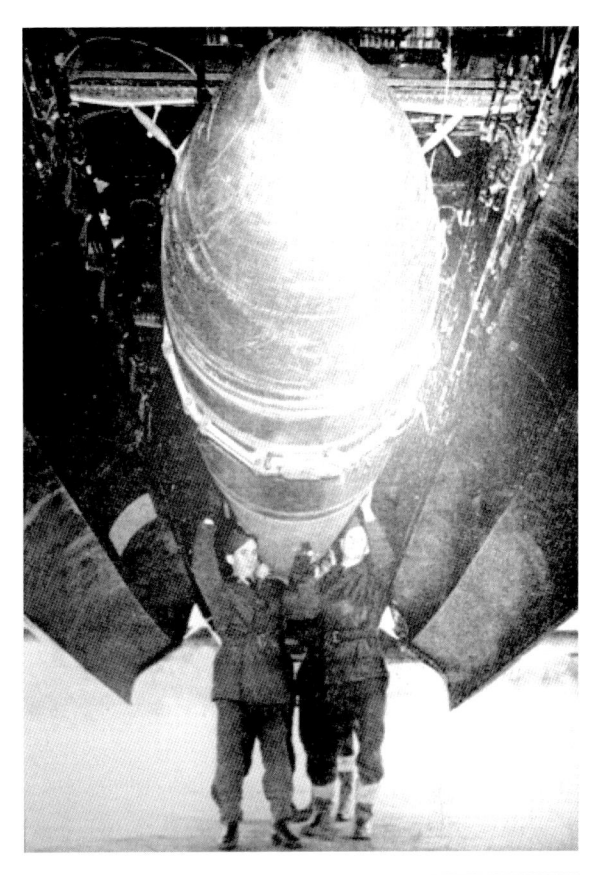

RIGHT: A Tallboy, 12,000 lb is a snug fit in a Lancaster's bomb bay

ABOVE: Woodhall Spa November 1944, Left to right:
Top Row: Norman Lambell (R/G), Basil Fish (Nav), Frank Tilley (F/E), Arthur Joplin (Pilot), Ground Crew Member
Bottom Row: Ground Crew Member, Gordon Cook (W/Op), Lofty Hebbard (B/A) and another Ground Crew Member

Kiwis Do Fly

ABOVE: The Kembs Barrage raid pictured by Keith Aspinall with 306 Squadron Mustangs on flak suppression duties. Shown is KC-O (DV391) piloted by F/O Phil Martin *(A. Joplin Collection)*

"The front guns were removed in November 1944 so from then the bomb aimer never had a seat! The mid upper turret went, the pilots armour plating went too, some aircraft lost their wireless operator, communication then being by R/T to the wireless equipped aircraft. By January 1945 even the bomb bay doors had gone. In exchange we got a 200 gallon fuel tank fitted into the fuselage. We were then literally a flying bomb with four engines and five or six bods along for the ride."

The first raid for the Tirpitz was planned for 29th October 1944 and both Squadrons found heavy cloud cover. "The Tirpitz was obscured by mist and smoke from generators so we aimed at the flashes, knowing that 10,000 lb of Torpex going off anywhere near the ship would give them a bit of a hurry up."

RIGHT: The Kembs target photo published in the Morning Post newspaper of October 9th, 1944 The accompanying article was headed 'Earthquake Bomb.' The burst marked 'X' was claimed by Arthur's bomber aimer, Lofty Hebbard

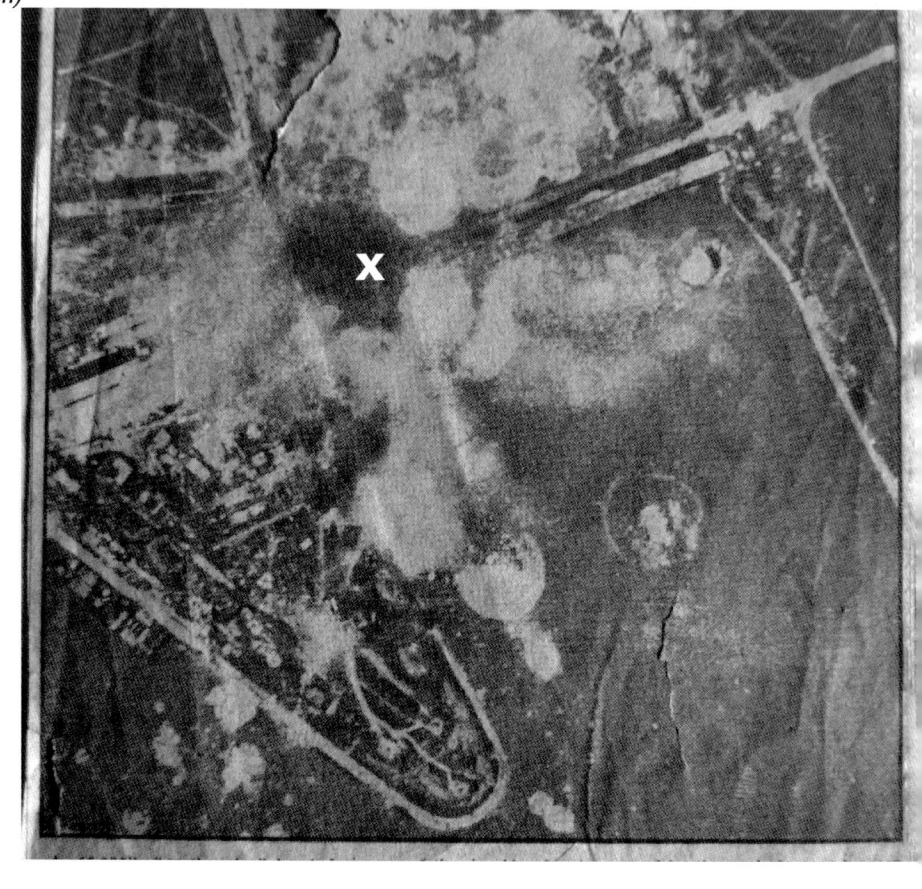

Chapter 10 – A Wizard Show

LEFT: Log book entry of the Urft raid December 11th 1944

However, the Tirpitz was not out of commission yet, reconnaissance showed the Tirpitz still safely in Tromso fiord, another raid was scheduled for November 12th.

"Our briefings were extensive, twice at Woodhall Spa before I took my KC–T (ME561) to Milltown in Scotland on the Saturday morning. That night we were again briefed and taken back to Milltown for a 3 am take-off and a fourteen hour trip."

The raid consisted of thirteen aircraft from 9 Squadron and eighteen aircraft from 617 Squadron.

"We flew north at low level up to the Shetlands then tracked across the North Sea, over Norway and into neutral Sweden. We kept low and the odd salvo from Swedish flak batteries wasn't accurate. Perhaps on purpose!"

Approaching Tromso the formation gathered and climbed to their allocated bombing height. The flak became very heavy. The visibility was perfect, none of the predicted fighter cover materialised and the early bombs bracketed the Tirpitz. Two were direct hits. Bombing at 0843 hours, Arthur's bomb aimer Loftus Hebbard could only aim for the centre of the smoke. He later commented; "I was on my knees at the SABS and while I was the only crew member that could see everything going down, I was the only one seeing everything that came up."

Two Tallboys hit the Tirpitz near mid-ships and later analysis showed a further four had landed within the protective torpedo net.

At 0942 hours the Tirpitz capsized, there to remain until Norwegian salvage crews scrapped the hulk during the late 1940's.

On the 50th anniversary of the raid in 1994, Arthur was presented with a mounted section of the battleships deck as a memento from the Norwegian Forces.

Of the 108 members of 617 Squadron on this raid, the crews knew of none who were decorated. Eight New Zealanders were among the 168 aircrew from 9 and 617 Squadrons on this raid including four of the thirty-two pilots.

Only one aircraft was lost, a 9 Squadron Lancaster with three New Zealand crewmen, Flying Officer Coster (Pilot) and Flight Sergeants Black (Nav) and Boag (B/A).

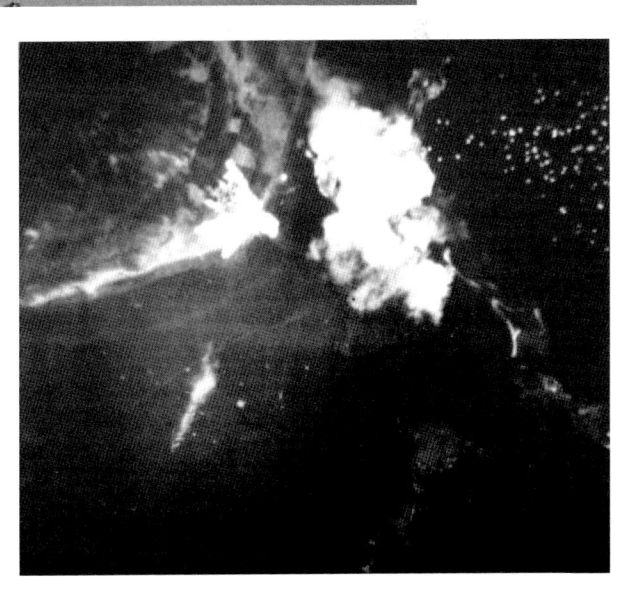

ABOVE: Target photo of the Tirpitz during the attack on 12th November 1944, taken from AJ-T (Arthur Joplin's Lancaster) at 12,000 feet. The explosion indicates a near miss

Reported by the New Zealand Press Association on 28 November Flying Officer Coster said during the 'interview' they had been hit lightly by flak but both starboard engines began to fail. The starboard inner caught fire and was feathered. "We had little hope of reaching the base so we either made a forced landing in Sweden or took the risk. We took a vote over the intercom, five to one for Sweden."

"We spotted four Fw190 fighters which seemed to ignore us then an Me109 put in an appearance and

Kiwis Do Fly

made four attacks. All missed but my Welsh rear gunner (WJ Jones) fired a few shots. We came through clouds then made a 'wheels up' forced landing beside a river. Nobody was hurt at all and we were given a great welcome by local villagers."

After two days in a Swedish Army camp, the crew enjoyed nine days of freedom in Stockholm before returning to England. Costers crew were on their seventh operation of their tour.

Dropping 12,000 lb bombs was a specialty of 617 Squadron and even as a Sprog crew, Arthur's team set about transporting large quantities of high explosive to Germany. A Lancaster with a Tallboy carried as much as much as several B-17 Flying Fortresses but the impact of this one great bomb literally caused an earthquake which shocked and overstressed the structure, causing it to collapse.

On 8th December again in ME961 Arthur targeted the Heinback dam but weather forced a recall. The attempt was repeated three days later this time using F/Lt Sayer's DV402. On December 15, the E-Boat pens at Ijmuiden were attacked and on the 21st (the fourth Op in twelve days) the synthetic oil plant at Politz was the target.

Returning after a ten hour trip in faithful ME561 bad weather forced Arthur to divert to Ludford Magna and its FIDO equipped runways but things didn't go to plan.

By then Arthur Joplin and his crew had dropped six Tallboys over a ten week period. Arthur's aircraft crashed on returning to England, his crew having dropped over 100,000 lbs of explosive in nine sorties.

– Arthur Joplin

ABOVE: The Tirpitz being scrapped post-war with the results of a 12,000 lb miss in the foreground

ABOVE: A section of the Tirpitz teak decking presented to Arthur Joplin at 617 Squadron reunion in Lossiemouth, 12th November 1994 on the 50th anniversary of the attack

RIGHT: Arthur's escape kit labelled 'N' for Norway. Then worth a fortune in Krone. This kit went on both Tirpitz raids and its return was 'overlooked'

October 2	Walcheren	1 x 12,000 lb DNCO	DV393/T
October 7	Kembs Barrage	1 x 12,000 lb	DV393/T
October 29	Tromso	1 x 12,000 lb (Tirpitz) Via Skatsha	DV393/T
November 12	Tromso	1 x 12,000 lb (Tirpitz) Via Sumburgh	ME561/T
November 24	Night Bombing		
December 8	Urft Dam	1 x 12,000 lb DNCO. Badly shot up	ME561/T
December 11	Urft Dam	1 x 12,000 lb	DV402/X
December 15	Ijmuiden	1 x 12,000 lb	ME561/T

Chapter 10 – A Wizard Show

Flying in Oblongs, Operation Taxable

"On 5th June 1944 we were summoned to the briefing room and were told that we would be operating that night supporting the Normandy landings. The operation followed the training we had been carrying out over the past five weeks and was code named 'Operation Taxable.'"

"'Operation Taxable' was a spoof exercise, designed to simulate an invasion fleet on enemy radar screens, in the Pas-de-Calais area. No details of that highly secret operation were ever entered into the operations record book. As there are several different versions, all recalled from memory, the exact details are as I remember."

"The direction was a point between the towns of Fecamp and Le Treport, some 60 miles North East of the Normandy coast. The plan required a first wave of eight aircraft to head toward the French coast off Cap d'Antifer eighty miles away from where the real landings were taking place. Each aircraft flew parallel oblong circuits at 180mph at 3,000 feet with two miles between each aircraft, creating a 16 mile front. From the commencing point, each aircraft flew a straight course towards the French coast for two minutes and 30 seconds, then executed a slow 180 degree turn to port lasting one minute before returning towards the English coast at an exact parallel to the outward leg. After two minutes and ten seconds the aircraft then carried out another 180 degree turn to port again, lasting one minute arriving back over the track of the original leg. The difference in timing between the outward and return legs of each circuit when repeated by the eight aircraft resulted in the whole pattern advancing towards the French Coast at the rate of eight knots, the average speed of a naval convoy."

"To create the impression of an advancing armada on German radar screens, each aircraft dropped bundles of 'window,' of predetermined sizes down the flare chute every five seconds, the size of the strips increasing as the aircraft flew towards the French Coast and decreasing as they flew back on the return leg. No window was dropped on the turns. The directions to the crew manning the flare chute when to commence dropping the bundles of window, when to cease and when to change the size was

ABOVE: The crew of KC–W (LM482) Left to Right:
Standing: S/L Les Munro (Pilot), Jimmy Clay (B/A), Bill Howarth (M/UG), Harvey Weeks (RG)
Kneeling: Jock Rumbles (Nav), Frank Appleby (F/E), Percy Pigeon (W/Op)
Except for Clay and Weeks this crew served together since 97 Squadron days in 1943

ABOVE: Lancaster B Mk III KC-W (LM 482) issued post Dams Raid. The nose art depicts Admiral Harpy

done by a system of red and green lights operated by the second navigator."

"Because of the tedious and repetitive nature of the operation each crew was doubled up so that individuals could be rested periodically. As a result every aircraft carried 13 or 14 crew. CO of the Squadron, Wing Commander Leonard Cheshire, flew as my second pilot in LM482 (W William)."

"We had to adhere to the exact airspeed and the exact compass bearing on both outward and return legs. The concentration required was only relieved during the turns at each end of the circuits. The operation certainly wasn't boring. Navigators had the most important role, to maintain the accuracy of the circuits and the dispatch of window. By using Gee, straight tracks for each of the continuing circuits could be laid along two grid lines of the system. Timing was of the essence."

"A second wave of eight Lancaster's took over from us two hours into the operation with each aircraft of the second wave joining the circuit at precisely the same time as the aircraft of the first wave were starting their last circuit but 500 feet above. Both aircraft then flew the same circuit together, with the aircraft of the first wave leaving the circuit at the end of the return leg. The second aircraft then lost height to 3,000 feet and commencing its first circuit on its own. This change over had to be completed within a margin of 90 seconds."

"While the Lancaster's were flying their continuous circuits a number of naval ships below were advancing at the same eight knots using radar counter measures and broadcasting sound effects to simulate a large convoy at sea."

"I always considered this operation was one of the most important that the Squadron carried out. Not because of bad weather, not because of any risk of enemy action and not because of any tangible result on the Germans infrastructure, but because of the very exacting requirements to which we had to fly and navigate. There was absolutely no latitude for deviation from ground speed, compass bearing, rate of turn and timing." Afterwards it was recorded, "While 617 Squadron's contribution to D-Day, was perhaps the least spectacular of all its operations, it was however one of the most exacting, arduous, and certainly, one of the most important."

"Flying in circles or rather oblongs so precisely demanded all our skills as pilots and while we didn't bomb anything it confirmed what precision flying could do."

– *Les Munro*

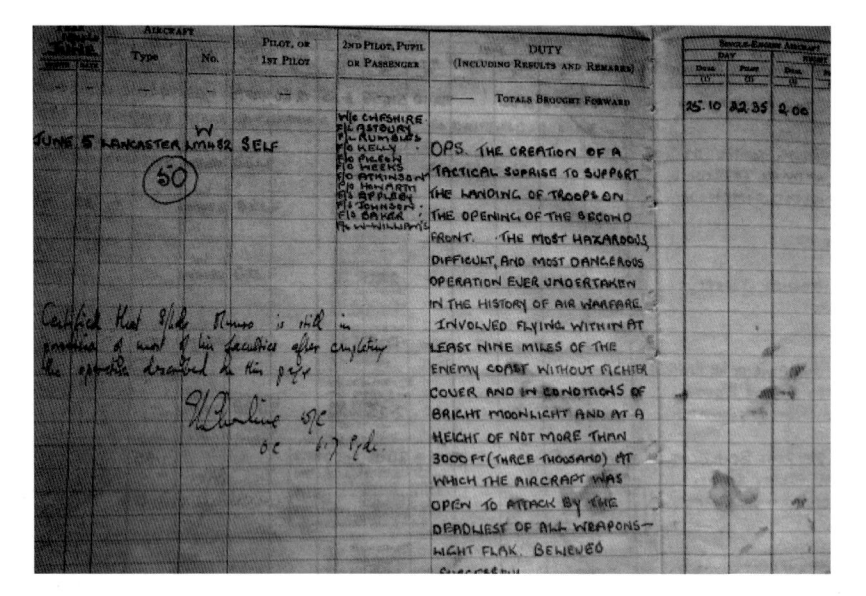

ABOVE: "The creation of a tactical surprise to support the landing of troops on the opening of the second front.
The most hazardous, difficult and most dangerous operation ever undertaken in the history of air warfare. Involved flying within at least nine miles of the enemy coast without fighter cover and in conditions of bright moonlight and at a height of not more than 3,000 feet at which the aircraft was open to attack by the deadliest of all weapons – light flak. Believed successful"

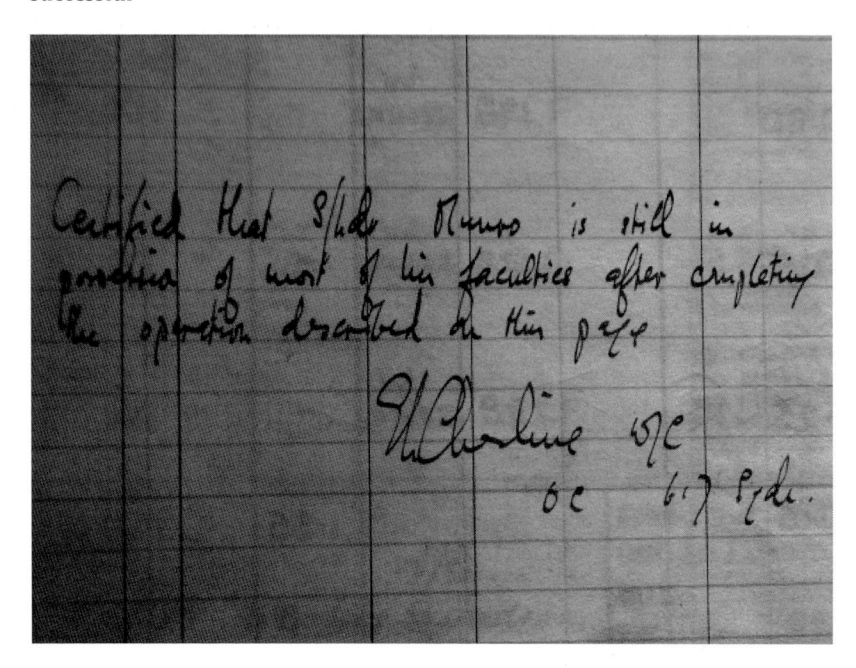

ABOVE: Having your Officer Commanding aboard as second pilot was unusual but when it was Wing Commander Leonard Cheshire it was special. Along side Les Munro's comments, Cheshire wrote:
"Certified that S/Ldr Munro is still in posession of most of his faculties after completing the operation described on this page."
G.L. Cheshire W/C OC 617 Squadron

Operation Taxable June 5, 1944:
Along with other senior pilots Les Munro was taken off operations for almost a month before D-Day to undergo the training needed to fly precise orbits. After the Op a rather disgruntled Squadron Leader Munro wrote in his log book in red ink (see left).

Chapter 10 – A Wizard Show

Daylight Raid

During 1945 daylight raids became more common for RAF Bomber Command and 75 (NZ) Squadron carried out daylight attacks on transport and petroleum production centres.

75 (NZ) Squadron 'A' and 'B' flights carried AA fuselage codes while 'C' flight were allocated JN codes.

Field Marshal Montgomery had called for Bomber Command assistance to neutralise potential German strong points along the Rhine hoping to minimise casualties during the crossing, an important point with the war in Europe about to end within weeks.

On 23rd March 1945, 75 (NZ) Squadron were part of a raid on Wesel, its GH equipped lancasters acting as lead navigators and 'trigger' aircraft for simultaneous bomb release.

This collection of photographs came from Neville Selwood and Colin Emslie, both navigators in 75 (NZ) Squadron.

– Neville Selwood

ABOVE: AA-C Lancaster PB132 fuels up, the tanker aptly named Dumbo

RIGHT: 75 (NZ) Squadron crews join the bus bound for their dispersal. The navigators with their large sachels include Colin Emslie and Neville Selwood 23 March, 1945

LEFT: 75 (NZ) Squadrons 'C' flight JN-V on the perimeter track at RAF Mepal on the afternoon of 23 March, 1945

LEFT: Close up from the rear turret of AA-C showing AA-G

ABOVE: Neville Selwood's log book showing some of the last operations of 75 (NZ) Squadron during March and April 1945

LEFT: Neville Selwood emerges from the curtained navigators precinct to do a 'visual.'

RIGHT: The crew returns after the Wesel Operation. A well known photograph of:

AA-C (PB132) sharing 98 operations

Left to Right: P/O W Russell (Pilot), F/O V. Hendry (B/A), Sgt F Jillians W/Op), F/O Neville Selwood (Nav), F/O Howells (M/UG), Sgt G. Robson (R/G), Sgt J Hunt (F/E). The ground crew add victory signs

Chapter 11

Welcome to the Caterpillar club

Aircrew forced to abandon their aircraft and parachute to safety automatically became members of a very exclusive club, the Caterpillars.

The 'Caterpillar' represented the silk worm whose woven fabric was manufactured into parachutes by the Irvin Air Chute Company and saved many thousands of lives during WWII and since.

Along with a certificate of membership the survivors were issued with a small gold caterpillar pin.

Jack Shorthouse "earned" his membership card when he parachuted from his Fairey Battle (L5324) over France, June 11, 1940

Kiwis Do Fly

Into the Frying Pan

"I originally applied to train as a pilot, but with entry delays, I re-applied to become a navigator. I was refused. At ITW training in Rotorua I was asked to change from pilot to navigator – this time I refused."

"My flying career was intense and really quite brief, just over 600 hours in total." Having soloed on Tiger Moths at the RNZAF No.1 EFTS in early 1943, Stan and some of his class mates shipped to Canada for multi-engine training and then on to England. "It was a production line; firstly PRC at Brighton, then NCO's school at Whitley Bay then back to Brighton. Then flying at 24 EFTS (Sealand) on Tiger's again, Brighton again, 15 AFU (Castle Combe), 12 OTU (Chipping Warden), 1653 HCU (Chedburgh), 3 LFS(Feltwell) and finally to 75 (NZ) Squadron at Mepal, a process taking fourteen months. Imagine the paperwork involved."

"I joined 75 (NZ) Squadron on December 2, 1944. It had a gung-ho reputation and was full of press-on types. That showed in 75's casualty rate. I was a bit fortunate that my cousin, Wing Commander Ray Newton was Officer Commanding. By all accounts the previous Commanding Officer had been a bastard and had to be replaced. Ray didn't last long, being killed on New Years Day 1945 flying with a sprog crew on their first operation."

"Such was the pace of operations my log book shows no daytime flight tests or training flights, just day or night Ops. We flew seven Ops in just sixteen days in January despite the bad weather. If we could see halfway down the runway we took off. Being the time of the Battle of the Bulge, our bomb loads were needed to hinder the German's re-supply lines."

"The raid scheduled on February 14 to Chemnitz was to be our 25th Op in just eight weeks and we were

ABOVE: Pilot Training RNZAF, Taieri, March 1943

'dog tired' It was to be our last."

"At 2032 on 14 February 1945 we took off from Mepal. We were nominated as an H2S crew for the raid and as our own aircraft AA–H was not equipped with H2S navigational radar we were flying a borrowed kite: AA-D (NG113)."

'Unknown to us at the time, the previous night's crew of 'Dog' had reported some problems with it. Regrettably it let us down when we were north of Karlsruhe which was about half an hour into enemy territory. A fire developed in the starboard wing, possibly from a broken oil line. We were unable to feather the prop or subdue the fire."

"After jettisoning the bomb load I trimmed the aircraft as best I could and gave the order to abandon in the normal way. This involved all members of the crew coming forward to the cockpit and being counted before bailing out through the front hatch. Johnny Maher, the rear gunner did not appear and without hesitation the wireless operator Tommy' (Flight Sergeant White) went back to check that Johnny hadn't been trapped in his turret. He wasn't. Unthinking of the consequences he had carried out the emergency bail-out procedure by turning his turret and dropping out backwards. I was relieved when Tommy reappeared in the cockpit and we were then both able to leave the aircraft. His trip to the rear turret and back would not have been easy in the dark. It involved twice clambering over the main spar. The return trip probably took at least two minutes – a

ABOVE: Flight Lieutenant Davies 1944

long time in a burning aircraft."

"Just before I dropped head first through the hatch I carefully took hold of the parachute ripcord, perhaps with the thought that I mightn't be able to find it afterwards. That was a mistake, because as soon as I hit the slipstream of possibly 140 knots, the force of the slipstream pushed my arm strongly backwards. This immediately pulled the cord and released the chute. In

Chapter 11 – Welcome to the Caterpillar Club

LEFT: 12 OTU training and crashing. An overshoot in Wellington LP460 resulted in a night time wheels up landing on only one engine

the normal way should have counted for some seconds and been well clear of the aircraft before pulling the cord. Fortunately, no harm was done. Claude (Flight Sergeant Greenough), our navigator, did the same as me and wasn't so lucky. Lancasters had fixed tail wheels and when his chute also opened early it got torn 'en passant' by the tail wheel, with the result that he had a quick trip to the ground. He landed quite heavily but happily without any broken parts; My pilot's flying gloves were actually a 3-in-l. First were long silk gloves, then woollen mittens without fingers, and then long leather gauntlets. The force of the slipstream tore them all off!'"

"My drop to the ground from about 10,000 feet, was uneventful. I remember seeing the aircraft circle away but not the crash. At first it was just stars and the silence, and then suddenly the darkness became blacker and there was a wood coming up at me. To my great relief I drifted over it and landed in a field, missing the nearest trees by about 20 yards. I have often wondered how my life may have altered if I had dropped into the branches of one of those trees. Would I have survived?"

"After dumping the parachute in the wood I walked for about three hours and then spent the rest of the night shivering and dozing. It was still winter and very cold and I was dressed only in my battle dress. My intention was to try and make the Swiss border and so I set out the next morning. Unfortunately, Claude, my navigator had been caught and that brought out the local Volkssturm to search. I walked into one on the edge of a wood and never had a chance of getting away. He was armed, I wasn't."

"I was first taken to the local village where I met Claude. We spent some hours in the village lock-up and were then paraded on the village green. Claude later recalled being scared stiff of a young lad with a bow and arrow who he was sure was going to fire at him. A policeman then escorted us to a Luftwaffe base a mile or two away. Claude and I pushed the policeman's motorcycle while he walked behind with a shooter – we didn't argue."

"At the Luftwaffe base we were taken to an operations room which I recall as being well-manned. The Commanding Officer was in his late twenties, had an injured leg, and wore an Iron Cross. He spoke to us through an interpreter and told us that we would have to stay with them in Germany for three months (Note: Bearing in mind that at that time Allied forces had still to cross the Rhine, his forecast was remarkably accurate. The date was February 15. The war ended on May 8 and I returned to England on May 13.) In retrospect I have wondered why the Luftwaffe officers received us at all instead of our being bundled straight to a detention centre. Our reception was courteous and correct and I did not detect any antagonistic feelings. I suspect that in 1945, being in Luftwaffe custody was the safest place in Germany for RAF personnel. I would certainly not have liked to have had to take my chances with the civilian population."

"On leaving the Commanding Officer's presence we were taken downstairs and while awaiting transport the escorting officer demanded that Claude and I hand over our watches. I refused and it became a bit heated. I finally agreed that if his Commanding Officer upstairs supported his request he could have them. Nothing more was said and we were relieved when a truck arrived and took us to a military prison where we arrived about 7.00 pm. Imagine our surprise when we were put into a cell and found Jock (Flight Sergeant J Chalmers our bomb aimer) already there. We stayed there for five days and again were well treated. The guards were fairly friendly to us, but from what we saw they treated other prisoners like dirt. Strangely, they respected my rank and refused to let me help Jock or Claude (both Flight Sergeants) carry the night soil can from our cell to be emptied."

"We were then sent to the Luftwaffe Interrogation Centre in Frankfurt. The central railway station was a bit of a mess, presumably from bombing. Travel from there to the Centre was by tram. We had five days in solitary confinement and I was interrogated twice, the second time being awoken from sleep in the middle of the night. Our next stop was Dulag-Luft at Weitzler, where we arrived on 27 February and spent two days resting

Kiwis Do Fly

from our solitary."

"From Dulag we were moved by train to Nuremberg, the journey taking four and a half days. The distance wasn't great but the area was chaotic from the Allied bombing and strafing. Tragically, we had first hand experience of this. Our train consisted of a locomotive, passenger carriages, goods cars, and a flak wagon, and then either three or four unmarked box cars containing RAF and USAAF POWs. On our first day of this journey an Allied fighter attacked the locomotive and of course the gunners in the flak wagon opened fire on the fighter. This brought a second fighter to attack the flak wagon, and regrettably its cone of fire covered the POW box cars. I have never been more scared in my life and even today I can still hear the shells tearing through the cars and hitting the wheels. By this time the train had stopped and the exodus from the box cars into the adjacent fields must have broken all records. If I remember correctly some twenty-odd RAF and USAAF men were killed in that strafing on 2 March 1945, including Jock Chalmers, our Scottish bomb aimer. Jock was in the box car in front of the one that Claude and I were in."

"The Germans were very proud of the stadium at Nuremberg and while marching us from the railway station to the prison camp forced us to do a complete circuit inside the stadium. Our new prison home at Nuremberg was Luft 3 and under Luftwaffe command. To my great joy the rest of my crew was already there and in good heart so except for Jock we had all survived. Ian Evans (Flight Sergeant) told me that the morning after our bail-out his German captors had marched him past the wreck of our aircraft and he was shown my flying helmet with my name inside, so he knew then that I had got out too."

"The camp we found to be in a terrible mess. There was scarcely any food and for the first eleven days our daily food ration consisted of one slice of bread, a mug of very watery soup, and a cup of erstaz coffee made from acorns. On this diet our health was rapidly deteriorating and I reached the stage when, on standing up, I supported myself on the wall until dizziness wore off. Fortunately Red Cross parcels started to arrive and from then on we had sufficient food to keep going."

"During our first days in Nuremberg it was very apparent that Germany was angry at the destruction of Dresden on 13 February, in which attack we had participated, and rumours of reprisal circulated freely. The strongest 'rumour,' which was reputed to be based on advice from the Camp Commandant to the SBO (Senior British Officer), was that Hitler was ordering that all RAF prisoners be shot. According to the rumour, the Camp Commandant (a Luftwaffe officer) had stated that if such an order was issued, the SS would be given

ABOVE: 1945, 75 (NZ) Squadron's busy January in very poor weather during support operations of the Battle of the Bulge. On January 13, following the raid in Saarbrucken, the Squadron was diverted from Mepal to the coastal airfield at Portreath in Cornwall and did a stream landing much to the worry of the Scottish Controller, who in the end just sighed and said "och, land yourselves you're not listening to me!"

Chapter 11 – Welcome to the Caterpillar Club

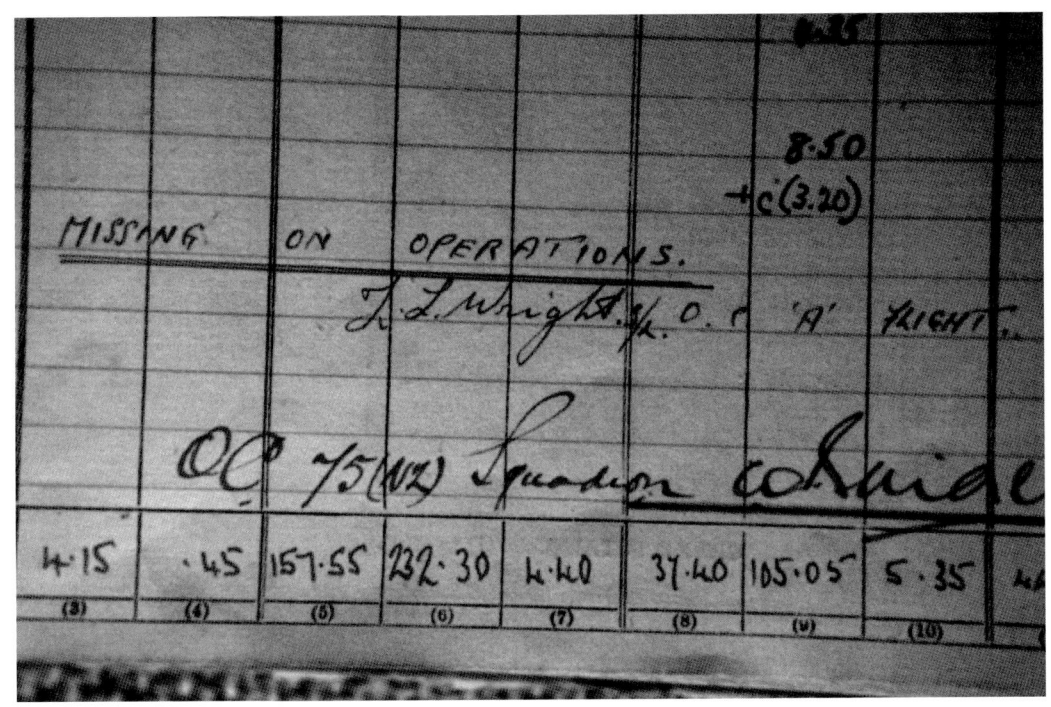

LEFT: Missing on operations. OC 75 (NZ) Squadron, Wing Commander Cyril Baigent, records the crew's loss in Stan Davies log book. The low number accumulated hours are of note

the job of carrying it out, the Army might go along with it, the Navy would do nothing, but the Luftwaffe would actively defend the prisoners. The next rumour gave Himmler the credit for the order not proceeding."

"I was only at Nuremberg for a month during which I started to learn the intricacies of POW life: how to stretch the food parcel contents by using them sparingly as spreads; how to re-slice a half inch thick piece of bread into four or five slices to put the spread on (I still had my escape issue pocket knife which the Germans hadn't found); the interminable search for dry twigs, paper or cardboard as fire material for cooking. Personal hygiene care was difficult. The ablution block consisted only of cold water and a long-drop where we sat like a row of sparrows on a branch. A goon (German guard) stood outside and gave us two pieces of toilet paper each as we went in.'

"The camp was some six miles from Nuremburg city itself, which was heavily bombed on the night of 16/17 March. During the raid we were shut in our huts and so could hear but not see."

"Another event was the arrival in the camp of a number of US Army tank crews. The tanks had been ranging behind German lines and had come across a prisoner of war camp. The tanks succeeded in releasing the prisoners and proceeded to shepherd/escort them back to allied territory. The convoy could only go as fast as the prisoners on foot which meant that the tanks had to use a low gear with consequential high fuel consumption. The gas ran out and the tank crews and the released prisoners were rounded up by German forces."

"By the beginning of April Allied armies were pushing well into Germany and the Germans decided to evacuate our camp. We were given one or two days notice – long enough for the undistributed Red Cross parcels to be opened up and the 'cookable' ingredients mixed up by the kitchen staff who produced a highly concentrated concoction of which we were each given a 'cake' to be a stand-by on our march."

"We moved out of the camp on my 22nd birthday, April 4 - umpteen thousands of us. After having been shut behind barbed wire for a month it was a change to be on the road. But the countryside peace didn't reign for long. We had covered only a few miles and were on a road that paralleled a railway line when there was a roar of aircraft and the din of exploding bombs. What a scatter! Everybody took off into scrub on the other side of the road as several USAAF Thunderbolts shot past. We assumed that they were attacking rolling stock on the railway and didn't see us in time – or did they originally identify us as retreating German troops – but they did manage to throw their bombs clear of us. Thereafter the idea of one long column was given away and we were broken up into small groups (perhaps 30–40 per group) with a couple of guards per group. There was no question of our escaping as we were under allied orders to stay together as the advancing allied armies did not want to be hindered by POWs on the loose, and additionally German forces could have been a bit trigger happy. In the late afternoon our guards disappeared so we continued on our own until we found some rough scrub where we sheltered for the night. It rained. Next morning we had fires going – cooking porridge and brewing up when our guards ambled up. They had apparently spent a pleasant night and kept dry."

"For the next 14 days we strolled through the Bavarian countryside. It was spring, the weather had cleared, and the countryside was beautiful with its wooded valleys and hillsides. Regularly, twice a day, an allied spotter aircraft kept tabs on us. We crossed the 'blue' Danube at Regensburg – it was actually a dirty brown. We slept in barns, we slept in churches; we slept anywhere. There were no toilets and I often wonder who cleaned up after us. Eventually we arrived at Moosburg, about 30 km north east of Munich. Moosburg was a huge camp which had been filled up with prisoners being evacuated from other camps. It was organised into separate compounds for officers and NCOs, so unhappily Claude and I were separated. We had first teamed up at OTU at the end of May 1944 and had stayed together since then, including shared leaves.

Strangely, although we were together, my only memory of him on the march from Nuremberg was when we mutually agreed 'that now was the time to start eating our concentrated concoctions. He ate his all in one go, whereas I spread mine over two or three days."

"Moosburg was a real hotch potch and we newcomers were mixed in with old hands. Two of the old hands in our hut were 'RAAF. A couple of us became friendly with them, but we became suspicious of some of their chatter about aircraft. When we deliberately asked them some loaded questions they came clean and admitted that they were Australian army privates who had exchanged identities with two RAAF officers who wanted the 'freedom' of being on work parties to escape."

"There was excitement on 28 April, when some US Army officers entered the camp to discuss with the Germans whether they were going to defend the camp or not. Fortunately the Germans agreed that they would surrender, and at five to twelve on Sunday 29 April a couple of US tanks rolled in. Shortly after, the German guards marched out to formally surrender and join the next generation of prisoners of war."

"We were extremely relieved when the Americans arrived because right up to the end the Germans were considering moving the airforce prisoners on again, presumably into the mountains – there was a suggestion that we were to be used as hostages."

"After the camp was liberated on 29 April we were officially in the camp for another nine days. Unofficially there was no impediment to our going outside and several of us visited a farm house and were invited inside. The family was understandably very nervous of us and they took care to keep their dogs by them. As far as the future of Germany was concerned they thought that it could revert to smaller states and they obviously would have liked to see Bavaria on its own."

"From Moosburg camp we moved to Straubing airfield which was a Luftwaffe base, and there we watched Luftwaffe aircraft flying in to surrender, the war in Europe having officially ended the previous day, 8 May. One of the aircraft even contained a live pig. Straubing must have been a substantial base as it contained permanent residential quarters. The married quarters seemed to have been occupied until very recently, unlike the RAF stations where you didn't see civilian wives. We wandered through many of the buildings; the rooms were a shambles. We were puzzled to find in one of the messes a supply of small whips and couldn't imagine what they had been for – perhaps some ceremonial use. I acquired half a dozen beer steins but to my everlasting regret abandoned them later when they became too heavy to carry."

"On 10 May the Yanks flew us in Dakotas to Nancy and for the first time we really realised that the war was over. Here we sat down to a three course meal served by French girls. They even had an orchestra playing. From Nancy we went by train to Epilan for a shower and fresh clothes. This was quite an amazing experience. We entered a building where we stripped off completely, and I said goodbye forever to the clothes that I had lived in for three months – how they must have stunk – thence into a glorious hot shower. The shower room exited into an equipment store and we came out the other end DDT'd and fully clothed in US army uniforms and even kitted with blankets and sleeping bag. What a glorious sleep I had that night. I had quite a dose of tinea on my feet which a doctor kindly attended to, but a temporary cure only as it wasn't until 1996 that it cleared up as a result of a treatment for pneumonia."

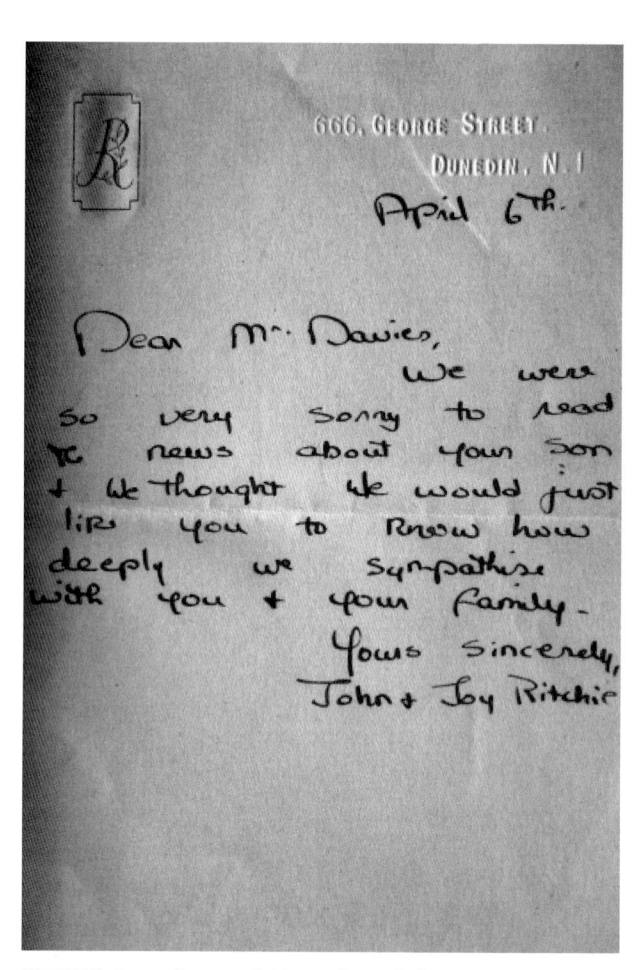

ABOVE: One of many letters of condolence sent to Stan's Mother

"The next night we moved out by train bound for Littavre but we became stuck in a siding for some hours. Fed up with the delay, when we saw some of our Group's Lancasters landing a few miles away, two of us scrounged a ride in a jeep and went to the airfield. The other chap knew quite a few of the pilots and we were made very welcome. We spent the night at the airfield and flew back to England with the Wing Commander the next day. Dover's white cliffs showed up through the haze, what a wonderful sight. We landed at Wing, north west of London on 13 May 1945. Our transport to the railway station was stopped by a milkman who insisted on giving each of us a pint of milk to drink there and then."

"My final move was to Brighton's reception unit. The circle from my leaving Brighton to my return there had taken 15 months, during which I had flown Oxfords, Wellingtons, Stirlings, and Lancasters; completed 24 operations, being scared stiff in the process; advanced from Sergeant to Flight Lieutenant with DFC; and been an unreported POW. But, above all, it was a period of association with so many wonderful people."

– Stan Davies

Chapter 11 – Welcome to the Caterpillar Club

Bail Out

Arthur Kirk (Winkie) became a member of the Caterpillar Club at 1.30 am on July 29 1944, when his 75(NZ) Squadron Lancaster AA-M (ND657) caught fire after being hit by a Ju88 night fighter. It was just his fifth operation. The crew became one more to face the chop early in their tour. Winkie survived and tells his own remarkable story.

"When I was born in the early autumn of 1923, I am sure my mother never would have dreamed that her eldest child (Jim) Aubrey Charles Kirk would be seated in a recruiting office on the eve of his eighteenth birthday waiting to sign up to join the Air Force. I wanted to see the world especially Canada, and if that meant joining the Air Force to fight in the war, that is what I would do."

"My mother was quite relieved when I was sent to Burnham because in one of her weaker moments and against her better judgment she signed the papers allowing me to go overseas with the Air Force. When I was sent to Burnham she thought that meant I wouldn't be going far afield but I wasn't in the army very long. After six weeks, my name appeared on Daily Routine Orders listing men to report to RNZAF Ohakea for Aerodrome Defence Unit (ADU) duties and a continuation of our aircrew assignments."

"I had signed up for the RNZAF on the 23rd March 1941. It took until the 30th May 1942 before I was finally attested at Ohakea as an AC2, the lowest form of life in the Air Force."

"After completing our initial ground training at Rotorua on the 19th November 1942, I was posted on final leave until we left New Zealand in January 1943."

"While at Number Two Wireless School, I requested that I be reassigned to be a straight Air gunner. I did not enjoy nor was very good at sitting down at a desk sending and receiving Morse code all the time. A number of us thought that the war would end before we got to England which shows how young and naive we were in those days. We wanted to have a piece of the action before it ended."

"After training I was posted to Halifax, Nova Scotia to embark on a ship called the Mauritania. The ship sailed for England not in a convoy like most other ships that sailed because it was too fast for convoy protection and safer alone. We arrived and docked in Liverpool, England on the 2nd December 1943. I was sent to Brighton and was billeted at the Grand Hotel while waiting to be posted to an Operational Training Unit (OTU). It was while I was there that I had my first taste of war. I saw an enemy aircraft shot down onto the beach at Brighton."

75 (NZ) Squadron Lancaster AA – M (ND 657), destined to be shot down by a nightfighter over France on 29 July 1944

Kiwis Do Fly

Operations:

"A month later I arrived at No 11 Operational Training Unit Westcott. Crewing up was on a voluntary basis but we got four Kiwis together."

IAN BLANCE	Pilot	New Plymouth	FRED CLIMO	Wireless Operator	Timaru
COLIN GRIEG	Navigator	Taupiri	FRANK JENKINS	Air Gunner	
MAC MAAKER	Bomb Aimer	New Zealandww	WINKIE KIRK	Rear Gunner	Christchurch

"After OTU, we went on leave and were told that we would be posted to India and did not require a bomb aimer so Mac was taken from our crew. When we returned from leave our posting to India had been changed to Bomber Command. So off to a heavy four engine aircraft conversion unit where the skipper was to be trained. We then had to get another Bomb Aimer and a Flight Engineer."

| OSCAR SPENCER | Bomb Aimer | Walsall, Staffordshire | Bill Hyde | Flight Engineer | Manchester |

"Once converted we were posted to 75(NZ) Squadron on July 10, 1944. The crews were all allocated their own aircraft, ours being AA–M, (ND 657)."

"Every morning after breakfast we checked the Battle Order for the day. This was a list of crews that would be flying that night and if we were on it we wouldn't go to the pub."

"I would always feel apprehensive with butterflies in my stomach before boarding the plane but once we were in the air all these feelings disappeared. Our trips did not seem long at all, most were between three to four hours and the longest trip eight hours and forty minutes. I was always glad to reach the target, drop our bombs, and be on our way home again. When flying I hated to be down on the ground but when on the ground I would want to be up flying. I found every trip very hard."

"Our fifth operational sortie was on the night of the 28–29th July 1944 to Stuttgart. We encountered a lot of cloud, the flak was quite heavy and our Lancaster bumped about now and then from the flak bursting beneath us. As we approached the target, the cloud cleared and Oscar, our bomb aimer, had a clear run into the target. There seemed to be dozens of searchlight beams trying to pick up our aircraft but I didn't feel any hits."

"I could hear Oscar give our pilot bombing run instructions then the report from him "bombs gone." We always knew when the bombs had been released as the Lancaster would rise and the pitch of the engine noise changed. We passed over the target to see all the marker indicators from the Pathfinders and the bomb explosions and fires in bright and vivid colours."

"We were thirty minutes on our return leg home and then came a sound above the noise of our engines which sounded like rolling thunder. All of the cloud lit up with a bright orange glow."

NB: Winkies's comments are a rare first hand description of a 'Schrage Musik' attack from cannons fired upwards by a Luftwaffer night fighter firing beneath the Lancaster. Few survived such an attack and those that did were unaware of what hit them. The RAF also remained unaware of this type of attack for some time.

Bail Out 1.30am 29/7/44:

"When I saw all the fuses light up on my panel I knew that we were on fire. The fire was so intense that the flames began to set off the ammunition to my guns stored in four special ducts in the fuselage. The turret hydraulics were not working and the aircraft's intercom system failed."

"When the smoke and flames began to come up through the bottom of my turret I decided to bail out. I had always said I would never parachute out of a plane even though the chances of a parachute opening were 99.9 percent, but the fire and smoke certainly changed my mind. I had to rotate the turret around by hand so I could open the doors. I reached into the fuselage to get my parachute from near the turret doors and as I was about to put my chute on, our aircraft broke through the cloud with a Ju88 German night fighter following us down. I did not want to bail out while the fighter was there. I could see the pilot and I thought he might try to shoot at us again if he saw me trying to get out of the turret. I was in his line of fire and it would have been impossible for me to go back through the fuselage because of the fire. I dropped my 'chute back into its storage position and released my guns from the hydraulic mechanism. As the turret was facing dead astern I did not have to turn it at all but had to get a sight on the fighter. Raising the guns I opened fire and one of the engines on the German fighter plane caught fire. He peeled away."

"I then turned around and retrieved my parachute and managed to engage one of the harnesses on my 'chute but I just could not seem to get the other one on. For a split second I stopped trying and thought of the old saying 'more haste less speed.' I tried again and then I heard another click my 'chute was on. Turning the turret around to port by hand I tried to bail out. By now we were going down in a dive and when I put my head and shoulders out of the turret I was pinned hard against the side of it. I moved back into the turret and managed to get my feet up onto the seat and with my hands grasping the top of the turret antenna I heaved myself out into the open space. It did not feel as though I was falling but rather felt as though I was going upwards. I think that me being small in build saved my life as had I been any taller I would not have been able to get my feet onto the turret seat."

"I desperately tried to find the ripcord of the parachute so I could pull it open but it wasn't there. I had always stored my 'chute with the ripcord handle so that it would finish up on the right hand side of my chest that way I could pull it with my right hand. But in this case I must have dropped the chute back in the storage compartment upside down after I had seen the fighter. Anyhow my left hand found the ripcord and I pulled and the next moment I had a lovely big white canopy above me."

France:

"Everything was so black; all I could see was the parachute. I did not seem to be coming down. I thought maybe that I was too light, so I began to pull on the parachute cords to let some of the air out. Next thing I went down through some trees very fast and came to a sudden stop, which left me swinging in the dark. After a little while I thought I would swing myself to see if I could catch hold of a branch in the tree. I thought I might be able to sit on a branch, as I was not in a very comfortable position hanging in my 'chute. Each time I tried to swing myself to get a branch to sit on, my 'chute dropped a foot or two more, with the snapping of branches above me. Finally, I tried again, my feet touched the ground I was down."

"After I got my 'chute down I began to cover it with leaves, but found their underside glowed like the face of a luminous watch. I picked up a leaf and held it over my wristwatch and although my watch was not luminous I could read the time. It was 1.40 am."

"I found that it was impossible to walk out of the forest because I just walked into the trees and fell over logs, so I spent the rest of the night sitting up against a tree."

"When daylight came I looked to see what my escape kit contained. It was in a clear plastic box. There was one concentrated fruit bar, which was very hard, in fact so hard, that it was impossible to bite it. I could only gnaw a little of it at a time. Also Horlicks, wakie-wakie energy and water purifying tablets. A fishing line and hooks, a plastic bag for carrying water in, a compass, matches, needles and threads. I also carried a silk and rubber map of the area. Sewn into my battle dress were nine photographs of myself, three each of three different views. These were carried to help the resistance movement with identification papers, as having the photos taken for them was difficult. I also had various types of compasses hidden as buttons, sewn on my battle dress. I finally removed my three flying suits and headed south."

"After about an hour I came across an unused narrow track and followed it for about four hours when I spotted an old letter on the ground. It looked like it was written in French as at that stage I didn't know if I was in Germany, France or somewhere else."

"While I was deciding which way to go I heard voices and two men came walking along the path so I hid. Once they had gone I then went in the opposite direction and finally walked out of the forest."

ABOVE: The photograph of the crew's funeral in France taken by the Maquis. The graves are decorated with flowers and aircraft wreckage

"I decided to and walk as far as I could, whether I was in Germany or France. I checked the silk escape map, took a compass bearing and I headed off towards Spain via the Pyrenees."

"I walked for most of the first day keeping off the roads as much as possible. My first sighting of Germans came when I was about to cross a road. A platoon of German Soldiers came around the bend. Fortunately there were some cattle in the paddock I was in, so I just began to move them back the way I had come and the soldiers passed without taking any notice."

"After they had passed, as the Corporal of the platoon gave a command and suddenly all the soldiers began to sing. When they were further the road another command was given and they all stopped singing."

"That night I slept in a haystack, but during the night it rained causing earwigs to fall down on me, so as soon as it was daylight I began to walk again."

"By this time I was very hungry, so I opened my escape kit and tried to eat some of the fruit bar. I could not get my teeth into it, so I cut it up in little squares, and after eating some I began to walk again, still hungry. We were told the fruit bars, plus the other contents of the escape kit should last us seven days but by the second day, I had eaten all of the food and I was so hungry. I found a little pool of water, but it was too shallow to draw from and it had little bugs and tiny insects swimming around in it, so I put some of the water purifying tablets in, waited for half the time that it suggested on the instructions, and drank the water, bugs and all. It did quench my thirst, for a while."

"I was hungry again and I found a paddock full of potatoes. The tubers were still green but I bit into them. My mouth dried up I needed quite a lot of water before my mouth lost the taste."

"Later I found apple trees with green apples. They weren't ready for eating either, but they were not as bad as the potatoes."

"It was a nice warm sunny afternoon and all I wanted to do was rest, by a wall surrounding a cemetary I found a nice place to conceal myself, resting in the sun. I was awakened by voices, not too far away. I was certain that the voices were only from children, they wore red, white and blue ribbons pinned to their clothes. For a while this had me confused. Why were they wearing British coloured ribbons? It then occurred to me that I was misreading the colours. They were blue, white and red, the French tricolours. I was in France after all."

"I took out my translation card and climbed over the wall, calling out to the boys."

"I called out "Hey there!" The boys stopped playing and started running away. They must have thought I was the owner of the apple orchard. So I called again, "Come back," "Parlez vous Anglais?" This was the only French phrase I knew. One of the boys stopped and said something to the others and they stopped running too. I waved them over to me and pointed to the card I held in my hand."

"At first the boys approached cautiously, the elder of the three coming a little closer while the two younger hung back. They would have been about nine to eleven years old. The elder boy came close enough to read the card, I pointed to the phrase in French, "Where am I?" The boy took the card from me, and then called the other two boys over to him. They looked at the card and then at me, then back to the card again. They pointed to a French phrase; translated to English it was "are you hungry?" I just nodded. The boys then relaxed and began talking excitedly to each other. One of them pointed to the card again, the translation was, "do you want help?" The two younger boys sat down on the ground and indicated I should do likewise, so I did. The older boy then turned and pointed up at the sky then fluttered his hand down until it touched the ground. He pointed to me. I nodded. Yes. He then shook my hand and said, "Bon Comrade.""

"The elder boy pointed towards a village near the bottom of a hill we were on, and pointed back to him. Before I knew it, he went running down the hill towards the village, leaving the two other boys with me."

"About an hour later the boy returned with two men and we tried to communicate using our hands. I tried to explain that I had parachuted down three days ago. Both men seemed very pleased and tried to tell me something with their hands, but I could not understand them. A little while later some more men arrived. One of the men had brought an English/French dictionary with him and some writing paper. We began communicating with each other via the dictionary."

"Quite a lot of other people arrived, bringing food and drink. Everyone who arrived had something, black bread, pressed beef, biscuits, cubes of sugar, and bottles of wine. I would have had to stay for weeks to eat and drink it all. As each person arrived I was shaken by the hand and welcomed. While I was trying to translate English to French on paper and vice versa, a voice spoke to me in English. These were the first English words I had heard since our navigator had spoken to our skipper telling him we would soon pass over Strasbourg. The man, who was well dressed, had an air of authority about him. He asked me where was I shot down. I pointed in the direction from where I had walked for the last three days."

"The man told me his name was Maurice, but no surname was given. (I was never given any surnames the whole time I was with the French Resistance). He wanted certain information from me to confirm who I was. I told him that I was not able to give details of my Squadron, only my rank, name and number. He said he understood but also had to be very careful whom he and his friends helped. I knew then, had I not been who I said I was, but perhaps a German posing as a British airman, I would have been doomed."

"Maurice asked me how many of my crew had bailed out. I told him that I did not know, as we were on fire and I had bailed out of my turret. He then really shocked me, by telling me the identification letters of our Lancaster. He informed me that my plane had crashed only a few miles away. The fighter, that had attacked us, had crashed near our Lancaster. He told me that three of the crew had bailed out. The Flight Engineer, Bill Hyde was already in the hands of the French Resistance and the third member, the navigator, was still missing."

"The other four members of the crew had died, and had already been buried in the local cemetery, by the Germans. Many French locals had attended the burial and covered the graves with flowers and laid parts of our Lancaster and parts of the German plane on top. A photograph was taken of the graves by one of the French locals, which was a very risky thing for them to do. This photo was given to me a few days later. After being given all this information, I felt that I should confirm it was my crew. What good would it do not to?"

"Maurice and I continued to talk. Meanwhile people were still arriving and coming up to shake my hand. It seemed the whole village had come up this little hill to meet me. I could not understand how the Germans did not hear about this English Aviator."

"As some of the locals began to leave, Maurice told me the name of the person that I would be staying with that night. As more locals left, the place where I was to stay was changed, this was done a number of times, until in the end nobody knew where I would be staying with. In fact I was to be moved from one safe house to another."

"While all the arrangements of which house I was to stay in was being sorted out, I was asked by Maurice if I would mind changing out of my uniform into French civilian clothing. I gave this matter a lot of thought. Once I was out of my RAF uniform I could be shot as a spy as the French people were risking their lives by helping me evade, if I were dressed as a Frenchman it would be easier for them to move me from place to place so I agreed. The village people then produced lots of different clothes for me to select from. I picked out some of the clothes that I thought would

Chapter 11 – Welcome to the Caterpillar Club

fit me and I then asked Maurice which of the clothes would be most suitable for me to wear. Between us we selected what clothing I needed."

"The fun then began. I began removing my top clothes, starting with my 'not so white' flying jersey, as soon as I had put it down on the ground it disappeared, almost before I had taken my hands off it. Then I took off my battle dress tunic, and this was even more amusing. The Locals all wanted a souvenir from it. A knife and a pair of scissors appeared and the brevet and the Brass Crown of my Flight Sergeant's stripes were removed, then the stripes and finally the eagles off the shoulders. I remember thinking to myself how it had taken me quite a while to sew them on. It certainly did not take long for them to be removed. Next I removed my shirt, flying boots and my big white flying socks."

"There I was standing stripped to the waist. I was then told to remove my trousers, but I felt too shy, as there were still a lot of girls and women around. When I pointed to them then to my trousers they thought it a great joke and just laughed and laughed. Maurice must have felt sorry for me, as he said something in French and immediately I was handed a shirt to put on. When I had the shirt on I removed my trousers and changed into a French pair, which were too long for me. They all gave me a big cheer when I had finished dressing, I then felt and looked like some of them."

"I remembered my photographs sewn in my battle dress waistband. I explained to Maurice that I wanted my top back and why. He gave an order and it reappeared, stripped of everything, even the brass buttons off the shoulders, one of which concealed a compass."

"I cut the waistband of my flying jacket and removed the photos, which were still dry and in good condition. I showed them to Maurice and he said, "Good, don't lose them, we will be able to use one of them soon.""

"When most of the people had left I was introduced to a man whom I shall never forget. He was a little taller than I was, of slight build, and was known as Ugo (spelt Hugo). He was to be my escort from place to place. All of the French that I was associated with during my time in the Resistance were brave, loyal people and of all of these courageous people Ugo would top the lot."

"After being introduced to Ugo, I was informed that I would be staying with Maurice and his wife for a day or two. Maurice asked me to explain in detail where I thought I had left my parachute and harness and wrote it down for Ugo. When I mentioned a water tank, Ugo said he knew of two or three in the area. I also mentioned the potato field and the path I had followed out of the forest and how long it had taken me to walk, after leaving the unused track. I also mentioned the letter I had found and thrown away again."

"Armed with the information I could give him, Ugo set off the next day to find my parachute. He found it just as I had described it and brought back all the silk from it. Maurice's wife made a scarf for me to keep and a small handkerchief for my sister."

"On the way down the hill we met a lady coming towards us. Maurice spoke to her, then introduced her to me by saying this is "my woman," meaning his wife. On the way down, the lady would stop every now and then to pick up large orange slugs, approximately an inch to inch and a half long, plus other types of slugs. I asked Maurice, "What does your wife want them for?" He told me that they salt them in a barrel along with snails, to be eaten."

"Maurice was a man in his fifties, nearly six feet tall, well built and was manager of the steel works in Pompey. He had lost part of his fingers on one hand, which unfortunately was a very positive means of identification if any person was to betray him to the Germans."

"As we approached the village of Pompey I was told not to speak at all, but just walk along with Maurice until we reached Maurice's home. In the basement, where Maurice showed me three large barrels, two were full of snails. Maurice explained that a layer of snails and these other slugs were covered with salt, and then another layer of slugs and snails would be added and so on until the barrel was full. I was asked, "Would I like to eat some?" I said, "No, I'd rather not.""

"Finally to bed and I just did not remember anything after settling down between the sheets. A very old man, with a beard, was gently putting something on my chest, awakened me. For a moment or two I thought the Gestapo had been informed and we had all been caught. But to my relief it was not the Gestapo but as I had slept all the previous day, Maurice and his wife became quite worried as they could not wake me and so they brought in a doctor."

"I had only turned twenty-one and I was young for my years regarding life, not having experienced things like many of men of my age."

"At dinner that night, one of the guests that I was introduced to, was a very pretty girl with long dark hair, who would had been about my own age. She had been seated beside me at the table and although she could not speak English and I could not speak French, we enjoyed each other's company. Every now and then Maurice asked me a question on behalf of one of the guests, which I answered looking at the person who Maurice had translated for."

"I noticed that Marie, the young girl who had been seated beside me, was wearing an engagement ring, I pointed to her, then to the ring and then to the other guests. She looked quite sad and she turned to Maurice. After having spoken to Maurice she turned to me and then pointed to Maurice who explained that she had been engaged to a boy in her village for about two years. The Germans sent him to Germany where he had been put into one of the work camps and she had not seen or heard of him since. I was so sorry for them both and she took my hand, squeezed it and just held it for quite a while. I felt so sorry for her."

"When it was time to go to bed, I said good night to Maurice and his wife. I then turned to Marie and said good night and I kissed her on the cheek. I went up to my bedroom and no sooner had I entered the room Marie appeared at the doorway. She came into the room and took my hand and just stood beside me. I began to feel uncomfortable, for two reasons. I wanted to hold and cuddle her, as she looked sad and also very pretty. But then on the other hand, she was engaged to another man. How would I have felt if I was him? I did not know what to do. I gave her a little hug and once again kissed her on the cheek, then said "good night." I put both my hands together, held them against my face and said, "very tired" in French I indicated I wanted to go to bed. She then indicated that she would come to bed too, but I took her hand, pointed to the engagement ring and back to myself and shook my head. She seemed to brighten up. She then kissed me on the cheek and left my room."

"The next morning Maurice asked me how had I enjoyed the evening, had Marie and I enjoyed each other's company. I told him it had been a very good evening and I thought Marie was lovely. He said, "We thought she would please you." I then understood it all. The whole evening had been to entertain me and to provide me with company for the night. This lovely girl Marie had been willing to oblige, because she had been requested to do so by the Resistance. I would have loved to know if she and her fiance ever met again and married. I hope so. When I look back on that night so many years ago, I wonder if I made the right or wrong decision. I think I made the right one."

"That night, I was told that I was being moved to a new safe house and Maurice told me to always follow instructions, even if I did not understand why. I said, "I will.""

"Then Marie, who had come to say goodbye, came into the room and we both hugged each other for the last time, and said, "Au revoir." I had liked her very much. I wondered if Maurice ever knew what had not happened between us that night."

"Ugo arrived to take me to the new safe house, with sadness in my heart, we left Maurice's home and Marie forever. I never saw either again. While we walked to my new home Ugo talked away, as if I knew what he was saying. I was told not to speak at all, not even French, of which I knew a few words. Ugo would hold a one sided conversation to avoid any suspicion. Ugo stopped once to talk to a couple of men that we met on the road, he mentioned something to them and they put out their hands and shook mine. I just nodded and then we moved on again. We did not have much time because there was a curfew between 10 pm and 6 am. I think, that was one reason we left it so late, so that there would not be many people on the road who might have stopped to talk to us."

"We reached my second safe house, which was a boot shop. Ugo took me inside and introduced me to the couple that owned the shop. I was not told their names. They took me upstairs to a small room. In the room there was a single bed and a dresser, plus it had an alcove behind a curtain to hang clothes. The window of this room looked down onto the street and although the couple could not speak English, I was told by signs to keep away from it. I was kept in this one room for the two days of my stay."

"On my second day in the boot shop, Ugo arrived and brought out a packet. Inside was a French identification card with one of my photos, glued inside and stamped. Ugo handed me two other certificates, one a travel permit and the other a certificate that exempted me from forced labour. They used the name Charles Leroy. As my own first name, Aubrey, was not so suitable they had used my second name Charles, and so I became Charles Leroy, Agricultural Worker."

"I was to be moved again to another safe house quite some distance away and was quite pleased because the people in the boot shop were a bit nervous with me there. German soldiers often passed during the day and the couple were worried that they might decide to enter the shop and search. When Ugo arrived to collect me, he had brought travelling clothes, not so noticeable as the lovely suit I had on. It was a shame that Maurice's wife had gone to so much trouble altering the suit to fit and I was not able to wear it for very long."

"Ugo pointed to my wrist chain, which had a greenstone heart hanging from it, which my mother had given to me before I left New Zealand, and then to my service dog tags and indicated that I should remove them. I was upset that I had to leave them behind, without the dog tags I had no way of proving I was an RAF evader if the Germans had caught me. But, I could also understood that if I was searched and they found the dog tags, the men who were with me would have been taken by the Gestapo and most likely be shot. Unfortunately, this did happen to people who helped evaders escape. Not only were they shot, but they would first be tortured for information. So I removed my chain and dog tags and gave them to Ugo. He put them in a little tin then went outside the back door of the shop and buried the tin in a little flower garden."

"My next safe house, was in a township called Pont-a-Mousson, twenty miles from Pompey."

"We went into a cafe and although it was still light outside, it was quite dark inside and the room was lit by candles in bottles on the counter and also one on each of the alcove tables. While we were drinking our coffee, two German SS officers came in. One of them spoke to the man behind the counter and he then turned around and walked over to our table and put his hand on my shoulder. It was a wonder he didn't hear my heart it was thumping so hard. He reached over with his other hand and took the candle off our table and walked back to the counter, and began to read some papers he had. When he had finished, he returned the candle to our table. "Merci monsieur," he said. He and the other officer finished their drinks and left."

"I do not know what my two companions felt when this happened, but I thought we had been recognized or been betrayed. My companions may have heard what the Germans said to the man behind the counter, because neither one of them looked worried at all."

"We left the cafe and climbed into an old car, my first ride in a motorcar in France."

"Once we were out in the countryside Ugo stopped, lifted the seat up, revealing an array of rifles and handguns. Ugo gave us a rifle each, which we put under our legs, and then he gave us a handgun. They were all different makes; the one I was given was very old looking, but nice and small. I checked that the safety catch was on, and then put it in my pocket. 'Armed to the teeth,' as the saying goes. I hoped that we would not have an occasion to use them, but I did know that Ugo would not hesitate to use his. It would not have been the first time either, according to what Maurice had told me about Ugo."

"After we had driven along this country road for quite a few miles, when we came up behind a platoon of German soldiers marching in the same direction. The driver of the car, instead of slowing down and waiting for the soldiers to make room to let us pass, just kept going at the same speed and sounded the car horn all the time. I was surprised when they all moved over to the side of the road to let us go through."

"The safe house I was taken to in Pont-a-Mousson was quite large, and belonged to another Maurice this one being a veterinary surgeon who spoke English quite well. I was taken into another room and what a surprise when one of those in there was our Flight Engineer Bill Hyde. How wonderful our meeting was."

"The 'stranger' was an English army captain 'Emile' and could speak French fluently. How he came to be here I never found out, except that he had been in the Tank Corps before joining the Resistance. He came and went from the house as he pleased."

"When Bill and I were finally left alone we began to tell each other what we experienced after the attack on our Lancaster. Bill recalls he was checking the engine gauges and temperatures when all of a sudden we were on fire. "I turned to Ian to see if there was anything I could do to help. The intercom was broken, because he was waving to get out. I put my parachute on and passed Ian's 'chute up to him; he was trying to keep the plane straight and level. I opened up the escape hatch and went to throw it out when it got stuck against the sides. While I was trying to free it, Oscar had come up and was helping to get it out, but it wouldn't budge. I stood up and began to kick with my foot, next thing everything went black. When I came to I was floating down with my parachute. I think the hatch must have suddenly become free and I followed it. I don't remember pulling the ripcord but I must have. As I began to gather in my 'chute some men surrounded me and started helping me with it. I was taken away to a house for the night and transferred to another house a couple of days later."

"Bill, Emile and I stayed at this house for nearly a week. The little three-year-old girl, after hearing Bill and I talking, had learned to say the English word "yes." She would then repeat it when she spoke to her parents. Of course, this was very dangerous because Maurice had German army officers visit, and if they had heard the little girl speak English it would have been very suspicious. So Bill and I had to stop speaking to each other when not in our room that afternoon we were halfway up the stairs when a rifle shot fired through the window by the staircase landing. We quickly hid in a special hiding place behind some panelling on the stairway. After a few minutes we were told to come out, a blackout warden had seen light showing though the stairway window and the shot was a warning to make sure that the blackout curtain was in place."

"On our last evening Maurice held a dinner to celebrate the liberation of Paris. It was a very posh affair, crystal glasses, crystal knife and fork sets, which I had never seen before, nor since. I can't recall all of the evening after being given some lovely sweet red wine. I really enjoyed this and my hosts kept my glass full all the time. Bill told me the next morning that we had drunk champagne and I woke up in bed, no headache or any ill effects, except I could not remember the last part of the evening."

Maquis:

"We had been told that retreating German soldiers had been breaking into homes looking for food; and we may be caught if we continued to stay at Maurice's, so we left late in the afternoon. After a ten minutes we drove into an empty warehouse. There was a covered truck loaded with men all dressed like Bill and myself. Emile, who was also with us, had dressed up like a very dapper Frenchman. Two of the men were Americans, who had walked out of Germany after their Fortress had crash landed. There were also three Canadian soldiers, escaped POW's, and a Polish boy who looked about 17 years old."

"The truck left almost immediately and travelled for about an hour. We stopped at the foot of a tree covered hill, and we were given sugar-sack like bags. We set off up the hil, it took us about twenty minutes to reach the Maquis Camp."

"The camp shelters were made from trees and surprisingly quite dry. In the bags we carried was food, tobacco, and vegetables. Bill, the two Americans and I bunked together."

"In the camp were a number of wounded French Senegalese soldiers who had been prisoners of the Germans. Ugo, alone, had gone into a German camp where the Senegalese soldiers were

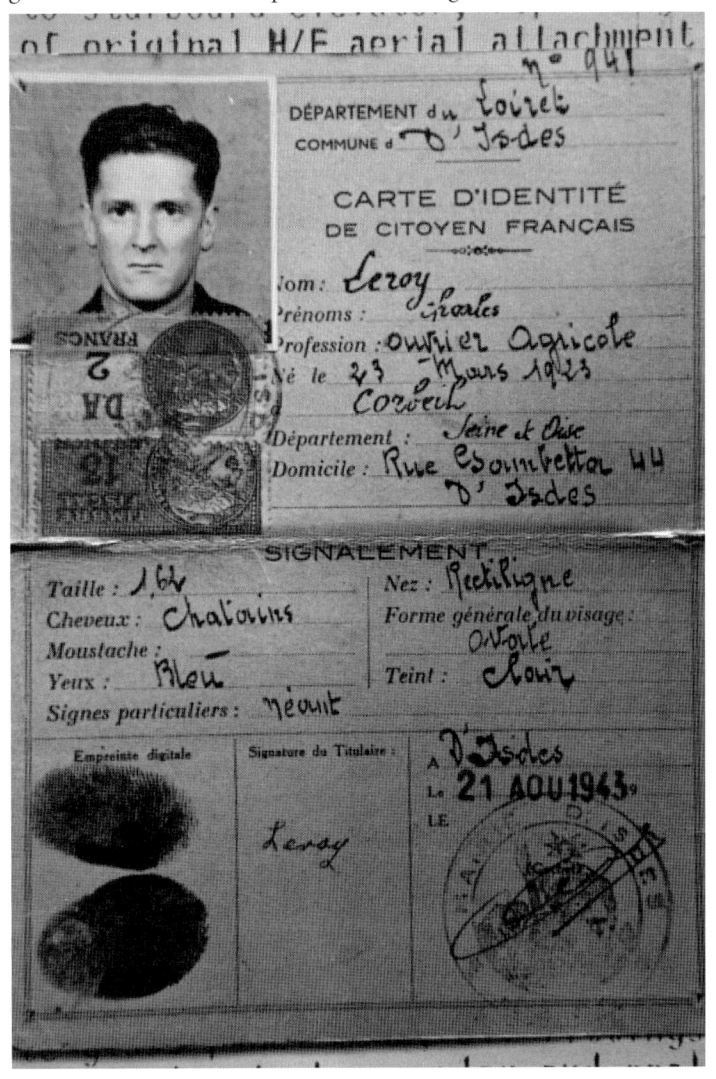

ABOVE: Winkie's forged French ID card

held, and dressed as a German soldier rescued them. He killed the guards on duty and brought all the Senegalese soldiers back to the camp. Also in the camp, were about twelve other Frenchmen. The French members of the Maquis were there because they were known and wanted by the Gestapo, so they now lived with the Maquis to avoid capture."

"The French Resistance was an organization which fought against the Germans while still living their normal daily lives, but once a member was suspected or known to the Germans, they had to leave home and live with the Maquis. Sometimes the whole family would have to move."

"The Maquis was run under very strict discipline. The camp itself was nestled amongst fairly tall trees and surrounded by a lot of bush, and was camouflaged from the air. Fires were only lit at night. String was threaded all through the bushes and trees with bottles and tins tied to each other. This was set up all around the camp and for about fifty yards down the hill. It was all part of an alarm system that worked very well, both day and night."

"All members of the camp took turns on guard duty, but otherwise were allowed the freedom of the camp."

"When I arrived at the camp there was a Frenchman being held prisoner. He had been in another Maquis camp and had betrayed it to the Germans. The Germans then raided the camp with tanks and wiped it out. They killed most of the Maquis and took the two survivors to the Gestapo. One of them died and the French Resistance rescued the other man, who was nearly dead. He survived, was able to talk and gave the Maquis information about the traitor. The traitor was captured and questioned, as if in a court, and found guilty. The next morning after 'the trial', we were all put on parade, the traitor in front of us, and he was hanged. What a lesson to anyone who might have had any thoughts of betraying the Resistance."

ABOVE: Forged Exemption from Compulsory Labour Pass

"The leader of our camp had a shelter to himself and a few home comforts, but not much more than us. He was a very busy man, organizing operations against the Germans. When in camp he held parades where we all were given the latest war news. He would then select a number of men for a job that was planned for that night and dismissed the rest of us."

"Our jobs varied: One night we might be sent to collect arms dropped by the RAF, the next night sent to 'rob' a farmer of his potatoes. The farmer would have already put in sacks ready for us to steal. Other nights we could be sent to derail a train line or blow up a bridge. The only problem for the English-speaking members of the party was that whenever a plan was changed, it was difficult for us to know what the change was, unless Emile was with us to interpret but we managed to carry out our assignments."

"My job in the camp was maintaining the rifles and pistols in the armoury, as I was an air gunner. Most of the weapons were strange to me, some were very old and so was the ammunition. I was glad that I did not have to prepare any of the explosives as I had no training on how to handle 'plastique!'"

"When a party went out to blow up a bridge or railway line, Ben, Dan and I would go with them as part of the escort and act as guards while the 'experts' laid the explosives and set the detonators. When I say 'experts' that might have been an overstatement, because sometimes I wondered how we weren't all blown up as well! At times we were too close to the explosion and at times the bomb wouldn't detonate at all. The men who set the charge would return to see why it hadn't gone off. They never waited the correct period of time for safety, and one time when nothing happened, one of the men went off to check and his mate pushed the handle down again and up went the charge. His friend was lucky, but a few feet closer and he could have been killed."

"Emile, the British second in charge of the camp, was not very popular. I didn't have much time for him. I thought he should have been able to get himself back to England long ago but it seemed as though he enjoyed living a very comfortable life with the French. To be fair, I later realized that maybe he was doing his duty in some other way that we knew nothing about."

"After we had been with the Maquis for three weeks, with Dan, Ben and I in the same party, we could sense what each other were going to do or say and this built a very strong bond between us."

"Emile and I never really became friends. When we were living at Maurice's home we were sharing the bathroom. Emile normally used the bathroom first, then Bill then me. One day I went into the bathroom after Emile, and found that Emile had not cleaned up the washbasin. Well, I got really uptight and went to Emile. Why hadn't he cleaned up after himself? He said Bill always did that. After all, Bill was only a non-commissioned officer and he was a captain, holding the King's commission. He told me that Bill and I were under his command. Well, I saw red and told him that Bill was not his batman and nor was I. Furthermore, when we parachuted our of our aircraft we were on our own and our only duty was to try and return to England. I added; "So you know it is also your duty to do the same." I mentioned the confrontation to Bill; I think he had heard some of it. Poor old Bill, he said that he and Emile were both English and I was different being a Kiwi. I said no more and Bill still washed up after Emile. So much for the class system."

A Maquis Mission:

"One night I went with a party into town for supplies. As usual, the person we were going to 'rob' had the supplies packed and ready. The 'theft' could be reported to the German authorities. The leader of our party paid the man who 'gave' us our supplies and once he had put the money away, we ransacked his shop, tied him to a chair and left with the goods. What some of the French people went through to help the French Resistance never ceased to amaze me!"

"As the Allies pushed the Germans out of the various towns and villages in France, the French people who had willingly helped the Germans, and those who were pro-German, were hunted down by the local pro-Allied French and executed. Unfortunately there were a lot of Frenchmen who were seen as to be helping the Germans. In fact they were, but it was so they could get extra food so they could to help hide and feed escaped prisoners of war and evaders, like myself. A number of these people were executed because at the time they could not prove what they said was true."

"One night Ben and Dan went with other members of the Maquis to a house in the local town. The two French members of the party went up to the front door of a house leaving Ben and Dan on guard. They knocked on the door and the man who answered was questioned, and then told that he was being taken on order from the Resistance to stand trial for betraying two of the local resistance men to the Gestapo. He was not allowed back into the house to say goodbye to his family or even to get a coat. Back at camp he was interrogated and the man admitted to giving information to the Germans about two resistance men that the Gestapo had killed. If the French Resistance found a person guilty of willingly helping the Germans and no life was lost, they would demand money or the person's life. The choice was the person's. However, if a life were lost due to information or betrayal, the traitor would be executed with no choice. The man they brought in this particular night admitted his betrayal, so he was given no choice. He was given a pen and paper to write to his wife, to tell her what had happened to him and he admitted his guilt on paper."

"He was to be hanged the next morning. After sentencing, Emile thought that the man should not be hanged, but rather shot by a firing squad. The leader of the camp and others did not seem to agree, but it was decided to ask the man who was to die which method he preferred. He chose to be shot. The next morning a firing squad of five men was to be chosen to carry out the execution."

"He was tied to a tree but he was able to sit down or sleep. With his hands tied behind him it would not have been very

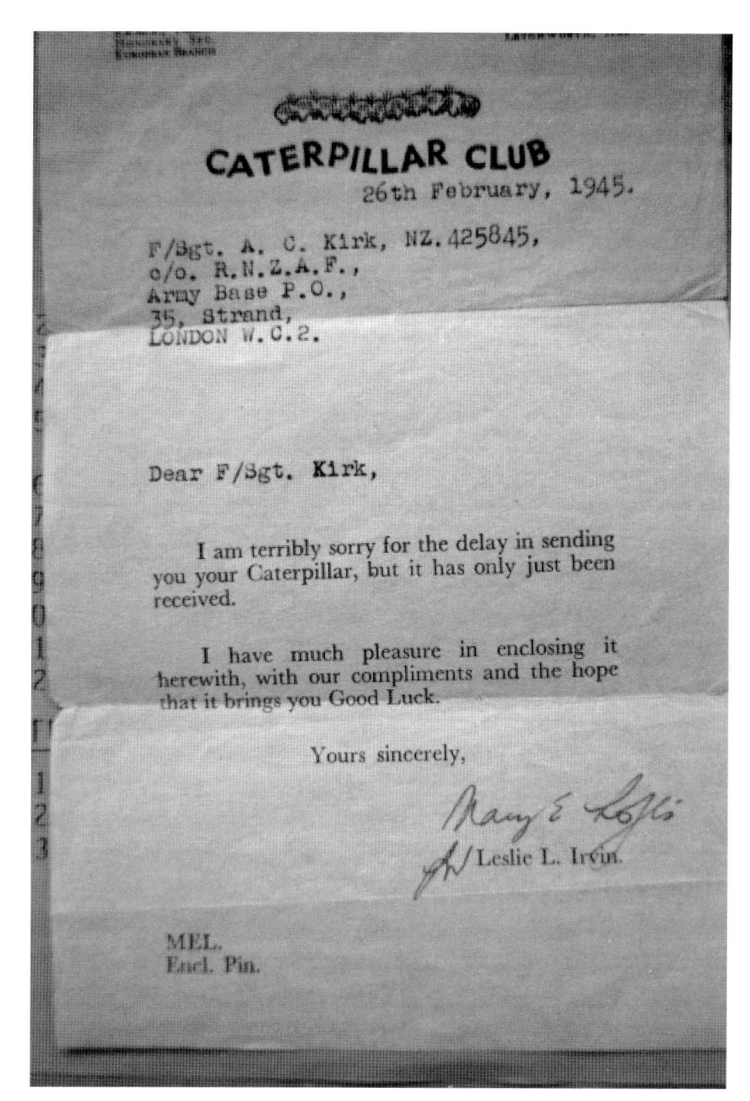

ABOVE: Winkie's Caterpillar Club Certificate

comfortable. A guard was posted to watch him all night, so he had no chance of escaping. I just could not help looking at him and feeling for him."

"The next morning at 9 am the whole camp was put on parade to witness the execution, which was carried out as per sentence. What upset me, after the shooting, the body was left lying on the ground all day and overnight."

"Following the execution, I was on guard duty. I sat listening for any noise from the bottles and tins but all I could think of was the chap who had been shot and still lying nearby. It was dark, every now and then a bird or something would rattle one of the tins. Not wanting to raise a false alarm I had to see what had caused the noise, and make sure it was not an intruder. I again heard the sounds of a tin rattling, and then I felt a hand on my shoulder and nearly died of shock. It was one of the Senegalese men. He sat down beside me and all I could see was his white teeth shining in the darkness. It was a great comfort having him there, he stayed with me right through my shift on guard. I couldn't speak his language and he couldn't speak mine, but afterwards we some how managed to communicate with each other."

"Later I was paired up with the tall 6'8" Senegalese Frenchman, who had sat with me that night. The detail allowed for two men to each carry a sack of potatoes. That was okay for most of the pairs, most of them were about the same height. But all of the Senegalese men were very tall and this was one of the duties that they took part in. My partner and I must have been the funniest looking pair, with him six foot eight and me only five foot three. When I went to pick up the sack of potatoes he just gently pushed me aside and took hold of the sack with both hands and lifted it above him. He then rested it on his head and away we went, with me walking beside him. Each time the party stopped for a rest he would sit beside me. I could have managed to carry one, but not very far. My partner, although wounded and wearing a bandage around his head, was a very strong man, but very gentle. He carried that sack all the way up the hill to camp and never looked like tiring."

"Ben, Dan and I were tiring of camp life and decided that we would try to get through to the Allied lines. We informed the leader what we intended to do but he told us that he would not permit us to leave. He called two of his senior men, who were armed with sub-machine guns, into his quarters. We were told that if we attempted to leave the camp by ourselves, his men had been given orders to shoot us. Strangely, he took our word not to leave, said he understood how we must feel, but it was all for the best. He spoke to his armed men, they smiled at us, then shook our hands and left."

German Retreat:

"We could hear heavy gunfire way in the distance and that night were sent out on a mission to ambush some German Tiger tanks that were retreating from the Americans. With anti tank guns. Our members were very keen to use them on the Germans. I was not so sure that they would inflict much damage on a tank but to my surprise they were very effective and the sudden attack confused the enemy without any loss to our own people."

"The next night the gunfire sounded much closer to our camp and we were detailed for a new type of mission. We were taken to a two-storied house and told to cause as many casualties to the enemy as possible, who were now retreating from the American Forces. We were set up on the ground floor and were positioned at a window that faced directly down the road."

"The retreating Germans were running on foot, some on motorbikes and some in trucks. But most were on foot and our job was to stop them. The Polish boy, who was with Bill, had an old First World War machine gun, with ammunition just as old, and the gun would only fire three or four rounds at the most, and then stop. It was Bill's job to feed the ammunition into the gun while the young boy was firing it. We all had rifles and various types of small arms. I felt sorry for the German soldiers because they were on the run and the French people showed no mercy. Many Germans were unarmed, but it did not make any difference to the French who killed them showing their hatred for the Germans."

"I remember the young Polish boy telling Bill to try and hit the Germans in the shoulder, because it would make the victim spin around. I don't know if Bill was shooting at anyone or not. I could understand the French hating the Germans so much because of all the terrible things that happened to their friends and families, but I could not bring myself to kill in cold blood like that. If it were us it would be different, or if they were trying to shoot at us, but they weren't or at least these soldiers weren't."

"While all this was going on a German Tiger tank came down the road. When it was about fifty yards away from us the Polish boy opened fire on it with the old machine gun. He might as well fire at it with a peashooter. Next thing I saw the 88 mm tank gun swing around at our house. I called out to Bill, "Let's get out of here now!" The room we were in had another window, and fortunately it was open. I dived out, with Bill just behind me. I got up and started to run but I seemed to be not moving. Then there was a huge explosion as the tank shell hit the top half of the house. Most of our men seemed to pour out of the house unhurt. They were lucky they did because the second shell hit the bottom of the house."

"I lost Bill that day. The next time I saw him was in England. I asked him if he ever used the hand grenade that he had. He said, no, he had been too afraid to use it in case it blew up in his hand or something, so he had dug a hole and buried it. Very wise."

"After the house was blown up, Ben, Dan and I went on to our next detail to stop any Germans from leaving the area. When we arrived at the specified road intersection, none of the Maquis had arrived, so we decided to return to our camp."

"When we finally got back to the camp the only people there were Senegalese soldiers and one wounded man. The French were out in the front line."

"From our camp we could see a road in the distance, and we could see some vehicles with big white stars on them. Wow! Americans! The vehicles were Greyhounds, like overgrown jeeps."

"We rushed around the camp and tried to tell the everyone that the Americans were here. I picked up a few belongings, and took off down the hill as fast as I could. When we reached the bottom of the hill we had about 100 yards of flat land to cross before we got to the road. We began running waving our arms and we hoped the Americans would recognize the Maquis armband."

"When we were about 50 yards away, the leading Greyhound stopped and pointed a 50 calibre machine gun at us. We all put up our hands and approached them very carefully. We would have hated to be shot at that stage of the war. When we got close enough, Dan called out to the men in the Greyhounds, "God, we are sure glad to see you guys." One of the men in the front vehicle said, "You speak very good English," Dan replied, "I should do, I come from the same place you do." We were told to approach their vehicle with the machine gun still trained on us. "Who are you?" We were told that they were only an advance party and the front line was back about ten miles but one of the other vehicles would take us back. We were searched first and were then taken to their HQ."

"When we arrived at HQ, a Two Star General, General White, interrogated us. Once he was convinced we were, who we said we were, he told us that he could not get us to Paris unless we were prepared to go back as guards with four truck loads of German prisoners. We agreed. We were given a meal, the bread being baked on site and it was the whitest bread I had ever seen ever."

"Uniform issue came next and we were asked for our ranks. Ben and Dan were Sergeants. I was asked my rank, which was Flight Sergeant, they did not know the American equivalent so they gave me First Sergeant stripes, that is three up and three down. So for a while I was in the American Army as a First Sergeant, though unpaid."

"We slept well that night, well dressed and well fed for the first time in a long time."

"The next morning the German POW's were put into trucks and we were each given a loaded carbine. The Germans were no trouble and seemed quite happy being POW's, but whenever we went through a French Village we had to protect the Germans from the French. The French villagers would start climbing up onto the trucks calling out, "kuput, kuput" and twice we had to fire our rifles above the heads of the French people to keep them off the trucks."

"That night, all the POW's were put into a big compound, with just standards and ropes around them. Although there were guards posted during the night. By the morning, when we did a head count, we had more prisoners than the night before. It was a real drag, because we then had to search them all again. There were more prisoners in the morning as a lot of Germans were still fleeing and if the French had caught them, they most likely would have been killed so it was safer to try and sneak into an American POW camp."

"During the search of the POW's, we were given hundreds of French francs, which were very useful later on."

"A number of German prisoners could speak English quite well. These men were ordinary soldiers, just like me, who were fighting for their country and when I asked a few of them about Hitler, they told me they thought he was a great man who did a lot for Germany before power went to his head. I wonder if our positions had been reversed would they have been so friendly to me. One will never know."

"Once the POW's had been delivered we were taken into Paris, and the American HQ where we were interrogated again. Once that was over, Ben, Dan and I were given a lovely suite to share in none other than Hotel Maurice. We stayed indoors because there was still a lot of sniper activity in the street."

"That night we sampled champagne the hotel was selling for 300 francs a bottle, or two bottles for 500 francs. We bought two bottles each. It was the second time in my life I had drunk champagne but this time I remembered it for a while. Later that night we thought we would have a look at the city. Down in the street a little boy came running up to me, holding what I thought was a water pistol, I pointed to Dan, and so the boy gave it to him. The next morning I saw that it was a German Luger, which the boy had found under an upturned vehicle. So much for champagne!"

"After two days wait in Paris we were flown to England and arranged to meet in London the next day for a drink together.

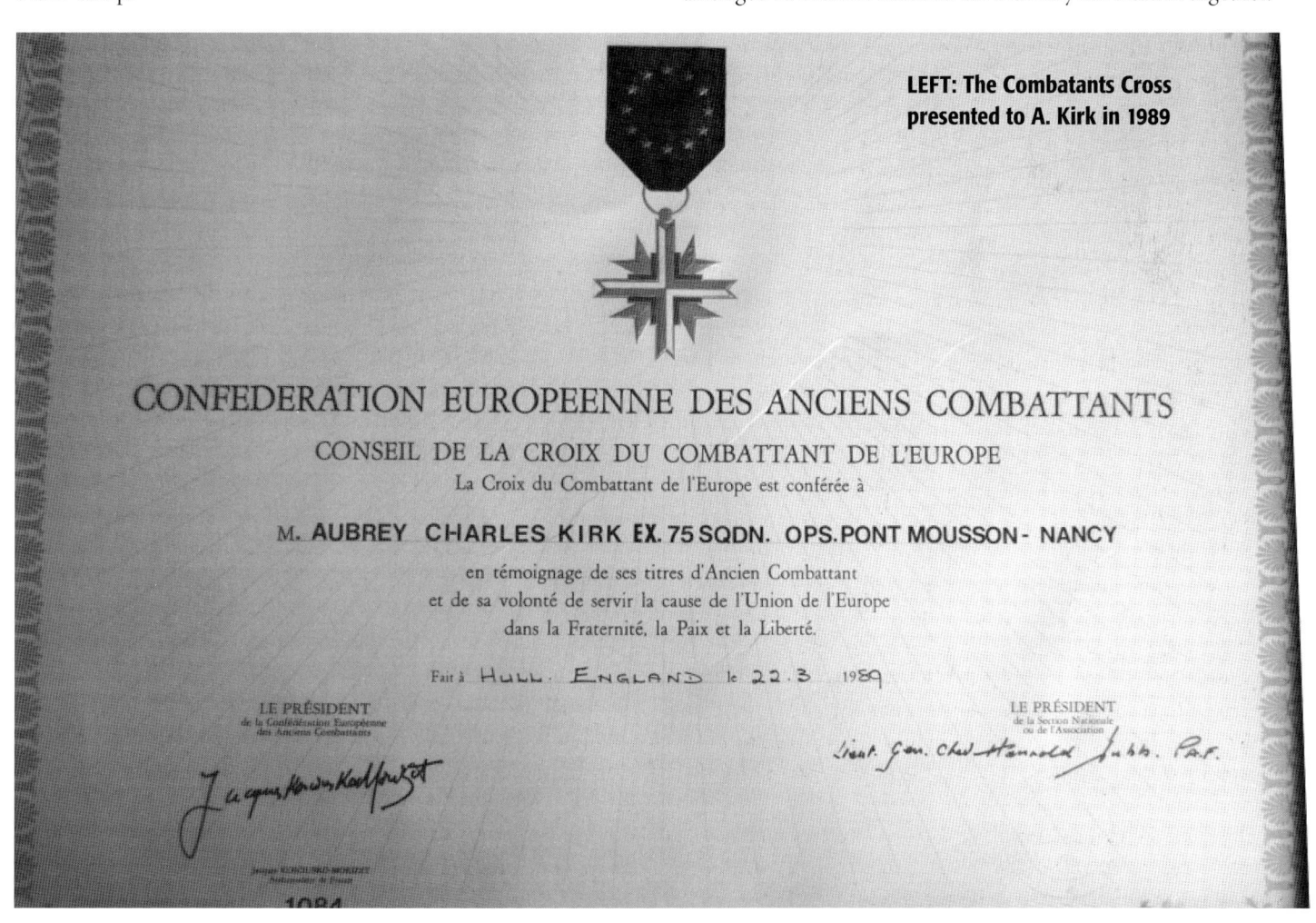

LEFT: The Combatants Cross presented to A. Kirk in 1989

Kiwis Do Fly

We had been together for only a matter of a few weeks, but we'd seen. Because I had been with the French Underground I was not permitted to fly over Europe again."

Surprise:

"Before Christmas 1944 I made my way back to Mepal and 75 (NZ) Squadron and was greeted with a lot of "hello's" and arranged to meet my best cobber Jock, who was still going strong on operations. He had leave due to him on the following Friday so I arranged to meet him in Aberdeen."

"That Friday night is one I shall always remember. I was walking to the railway station just before midnight to meet Jock, I had this feeling that he would not be on the train, he wasn't. Such feelings are something you just can't explain in life, but they do happen. My friend Jock Biggar had been killed on a mining operation the previous night. In the same crew as Jock, I had another very good friend, Paddy Giles, who I had been with since my very early days. We were both in the Army together for six weeks and then both of us transferred to the Air Force. We had trained together in Canada and finished up on 75 (NZ) Squadron. Paddy was one of the Army guys who gave me the nickname Winkie. I was known as Winkie all through my service life and occasionally even now. Sadly, Paddy was killed on this operation too."

"In February 1945 I was posted as a gunnery instructor to RAF Dalcross in Inverness. After a few weeks I was reposted to the Far East Air Force in India as a gunner on Mitchell Aircraft, but before I was transferred the war in Europe ended."

"I applied for a repatriation to New Zealand, and finally returned to New Zealand on the 'Vulcan.' I was demobbed, but left on the General Reserve for four years with the rank of Warrant Officer. It had been an exciting journey."

— *Arthur (Winkie) Kirk*

This account was compiled by Winkie Kirk's children Vikki (now Mrs Pflaum) Debrah and Zane from recorded interviews with their father before his death in 2008.

ABOVE: Winkie's Crew: Left to Right:
Standing: Oscar Spencer B/A (2nd tour)*, Bill Hyde, (F/E), Colin Greig (Nav), Frank Jenkins (M/UG)*
Seated: Winkie Kirk (RG), F/O Ian Blance (Pilot)*, Fred Climo (W/Op)*   * Killed in action

Chapter 11 – Welcome to the Caterpillar Club

Home via the Pyrennes: an Evader

Following Harry's crash on take-off at Skellingthorpe in July 1943, he became 50 Squadron's fill-in Flight Engineer flying with different crews on operations.

On 25 February 1944 Harry was allocated to VN-Q (LL791) as Flight Engineer for a crew he'd never flown with before.

"All crews had a feel about them, the pilot especially set the tone. Some were smooth and relaxed, others stiff and jerky perhaps with nerves. Some left the throttles to me, others shared control as a pair. I wasn't too happy with this Skipper. He seemed a bit slow somehow, anyway I kept to my work. About 50 miles from the German border, a shower of cannon shells cleaned up the rear fuselage and set one engine on fire. There was no call from the gunners. The Lancaster just nosed over, shaking and shuddering all the time and obviously out of control."

"Get out," "came the skippers call. The bomb aimer was a big chap but couldn't release the front hatch because of the negative gravity so he jumped on it and promptly disappeared. I followed with the pilot still shouting, "get out, get out." "I never saw either of them again."

"My parachute opened with a real crack. I saw our aircraft go in and heard our attacker flying off. Then all was peace and quiet, rather a nice experience. I made a soft landing in the snow, buried my parachute, and on hearing a train whistle, made my way towards a railway line. I thought I'd hop on a passing goods train. Some thought, they were all going like the clappers."

"After the effort to board a train, I walked along the railway lines for quite some time. I hadn't a watch so had no idea of the time but guessed it was late evening.

I heard dogs barking and thought I was going to be caught. Anyhow, I reached this small railway station and peered through the window and saw this man in railway uniform at a desk. It had the name Embermenil on the station board which sounded French to me and we had been told on escape lectures how patriotic the French Railway men were. So I entered the room and he was speechless. I said "RAF" and as he didn't seem too savvy so I pointed to a map on the wall which showed a corner of England. He obviously knew what I meant and put his finger to his mouth and said, "Ssh, La Boche" (meaning German lived close by). He led me to this single storey cottage which I presumed was his, and with a lady inside. After getting over her shock, in sign language, she wanted to know where my 'chute was. I could only vaguely point the direction. I don't know if she ever found it."

"George mimed, 'time to sleep' and took me to their bedroom and to a great big feather bed. I'd never seen anything like it, but I was a bit stunned when both Monsieur and Madame climbed in with me after offering me the privacy of the 'psst' china pot that hid behind a curtain in the corner of the room. Madame even demonstrated a man peeing into the pot. I got the idea quick enough."

"Next morning my uniform had gone and been replaced with a French Railway porter's uniform. The trouser legs were two inches too short but it came with black patent leather shoes. Quite a smart ensemble, and one I'd wear for two months."

"That morning a gentleman from the underground

ABOVE: Kitted up on a flying test, the white submarine jersey used on Ops is not being worn

BELOW: One of many 50 Squadron's Lancasters that Harry flew in as a stand-in F/E, VN-T

Kiwis Do Fly

called, sat me down and asked a number of questions, not just name, rank and serial number but my Squadron, my crew role, our base and the names of the other crew. Of course it was easy to answer some, but not the names of the crew; I just didn't know. I tried to explain the role of standby aircrew and all I could recall was that the navigator had 'Gilly' on his flying helmet. Obviously the escape organization was going to check me out before releasing one Harry Cammish, Flight Engineer, into the system. A day or two passed when they obviously radioed England for confirmation. It must have come because then I was accepted. If the details hadn't come back I am sure I would have been summarily dispatched as a mole."

"It seemed the French Railway staff were very pro-Allied and very anti-German. Three days later a courier called for me to follow him. From now on I never walked with these anonymous couriers, but always some way behind in a slow, casual way. I certainly didn't feel either calm or casual."

"On February 28th, I was moved about five miles to another village (Luneville) to be put up with two old dears who didn't turn a hair at my arrival. Madam Chapleur ran a small shop and I stayed out of sight and away from the windows upstairs. The escape network arrived with a new ID card, I now was Louie Blanc, painter, this despite my railway uniform!"

"The following day I continued on my trip via safe houses to Nancy, where my minder this time was a policeman complete with pistol. He delighted in pulling this out of his holster and saying "arrete, stop!" The humour was beyond me but he was very proud of the key he had to the German Armoury."

"On March 6th, I moved from Nancy to a farm at Mazerville. The farmer was the head of the local Resistance Movement and I listened to the BBC broadcasts with him. He told me the Germans in the area were second grade troops and who had even told him that when the invasion came they would immediately surrender as they weren't really Germans but Polish and Czechs who had been conscripted into the army as occupation forces. He had a wardrobe full of weapons and hand grenades supplied by parachute drops from England. To see the way that they handled Mills grenades scared me stiff. The Germans called regularly for milk and eggs while I stood behind the curtain and watched them. He told me he would never be taken alive and I believed him."

"Next stop was Paris. I moved around quite a bit and had several close shaves on the metro underground, once being entirely surrounded by German soldiers in full gear. Luckily no-one spoke and I was glad when my guide got out of the train and I quickly followed."

"I was picked up by another guide and taken to the railway station.

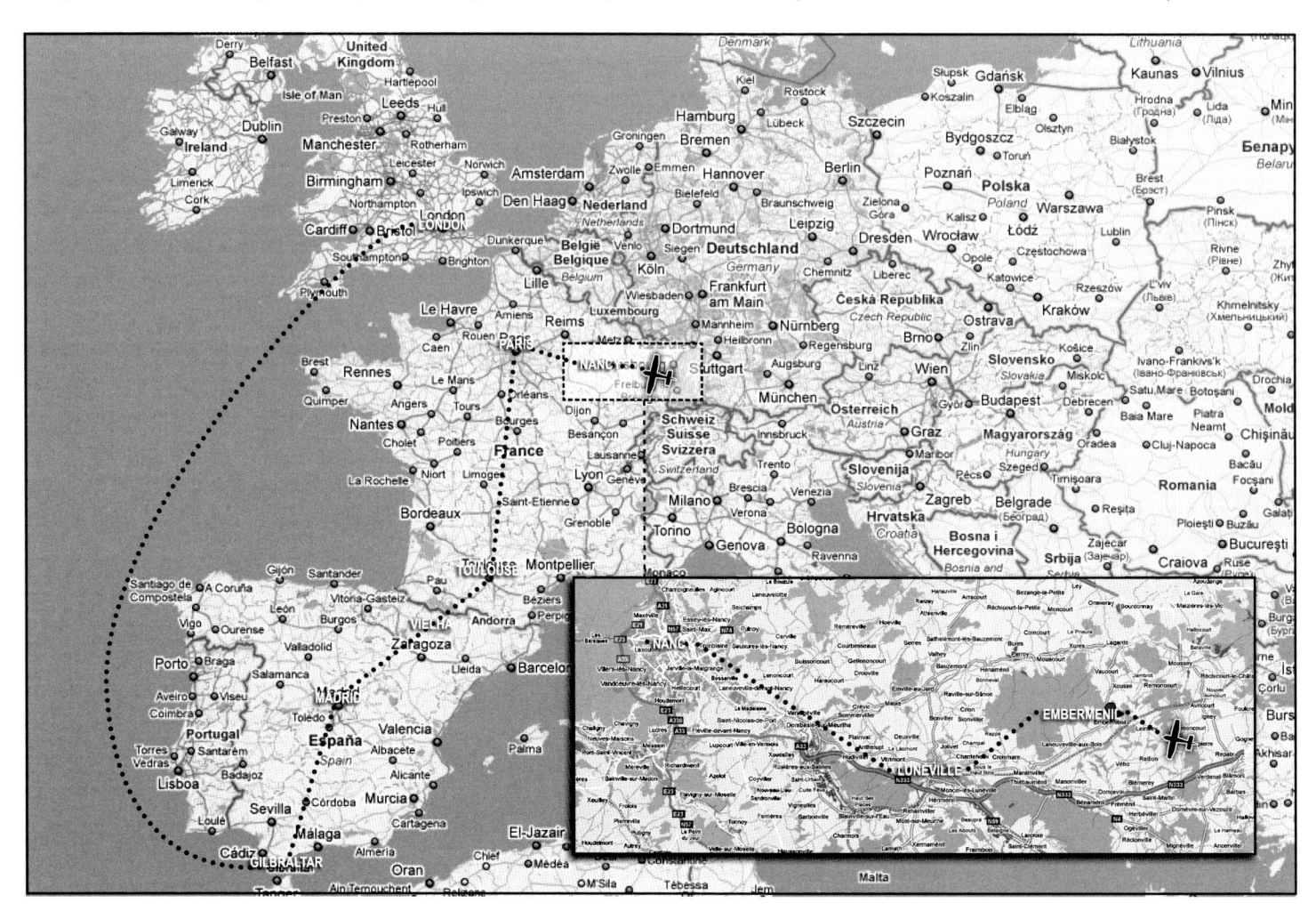

ABOVE: A map of Harry's travel

Chapter 11 – Welcome to the Caterpillar Club

We were going to Toulouse. As I got to the train there was this big German with a brass plate around his neck and a machine gun over his shoulder watching us all board the train. He got on too. My guide put me into one compartment with my ticket and he went into another compartment. It was a corridor train and I sat in the corner and closed my eyes, not wanting the other French passengers to speak to me. As we got on our way in came the ticket collector. He asked me something, I hadn't a clue what he was on about. There was this awful suspense when my guide popped his head in and said "Anglais Aviator." The collector clipped my ticket and shot out of the compartment. The other passengers acted quite normally having this aviator in their midst and the journey was completed without any further conversation."

"From Toulouse, we took a branch line train to the Pyrenees foothills where I was gathered up with about 30 others and moved into the mountains. Here we all were locked up in a barn. Outside there were patrols of Sten gun-carrying Resistance members. A very stern looking lot. Everyone kept much to themselves although there were certainly some Americans in another group. Who the others were, I never knew." (See the footnote for a surprising list of who was there).

"That evening all hell broke loose outside, lots of automatic fire and rifle shots. There seemed to be Germans everywhere shouting "Raus, Raus" and I believe they were trying to encircle our barn when the Resistance opened up. Most of the prisoners just stood with hands rasied but I thought bugger this and ran like hell just as I did after my crash landing. Up the hill I went as fast as I could run until all was quiet. What happened to the rest I don't know. So twice in my life self-preservation and fear saved me. I was determined to reach Spain and freedom so knew to just keep going uphill, there was snow everywhere and patches of forest. What I didn't know was that Pyrenees reached several thousand feet high here and the Spanish border was unmarked. (In fact it was over 50km from the French barn to the first Spanish shelter)."

"So here I was still in my porters uniform and patent leather shoes treading through the snow. The cold must have been intense but it didn't worry me as much as the long trail of footsteps I left in the snow."

"Anyone, especially German patrols, would see them clearly. Walking the next day began easily with the frosted ice crust but as the day warmed and the crust melted I sank to my ankles and then to my knees."

Harry kept this up for two and a half days, without food and with only handfuls of snow to relieve his thirst. "I went from a young lad to an old man during that time."

"On April 23 Harry saw a sign of life, a man working in the snow. "Espania" I called. He replied in French

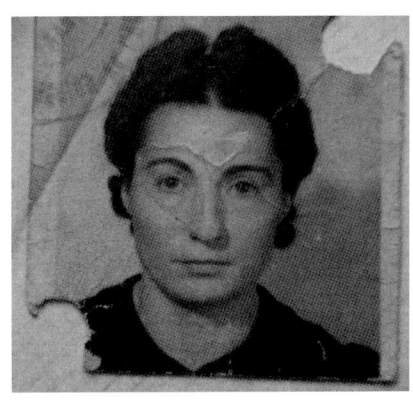

ABOVE: Madame & Monsieur Collins who gave Harry very personal shelter by taking him into their bed

ABOVE: Missing in action, the telegram no mother or parent ever wanted to receive.

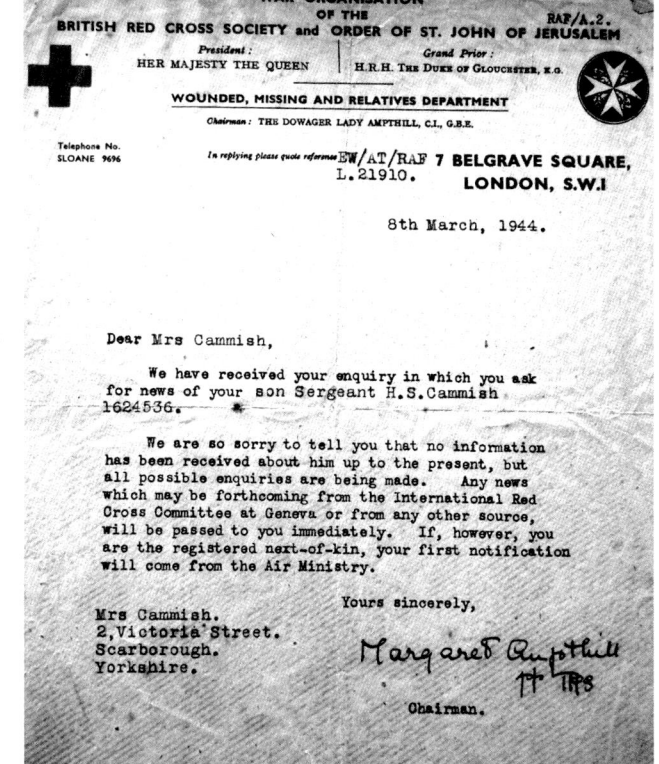

RIGHT: Hope or despair, the Red Cross confirm in March 1944 that the Red Cross has not been able to track Mrs Cammish's son down, not a POW, perhaps KIA?

Kiwis Do Fly

"But yes." For a moment I thought I was still in France and had walked a large circle. But no, so I headed on down to the nearest village."

The village was called Vielha, situated at 3,000 feet in the Pyrenees and it was snowed-in over winter. That year Vielha was isolated until late April 1944. Even today the area is heavily wooded and is now an alpine resort. As Harry reached tentative safety in Spain his crew mates were being captured on the French side of the mountains.

"I was badly frostbitten on the hands, feet and lips and must have looked a real sight but the local police took me in and called a nurse. As they removed my shoes, I remember the skin came off like a sock and my lips had all curled back leaving my teeth bare."

"With the help of a dictionary I told my story and the English Consul was contacted. I was moved into a lovely little hotel and well nursed, so that after a day or so I took a bottle of wine down by the river to celebrate. A few mouthfuls and I was gone, fast asleep. A soldier was appointed as my guard while I went out on daily rambles but so paranoid was I that I kept close behind him as I feared being shot in the back. On the third day he unshouldered the rifle and I thought "this is it" but he was merely passing it to me to take a pot shot at a rabbit."

"By May 9th the thaw had progressed enough for me to be taken down to the township of Sort where a British Consulate official was waiting and kitted me up with civvy clothing. Goodbye at last to the porters uniform and patent leather shoes."

"I was really well treated by the rank and file Spanish Police and once the British Consulate had taken me in, he impressed on all officials that I was an evader not an escaper as the Spaniards looked rather differently at those poor bods, usually keeping them locked up. They had to consider the German point of view of harbouring an enemy who had been held as a prisoner of war but I had never become a POW."

"May went by quickly as I recovered, and by the 30th I was in Madrid. The Embassy arranged a minder (presumably MI6) and we spent time enjoying the food, markets and all of the bright life that was missing back home."

"The Consul came across with some cash (being quite sympathetic to me) and I duly spent it on essential consumables for back home, like cigars, 4711 Cologne and nylons. While the former were readily available, Spanish men apparently didn't shop for nylons and I had to wait for a very senior lady in the shop before being allowed to purchase these unmentionables. Even better, the advance on my wages paid by the Consulate was never sent through to the RAF pay office, so these luxuries were gratis. The day before my final move, my minder, who had never introduced himself but was obviously Cambridge or Oxford educated, simply shook my hand said "all the best" and disappeared."

"On the second of June 1944 I crossed from the heavily fortified and guarded Spanish side into Gibraltar to be met by a lone Scottish guard complete with fixed bayonet and kilt. When I told him what was facing him just a hundred yards away he just shrugged and said, "Och they're no problem!"

First stop for Harry was the RAF stores and back into uniform. The RAF Stores Sergeant tried his best to lift the nice Spanish made civvies. On D-Day Harry was issued with air tickets and taking his kit bag (with cigars, nylons and clothing) and a large bunch of bananas, joined a dozen high rankers on a Dakota flight to England.

"I was coming right by now and seemed to be given special consideration where ever possible.

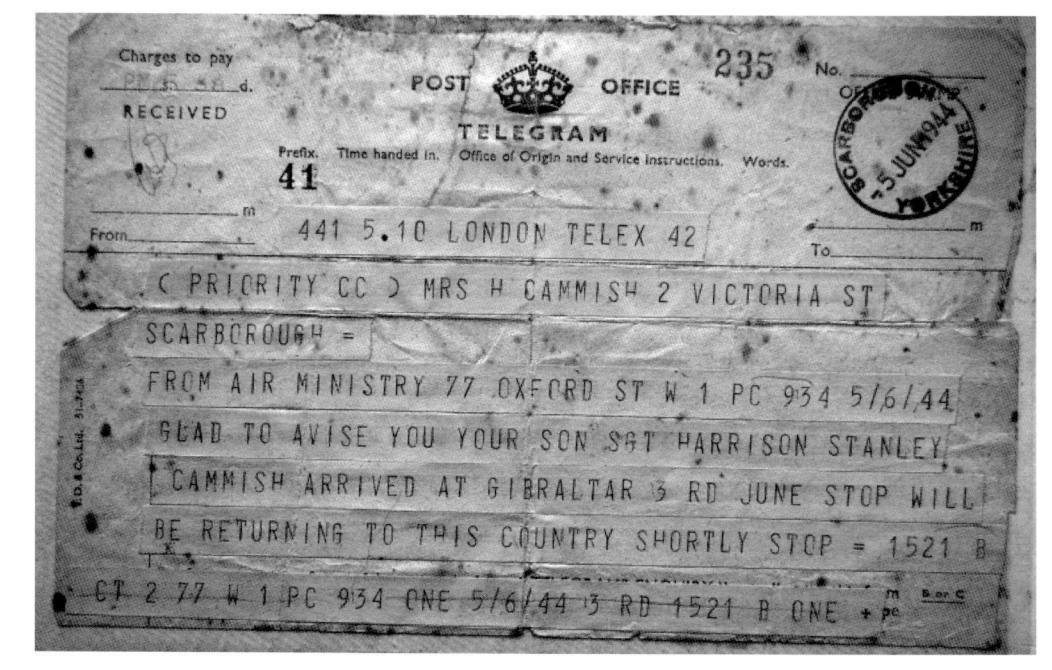

RIGHT: May 1944, in the high street, Madrid. Harry (Left), A Patterson (an English Civil Engineer) and a MI 6 Minder

BELOW: He's safe! Confirmation from the Air Ministry who waited until Harry was back on Bristish soil in Gilraltar to advise his mother, three months after he crossed into Spain

Chapter 11 – Welcome to the Caterpillar Club

took a refresher course at St. Athan, Wales, on aero engines."

"This course led to an instructors post at Fighter Commands High Ercall, Shropshire HQ where I lectured pilots on the finer points of Merlin engines. With seniority (now a Warrant Officer) I moved into running Flying Control offices (ATC vans and control towers) and with that post came a whole host of inherrant perks including the use of a flight van. Enough said."

In Harry's final year in the RAF he became the 'shutdown' air traffic controller as many RAF airfields were being closed. Harry finally went back to the building trade in 1946.

– Harry Cammish

When we landed at RAF Whitchurch, near Bristol, the Customs Officer said, "You are an escaped POW," and chalked a big X on my bag, "just go straight through."

"Two civilian dressed men met me at the airport "come with us" and I was taken to MI6 in London for debriefing. Amongst all of the who, what, and when, they were interested in small details like radio reception, the resistance paperwork and morale. They issued me with a pass and ID stating that all inquiries were to be directed to the London Area Commander. The next desk in the MI6 building was the pay office where a very considerate WAAF reimbursed me for back pay, lost items and even insisted on paying out £10 for the lost watch (which I never had). After being instructed not to speak to press, family nor to go near my old base at Skellingthorpe, I went out onto the streets of London with £30, a kitbag full of luxuries and a bunch of bananas. Soon a big older Bobbie pulled me up stunned by the sight of bananas. "I've not seen one for four years, could I have one to show the grand children." So less one banana off I went only to be pulled up by two Service Police."

"Why are you in battledress and not dress uniform if you are on leave?" – "The MI6 pass was flashed and they didn't know where to look. "Carry on," was all they said."

"A long train trip back to Mum and Dad's followed and when I walked in they nearly died. After the first MIA telegram, they received another to say I'd arrived in Gibraltar and that's all."

"I was on six weeks evaders leave, but with recurring nerve problems, stress and nightmares, three of those weeks were spent at the trick cyclists (Psychiatrists). Of course, Post Traumatic Stress Syndrome hadn't even been invented then."

"Being off Ops (as an evader) and banned from ever flying over Europe again, the Air Ministry offered me a posting to Transport Command. I declined and instead

ABOVE: From a lad to an old man, Harry Cammish on survivors leave 1944 with sisters Nora (L) and Elsie (R) both WAAFs

BELOW: Harry's escape kit, still almost new after 60 years. It includes French, Dutch and Spanish currency. It was never needed, nor returned

During the research for Kiwis Do Fly Harry finally learnt the fate of his crew mates.

RAF records show that VN-O (LL 791) was lost on the night of 25th February 1944 having flown just 37 hours. Attacked by two night fighters the aircraft crashed near Embermenil (40 km ESE of Nancy). With Sergeant Harry Cammish, the crew were:

Sgt KE Gilson (nav) (14 Ops) KIA killed during the attack, (Buried at Embermenil). 'Gilly' to his crew mates.

Pilot P/O W Taylor	POW
F/Sgt D Balmanno	(RAAF) POW
F/Sgt Ansell	(RAAF) POW
Sgt J Acthim	(RAAF) POW
Sgt T S Taylor	POW

Unknown to Harry Cammish the Pilot Sgt T.S. Taylor, along with Sgts W. Taylor, J. Acthim and F/Sgts Balmanno and Ansell had also evaded capture and were in the same Pyrenees camp on 21st April 1944.

Sgt Acthim was 'savagely beaten' by the Gestapo for information before being sent to Camp L7. The other three were sent to prison in Frankfurt.

The secret location of the Maqui camp had been betrayed to the Gestapo by a member of the French underground.

Courtesy www.lostbombers.co.uk

Chapter 12

Remember This

Fun and laughter was as much an essential part of wartime service as was the operational side. Humour provided an escape from the daily dangers – whether it was pranks played on crew mates or games in the mess.

With aircrew either being teenagers or in their early twenties a sense of fun was natural and this appeared often in print and even official prohibitions.

Chapter 12 – Remember this?

Form 700

*Just as a good 'line' needed thought and nurturing, so did the one-liners left in Form 700s.
Assume P is the pilot; S is the ground crew Sergeant.*

P: Left inside main tyre almost needs replacement.
S: Almost replaced left inside main tyre.

P: Test flight okay, except auto-land very rough.
S: Auto-land not installed on this aircraft.

P: Something loose in cockpit.
S: Something tightened in cockpit.

P: Dead bugs on windshield.
S: Live bugs on order.

P: Autopilot in altitude-hold mode produces a 200 feet per minute descent.
S: Cannot reproduce problem on ground.

P: Evidence of leak on right main landing gear.
S: Evidence removed.

P: DME volume unbelievably loud.
S: DME volume set to more believable level.

P: Friction locks cause throttle levers to stick.
S: That's what friction locks are for.

P: IFF inoperative in OFF mode.
S: IFF always inoperative in OFF mode.

P: Suspected crack in windshield.
S: Suspect you're right.

P: Number 3 engine missing.
S: Engine found on right wing after a brief search.

P: Aircraft handles funny.
S: Aircraft warned to straighten up, fly right, and be serious.

P: Target radar hums.
S: Pre-programmed target radar with lyrics.

P: Mouse in cockpit.
S: Cat installed.

P: Noise coming from under instrument panel. Sounds like a midget pounding on something with a hammer.
S: Took hammer away from midget.

P: The autopilot doesn't.
S: It does now.

Notices to Airmen (NOTAM)

Anderson Shelter	Your backyard's tin hat.
Ashes	All that's left of Hamburg.
Barrage Balloon	Catches drifters unawares, thought to squeak if molested.
Berlin	See ashes.
Bremen	See ashes.
Blunderbuss	The weekly London-bound wagon taking 'fallen' WAAF's off to London for discharge.
Calvary	Training ground of modern Generals.
Censorship	Never were so many words, telling so much, suppressed by so few.
Cologne	See ashes.
Dornier	A large winged bird, almost extinct.
Dusseldorf	First class building site, recently cleared at enormous cost.
Essen	Large ammo dump used by RAF.
Goering	Collector of medals.
Hamburg	Something ground, pounded and then grilled.
Horrors of War	No silk stockings.
Incoming Fire	Has right of way.
If the enemy	Is within range so are you.
Junkers 52	Carries two crew and 27 paratroops or Herman Goering.
Kiel	One time site of a canal.
Munich	A tourist town many Englishmen still fly to.
Munitions	Where the money we didn't have before the war now goes to.
No Ops Plan	Survivors contact with unexpected weather or enemy.
Objective	Where we aim at and the Germans hit.
Peace Treaty	An agreement not to fight until hostilities break out.
Secret Bomb Sight	Converts near misses into near hits.
Take-offs are Optional	Landings are compulsory.
Try to make the number	Of take-offs equal the number of landings.
The propeller is in front	To keep you cool, sweat only when it stops.
Try to remember	Jerry does attack head on.
	Who said the wind had swung round.
	The bomb doors, of course.
	Where the ammo is, where your parachute is and where you are.
	Twinkling lights coming towards you are not pretty.

The Aircrew Alphabet

A for Horses	Able	N for dig	Nan
B for Mutton	Baker	O for The Garden Wall	Oboe
C Forth Highlanders	Charlie	P for Relief	Peter / Popsie
D for Dumb for Ensail	Dog	Q for Rations	Queenie
E for Brick	Easy / Eddie	R for Mo	Roger
F for Vescence	Fox	S for Williams	Sugar
G for Police (Gosh Sakes)	George	T for Two	Tare
H for Ome	How	U for me	Uncle
I vor Novello	Item	V for France	Victor
J for Oranges	Jig	W for nothin	William
K for Answers	King	X for Breakfast	Xray
L for Leather	Leather	Y for Husband	Yoke
M for Size or SIS	Mike	Z for Breezes	Zebra

TEE EMM

Tee Emm (Training Memorandum) was published by the Air Ministry from 1940 and covered subjects that airmen ought to remember but often forgot. Its serious tone was lightened by the cartoon activities of Pilot Officer Prune. This character was created by Bill Hooper and Prune became famous in his own right. 'Removal of the digit' joined RAF slang vocabulary. The magazine always carried the warning 'NOT TO BE TAKEN INTO THE AIR.'

LEARN FROM THE OTHER FELLOW'S MISTAKES

P.O. Prune says, Did I bJob?

While a squadron of fighters was on offensive patrol over France the Squadron Leader had trouble with his R/T and tried without success to hand over to another pilot. At this point the squadron was warned of Me.'s on the right, but at the same time the Squadron Leader saw aircraft to the left, dived away and lost the squadron. He found the aircraft, however (Me. 109's), attacked by himself, shot one down, and then went home. But the rest of the squadron, though they saw many Me. 109's, did not engage and came home without their leader. This story shows the enormous importance of arranging an emergency scheme for a deputy leader to take over in case of R/T failure. Had such a scheme been in force in this particular instance, heavy punishment could have been inflicted on the enemy. But the snake's body, as it were, having lost the head, was powerless to grow a new one and so became ineffectual—though the missing head at least got in a good bite.

1941 TELL US,

You can't tell P.O. Prune anything.

From the moment when Special Flying in the last established for themselves Up to the war the results of flying was high : the ac

The aircraft now bein sarily more difficult to f There is less time for thi and there are more things has come for one of the per There is no intention of c instruction ; but as the keep pace.

Among the people who read this note teaching others to fly, or have recently learnt who have both the time and the inclination piece of paper and jot down those points wh either as an instructor or a learner. If instru difficult to teach : have you any devices or understand : have you any subtle or special If a recent learner, what things did you find fences you were asked to take too high : did being asked to do : if you found it difficult fly by instruments, how did you finally get o

Chapter 13

Gallery

In compiling 'Kiwis Do Fly' veterans scrap books and albums yielded many more photographs and souvenirs than could be included within the appropriate chapters. The images are unique, often taken without permission, yet other moments were captured by station photographers who often enjoyed a side line business in selling prints of very fine quality. This gallery is a diverse selection of images covering the many facets of a New Zealander's life in RAF Bomber Command.

Kiwis Do Fly

Gallery

Leaflets

Propaganda leaflets, dropped in their thousands by Bomber Command, were not often read by the aircrew but certainly were by the civilians they were intended for. The propaganda varied from polite warnings to the very graphic. Interpretive translations are:

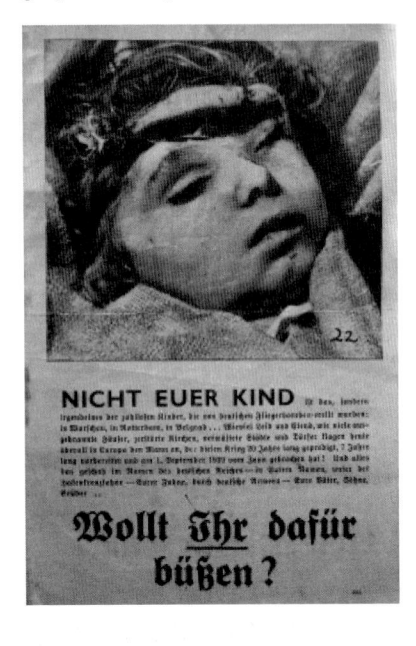

FAR LEFT: "Why let the helpless suffer? Don't let this be your child"

ABOVE: Total War against helpless civilians doesn't hurt you

LEFT: "Women of France, today they are polite but they are the same boches as yesterday. Three months ago German officers and men machine gunned, without pity, refugee convoys killing French women and children. Now they are polite." Never forget that these same Germans have a sole aim, to subjugate France. Hitler has said "France is our eternal enemy"

Fighter Attack

Stirling III BF517, AA-O, of 75 (NZ) Squadron forced landed at Newmarket. On 26th April 1943 nineteen year old Pilot Officer P Buck and his crew were on a raid to Duisburg when the aircraft was attacked by a night fighter. The cannon fire killed the rear gunner, Sergeant Rogers and badly damaged the rudder and fuselage. Mid-Upper Gunner, Sergeant Watson, and wireless operator Pilot Officer Symons were wounded but continued to obtain positional fixes. The bomb load was jettisoned, and following an engine failure the undercarriage could not be lowered forcing the pilot to make a wheels up landing. The aircraft was dragged from the runway to allow the remaining Stirlings to land. Pilot Officer Buck was awarded a DFC for his courage. The aircraft's Captain, Pilot Officer P Buck survived two tours and instructed at 11 OTU before returning home.

This photograph taken on 27 April shows Squadron Leader Dick Broadbent, 'C' Flight Commander, with Wing Commander EP (Hawkeye),Wells, DSO DFC, a New Zealand fighter pilot with 485 (NZ) Squadron. Wing Commander Wells by this time was a fighter Ace with thirteen enemy aircraft claimed destroyed. By August 1943 he commanded the Kenley Fighter Wing. Later as a Group Captain he served in the post-war RAF until 1960.

75 (NZ) Squadron

During the first eight months (1942–43) that 75 (NZ) Squadron flew Stirlings, at least forty nine were lost on operations. 75 (NZ) Squadron was unusual in having three flights totalling 27 aircraft plus an Oxford for communications, 'A' and 'B' flights carried the code letters AA, while 'C' flight (commanded by an RAF rather than an RNZAF Squadron Leader) carried JN codes. In mid 1943 the RNZAF HQ in London insisted that the third flight also be New Zealand led and Squadron Leader Dick Broadbent DFC took command.

Poised in front of JN–G (BK 810) at Newmarket to record the event in June 1943 are:
5th from left S/L Broadbent; 7th, Pilot Officer Jack Fabian (Nav); 9th, S/L Guy Hayward (Squadron Gunnery Leader) and far right Flying Officer Thompson.
This aircraft failed to return from a raid on Mulheim on 22 October 1943.

162

Chapter 13 – Gallery

H2S Leader

Lancaster III DX - Q of 57 Squadron, East Kirby (Base 55 of 5 Group) on 4 April 1945.
The red/black rear tail markings signify the aircraft as an H2S radar leader.
Flying Officer Douglas Taylor was Mid-upper Gunner and that night Queenie carried a 4,000 lb and 12 x 500 lb HE bombs to Nordhausen (an underground rocket and jet factory). Of note are some of the 500 lb bombs lying in the grass prior to leaving. The trolley ACC (battery accumulator) is drawn up ready to start the all-important starboard inner Merlin engine.

Heavy Bomber Group – Middle East 1942

While the Wellingtons of 205 Group struggled with landing strips that were just stretches of flat desert marked with petrol drums, LG 224 in Egypt was equipped with some tarmac and drew a variety of interesting four engined heavies. Roy Montrowe stationed nearby visited this landing ground to inspect the new 'heavies,' so much for security!
Shown (bottom right) is Halifax, ZK–J of 10 Squadron on detachment to the area is part of a trial heavy bomber element. Its liquid cooled Merlins would have had a short life in the desert conditions.
Also shown are early model B-24 and B-17 (right) aircraft, the black painted Liberator (below) being used for SOE operations while the B-17 was part of 220 Squadron's anti-shipping detachment. That this aircraft is in Egypt suggests it flew from Gibraltar rather than Malta as the Group there habitually held onto good aircraft, crews and spares for their own operations.

Kiwis Do Fly

Whitley

Very early RAF Bomber Command operations included a New Zealand pilot from War Course 1, Flying Officer Bill Mackley whose GE-H 'Harry' (NI469) of 58 Squadron (Linton on Ouse) completed half a tour. The Whitley had a nose down flying attitude laughed at by others but Bill Mackley always smiled as he overtook Wellingtons and Hampdens struggling along 4,000 feet lower. Transferred to 19 OTU at Kinloss NI469 crashed on January 3 1943 when it flew into high ground at Mannock Hill, NW of Archiestown. Bill Mackley returned to New Zealand transferring to the SW Pacific theatre and Catalina flying boats. After a long career with TEAL and Air New Zealand, Bill retired in 1980 with over 20,000 hours in his log book.

Bomber Boy, Now a Fighter Pilot

Returning to England following a 42 Op tour in 148 Squadron Wellingtons (205 Group) in the Middle East, Flying Officer Roy Montrowe was posted to 11 OTU Westcott as an instructor. A rugby tackle in the Mess damaged Roy's hand with it went his green endorsement for heavy bombers. OTU flying was limited to the Fighter Affiliation Flight with its Hurricanes and Martinets. That tackle changed Roy's life, as his next posting was to 692 Squadron (LNSF) and its Mosquitos. Converting to civil flying post-war saw Roy accumulate over 22,000 hours with NAC before compulsory retirement.

Chapter 13 – Gallery

Tiger Force

Lancaster RE157 was Yeadon built and one of the final production Mark IIIs constructed, the line changing to Lincolns mid batch. Taken in May 1945 at Ludford Magna RE157 now a 101 Squadron aircraft is being undercoated before repainting in Far East White. Navigator John Barton was preparing to be posted to Tiger Force when Japan surrendered. *(J. Barton)*

The finished product, 207 Squadron Lancasters now painted in all-over Far East white, practice low level daylight formations. In the event the Lancasters were replaced shortly afterward with Lincolns.

Post VE Day

With cameras and particularly film now readily available, John Barton photographed 101 Squadron and USAAF bombers during daylight sorties. Shown, are B-17E 46910 and Lancaster NN761. John's pilot was Sergeant Roy Barlow from Invercargill, New Zealand. *(J. Barton)*

165

Kiwis Do Fly

Middle East Air Force

Wellington Ic of 148 Squadron (205 Group) photographed from Roy Montrowe's aircraft during the Squadron move to LG 106. The photograph was taken 13 November 1942.

Pathfinder

A remarkable photograph of PFF HQ Ops board of April 4 1945 when Lutmendorf, Levna (near Prague), Harburg (near Hamburg), Berlin and Magdeburg (between Leipzig and Berlin) were raided by 93 Mosquitos and 96 Lancasters drawn from thirteen Squadrons. Losses amounted to four aircraft, one each from 7, 142, 571 and 635 Squadrons. The loss rate (2.1%) was a fraction of that suffered during the 'bad years' of 1942 – 43. Enlargement of the original print shows the aircraft were drawn from Oboe Mosquitos 105 (Bourn,) 109 (Little Staughton), LNSF Mosquito Squadrons 128 (Wyton), 139 (Upwood), 142 (Gransden Lodge), 162 (Bourn), 163 (Wyton), and 571 (Oakington).
Lancaster Squadrons are 7 (Oakington), 35 (Graveley), 405 (RCAF), 582 (Little Staughton), 635 (Downham Market).

Left Hand Column, Target: Harburg four aircraft from 635, 7, and eight from 105 Squadron.

2nd Column:
LEVNA	109 & 105,	4 Oboe Mosquitos each
	1409	1 met recon Mosquito
	162	6 EAR & Windowers Bourn LNSF
	35	16 Blackadder crew cancelled Rear Turrett U/S LeGooda, Douglas attacked while sky marking
	582	3 Lanc III Little Staughton

3rd Column:
	405	16 Missing 4/GL
MAGDEBURG	139	6
	128	6 LNSF Mosquito Wyton
	142	6
	162	1 Pudsey, no news
	571	6 Clarke, no news Downham Market LNSF Mosquitos

4th Column:
MAGDEBURG
BERLIN Mosquito	139	6 Calder, no News. Upwood
CODE 'WHITEBAIT'	128	6
	162	5
	163	6 Wyton
	571	6

Of note is the Operations code name for Berlin 'Whitebait,' a speciality New Zealand dish.

166

Chapter 13 – Gallery

Pere Morgan

Taken from an Oxford flown by Flying Officer W. Simpson, at 14 AFU, of another Oxford flown by a fellow Kiwi Pere Morgan is photographed on a rare daylight flight from RAF Ossington. Perenara Morgan was one of the few New Zealand Maori aircrew to serve in RAF Bomber Command.

He was eventually posted from AFU for Mosquito training 1655 MTU and then joined 692 Squadron (8 PFF Group). He completed 29 operations before being killed on 15 January 1945. Caught in bad weather and with little fuel he bailed out and is thought to have been knocked unconscious as his parachute had not been deployed when his body was found.

Flying Oficer George Wirepa was another New Zealand Maori who served as aircrew, flying as a bomb aimer with 514 Squadron. He completed a tour and retired to Te Kuiti.

Ludford Magna, 101 Squadron 1945

RIGHT: A timeless and unstaged photograph by John Barton (Navigator) on return from a test flight. The pilot has questions of the flight engineer while the ground crew 'make good'

LEFT: These will not be needed. John Barton resting on a small pile of 4,000 lb bombs, while stacked 1,000 pounders keep them company. This was 101 Squadron's ready use bomb dump, very close to the airfield. Fortunately by that time Luftwaffe raids were extremely rare

Kiwis Do Fly

The Grim Reaper

109 Squadron (PFF) based at Little Staughton was one of two Oboe equipped Mosquito Squadrons (105 Squadron being the other) with the Pathfinder Force. Of the twenty eight pilots in Squadron, ten were New Zealanders.

Posed in front of Bar Peter, 'The Grim Reaper,' are eight of the New Zealand pilots:

A Relph, B Dalcolm DFC, F Beswick, WJ Simpson DFC, AG Wigley, A Stevenson, N Roseman and JT McGreal DFC.
Flight Lieutenant McGreal was killed on Anzac Day 1945 (25th April) attempting a forced landing at Phelsbroek airfield in Belgium. He was the last New Zealander killed on Bomber Command operations in Europe.
Absent were A Dray DFC and K Boles DFC.

This photograph was taken early in 1945 when Bar Peter (HS-P) MM 295 had already carried out over 120 Oboe operations.

RAF Lakenheath 1943

199 Squadron Stirlings line up ready for HRH Air Marshal the Duke of Gloucester's inspection. The censor has roughly covered the Squadron markings in all but the clearest photograph!
The Duke made a round of Stirling Squadrons during early 1943, visiting 75 (NZ) Squadron at Newmarket Heath on 8 March.
Robin Craw was a pilot with 199 Squadron and flew Stirlings until volunteering for the 'safety' of the Pathfinder Force.

Chapter 13 – Gallery

Lancaster ED930 and Liberty Loan Flights

The Lancaster, ED930 was brand new and captained by Flight Lieutenant PS Isaacson DFC, DFM. They were the first RAAF crew to return home from operations in the UK with 40 Ops completed and also the first all Australian Pathfinder crew. Two passengers, Lord Burghley, British Controller of Repair and Overseas Supplies and Gp Capt CV Wincott, British Air Mission to Washington were aboard.

The Lancaster left England 22 May 1943 and landed in New South Wales on 4 June, with a flying time of 72 hours 12 mins, a record for one crew, and on such a route over North America and the Pacific.

ED 930 later flew to RNZAF Ohakea New Zealand from Bankstown and during 11– 20th June it flew throughout the country on wars bond fundraising displays.

The leaflets the aircraft dropped could be sent to Wellington and exchanged for a Bond worth £1. Some were autographed by Lord Burghley, Mr Walter Nash and the son of Lord Newall, the Governor General. These Lancaster flights helped to raise £1.5 million for the Liberty Loan in New Zealand. During a number of War Loan tours in Australia from October 1943 to May 1944, ED 930 helped raise £3.25 million: Suprisingly, this was a rather less proportionately than from New Zealand. The aircraft remained in Australia on experimental work and was finally reduced to scrap in August 1948.

RIGHT: This flyer was dropped over central Auckland on June 14 1943 by a touring RAAF Lancaster

LEFT: ED930 photographed at RNZAF Ohakea June 12, 1943 wearing an Australian roundel and named Queenie VI complete with a bomb-carrying winged kangaroo. Behind the Lancaster is a P-40E from the Fighter Pilot's School, RNZAF

Servicing in all Weathers

Ground crews and engineering staff were expected to put up the maximum number of aircraft for the nights operational regardless of conditions and supplies.

BELOW: 75 (NZ) Squadron Wellingtons being serviced during a snow storm at Mildenhall in January 1942.

RIGHT: now with Lancasters and at Mepal, servicing continues in the Summer of 1944. AA-U (ND782)) Captain Jake Aitken and B/A Ron Mayhill (on the bike) check with ground crew who are applying anti-icing paste to the propellors. *(R. Mayhill)*

Kiwis Do Fly

Oakington 1944

Often crew photographs are hurried and aircraft pictures blurred, however the Oakington station photographer captured Robin Craws 7 Squadron crew poised for a raid in 1944.

ABOVE: Navigators briefing. Robin's Navigator takes notes, while alongside their Bomb Aimer checks his notes

ABOVE: 'Gibbo looks for the target' is writtten on the back of this photograph

ABOVE: Operation over and debrief, smiles all around as tension, nerves and fear fade

ABOVE: Left to Right: Suitably freshly combed Johnny (Ron Johnson, Nav), Gibbo (Gordon Gibson, B/A), and Smithy (Ron Smith, W/Op). Their Skipper's caption is: "Look intelligently at an Operations chart or perhaps it's a London Street map"

ABOVE: The crew pose: Robin Craw (Pilot) in the cockpit with F/E Jack Owen standing in the escape hatch.

Sitting on the port inner, Left to Right are: Bert Fox (M/UG), Ron Johnson (Nav), Gordon Gibson (B/A), Bob Harpur (RG), Ron Smith (W/Op). Taken following their last operation the 50th, on August 1944

Chapter 13 – Gallery

For the Record

This group of photographs is held in the New Zealand Bomber Command Association 'Ops Room' in a file labelled Harry Russell. Harry served as a Bomb Aimer with 90 Squadron flying Lancasters from Tuddenham and the photographs depict post VE day target damage assessments.

RIGHT: The crew, including WAAF photographers, all kitted up, prior to their daylight low level operation

ABOVE: Cologne

ABOVE: Wesel

ABOVE: The Krupps Steel Works, Essen

ABOVE: Dusseldorf

ABOVE: Essen

ABOVE: Hamburg Marshalling Yards

171

Honoured Airmen

This rare photograph depicts two RNZAF Sergeant Pilots on final leave in Auckland, January 1941 prior to embarking on the Aorangi for England. They were to become amongst the most highly decorated New Zealand airmen in RAF Bomber Command.

On the left with his sister Patsy is Fraser Barron. He was awarded the DFM with 15 Squadron (Stirlings) in May 1942, the DFC in February 1943 (7 PFF Squadron), the DSO on March 2 1943 for exceptional gallantry over Cologne, and as a Wing Commander and Commanding Officer of 7 Squadron a bar to his DSO in June 1944.

He was the first New Zealander to be awarded the DSO, DFC and DFM. At one stage in 1943 he flew on three raids to Essen in the Ruhr within 24 hours.

Fraser Barron was killed in a mid air collision over Le Mans on May 20 1944 on his 83rd Operation.

On the right is Jack Ward, the first New Zealand airman to be awarded the Victoria Cross. He was posted to 75 (NZ) Squadron in 1941 as a second pilot on Wellingtons. Returning from a raid on Munster on July 7, his aircraft was hit by night fighter fire setting the starboard engine and wing alight.

Jack climbed from the astrodome across the wing to the engine and using a canvas cover he was able to smother the fire. He returned safely to the inside of the aircraft which returned to base. The Wellington carried two other New Zealanders, the Rear Gunner Sergeant Box, who was wounded in the attack and received a DFM for his action, while Sergeant Lawton, the navigator, helped Jack Ward climb out of and back into the Wellington. The aircrafts RAF Captain Squadron/Leader Widdowson was awarded the DFC for his airmanship. Jack Ward's VC was gazetted within a month of the action but just nine weeks later he was killed over Hamburg on his eleventh operation. His aircraft (X3205) was hit by flak and four of the six crew died. Fraser Barron's uniform and ribbons form part of a special cabinet at the NZ Bomber Command Association display at MOTAT 2, Auckland.

Merry Xmas

Christmas 1944 at No. 3 LFS Feltwell showing the severe conditions aircraft were serviced and flown under. At time the entire station would turn out to clear aircraft and runways in an effort to return the squadron to operational staus for that night's raid.

(Photos: J.K. Aitken)

Chapter 13 – Gallery

A Veteran Lancaster

Built by Avro at Manchester PB 132 joined 75 (NZ) Squadron as AA-C at RAF Mepal in January 1944. Allocated to Flying Officer in January 1945 its Navigator Neville Selwood recalls that it was a real old timer with narrow propeller blades. "Enough to get us to 19,500 feet and no more. It certainly did over 100 trips but that may have included some DNCO and the Manna drops of 30th April and 7th May 1945. "It was a lucky kite and eventually was re-engined. We did 23 operations in her, the last being a 5 hour 25 minute trip to Keil with 10,092 lbs.
My last trip with 75 (NZ) Squadron was with PB132 on 29th June 1945 when we flew a 'postmortem' run to Flensburg.
Apparently 'C' went to 514 Squadron and was scrapped in March 1948. What a shame, she had looked out for us.

ABOVE: PB 132 (AA-C) at its dispersal RAF Mepal, March 1945. It carries the tail markings of a GH leader for 'A' flight 75 (NZ) Squadron

LEFT: Close up of the cockpit section showing 100 operations

RIGHT: Flying Officer Wynn Russell (Pilot) RNZAF left and Flying Officer Neville Selwood (Nav) RNZAF with AA-C

Green Endorsement

While a red endorsement of a log book meant trouble, a green inked endorsement meant congratulations and was a rare event.
A notable entry in Flying Officer Watt's log book, part of the flying summary for January 1942, a green endorsement by 77 Squadron's Commanding Officer, Wing Commander Bennett. "On 6th September 1941, as second pilot of a Whitley, Pilot Officer Watts successfully piloted a badly damaged aircraft back after an attack by an enemy fighter.
On 21st October 1941 as Captain of a Whitley aircraft, Pilot Officer Watts piloted his aircraft safely back to base, after the rudder controls had been shot away but unfortunately the aircraft was badly damaged on landing. On both occasions Pilot Officer Watt's displayed outstanding coolness and devotion to duty.
    Signed D.C.T. Bennett
    Wing Commander
    Commanding 77 Squadron."

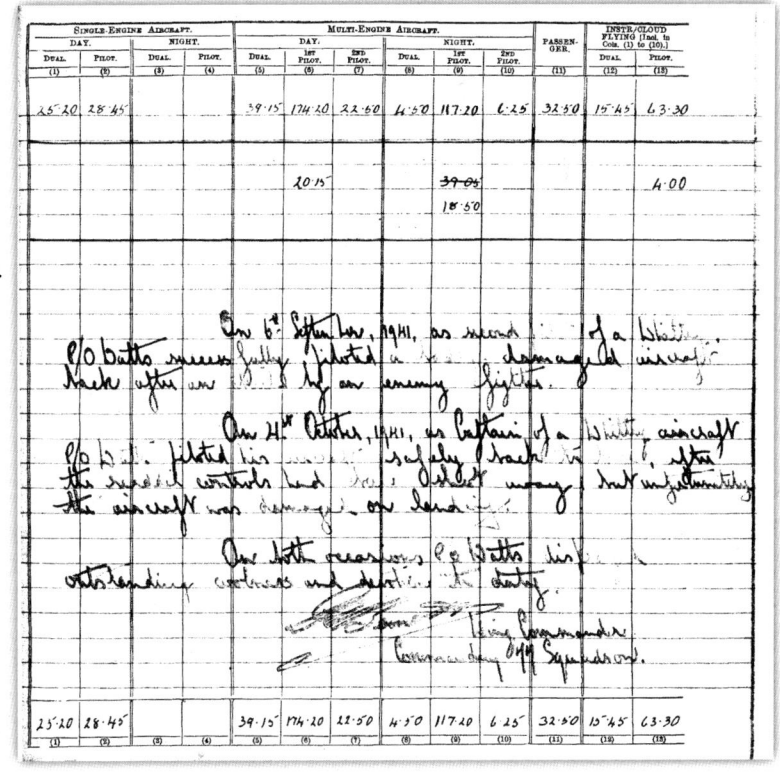

When 77 Squadron was shifted to Coastal Command in April 1942 Pilot Officer Watts had 22 Ops on Whitleys and transferred to 24 OTU. In September 1943 he was posted to 1655 Mosquito Training Unit and by November was in 139 Squadron (Wyton) again commanded by Wing Commander Bennett, as an early part of his Pathfinder group. It is apparent that Bennett thought highly of Watt's skill and had marked him down early on for PFF service.

Kiwis Do Fly

SOE Operations 148 Squadron Brindisi, 1945

While most RAF bomber Squadrons concentrated on dropping high explosives selected 'secret' Squadrons supported Special Operations Executive work, 148 Squadron specialised in it.

This series of official and unofficial photographs were collected to provide a sequence of a days operations. While in Europe virtually all drops were night affairs, many of the Southern Ops were made during daylight.

Phil Small who trained as a W/Op for RAF Bomber Command never did drop any armed explosives.

ABOVE: The Operations Officer plans the Squadrons tasks with Group Captain Woodhall (centre) and Wing Commander Haywood CO 148 Squadron

ABOVE: The Wing Ops board records 67 sorties that day over Southern Europe, most to Yugoslavia

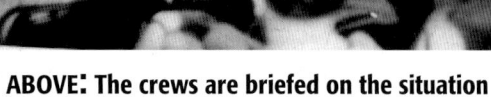

ABOVE: The crews are briefed on the situation

ABOVE: Phil Small (far right) ready for his last wartime Operation as a dis-patcher flying with F/L Ross and his crew on Halifax FS-N (LL290). Note the sidearms

ABOVE: Fuelling up and loading stores mainly radios, explosives, weapons and ammunition

174

Chapter 13 – Gallery

LEFT: Drop zone marked by a white pattern, charged each day and advised by radio

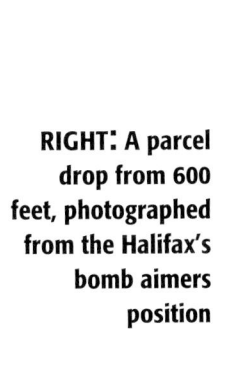

RIGHT: A parcel drop from 600 feet, photographed from the Halifax's bomb aimers position

ABOVE: Landing over the sea wall at Brindisi airfield, Southern Italy

ABOVE: 148 Squadron Captains after a sortie, F/L Dickie Prior (centre) who had been on the Warsaw Operation, C/O Wing Commander Haywood (right) and F/L Dobbin (left)

ABOVE: F/Lt 'Blackie' Black with Harry Wild and pilot Charlie Hall (DFC) in the background

ABOVE: Halifax FS-U crashed on take-off 26 December 1944. Captained by Don Solin, the navigator was killed and Phil Small still had bruises two weeks later

175

Farewell to War

In September 1945, the SS Andes left Southampton carrying many hundreds of RNZAF and RAAF veterans home and eventually to demobbing.
75 (NZ) Squadron was given the honour of farewelling the ship on behalf of RAF Bomber Command.

RIGHT: Now operating Lincoln II aircraft from RAF Spilsbury, 75 (NZ) Squadron allocated AA-A (RF 389) and AA-N for the farewell. Take-off 1400 hours, on route to Southampton

ABOVE RIGHT: A newspaper clipping showing the final flypast. "As the Andes was eased out into the stream, we lined up side by side and dived down to 500 feet over flying the Andes from stem to stern. With 270 degree turns one to port, the other to starboard brought the two Lincolns over the ship from opposite directions at the same time. Another pair of 270 degree turns brought us together for a final pass"

ABOVE: The Andes leaving the dock. Taken from AA-N at 1,500 feet

ABOVE: Farewell

Mepal the Wartime Home of 75 (NZ) Squadron

RAF Mepal (Cambridgeshire), was home of 75 (NZ) Squadron from June 1943. This photograph was taken by Squadron Leader R Broadbent on 28 June 1943 from 6,000 feet and shows 29 of the Squadrons Stirlings dispersed around the airfield having arrived from RAF Newmarket.
At the top of the picture is Mepal Village and at the bottom Sutton village, home of Percy's Pub, a popular spot with 75 (NZ) Squadron crew.
The canals (bottom right) were often followed by USAAF B 17 and B 24's returning to their bases in Suffolk. Little remains of the airfield today save some hard standings and foundations from a missile base.

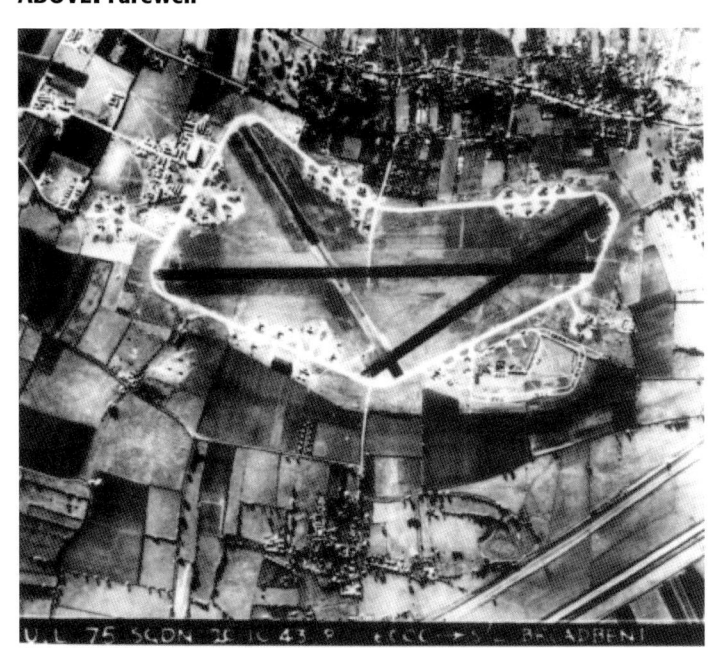

Chapter 14

Special People

During the research and interviews for this book, the Operational careers of two exceptional pilots and one exceptional family were uncovered.

All Served with great pride, dedication and bravery, two of the five pilots being killed on operations. Yet none of them have been widely recognised.

Thus, their careers are covered in this chapter in greater detail than others.

They all were very special people.

Kiwis Do Fly

Brothers in Arms

Many families had brothers join the RNZAF, the boys being especially keen on the prospect of overseas service. Often one brother became aircrew while the other was posted to a technical trade. There were no brothers who served together as aircrew, the Air Force system randomly splitting them up amongst different Squadrons, Commands or even Theatres.

Hence the Sheddan family lost one son in 1943 on his first Op with 166 Squadron (RAF Bomber Command) over Germany while his brother Jim, a fighter pilot, became an ace and finished his war as Commanding Officer of 486 Squadron on Spitfires.

The Shorthouse family however was quite remarkable. Jack Shorthouse (Snr), a Royal Navy Man, emigrated from Portsmouth, England in 1926 with his wife and three boys (Jack b. 11/4/20, Eric b. 24/5/21, and Robert b. 9/8/22).

With only 30 months between the three, the boys were a fiercely competitive trio. Jack senior became manager of the Foxton Hotel while his sons directed some of their energy into Surf Life Saving. This determination to be the best would eventually give the RNZAF three highly skilled pilots dedicated to being the best.

The family moved to Waimauku, north of Auckland, and in 1939 Jack was accepted for a short service commission in the RAF. His two brothers would follow him into the Air Force and all three became distinguished pilots, two on fighters and one on bombers. The two survivors of the war would have distinguished civilian flying careers go on to accumulate over 30,000 hours in the air between them.

As detailed elsewhere in this book, the eldest son Jack joined the RNZAF in June 1939 and just six months

ABOVE: Junior Lifesavers Foxton (NZ) Left to Right: Eric (Peter), Robert (Bob), John (Jack)

ABOVE: The Shorthouse Military Family 1942: Peter (in NZ Army Uniform), Jack senior (Royal Navy), Jack junior RAF, mother Marguerite, Robert in RNZAF (Pilot under training) uniform

ABOVE: Bob Shorthouse, Fighter Pilot, 164 Squadron (May 1942, Peterhead). His Spitfire carries the picture of a flying eagle carrying a bomb

later his Fairey Battle was shot down in flames over France. Jack finished the war as Officer Commanding 189 Squadron with a DFC and was Mentioned in Dispatches. He later went on to fly long-haul trans-Pacific routes in a career with TEAL (later Air New Zealand).

Two years younger than Jack, the youngest brother Robert became the second Shorthouse to join the RNZAF, entering No 17 Pilots course in May 1941. After going solo six weeks later Robert was posted to Canada for further training on Harvards.

Eldest brother Jack, was by then also in Canada flying Ansons and instructing future RAF Bomber Command pilots at the 32 SFTS at Moose Jaw (Saskatchewan). However Bob joined 2 SFTS based at Uplands (near Ottawa) some 1,500 miles east and their paths never crossed.

Bob graduated from 2 SFTS with 150 hours logged, promoted to Sergeant Pilot and posted to England arriving at 58 OTU (Grangemouth, Scotland) just before Christmas 1941.

Twelve thousand miles away, middle brother Eric had also volunteered for RNZAF service but was suddenly conscripted into the NZ Army on coastal defence.

Following Japan's attack on Pearl harbour in December 1941 and the immediate invasion of a number of SE Asian countries, New Zealand (and

Chapter 14 – Special People

ABOVE: Line up of 164 Squadron with Bob second from right
SITTING ON WING: (Left to Right) Jimmy Butler, Ron Stillwell, Jimmy Diack*, F/L Tarrant (I.O) Ian Smith, Bob Cunningham, Bobby Law *, Bob Tims OC
STANDING: R Brown, Tommy Burke, Doc Hartman, Ken Biggs*, Johny Long*, F/L Howlett OC A Flight, S/L MacMullen CO, F/Lt Kitson, Self, Bob Sarill*, MacQueen*, Alex Vale, Bill Beatley   *Later killed in action

Australia) became very vulnerable. With most of both countries front line servicemen already in Europe or the Middle East, homeland coastal defence was paramount and for a time all enlisted men were drafted into this service, often with little or no equipment, but each region being named a 'fortress.'

Meanwhile in England Bob Shorthouse continued training on Mk II Spitfires but the poor weather and high mountains in the region contributed additional casualties to the usual OTU losses.

Sergeant Pilot Bob Shorthouse added to the attrition rate by writing off his Spitfire during a ground loop which ended against a fuel tanker.

With 40 hours on Spitfires and a 'memorable dressing down,' a reformed Bob was posted on 12th April to the recently formed 164 Squadron based at Peterhead (near Aberdeen).

The Squadron was quickly moved further north to Skeabrae in the Orkney Islands where Bob completed just six convoy patrols before being posted to 43 Squadron in Essex at the other end of Britain.

With another dozen Ops completed Bob was on his way again, this time to 253 Squadron and Hurricanes. Having completed far north operations in marginal weather and with four postings in eleven months Bob Shorthouse should not have been surprised with the RAF system when Algiers in North Africa was to be his next destination (along with the rest of 253 Squadron).

By Christmas 1942, Jack was in Moose Jaw, Canada. Bob was in Algiers, while in New Zealand the arrival of American troops allowed Eric to be released back into RNZAF service and undertake initial training.

Flying from La Sabala, 253 Squadron Hurricanes were kept very busy, Bob claiming a Ju88 and two probables during the Allied invasion of North Africa.

The flying log book kept by Bob Shorthouse is quite unusual as it includes detailed comments on operations and results (something not encouraged in a Bomber Command Squadron).

With continuing problems with aircraft maintenance in the wet conditions of June – August 1943, Bob comments about his Hurricane IIc SW-G:-

"George is turning terribly, release the stick and she will half flick roll."

"Still bags of mag drop with plugs oiling up."

"Counted upwards of a dozen aerodromes between Monasti and Twins and wasn't looking for them. 'G' is misbehaving."

"RT duff, compass very duff, air pressure system duff, trimming very duff. In bad shape, the engine is still no good."

LEFT: B Flight Line Up

BELOW: The combination log book/diary Bob Shorthouse kept, June 1943 Tunisia

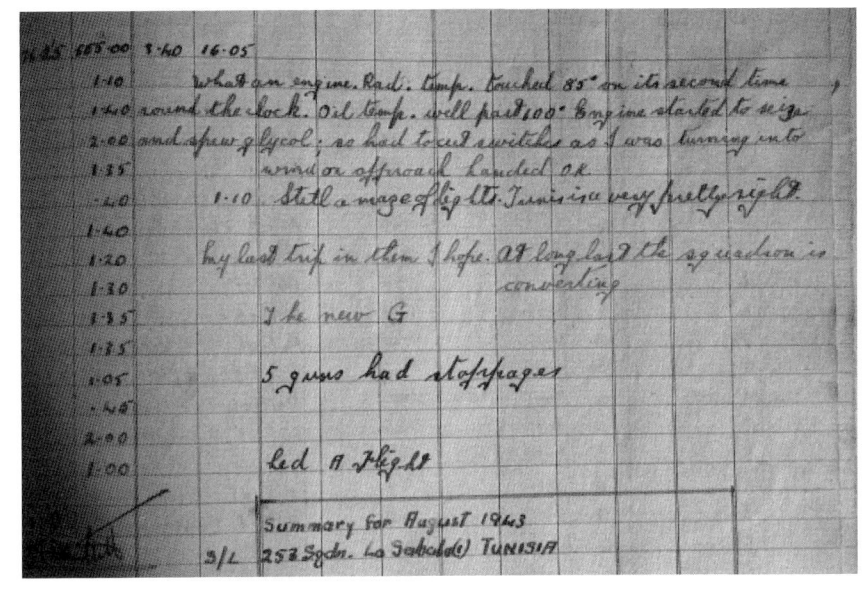

179

Kiwis Do Fly

"At last 'G' is AOG for a new engine."

Flying a clapped out fighter on daily patrols of one to two hours over both desert and sea, says much about Bob Shorthouse's determination. After five days of radio U/S, Bob notes the surrender of Italy in his log followed by:

"Radio keeps cutting, I'm off, HELL."

Bob's faith in fitters, armourers and Hurricanes were just about gone with a variety of ever changing failures:

15 July 1943   Starboard cannon stopped.
16 July 1943   Port cannon stopped.

Then on the 17 July, 'George' reappears with a new engine.

"Wizard! What an engine, goes like a rocket, at 25,000 feet 2050 rpm and 18 half lb boost about 410 mph."

"Gunnery Exercise. Good practice, lots of fun, had a very nasty spin from a high speed stall."

But a month later (August 1943):

"What an engine, radiator temperature touched 85° on its second time round the clock. Oil temp well past 100. Engine started to seize and spew glycol. Had to cut switches as I was turning into the wind on final approach. Landed okay."

On the 10th of August, Bob wrote up his 1.20 hour Op as "my last trip in them I hope." At long last the Squadron was converting onto the Spitfire Vc. Bob received his new 'G' on the eleventh and George was true to form on the 13th, "Five guns had stoppages." Perhaps the new George had a pre Op briefing from its predecessor.

This page of log book extracts shows just how difficult maintaining front line capability was in North Africa and how the Squadron had to press on regardless. The ground crews had a thankless task keeping worn out aircraft in combat, even if they were not airworthy. The bomber Squadrons flying Wellingtons out of Egypt faced identical problems.

Bob and 253 Squadron followed the invasion of Italy and by March 1944 he had become tour expired with 821 hours in his log book, 410 being on operations.

With all the Shorthouse boys, their comrades recalled their sheer determination on the job, but being bloody good mates all the same. Harry Carter who served with Bob in North Africa recalls great larks on leave and even a bit more fun on Ops.

Promoted to Flight Lieutenant, Bob Shorthouse was posted as an instructor to Abu Sueir (Egypt) but soon was repatriated back to New Zealand during November 1944. Following a spell with the Fighter OTU at Ohakea on Kittyhawks and Harvards, Bob was discharged from the RNZAF in October 1945.

Still with a lot of flying in his blood, Bob joined one

ABOVE: Bob demonstrating low level top dressing in a Fu 24. His license remained current until 1981 when he took ZK-CMY for a last flight

ABOVE: P-40 H-1 NZ3113 of 15 Squadron, Henderson Field Guadalcanal 1943

ABOVE: Log book entries for January 1944, recording two P-40 losses and Peter's own kill on January 1944

Chapter 14 – Special People

ABOVE: Peter Shorthouse's last log book entry Torokina/Rabaul S/L Clarke completing the entry, 620 hours flown as pilot

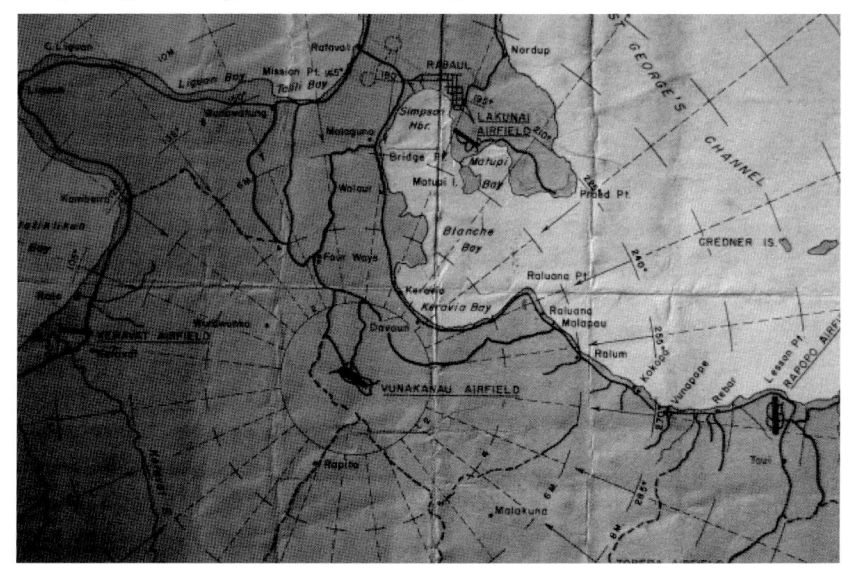

ABOVE: Peter's own operational map of the Rabaul area left in his log book. The concentration on Vunakanau airfield is obvious.
NOTE: the Courses marked are reciprocals, to get to Vunakanau

ABOVE: Kiwi F4U-ID Corsair NZ5218 at the Torokina fighter strip

of New Zealand's and the world's earliest aerial top dressing companies, Auckland Aviation Services. Using war-surplus Tiger Moths, dozens of ex RNZAF pilots developed this revolutionary method of applying fertiliser. Bob was a safe pilot in an industry renowned for its accidents and fatalities finishing four log books, 10,000 hours and surviving two prangs. On his retirement in 1984 he had 42 pilots working on FU-24 aircraft – more than enough for three of the old Hurricane Squadrons.

As more US forces began arriving in New Zealand during October 1942, Eric Shorthouse (or Peter he was called by the family) was released from the Army to take up RNZAF service.

Entering the Initial Training Wing at Levin as an Airman Pilot (U/T), Peter had passed through both Elementary Flying School and Service Flying Training School by June 1943. Promoted to Sergeant Pilot, he was selected for fighter school, joining No 2 OTU on P-40E Kittyhawks at Ohakea.

By this time Guadalcanal in the Solomon Islands was the centre of fighting in the SW Pacific and the RNZAF kept a rotation of fighter Squadrons in the region, based initially at Henderson Field. Peter's first of four tours was with No 15 Squadron in early December 1943.

The Squadron's tasks were air defence and increasingly as escorts for US SBD Dauntless dive-bombers attacking Japanese strong points and airfields.

On January 14 1944, the Squadron's target was Simpson Harbour (Rabaul), New Britain. Flying No 2 in P-40 Kittyhawk NZ3195 to F/L Boucher, Peter Shorthouse found a Zeke (A6M) chasing an SBD, "I managed to get on his tail and followed him firing bursts all the time. Smoke and flames came out both sides. I followed him down to 50 feet when he hit the water." Peter's kill was the RNZAF's 96th success of the hundred-odd air combat kills they scored in this region.

The Squadron returned to New Zealand in February 1944 and three months later returned to the Pacific, this time flying F4U-1 Corsairs. Peter saw more of the Pacific than he intended when flak damage on the 23 June and an engine failure on 7 July resulted in ditchings. The Squadron rotated back to New Zealand at the end of July, then returned for a third tour in September which was completed just before Christmas 1944.

15 Squadron again returned to the SW Pacific in January 1945 after the New Year, after just one month stand down. This time the Squadron was based fruther north on Green Island (between Bougainville and New Britain in the Solomon Islands), as the Japanese abandoned island forts or were by-passed.

Kiwis Do Fly

Peter's younger brother Bob arrived back in New Zealand at the end of 1944 but neither were aware of the others movements and had no opportunity to meet.

In the SW Pacific, large numbers of Japanese troops still remained at their major base in Rabaul. On April 12 Peter Shorthouse took off on his 120th Operation in NZ5317 and at 10,000 feet off the coast of New Britain encountered magneto trouble and turned back to Green Island. Fifteen minutes later NZ5317's motor failed. Peter reported to his No. 2 that petrol was entering the cockpit. The aircraft then nosed over and dived into a ridge exploding on impact. No trace of pilot or aircraft were ever found.

On 10 July 1945 Flying Officer EP Shorthouse received a posthumous Mention in Dispatches and on 25 September he was awarded the DFC. In part the citation reads: "A daring section leader who headed repeated attacks with extreme courage and determination." Such a citation could have easily applied to all three Shorthouse brothers. But for his dedication to duty and determination to do one more tour New Zealand could have seen a unique trio of pilots in Civil Aviation.

As it was, the Shorthouse boys did more than could ever be expected from one family, and their parents would welcome war's end more than others.

– *The Shorthouse Family*

RIGHT: Peter Shorthouse (left) with a fellow 15 Squadron pilot in tropical flying gear at Torokina airfield Solomon Islands.

ABOVE: Back row Left to Right:
Jack (John Sidney) 1920–2008, Mother, Mrs Marguerite Shorthouse, 1886–1970, Peter 1921–1945 (killed in action)

Front Row: Bob (Robert Clive) 1922–1999, Father, John Stephen Shorthouse 1885–1961

RIGHT: Bob Shorthouse, 14 Squadron 1944

Chapter 14 – Special People

Born to Lead

Stephen Watts was a WWI War orphan. His 40 year old father, despite his age and not passing the medical test, was still able to fight alongside his brother in the trenches of France and die.

Being left responsible for his widowed mother and two sisters meant Stephen Watts faced a difficult path, but he was able to attend Grammar School and matriculated at the end of the Great Depression.

The family's loyalty to King and Country was very strong. Grandfather Watts had originally fought in the 1860 Maori Wars, his father had died in the first World War so it was natural that Steven should also volunteer to fight for his country. He chose the RNZAF.

Selected as a pilot, he soloed on 28 November 1941 after just five and a half hours dual instruction at EFTS Harewood. He was a 'natural' and passed out with his flying badge from 2 FTS Woodbourne in March 1941.

By June he had arrived in England, training first at 10 OTU Abingdon, then being posted to 77 Squadron on Whitleys. His first Op to Essen was a rough introduction to the air war when a fighter attack damaged the aircraft's flaps and wing. The crew returned, if shakily, from their 'first one.'

Stephen was commissioned and won his first DFC on 6 September 1941. As second pilot he brought

ABOVE: 77 Squadron days – Formation practice

ABOVE: Log book entry recording the Whitley crash landing, to be followed by a DFC award

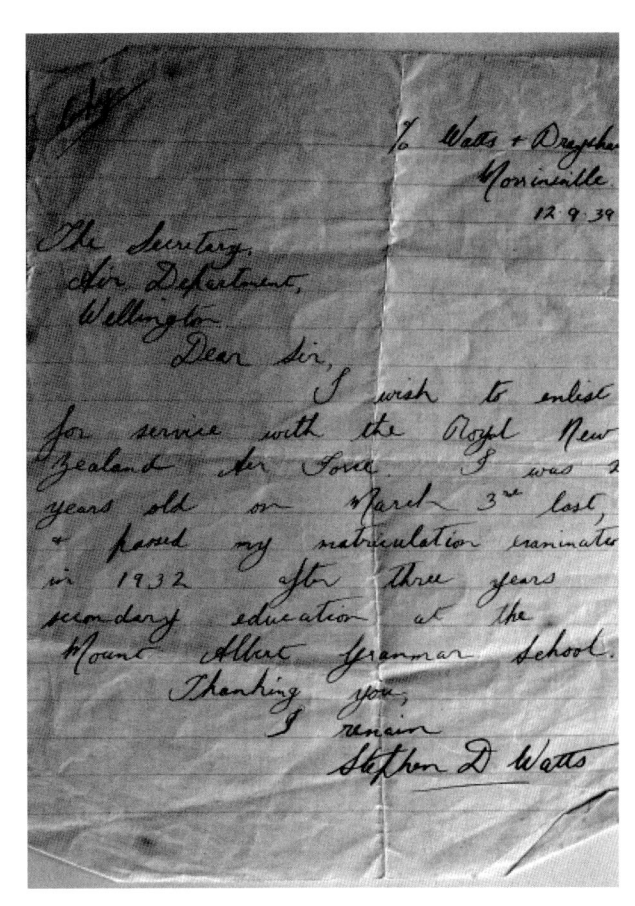

ABOVE: Stephen's application to become an airman 12 September 1938

Whitley Z6654 KN – V back on one engine following another fighter attack. The Whitley crash-landed on a beach just short of an anti-invasion minefield. There the crew were forced to wait until Army Sappers cleared a path through the mines. Flak damage forced a further crash landing in October and again there were no crew casualties. These actions earned Flying Officer Watts a green commendation in his log book, signed by Wing Commander Bennett OC 77 Squadron.

Sent on a BAT course, Stephen found some relief from the pace of operations before returning to 77 Squadron and a further 21 operations. During this period losses to the all important trans-Atlantic convoys were dangerously high and to meet an urgent need for anti U-Boat patrols, 77 Squadron was transferred to Coastal Command. Given the choice of a posting to Coastal Command or training, F/L Watts became an instructor at 24 OTU and OC 'D' flight. There he met up with his future navigator, Englishman Cyril Hassell. They would fly together on every operation from then on except the last.

This team was selected as potential Pathfinders and went to 1655 Mosquito Training Unit at Marham in October 1943. After training, they joined 139 (Jamaica) Squadron and completed 18 Ops over the next two months.

The Pathfinders AOC, AVM Bennett, had ideas to

Kiwis Do Fly

LEFT: Whitley days on 77 Squadron. Fighter affiliation practice with a Lysander! Flying Officer Watts flew 21 operations on this tour

ABOVE: Whitley postcard showing a 77 Squadron aircraft, sent to his mother in 1942

ABOVE: 77 Squadron days – Flying Whitley Z6956 on a daylight air test

ABOVE: 77 Squadron days – With navigator F/Sgt Hancock

equip a number of Squadrons with Mosquitos to form a Light Night Strike Force. Loaded with 4,000 lb 'cookie' high capacity bombs, they would disperse over Germany to numerous targets on a nightly basis causing not only damage but creating problems for night fighters of the Luftwaffe trying to locate the main raid being carried out by the heavies elsewhere.

The LNSF was a Mosquito-only force and their Mk XVI aircraft were modified with bulged bomb bay doors to accommodate a 'cookie.'

692 Squadron was formed on January 1 1944 at Graveley to trial this new high speed, low risk type of attack. 692 was commanded by the legendary Wing Commander Lockhart. Stephen Watts was posted in from 139 Squadron as Second in Command and 'B' Flight Commander. An Englishman John Sanderson, took over 'C' Flight. John recalls; "I was never too sure if Lockie was very brave or very mad. Even before the Squadron was declared operational, Lockie had grabbed our first B XVI, bombed up, and did a run to Berlin. What an inspiration."

W/C Lockhart DSO, DFC was posted to 7 Squadron on 25 March as Commanding Officer following the loss of their serving Commanding Officer. He was in command for little over a month before he was lost on operations in April 1944. His replacement was New Zealander Wing Commander J Fraser Barron DSO, DFC, DFM. The Squadron lost it's third Commanding Officer within two months when Fraser Barron was killed on May 20th during operations over France.

On February 23 1944, with Dusseldorf as their first target, the three commanders had a race. Steve Watts in DZ2637 P3-C wrote in his personal diary; "I wasn't going to be second, but it was a close thing, Sandy dropped his just 90 seconds after me and he was third."

John Saunderson and Stephen Watts became close friends. "Whenever we got time off we'd play a round or two of golf. He was a very fine pilot, commander and friend. I owe my life to him."

John recalls in his Squadron Report:

"ACCIDENT TO A MOSQUITO ON RETURN FROM A BOMBING OPERATION TO HAMBURG"

On 26 April 1944, 692 Squadron was detailed to attack Hamburg with 4,000 lb light case bombs ('cookies').

"I took off about midnight with my Navigator Flt/Lt (Dickie) Clarkson in Mosquito Mark XVI P3-E, (ML977)."

"The weather was overcast but did not present a problem and the trip out was no more nerve wracking than usual. At Hamburg, however, the heavy flak was very intense and we were 'coned' in numerous searchlights which were quite blinding."

"After dropping the bomb we weaved our way out of the area as best we could, the cone of searchlights followed us with ease and after evasive manoeuvres it was amazing how quickly the AA guns picked up one's new course and height. Hamburg was known by the crews as 'Chopburg' with good reason and I had very unpleasant experiences of it when operating in Wellingtons."

"We got clear and I had no indication that there was any damage. It took some time to get clear of the defences and when we did it became apparent that we had three problems; a complete failure of electrics and therefore no radio, the double windscreen badly misted up and

184

Chapter 14 – Special People

LEFT: 77 Squadron Flight Office, Abington

thirdly a shortage of petrol which, we estimated, would leave little margin for our return."

At this time, with D-day approaching, there was a lot of activity in the air and, although the rest of the Squadron had already landed at Graveley, there were a number of aircraft in the circuit including a German fighter firing at anything it could see. One Lancaster in particular was being attacked and the Norwegian Captain, in order to escape, made a rapid landing and put out his navigation lights. (This was ND413 of 35 Squadron which shared Graveley with 692).

"In the meantime, being short of petrol, I planned to land as soon as possible but had no way of communicating with Control."

"I knew that my friend Squadron Leader Stephen Watts was in charge of night flying and would probably be standing out on the airfield and indeed he was, wondering what had happened to me."

"Unable to communicate by radio, I decided to do a long low approach with 10° of flap and plenty of engine, the idea being to give Control the best chance of hearing me coming. During this approach I ordered a red light to be fired to confirm that this was an emergency landing. My Navigator, Dickie Clarkson, said the Verey pistol was jammed; never having heard of such a thing I swore and grabbed it from him only to find that he was all too right. I do not expect everyone to believe this occurrence because in retrospect, I find it hard to believe myself."

"Stephen Watts heard my approach and was aware that the Norwegian Lancaster was stuck on the runway with its lights out. He had a Verey pistol in each hand-loaded with a red and a green flare respectively."

"I landed with some difficulty,

MOSQUITOES CLOSED KIEL CANAL WITH MINES

1,500,000 TONS OF CARGO HELD UP FOR 10 DAYS

The Kiel Canal, most heavily defended waterway in the world, was mined by Mosquitoes of Bomber Command on May 12, just under a month before the invasion, and closed for 10 days.

Announcing this yesterday, the Air Ministry disclosed that a month before this exploit the Koenigsberg Canal, the Germans' important Baltic artery, was also mined and blocked.

For the Kiel expedition Mosquitoes of Bomber Command were loaded with mines for the first time since this aircraft came into service. In bright moonlight and from a very few feet above the sea the mines were laid in the Canal.

A diversionary attack against a land target close by was made at the time the mines were laid.

When the Germans discovered what had happened the canal was closed for seven days, reopened, though for less than the usual traffic, for three days, and then closed again for three days.

As a result, it is estimated that at a critical time, when it was all-important to block every possible route for German supplies, not less than 1,000,000 metric tons of cargo to and from overseas, and about half that amount of coastwise cargo were held up, the Air Ministry stated.

PEAK TRAFFIC BLOCKED
The overseas cargo, including iron ore from Sweden, coal with which to pay for the ore, and military supplies to Norway, were stopped at the beginning of the ice-free season when such traffic was at its peak, and much above the average level for the summer months.

Air photographs had been taken along the entire length of the canal and all the defences plotted.

To lay mines accurately in the canal the aircraft would have to fly very low, and the four-engined bombers which usually do this work would be in great danger from the ground defences.

The Mosquito seemed an obvious choice. It had the right speed and manoeuvrability, but no Mosquito had ever before carried mines.

MINES MODIFIED
Admiralty and R.A.F. experts studied the problem and found that if ordinary airborne mines were modified Mosquitoes could take them.

A single Mosquito squadron was given the task. It was led by Wing Cmdr. S. D. Watts, D.S.O., D.F.C. His D.S.O. was an immediate award given for his part in the operations.

In the event the crews navigation was perfect and the mines were laid right in the middle of the canal.

Only one Mosquito was missing, and it is believed that this aircraft hit the ground when flying very low.

KIEL CANAL MINED

DARING OPERATION BY MOSQUITOES

SHIPPING DELAYED FOR TEN DAYS

About a month before the landings in Normandy Mosquitoes of Bomber Command, in bright moonlight and from a very few feet above the sea, laid mines in the Kiel Canal, the most heavily defended waterway in the world. As a result the canal was closed for seven days, reopened, though to less than the usual traffic, for three days, and then closed again for three days.

It is estimated that at a critical time when it was important to block every possible route for German supplies, 1,000,000 metric tons of cargo were held up. The cargo included iron ore from Sweden, coal with which to pay for the ore, and military supplies to Norway.

All this was done by a single Mosquito squadron. The planning and preparation was a good example of swift but careful staff work. All the defences were plotted. To lay mines accurately in the canal, the aircraft would have to fly very low, and four-engined bombers, which usually do this work, would be in great danger from the ground defences. The Mosquito had the right speed and manoeuvrability, but no Mosquito had ever carried mines before.

Technical experts found that if ordinary airborne mines were modified, Mosquitoes could take them. The...

ABOVE: News release on the 4,000 lb load Mosquito a month before the Keil mining Operation as detailed in the text

ABOVE: Part of a PR series photographed by the Air Ministry now held by Hawker Siddley Archives their caption states '692 Intelligence Officer with an RAF Engineering Officer'. This engineer happens to be wearing a Flying Badge and a DFC and is actually 627's CO, Stephen Watts. So much for censorship

185

ABOVE: A BBC interview followed the successful Canal raid part of the PR campaign surrounding the Mosquito and its big bombs.

ABOVE: Grand Tour of Germany 1944 style, Wing Commander Watts briefing the Squadron. In over the Frisian Islands, then Hanover, Berlin, Hamburg and home over the Waddensee

RIGHT: Stephen with his favourite past times, golf and a pipe, photographed by his friend and second in command John Saunderson

taking into account a very dim flare path and a misted windscreen. We probably touched down at about 100 mph and I remember saying "I think we've made it Dickie."

Stephen Watts must have foreseen the inevitable disaster with considerable distress and he said afterwards, "It was not easy to do nothing and let you crash". He could not, of course, fire a green, and being intelligent and quick witted, he realised that if he fired a red, I would probably open up the engines to go round again and inevitably be killed."

"After saying those words (which might well have been my last) to Dickie, we shot on down the runway which, as far as I was aware, was quite clear. Shortly after touch down, however, I had an apprehensive feeling that something was in front of us and immediately applied full pneumatic brakes."

"We struck the Lancaster at high speed. I never saw it but one moment we were running down the runway and, I recall, it felt as if one had been trodden on by a giant."

"The undercarriage and one engine had been torn away and the port engine was still running over my head. Dickie Clarkson had been thrown out through the aircraft and I was trapped in the wreckage with something bent over my knee. I could feel blood running down my face and right leg and my left leg had been forced back behind me."

"I do not remember suffering any pain but I do remember feeling intensely alive and alert. When I became conscious of petrol fumes, I realised what could happen and made serious efforts to get free from the wreck. Somehow I managed to break away the piece which was trapping me and fell through the wreckage on to the grass. At this point I suddenly felt very dazed and staggered away aimlessly until two airmen caught me up and took me over. At this stage I can only remember two things; light was increasing with the dawn and I recall looking back and seeing my Mosquito embedded in the Lancaster. This was the first moment that I realised what had happened. As I was being taken away I caught a glimpse of Dickie Clarkson standing up with blood on his face and fumbling with a tin of tobacco which was squashed nearly flat."

Chapter 14 – Special People

ABOVE: The brief recording of the Kiel Canal attack on May 12 1944

ABOVE: The first 4,000 pounder gone, many more to follow

ABOVE: The last log book entry recording on air test prior to the operation on July 9th

"My next memory was sitting with my legs in a bucket of bloody water, being treated by a surly Scottish doctor. It was then that I learned that the Lancaster rear gunner had been killed and that the mid upper gunner was not expected to live. Tragically the rear gunner might have survived but had gone back to his turret to unload his guns."

"Neither Dickie nor I were badly hurt and, after a short time off, we were given another aircraft and had to get on with it. We had to get in some more practice before mining the Kiel canal on May 12th."

Having set up 692 Squadron, Wing Commander Lockhart DSO, DFC, was posted to take over No 7 Squadron which had lost its Commanding Officer and had suffered heavy losses. Stephen Watts was promoted and assumed command of 692 (Fellowship of the Bellows). The Bellows were a pro British society in Argentina who funded many aircraft for the RAF. The Squadron was kept busy prior to D-Day targeting German supply lines and railways to block their ability to reinforce any new front line in France.

The 4,000 lb bomb carrying Mosquito was announced to the public in March 1944 with the Telegraph newspaper on April 10 1944 carrying photographs of Steven Watts (described as a 'Technical Officer') and 692 Mosquitos.

Just a month later Wing Commander Watts lead his Squadron on one of the wars famous raids that made front page news.

> **"CANAL WITH MINES 1,500,000 TONS OF CARGO HELD UP FOR 10 DAYS"**
>
> The Kiel Canal, most heavily defended waterway in the world, was mined by Mosquitos of Bomber Command on May 12, just under a month before the invasion, and closed for ten days.
>
> Announcing this yesterday, the Air Ministry disclosed that a month before this exploit the Koenigsberg Canal, the Germans' important Baltic artery, was also mined and blocked.
>
> For the Kiel Operation Mosquitos of Bomber Command were loaded with mines for the first time since this aircraft came into service. In bright moonlight and from a very few feet above the sea the mines were laid in the Canal.
>
> A diversionary attack against a land target close by was made at the time when the mines were laid.
>
> When the Germans discovered what had happened the canal was closed for seven days, re-opened, though to less than usual traffic, for three days, and then closed again for three days.
>
> As a result, it is estimated that at a critical time, when it was all important to block every possible route for German supplies, not less than 1,000,000 metric tons of cargo to and from overseas, and about half that amount

Kiwis Do Fly

of coastwise cargo were held up. The Air Ministry stated:

"PEAK TRAFFIC BLOCKED"

The overseas cargo including iron ore from Sweden, coal with which to pay for the ore, and military supplies to Norway, were stopped at the beginning of the ice-free season when such traffic was at its peak, and much above the average level for the summer months.

Air photographs had been taken along the entire length of the canal and all the defences plotted.

To lay mines accurately in the canal the aircraft would have to fly very low, and the four-engined bombers which usually do this work would be in great danger from the ground defences.

The Mosquito seemed an obvious choice. It had the right speed and manoeuvrability, but no Mosquito had ever before carried mines.

MINES MODIFIED:

Admiralty and RAF experts studied the problem and found that if ordinary airborne mines were modified, Mosquitos could take them.

A single Mosquito squadron was given the task. It was led by Wing Commander S D Watts, DSO, DFC His DSO was an immediate award given for his part in the operations.

In the event the crews navigation was perfect and the mines were laid.

A rare air to air shot of a 627 Squadron Mk XVI with the bulged bomb bay. The aircraft is thought to be P3-J

"KIEL CANAL MINED DARING OPERATION BY MOSQUITOS SHIPPING DELAYED FOR TEN DAYS"

About a month before the landings in Normandy Mosquitos of Bomber Command, in bright moonlight and from a very few feet above the sea, laid mines in the Kiel Canal, the most heavily defended waterway in the world. As a result the canal was closed for seven days, re-opened, though to less than the usual traffic, for three days, and then closed again for three days.

It is estimated that at a critical time when it was important to block every possible route for German supplies, 1,000,000 metric tons of cargo were held up. The cargo included iron ore from Sweden, coal with which to pay for the ore, and military supplies to Norway.

All this was done by a single Mosquito Squadron. The planning and preparation was a good example of swift but careful staff work. all the defences were plotted. To lay mines accurately in the canal, the aircraft would have to fly very low, and four-engined bombers which usually do this work, would be in great danger. The mines could be considered one of the first smart weapons. The mixture of acoustic, magnetic and delayed action fuses caused on-going disruption to canal traffic. The Mosquitos were modified by having new attachments points fitted into the bomb bays.

Wing Commander Watts in DZ599 led the raid, his log book entry being somewhat subdued. Navigator Cyril Hassell received a bar to his DFC for the spot-on timing and navigation the Squadron achieved.

On 22 June 1944, the Watts and Hassell team completed their 50th and final Op of the tour, and Cyril left on leave the next day. Awaiting his replacement and promised repatriation to New Zealand, Steven

ABOVE: Wing Commander S Watts DFC, MiD with Flying Officer Archie Matheson DFM posing in front of PF380 10 July 1944, prior to their last and fatal operation. Notification of Wing Commander Watts DSO was gazetted three days later

elected to fly again, this time with stand-in Navigator, Archie Matheson DFM, a fellow New Zealander. Flying PF380 they joined a planned raid to Berlin on 10/11 July 1944 but did not return.

It was Watts' 18th trip to the German Capital. His surviving log book shows 1420 hours completed, 947 on operations. Archie Matheson was an experienced navigator, this trip being his 42nd Op on 692 (having completed a tour with 218 Squadron on Stirlings). Perhaps Stephen Watts was helping out a pilotless Kiwi navigator to complete his last tour. Later Steven's long time friend, John Saunderson heard they had been shot down in flames over Bonn, but nothing was ever found.

Archie left a wife waiting in his home town of Featherston while Steve's fiancee would not need her new wedding dress.

That he was held in such high regard has come from many veteran aircrew. Even after his death, new crews coming on to 692 learnt of the huge respect he held by Squadron members.

Over 60 years after his death his wartime friend and Second in Command, John Saunderson still remembered the debt he owed to Stephen Watts and sought out members of the Watts family to pass on photographs and press cuttings from 692 days. Such was the mana of this man as a pilot, commander and friend.

– Stephen Watts

Compiled from logbooks, diaries, letters and albums held by his neice Shirley Thomas.

Chapter 14 – Special People

An Exceptional Young Man in the Prime of Life

Combat Report 27/28 August 1943 156 Squadron

Lancaster III, GT - B JA 697
Bomb Load: 4 x TI Green, 3 x 1000 GP, 1 x 4000 HC
Target: Nuremburg

Aircraft 'B' Captained by F/L Thomson was detailed as backer-up in a raid on Nuremburg. On returning at 0210 hours, 2,000 feet, position 50 33J 04 07E, a burst of fire from a Ju88 on the starboard quarter hit the aircraft wing and damaged the front turret. The attack was over in two seconds and neither rear nor mid-upper gunners were able to open fire.

So 'a near thing' was duly recorded at debriefing. John Thomson's way of looking at life and war were summarised in his DFC recommendation: "He came to this Squadron with a very high reputation as a pilot and has displayed courage and determination in identifying the target and pressing home his attack."

Long John (as his friends called him, he was 6 feet 3½ inches tall) could also be laconic as his log book records.

1944 May, 13	Mosquito 'H'	Ops Bourg Leopald 1,000'	"Balls up"
1944 May, 31	Mosquito 'A'	Saumaur 3,000'	"Belly Landed"
1944 June, 12	Mosquito 'P'	Poitiers 800'	"5 holes"
1944 June, 15	Mosquito 'G'	Chatellerault 500'	"2 RSF"

ABOVE: The V1 depot at L'isle on 18 August 1944 after a visit by 627 Squadron (F/O Thomson)

ABOVE: Deelen Airfield Holland on 15 August 1944, part of a cine film taken by F/L Harris after two Yellow TI's had been dropped

LEFT: A further still from the cine film showing the raid developing, taken from 11,000 feet. The yellow TI smoke is drifting towards top right

Kiwis Do Fly

Obviously the lower John flew the less damage his aircraft suffered, but following his May 13 'balls up' John and his Navigator, Flying Officer Harris subsequently spent a few hours on dive bombing practice and after the belly landing his usual mount AZ-A didn't come back on to Squadron strength.

Two years earlier John had formed up with his crew at 25 OTU (Finningley) and joined 12 Squadron and its Wellingtons at Wickenby. He would go on to fly 87 operations and serve on four Squadrons.

Writing John Thomson's obituary in the 1990 issue of the Wickenby Register, his first navigator and life long friend John Wilkin said:

"Johnny Thomson was good looking, of slim build and had a liking for rum; but more especially he frightened the life out of us by continually landing on the airfield other than in the specified manner. His calm and calculated remark was always. "Shit she fell out of my hands." Eventually the crew were posted to 12 Squadron which had just moved from Binbrook to Wickenby. Our billet was a Nissen hut close to the solid fuel dump. It was in the cold dank atmosphere of that communal site and after many hours flying in the Wimpy that we got to know each other and to recognise that we had 'acquired' an exceptional man as Skipper."

"The first Ops over occupied Europe were naturally exciting but Johnny really showed his mettle after

LEFT: Long John with his three loves, beer, golf and Mosquitos. Drawn in 1950 during John's RAF commission

RIGHT: 627 Squadron HQ at Woodhall Spa

ABOVE: John's favourite pastime – to John's right is F/O KW Gale an RAAF navigator (killed over Rennes on 8 June 1944) and F/O Foxcroft DFC, an RAF Pilot who was also killed attacking a gun battery at St Valery on 27 May 1944

LEFT: It's 'Johnny Beade's not mine,' but on 31st May flying 'A' they belly landed on return from Ops to Saumar

RIGHT: John with Brian Harris's Sextant, 'What's this for?'

Chapter 14 – Special People

LEFT: John Thomson's Navigator Flt Lt Brian Harris DFC. Brian had a supply of 8mm Kodachrome colour cine film and recorded a unique set of scenes of 627 Squadron aircraft, Crews and John Thomson. The film was released as 'Mosquitos Airborne!'

ABOVE: Mosquito Pilot taken by his Navigator

LEFT: 12 Squadron Wickenby days

Left to right: Jock Craighead (Gunner), Charles Hamilton (B/A), John Thomson (Pilot) John Wilkin (Navigator), Fitz Farnell (W/Op)

we had converted to Lancasters in December 1942. Like other crews we had our share of heavy flak and the occasional clash with Bf110s and Ju88's but his skill in throwing the aircraft into corkscrews and dives enabled us to keep out of trouble most of the time and return safely, but shaken. During this period we were 'loaned' to No 101 Squadron, stationed at Holme-on-Spalding Moor, as they had sustained heavy losses but after just three Ops we were returned to 12 Squadron Wickenby, as they had suffered a similar fate."

"Halfway through our first tour of Ops we had pranged the Flight Commander's nice new Lancaster into a useless heap when Johnny suddenly announced that we should 'Opt' for the Pathfinders of No 8 Group. I don't think any of us were keen but we were loath to lose a first class Skipper."

"So Johnny Thomson and I arrived at Warboys to fly with 156 Squadron. We carried on to complete our first tour and were given three weeks leave before returning to start the second tour. During this period of leave I got married. Johnny was my best man and the rest of the crew were ushers – until they all fell down!! Johnny remember, was thousands of miles away from home yet he tried to insist that we should all go our own way.

Charles' parents would have none of this and he became one of the family for evermore. Such was his impact on everyone he met – a kindly, loveable and genial man in a world of chaos."

"The crew returned to Warboys and Johnny, Charles and myself, the survivors of the original Wimpey crew, eventually completed our second tour in September, 1943. Johnny went to 1662 HCU at Blyton, the satellite of 1656 HCU at Lindholme – where Charles and I ended up."

"After a month Johnny decided that he had had enough of HCU when a pupil pilot when told to re-start the two starboard engines proceeded to feather the two good port engines. Not a healthy exercise!! As a result Johnny returned alone to No 8 Group but this time to fly Mosquitos."

"Certainly Johnny regarded himself as just an ordinary bloke who wanted nothing out of life except happiness for his family and friends. We in the UK who knew him are confident that he achieved that end but to us he was an exceptional man. God bless him."

Eighteen months earlier on his first Op after being loaned to 101 Squadron, the trip to Essen was interupted by a fighter; "shot by fighter, pranged on return" was his log book entry and Lancaster W4792 PH-M went away for repair but like the previous 'interruptions' the operation was completed and the crew returned safely.

John Thomson was one of over 6,000 New Zealand volunteers who flew with RAF Bomber Command. He served from October 1945 through to war's end and somehow avoided the 'chop' that claimed so many lives. His targets weren't soft; on joining 12 Squadron in January he and his crew went to Essen three times and Berlin once within ten days, the odds were not in his favour.

Recommended for the DFC in May 1943 after finishing his tour with 156 Pathfinder Squadron, he

Kiwis Do Fly

Chapter 14 – Special People

ABOVE: 'M' showing over 75 Ops up, with its crew

ABOVE: 156 Squadron RAF Warboys, the PFF airfield Left to Right: Jock Craighead (AG), John Baxter, John Wilkin (Navigator), Charlie Hamilton, Titch Towson, John Thomson, Fritz Farnell

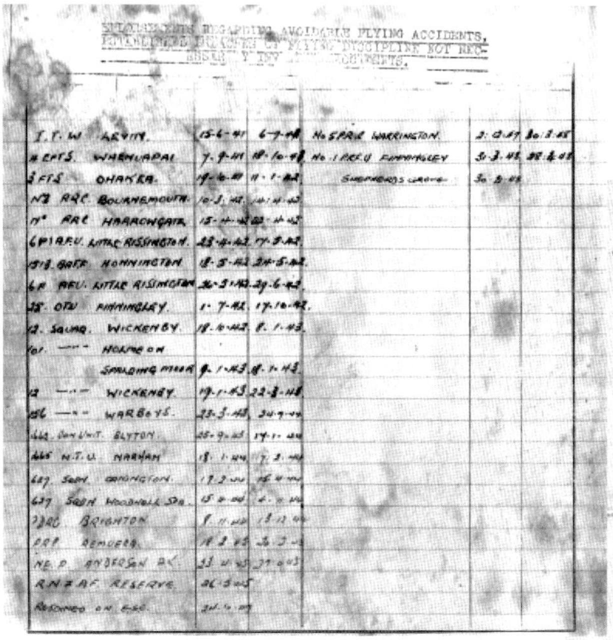

ABOVE: A flying career on a page

RIGHT: Letter from the New Zealand High Commissioner Bill Jordan to John's parents

met with New Zealand's legendary High Commissioner in London, Bill Jordan. Bill kept a fatherly eye on 'his' boys and would apply significant pressure in the right quarters to correct any perceived wrong.

After his brief spell with 1662 Heavy Conversion Unit at Blyton, John moved to the Pathfinder Mosquito Training Unit at Marham, then joined 627 Squadron at Oakington in February 1944 prior to its transfer to 5 Group. Here 627 became a specialist dive bombing and low level marking unit. John enjoyed every minute and brought back some exceptional photographs. In mid August 1944 he took several very detailed photos of the raids on Deelen Airfield and the V1 site at L'isle.

Wing Commander Guy Gibson VC of 617 Dam Busters fame had links with 627, borrowing a PR Lightning from Group HQ, he photographed Deelan four days after Johnny's raid. One month later with Coningsby's Mosquito unavailable, Gibson travelled to Woodhall Spa with Navigation Officer S/L J Warwick DFC. Here the Commanding Officer of 627, Wing Commander Curry, signed out a Mk XX Mosquito (KB 267) AZ-E[2]. This famous pilot wasn't to return. Perhaps hit over the target or with barometrically fused TI's hung up, Gibson's Mosquito circled Steenburgen in Holland, on fire before crashing and exploding. There was little to bury. Given that the navigator had no time on Mosquitos and Wing Commander Gibson had just eleven hours, neither were fully competent. 627 Squadron members felt the major cause was pilot/navigator unfamilarity with the new Mark XX. "Mossies were lovely to fly but you had to be on your game to fly them well, especially the later marks."

Long John was remembered by his crew mates as being a cheerful and likeable character so relaxed he was prone to going to sleep in a chair even with a party going on around him. A fellow New Zealand pilot, John Buckley, recalls him asleep by the fire with a cat curled in his lap. One of the lads popped a Verey cartridge into the iron fireplace. When it went off both Johnny and the cat were in mid-air heading West.

With 87 Ops completed Johnny was withdrawn from service and in spite of his grumbles his mates convinced him he'd done more than his fair share and deserved to be repatriated to New Zealand. Post-war John rejoined the RAF on a short service commission along with 200 other Kiwis pilots to enjoy another four years of flying, but without the bangs.

So often, others who served with the New Zealand volunteers spoke of the something extra they brought to a crew, a flight or even a Squadron. Free from class distinctions and confident in their physical ability, the RAF servicemen and women they served with, from ground crew to HQ, always seemed to be proud that they knew a Kiwi. But don't ask a Kiwi veteran that "Bullshit" would be the reply, but special they were.

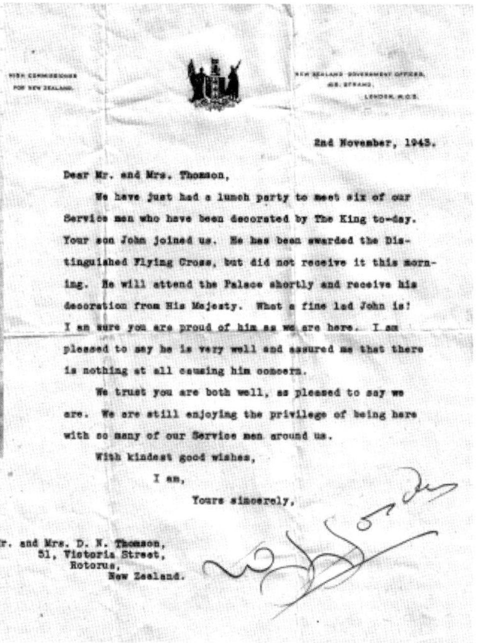

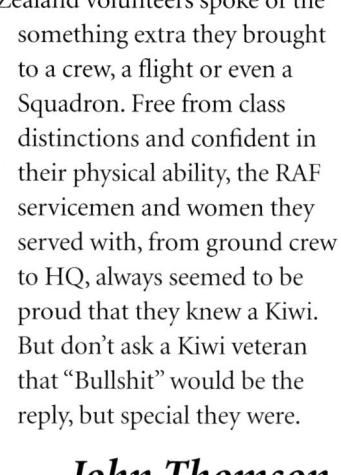

– John Thomson

Compiled from logbooks, photographs, diaries and albums held by his daughter Mrs K. Lawson.

Chapter 15

Keeping Lucky

Like the occasional Oops! referred to in Chapter Eight, service life in wartime was filled with the mundane, the funny, and the outright dangerous, but all crews who completed 'one' (one tour) smile, perhaps with relief of the time they were just a little bit lucky.

Kiwis Do Fly

What Oxygen

"Once I had completed Oboe beam training on Airspeed Oxfords a posting to 109 PFF Squadron followed. I was fortunate in being picked by a very good navigator at Warboys. Jeff (Flight Lieutenant Jeffery Watkins DFC and bar) saw us through a full tour without too much fun and games. However there are always little surprises and in a mid tour operation we were cruising along on track waiting to be called into the Oboe beam and holding 34,000 feet to pick up the transmission when Jeff asked "where is the spare helmet?" I replied, "behind me, why?" "Lost my oxygen" and as he turned to reach behind me he collapsed across my legs. Absolutely right out and quicker than you can say it."

"I undid my safety harness and parachute to give some freedom of movement so I could raise Jeff off my legs, but I just couldn't do it. My position was wrong and at that altitude I had no strength. This had all taken just a few seconds but the horrible rattling noises coming from Jeff said "down now!" I pushed the Mosquitos nose down and didn't reduce power and boy did we come down."

"Jeff's terrible noises gradually eased so I levelled off at 17,000 feet by using the trim tabs as the control column forces were just too great to do it alone. Jeff came round, sorted out his oxygen problem, so back up to 34,000 feet we went, but by then we were too late to be called into mark the target."

"It was a bit of a wake up call to see how hypoxia works very, very fast at that altitude."

– Keith Boles

ABOVE & BELOW: Roy Montrowe (Pilot) and Guy Soulsby (Navigator) in a 148 Squadron Wellington during a daylight run over the Western desert, October 1941. Low level and no flak permits their oxygen masks to be put aside, however on the nightly runs to Tobruk they were strapped up tight!
Later over Europe the intense cold created additional problems and rear gunners especially recall the long icicles growing from the masks like a beard

Chapter 15 – Keeping Lucky

Low Flying is Fun

"Before joining 617 Squadron, low level flying was taboo and a Court Martial offence if pilots were caught indulging. As an official part of our pre Dams raid training we tackled this phase with a great deal of pleasure. It was not without its moments and there were some close calls. Low flying at 200 mph plus came naturally to some pilots, those who were able to judge just when to pull up to clear the trees, buildings, structures ahead of them. Others had real problems during this early stage of training, clipping the tops of trees. The twigs and leaves sucked into the air intakes overheated the engines, so it was a matter of learning by experience how late to delay gaining height. I took to low level flying and became quite proficient flying well below tree top height. During all my time on 617 we engaged in low level training much of the time."

"On one of these training exercises, this time at night, we were flying down the North Sea in somewhat hazy conditions when, immediately ahead of us was a convoy of ships. I quickly requested Percy Pigeon, my Wireless Operator, to fire off the colours of the day. In the flare light I could see quite a number of barrage balloons attached to various ships. I pulled back and went shooting up through the balloons and cables and with Lady Luck on my side, or shoulder (which ever), I cleared the convoy without hitting anything. The convoy remained silent. We were very fortunate as the Navy would normally shoot at anything friend, foe or unidentified. They must have used different colours of the day because it never made any difference."

"Parts of Lincolnshire were designated for low level training. The county has a large area of fen country in the South East adjacent to the Wash. The area was inhabited by myriads of seagulls and water fowl and during our low level practices over the area they would take flight on the approach of low flying aircraft"

"One seagull was a bit slow in avoiding our monster of a plane and hit my windscreen almost dead centre. It smashed a hole in the screen and came through the cockpit like a cannonball between Frank Appleby, my Flight Engineer and myself and hit the curtain shielding the Navigators compartment. It ended up as a rather messy lump of feathers and flesh on the cockpit floor. If it had hit the screen dead in front of me I shudder to think what might have happened. At that height, maybe one crashed plane and no survivors."

"Over three days in May 1943, twelve of our modified Lancs were detailed to carry out a final trial, dropping inert 'Upkeeps' at Chesil Beach. We were to fly at 232 mph and 60 feet, on which Barnes Wallis had based his calculations. Because some pilots flew at the incorrect height or airspeed the splash from the Upkeeps as they hit the water was great enough to hit the aircraft. Six of the twelve were damaged, mainly in the rear turret area. I was one of the guilty ones with Harvey Weeks my Rear Gunner being jammed in his turret and unable to get out until we landed back at base. It put a huge strain on the station fitters to repair the aircraft in time for the Operation. As a result of that trial, the airspeed for the actual Operation was reduced to 220 mph."

"After the Dams raid the Squadron carried out a lot of high level precision bombing, but low flying had become second nature. On 30 October 1943, Nicky Ross returned from a training flight with debris in his air intakes. He was summoned to appear before the Station Commander and explain the reason for this! On being accused of flying at an unnecessarily low height, Nicky responded that he had not flown below tree top height, (the official rule), to which Station Commander said, "well, Ross, this is the first time that I have ever learnt that rabbits live in trees." There seemed to be a general acceptance that Nicky had indeed, bagged a rabbit!"

– Les Munro

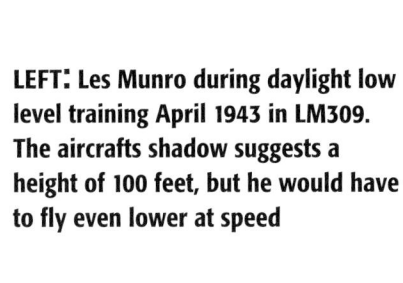

LEFT: Les Munro during daylight low level training April 1943 in LM309. The aircrafts shadow suggests a height of 100 feet, but he would have to fly even lower at speed

A Stuff-up is Always Fun

Having survived a tour on Lancasters with 100 Squadron (and a serious brush with Luftwaffe night fighters) Harry was looking forward to a quieter life at OTU.

"We were on survivors leave and a second tour on Ops was at least six months away depending upon losses. What we didn't know that six mis-delivered PBY Catalinas would lead us to a much pleasanter, safer world."

At this stage of the war the Lend Lease programme was in full swing with multi-engined aircraft for RAF service being flown directly from North America to Scotland.

In this case six PBY aircraft from the San Diego factory of Consolidated became caught up in the trans Atlantic ferry services, rather than the trans-Pacific service to Hawaii.

Rather than adjust paperwork, the Lend Lease board determined that the aircraft should be returned so Harry with a crew were 'volunteered' to return JX 629 from Preston in the UK to San Diego.

"The planned route was across the Atlantic, then down to the Bahamas, across the Carribean and finally into San Diego. The route was marvellous, the flying relaxed and we really only flew when pressed by signals from the Air Ministry. In all we were able to take three weeks to complete the trip. The RAF tended to lose chaps on ferry flights and we hoped we would go into limbo for a month or so in somewhere nice. Post-war, I recall a ferry flight of Oxfords to Norway where the crews were billeted out for three months before someone missed them."

"This long distance flying was very enjoyable and in the end we were told to wait in Los Angeles to pick up a new C-54 Skymaster from Douglas. We were officially posted to 231 Squadron and flew down to Australia. For the rest of the war we flew regular services from Darwin to the Cocos Islands and Ceylon. Certainly a pleasanter way to pass the war than as a Flight Engineer in a Lanc over Europe."

– *Harry Widdup*

Chapter 15 – Keeping Lucky

To Berlin in a Big Wind

Having survived a very dodgy first Op, Des Andrewes (Nav) and his crew captained by 'Chook' Struthers left Mildenhall on 24 March in GI-M ED619, a Lancaster III of 622 Squadron, on their fourth Operation.

Berlin was the target and that raid became infamous as 'the night of the big winds.'

"All of our plotting that night was based on the met forecast winds of around 35 knots. We seemed to keep in the bomber stream out over the North Sea then headed into the Baltic with a planned landfall over Denmark."

"Our gunners saw flak over to starboard and it seemed a bit heavy for a coastal fishing village. I hadn't twigged our drift was probably taking us nearer Rostock. As the broadcast update of wind speeds increased so at our level (20,000 feet) I made an allowance for twenty knots."

"The planned route called for a final timed 60 mile leg to Berlin but before I gave the pilot this heading our Bomb Aimer sung out," "there's a lake in a park ahead. It looks just like the briefing photo of Havelsee in Berlin."

"After my first Op when I was 35 miles out on my coast land fall, the Squadron Navigation Officer hadn't been impressed. The Commanding Officer recommended that to finish our tour we had better stay nearer the main stream (Chook had covered for me by saying he felt safer out of the bomber stream!) But now I thought, I've mucked it up again, back to OTU for me!"

"We must have been one of the first over Berlin that night as everything was dead quiet. No flak and no markers so I called up the skipper and suggested we head due east and orbit for a while. The crew were not impressed!"

"Our gunners were told to watch for the markers and as soon as they went off, so would we. My diary records our bombing run at a heading of 060° while the main stream force had 200° as their run in."

"We got a good photo flash but it was two days later when the photo interpretation bods could locate precisely where we'd bombed, just six miles off target!"

"Once we left Berlin I started a new air plot still using the updated wind data being broadcast for Osnabruk so we would avoid the Ruhr. Our

ABOVE & BELOW: Berlin Cathedral – the old and the new

ABOVE: Buildings in Berlin remain pocked by splinters even today

Kiwis Do Fly

skipper, Chook, kept asking for headings as there was a big flak belt up ahead. I still couldn't work out what the hell was happening. Anyway I gave a series of courses that took us up around the top of 'Happy Valley' (The Ruhr) and then out. The first Gee fix put us 45 miles south of track. Oh not again – it's back to OTU for sure and a new crew for certain."

"Once we'd landed the skipper asked me, "What really went wrong?" I didn't know."

"Des and his crew picked up the perimeter bus to go for debriefing and at the next stop the pilot and navigator of that Lancaster were having a heated argument about fixes. This navigator slumped down next to Des Andrewes, very upset "we didn't even get there." I was really pleased as he'd not be the only one reporting to the Navigation Leader next day."

"But at debriefing Des Andrewes and the crew were congratulated for finding the target in 85 knot winds. Apparently the Met Flight boys didn't believe their measurements so knocked a few knots off. These wind speeds being reported were not believed by the Met Flight Office either so they knocked quite a few more off."

"The next morning Des was amused to listen to the BBC announcing another night of successful Bomber Command raids on Berlin, Leipzig, Hanover and numerous targets in the Ruhr!"

"Some days later the navigators ran a plot on position and found some aircraft had encountered 138 knot winds."

"We'd never heard of jet streams (or even jets), but we never got into so much trouble again once the ground mapping H2S sets came into use."

Des and his crew kept lucky, completing 30 operations with 282 hours on night operations.

– Des Andrewes

RIGHT: *"This mercator plotting chart was kept on the wall of our room and filled in the morning after each raid. The shaded areas are heavy and light flak zones. The bomb symbols show our targets and each is dated"*

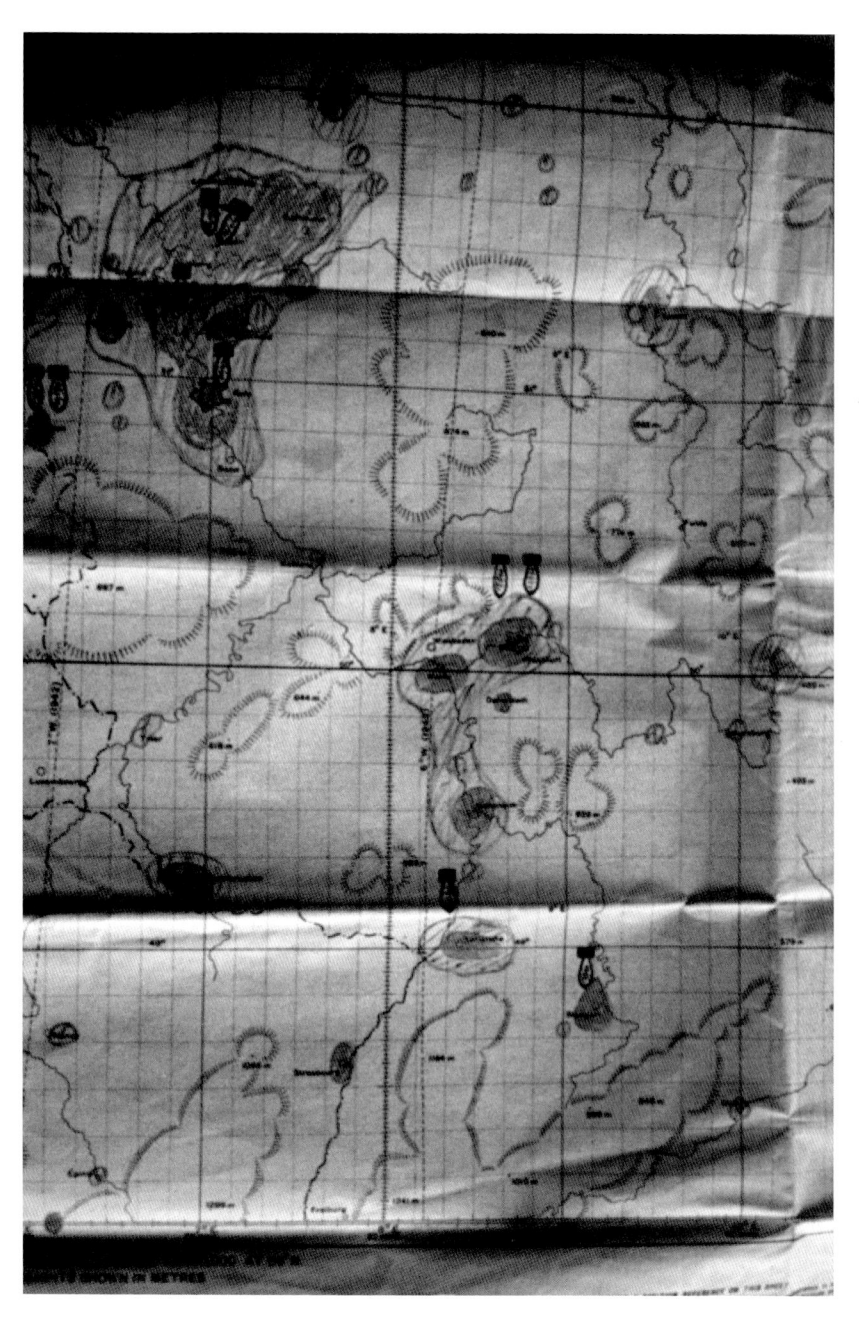

RIGHT: Reichstag restored but Des's crew hadn't touched it

198

Chapter 15 – Keeping Lucky

Our Last Op

A PFF tour was complete at 50 operations, presumably as a Pathfinder Operation was considered 'easier' than the normal bomber squadron requirement (30 operations). Robin Craw's final Op was to Stuttgart on August 18 1944 and was recorded years later by his Canadian Flight Engineer Jack Owen.

"Smithy the wireless operator appears fiddling with his pipe as usual. It has just fallen to bits again. He is looking a little unhappy which is unlike him. We have shared a few scared moments together. I sat on his lap once when the situation was very uncomfortable and sharp foreign pieces of metal were flying around us as he was supplied with armour plate behind his chair for protection from such things. There's always much laughter when we recall these times."

"We wend our way to the briefing room with the talking and laughing and the 'leg pulling' that goes on. Inwardly we are dreading what the target will be tonight and on what route. As we enter the briefing room the first thing we see is the large map of Europe which completely covers one wall. On it is pinned the 'black ribbon' indicating the route from the base to the target and the different return trip. I look at the route and groan to myself for Stuttgart is the target for tonight but WHAT a route has been decided to get there. First over France then the battlefront down towards the south to bluff the enemy of our objective then again turning up towards the target. This is going to be longer and deadlier than Berlin could ever be."

"I join my crew at our table and settle down to prepare my fuel log, calculating our loaded weight including bombs, fuel, load, equipment etc. Our estimated time of the trip and speed can be roughly calculated after allowing for the wind velocity and direction. If the wind changes, consumption can alter considerably."

"A hush descends over the room as the Commanding Officer commences his briefing orders and warnings, "Keep away from London and the barrage balloons." The Skipper and I glance at each other momentarily we remember a past experience when we found ourselves in the middle of our own flak and enemy aircraft which were attacking London."

"The Commanding Officer drones on about flying levels, shipping, cloud and other cheerful subjects such as:" "Enemy fighters are increasing their activity in this area and don't hang around the target area or the battlefront you'll be asking for the defence on the ground to line a bead on you." "As if we would give them half a chance."

"After a final warning to the air gunners not to shoot down any Lancasters, the Navigator Leader spouts away a mass of technical data followed by more details from the Bombing Leader."

"I have to write swiftly to take down the settings for the computer box. It's a large box of tricks which controls the bomb sight automatically, counteracting drift, variation of height, and speed of the aircraft. Then the Met Officer gives us all the gen on the weather. Cloud may be encountered over the target and may mean a change of height to gain visibility for aiming. I am not keen on another wrathful session from the rest of the crew caused by my missing the target initially and having to do another two runs over the target. The icing layer is at 20,000 feet which does not worry us as our heavily laden kite could never make that height."

"The Engineering Leader is next – more data on fuel load, armaments, equipment and centre of gravity positions. The Commanding Officer has the final word again regarding secrecy, target and take-off times and finishes off wishing all "happy landings.""

"After studying photographs of the target and drawing a rough diagram of approach I pack up and go to the Mess for eggs, ham and chips. While I sit eating, I look around and notice there are very few of the old faces left – losses from previous trips and transfers to other Squadrons have taken their toll."

"I don't delay long over the meal, have a final look around my room make sure I have my Saint Christopher and walk down to the flight's section. There I spend a little time studying forms and figures, pick up my parachute harness and Mae West (bless her), and take a ride out to our aircraft."

"It's a warm pleasant evening with a clear sky except for being a little dull high up in the sky. I pat the head of an Alsatian dog who is still waiting for his master to return from a trip several nights ago. He looks up but doesn't wag his tail. His eyes look very sad and I wonder what good is coming out of all the misery and grief caused by war."

"The driver of the bus sings out 'A for Apple' and stops on the tarmac near our Lancaster. I glance at the Alsatian once more, grab all my flying kit and clamber out."

"By the time I have loaded the front turret guns, set up the automatic bomb sight, checked controls, fuel cocks, gauges, switches, then checked the whole aircraft inside and out the whole crew have arrived. The skipper remarks on the condition of the aircraft we have been given for this trip and his face shows a dubious expression as he notes the dilapidated state it appears to be in."

"Judging by the rows of bombs painted on the nose it has done many trips and I console myself with the fact that it must be airworthy as the ground crew have checked and signed all the necessary forms for clearance."

"I squeeze through the small opening by the wireless operators chair and trip over his harness which he has left on the floor. I compliment him hurriedly and finally make it to the nose thinking to myself how quickly I can bale out if trouble necessitates such unpleasant action."

"I don my helmet and plug in the intercom to hear the skippers voice, "Are you ready Engineer?" I reply,

Kiwis Do Fly

"Just a minute Skip." Then Johnny the navigator's voice intercepts with, "Come on Knob Basher." Again compliments fly back and forth in a lurid fashion whilst I turn on the fuel cocks. I open the cockpit window and yell through to the ground crew below. "Stand by to prime port outer stand clear of prop." After all four engines have been primed in turn I yell out, "Contact port outer switches on" and press the starter button. The prop turns slowly and the engine coughs. "Come on you" I mutter and the engine comes to life with a healthy roar. With all the engines running I check the gauges and red lights for trouble. "Engines okay Skipper, bomb doors closed, cold air on, 'M' gear, flap 25°, trim zero lateral, nose heavy, booster switches off, ground switch to flight, okay to taxi out."

"The pilot and engineer complete the take-off check and the aircraft moves forward as the skipper releases the brakes. I write my first entry in my log book a duty which is carried out every 20 minutes throughout the flight. Engine conditions temperatures, pressures etc, fuel consumption and tank changes."

"We have now joined the long procession of aircraft moving around the perimeter of the aerodrome. I am constantly checking the gauges for any sign of impending engine failure or weakness. Maximum power is needed for take-off when the aircraft is loaded with fuel, equipment and bombs."

"At last it is our turn standing at the end of the runway. The engines have been tested and the Skipper calls out, "Okay, stand by for take-off." I slowly push the four throttles to the fully open position. The aircraft is now shaking badly from nose to tail and the engine noise is deafening. It slowly moves forward gathering speed and my eyes are trying to see everything at once. I feel the tail lifting as the speed increases, the bumping of the wheels lessens and the end of the

ABOVE: After their last op, the crew, hair combed, pose the next day for the camera at Oakington, August 19, 1944
Left to Right: **STANDING:** Gordon Gibbon (B/A), Bert Fox (M/UG)
SITTING: Ron Johnson (Nav), Jack Owen (F/E), Robin Craw (Pilot), Ron Smith (W/Op), Bob Harpur (R/G)

runway and the railway which runs across outside the perimeter rushes towards me. The Skipper eases back the control column and I pray to myself that the aircraft will answer. The bumping of the wheels on the tarmac changes to hefty ones and then stops. We are airborne and the railway rushes past underneath. The skipper calls out "Wheels up, climbing power." I snap up the undercarriage lever and ease back the four throttles and four mixture levers as I acknowledge his instructions. The roar lessens and settles down to an even tone as I synchronise the four engines, sit back with a sigh of relief and wipe the perspiration from my face. The worst part of the trip is over."

"This is the last trip when two whole tours will have been completed."

"I am staring down through the bombing window of our aircraft and can see many coloured specks of light in the black night ahead."

Johnny, the navigator's voice crackles over the intercom; "Estimated time of arrival over target two minutes forty five seconds time," I take a final glance over the bombing instrument dials and switch settings, remove the bomb release switch from its clip and answer the navigator. "Target sighted about four miles approximately at 11 o'clock" and settle myself comfortably on my stomach in the sighting position."

"The Skipper has a healthy respect for this area and is now violently weaving across the sky alternately swinging the aircraft onto each wing up port to starboard. As I lie waiting and watching the target coming closer for what seems hours I can hear the crump, crump of bursting anti-aircraft shells and the wind whistling past the opening beneath my chin."

"Curly, the mid upper gunner, reports flak at a thousand yards to port and an aircraft falling in flames. I look to port and see a ball of flame disintegrating as it drops towards the ground. If anyone manages to bale out of that kite it will be a miracle."

"The quiet voice of our hefty New Zealand skipper (six foot four inches in his socks) comes over the intercom; "What about opening the bomb doors Engineer?"

"I judge the distance again. The spots below are now larger and answer, "Just about another minute to go Skip, keep on weaving." As I finish speaking there is a heavy thump on the port side and the aircraft feels as if it is standing on its starboard wing tip. I feel very cold and shivery. My mouth is dry and there is a hard lump in my stomach trying to force its way upwards. I remember wondering afterwards why I had to wipe the perspiration off my face to clear my vision. I must shut out all other thoughts and concentrate on my bomb sight which is now almost sighting the first target indicator flares below. I call out to the skipper, "Straighten up now, bomb doors open, left, left." I am surprised at the sound of my voice which does not indicate how frightened I am. The Skipper's voice answers, "Bomb doors opening" the aircraft is still going to starboard and I repeat, "Left, left." The lights swing slowly onto the tracking line in the bomb sight. "Right, steady" the coloured lights are almost up to the cross as the line of track slowly aligns itself with the spots of light. "Bombs going now," I yell as I press the switch in my left hand. I feel the aircraft lifting under me as each bomb leaves its hook. I call out, "Bombs away" and press the switch several times to set the camera in motion. Each photo taken is indicated by a flashing light. At last the light goes out. "Bombs gone, close bomb doors, cameras stopped, get weaving Skipper." The roar from the wind rushing through the open bomb doors gradually fades away and I am suddenly aware of the crump, crump of shells outside bursting around us. The gunners are now busy reporting over the intercom. "Flak at nine o'clock Skip, flak at four o'clock." There's a blinding white flash directly ahead and I feel the floor fall away as the aircraft goes into a dive. I struggle up from the nose of the aircraft to my customary position in the cockpit beside the Skipper. I am still dazzled as I fumble around for the plug to connect my intercom. Then I hear the skippers calm voice, "Hello Engineer, are you alright?" When the aircraft dived I thought we'd been hit and as second pilot, my haste in regaining the cockpit can be clearly understood. I reply "I'm okay Skipper but I wish you wouldn't go into these fancy dives." He only chuckles and asks me if I've checked the bomb bay for any hang ups. I reluctantly leave and go below again to check the bomb racks through the observation windows. I notice many jagged holes in the fuselage which were not there before the action."

"As I climb up again I make a mental note to look for pieces of shrapnel in the aircraft when we land back at base."

"We are now well clear of the target. Ten miles away to the port side the coloured lights have disappeared and in their place there is a huge column of smoke rising far up above our height."

Reconnaissance Mosquitos returning from a bombing raid reported seeing sixteen square miles of flame on the ground below and flying through smoke at a height of eight thousand feet.

With 714 hours logged after volunteering for aircrew training and now a Flight Lieutenant (DFC) Robin returned to New Zealand and eventually to his reserved occupation as a Canterbury Farmer.

– *Jack Owen*

Flight Engineer RCAF on Robin Craw's crew recalling the operation from a Flight Engineer's and Bomb Aimer's perspective

Kiwis Do Fly

Diversions

Throughout his wartime career in Stirlings (15 Squadron), Lancasters (622 Squadron), and Mosquitos (487 Squadron) or as OC Admin RNZAF Fiji (in the 1950's), Bunny Burrows had an eye for the humorous and for what was going on around him.

Destined to be a tomato grower (but not before 20 years service had been served) his non Ops diary records some of the 'other life' most crews enjoyed.

New Year's Eve 1943 Westcott 11 OTU:

"We arrived from RAF Millom via Bournemouth to find no transport laid on. Being press on types we marched to Westcott and into the Officers Mess. Too late for breakfast, we cleaned up the sideboard goodies. A great start for OTU Course 63 but our staff officers went hungry."

15 Squadron (Mildenhall 1943):

"Most Kiwi aircrew had 'incidents,' being young, full of fun, no parents to please, and with beer, food and sometimes women on-tap and without centuries of a class system to conform to, we tried to have a great time. Mind you, you must keep away from Mildenhalls Chop WAAF even though she was good looking."

Andy Haden was a hard man, from Opotiki a 'Holy Coast Man' he would proclaim. Now a bomb aimer, he had been re-mustered from pilot to nav, then to bomb aimer. He loved his beer. Like every good rugby player, and he had a broken nose and cauliflower ears to prove it. Andy and bikes didn't go together once they were both fully fuelled. One night, thinking the bike was a horse, he crashed into the Mess building and lay outside covered in frost until woken by the kitchen staff. Andy survived, did another tour and won a DFC.

Bikes weren't an option for us as the Squadron Bulldog (naturally called Pilot Officer Prune) simply tore them to pieces. Our carefully cadged four gallon tins of petrol (always aviation grade) were also irresistible to him. Whether it was the reflection from the tin or the smell of petrol, we never found out but Prune would bunt these all over the station.

Returning to Mildenhall one night Andy (fully fuelled as usual) decided to give the Engine Wackers mobile crane a spin. A few of

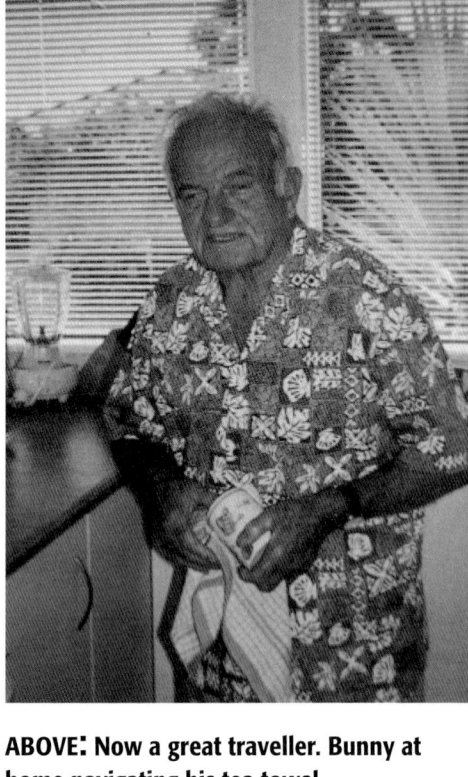

ABOVE: Now a great traveller. Bunny at home navigating his tea towel

LEFT: Mildenhall 1943, 15 Squadron and Bulldog Prune takes time off from petrol tin bunting for a Squadron photograph

ABOVE: A busy time on 487 Squadron flying from Rosieres, patrolling for trains and road transport while keeping out of trouble

his noble fellow officers spotted him from the Mess and arranged an issue bike, empty shoes and jacket and trousers right in front of the crane. Inevitably Andy ran smack over them. The crash and crunch saw him leap from the cab and rush into the mess, "Chaps I've killed an officer, squashed him flat, nothing left." Andy kept away from the beer for one whole day after that. The bike cost him 3/6.

Jan. 1945 2nd TAF, Rosieres (487 Squadron):

It's an ex Luftwaffe bomber station and the accommodation is an old run-down Chateau, but its got a great stock of champagne. We're having a shooting contest, trying to get the rats with our revolvers before they get back into their hole. Despite the beverages, our aim was poor. The Frenchies are trying to get us to drink their champagne but we've got the good ex-German stocks of Pilsener beer and Reserve champagne (one was kept for Bunny's wedding night and opened ten years later).

Brussels Melsbroek, 5 May 1945 (487 Squadron):

We'd been asked to host some admin types from London so we booked them into our local Bar and Bawdy House. It was all beer, bras, mattresses and boobs. The admin staff were appalled, especially as it was a very busy place and used not only by 487. They sent a very detailed signal back to London on the eve of VE day. The reply was swift, "please repeat which floor the mattresses are on."

– *Bunny Burrows*

ABOVE: Three of 487 Squadron's Mosquito FB VI's on patrol. Bunny navigating EG-T (MM 417)

Kiwis Do Fly

Altimeter Check

Robin had a busy war from the time he converted onto Stirlings at 1657 HCU Stradishall (in N3760 on 9 October 1943) until he finished his 50th Op with 7 Squadron on a raid to Bremen in August 18, 1944.

Starting on the Stirlings of 199 Squadron at Lakenheath, Robin and his crew completed 22 Ops without a problem including SOE drops near the Spanish border. "The run on March 7th 1944 was our longest with a 9 hour 15 minute outward leg but a 8 hour 25 minute home run. Perhaps it was down hill."

Robin recalls the PFF: "The official policy regarding PFF Squadrons was that as they were about to be formed, a selector (often Wing Commander Hamish McHaddie aka the 'body snatcher') would circulate all Squadrons in the Group and talk to those that had survived about 18 operations, or that had performed well. He gave a spiel about joining a select band, and out of the hum-drum of main force heavies. "Please just volunteer!" The chosen few would then be sent to training schools."

"For better or worse our crew was selected and we reluctantly had to leave a Squadron in which we were very happy. While all operations had hazards, on PFF, there was always the chance of creating a few more for yourself."

Robin and his crew did the obligatory week retraining at Warboys before arriving at Oakington where 7 Squadron was commanded by a fellow Kiwi, Wing Commander Fraser Barron. Their tour as bomb and flare dropping backer uppers or supporters didn't cause them a lot of concern but on July 5 on a run to Wizernes their antics to dislodge a hung up 1,000 lb bomb attracted a Ju88. "The Ju88 cannons caused enough damage to demand a visit to the emergency strip at Woodbridge in Suffolk."

"One episode is worth recording regarding altimeters. Before take-off altimeters were set at the barometric pressure of that particular airfield. During flight a figure plus or minus would be added to a figure on the wireless operator's briefing sheet – this was ostensibly to confuse the enemy. We were approaching Oakington in low cloud using beam approach when one of the crew yelled," "Hey Skip! There's bloody trees going past." "He was right, so I abandoned the landing and flew around again. The wireless operator (naughty boy) had added the figure given on the briefing sheet to the barometric reading on take-off. If we'd carried on attempting a landing it would have been underground. A serious talk to the wireless operator wasn't required, until after he'd stopped shaking."

– Robin Craw

ABOVE: Taken on passing out day from RNZAF Wigram's multiengine service course, prior to posting to UK as Bomber Command Pilots. John Tarbuck sitting beside the engine cowl of Oxford NZ 1288 just a yard away from Robin Craw, leaning from the pilot's seat. Neither would meet until 62 years later when this photograph was published in "Wednesday Bomber Boys" and Robin was recognised by his family

Chapter 15 – Keeping Lucky

It's all Over

RAF Mepal was home to 75 (New Zealand) Squadron. The Squadron had been formed in 1939 with Wellingtons purchased for the RNZAF. The Squadron remained in the 'front line' throughout World War Two. 75 (NZ) Squadron suffered a very high casualty rate with 452 New Zealand airmen being killed in action. On 24th April 1945 a raid to Bad Oldesloe was planned and this would be the Squadron's last operation. NE181 (JN–M) named 'The Captains Fancy' of 'C' Flight was on its 104th sortie and drawn to be the lead aircraft on a Gee-H raid.

Flying Officer Colin Emslie, the aircrafts navigator, kept a detailed log of this last operation:

Log: 24 April 1945

0200 hours – crew members awakened by Special Police. After morning ablutions off to respective messes for flying meal – Bacon & Egg.

0330 – Crews report to appropriate sections for first briefing. The navigators go to the Briefing Room and receive the details to prepare their Flight Plan.

0430 – The rest of the crews join their Navigators in the Briefing Room when we receive full details of the Operation.

0530 – Watches are synchronized and we depart to pick up our parachutes and other flying gear. Then wait for the transports to take us to our aircraft.
On arrival at dispersal the Pilot and Engineer make an external check of the aircraft. We all climb aboard and settle in.

0700 – Start up time and the engines roar into life. Pilot and Engineer go through the pre-flight check-list. Navigator checks all Nav. equipment is operating.
Taxi out to runway and join queue to take-off.

0711 – Airborne and fly to assembly area to complete formation of five flights of four aircraft headed by the leader for the day. Our aircraft Lancaster NE181 JN-M was the lead aircraft for formation No 5.

ABOVE: A copy of the Navigators log

0755 – Squadron sets course for target.

1042 – Arrive at target flights of four are in line astern. Guided by the lead navigator using Gee-H radar. The other three aircraft drop their load as the lead aircraft's load goes.

1107 – Squadron broke formation and aircraft flew back to base individually.

1257 – Arrived Base.

1320 – Landed.

"At no time was it indicated that this was the last bombing operation for the Squadron. I think it was a couple of days later that we knew there would be no more raids. We then commenced the food drops to the Netherlands."

– *Colin Emslie*

LEFT: The crew of NE181 after their last raid
Left to Right: F/Sgt J White RCAF (M/UG). F/Sgt S Heald RNZAF (B/A), Sgt R Wright RAF (R/G), F/O E Ware RNZAF (Pilot), F/Sgt W Cairns RNZAF (W/Op), Sgt D Carter RAF (F/E), F/O C Emslie RNZAF (Nav). This aircraft was earmarked for presentation to New Zealand but ended as scrap in 1947

205

Chapter 16

The Other Half

Aside from operations, fun in the Mess and going on leave, New Zealand airmen also had women in their sights. The station WAAFs, the local barmaids, civilians or perhaps the 'professionals' were all of interest.

Amongst the colonials who went overseas a few found ladies they loved. In the midst of death and uncertainty some took the risk and married. Their wives had no idea what awaited them in those southern islands of New Zealand, twelve thousand miles away and still a pioneering country.

To those fine women who took the chance and followed their man home, I have the utmost respect.

Chapter 16 – The Other Half

Canada oh Canada

Jack Shorthouse's operational tour was over on January 11 1940 when the Fairey Battle he was piloting was shot down by Bf 109s over France.

By August 1940, Jack had recovered and rejoined 12 Squadron at Binbrook. He took another Battle (this time P2321) up for a bit of local flying and re-familiarisation, to build his confidence and to confirm to himself that he still had 'it'.

Jack was quickly posted to 1 PRU at Heston and flew their sky-blue, camera fitted, Spitfires (P9310, and R6902) into occupied Europe. "Up there alone with one engine just wasn't me, I was somewhat unimpressed. The long flights at high altitude seemed to affect me, so I was then offered the chance to go over to Canada where the Empire Training Scheme was being set up. I welcomed this opportunity and shipped out on December 6 1940 with 32 Service Flying Training School, one of three RAF SFTS units sent to Canada.

"32 SFTS was located in Moose Jaw, Saskatchewan, near Regina, and I arrived as one of their first officers. With the promised Ansons yet to arrive, off to 35 FTS in Calgary I went."

Back in Moose Jaw on New Years Day 1941 the unit now had its complement of Ansons and began training dozens of pilots destined for Europe and Bomber Command.

In town, various local War Efforts Clubs organised suppers and dances for the staff and trainee airmen at 32 SFTS. Mary Stroud had a full time job as a bank clerk and with friends enjoyed the dancing club at the Armouring Hotel in 'down town' Moose Jaw. Pupils and staff from the 32 FTS came along for drinks. "They all looked much better in uniform, especially Jack who otherwise wore awful green civvies. I actually met Jack on a blind date. He didn't rush things and eventually rang back after about three weeks. From then we dated regularly for a year before becoming engaged in late 1941."

"When Jack was posted to 32 OTU on Vancouver Island (about 3,000 miles away) in January 1942, we decided to marry. The RAF gave its permission so Jack arrived from Vancouver on June 3 1942. We were married on the 4th and we both went out again into rented accommodation near the airfield."

"We settled into normal life for a few months until in November 1942 Jack suddenly was posted back to England. This was quite a surprise but Jack had to go. I was classified as a 'war bride' and had little choice but to stay in Canada presumably until the end of the war."

"But once Jack had settled into his new posting he got to work sending signals to the RAF and the New Zealand

ABOVE: Jack Shorthouse demonstrates close formation flying in an Anson

ABOVE: Navigation was just as important in winter with a thousand miles of flat snow covered plains in any direction. Jack in the Anson turret

RIGHT: Instructing on Harvards. 32 OTU, Vancouver Island 1942

Kiwis Do Fly

LEFT: 32 FTS Moose Jaw, Canada – Moose Jaw's instructors group, Left to right: Eric Outram, JS and Dusty Millar

ABOVE: Mary Shorthouse dressed for Moose Jaw's frigid weather 1941

ABOVE: Jack Jnr, Jack and Mary Shorthouse, England 1945

High Commission in London trying to get me over to join him in England. His tactics must have worked as the authorities eventually issued a passport and permit to travel to England. This was fairly rare and in my case I was listed as a 'Special NZ Government Assistant.'"

"So in early 1943 I travelled down to New York to join a troopship. Fortunately I was allocated a shared cabin with a Wing Commander's wife and we had our own private deck and were kept apart from the troops but those we did meet acted as proper gentlemen."

"The convoy reached Liverpool and I sent Jack a cable 'Bob's birthday, meet at the Aldephi Hotel. Poor thing, he hung around New Zealand House in London for two days not realising my cable had been posted. Finally we met up in London. Before leaving Canada, I had accumulated a treasure chest, full of nylons, coffee, nail polish and all the things on ration in Britain. Anyway we took a train up to Lincoln, with Jack sitting guard on the chest all the way."

"In Lincoln I shared a house while Jack lived on the Station, although he did move a great deal. First to Waddington, then Dunholm Lodge, Syeston, Winthorpe, Bottesford and finally Bardney when he was promoted to OC 189 Squadron."

"As an able bodied young woman I was drafted for war work and was allocated to an office in a company making machine tools. The pay was a pittance, £2 per week and the work was mundane, repetitive and eventually once the war contracts were cancelled, it was quite pointless so I gave up going in."

"We tried to live a normal life during Jack's leave periods. He really was a fatalist, saying that life should go on, so we made the best of it. Eventually our first son was born on the 12 April 1944, just a day after Jack's birthday (Strangely, Jack junior's first son, our grandson, was also born on April 11th)."

"I have lovely memories of the crew mates Jack would bring home on leave, but not so pleasant memories of always queuing for food, sometimes getting to the head of the line to find it was stale fish, NO THANKS!"

"Then there was the strangeness of VE Day with no blackout, not drawing the curtains at night, we felt so exposed being able to see the night sky after all this time."

"Jack continued serving with the RAF after VE Day as he held a pre-war RAF commission but things were running down rapidly. He only flew a few hours in December 1945. Jack's discharge didn't come through until mid-1946 and then we were soon on a troopship New Zealand bound, with our two and a half year old son and our Bulldog."

"Jack soon took up flying again but this time as an airline pilot."

– Mary Shorthouse

Chapter 16 – The Other Half

Arrested

When Jack 't Hart went to England and Cambridge University in 1939, he left behind his girlfriend Jopie in Heemstede, North Holland. After a quick visit back to Holland for Christmas 1939 Jack returned to Britain. He was expecting an invasion would soon occur and feared a repeat of WWI.

Jopie stayed in Heemstede with her parents and recalls the German invasion as being very quick. "It was over in just five days and other than requisitioning the larger houses for barracks for the German troops, there was little effect on day to day life."

In early 1941 Jopie wrote to Jack and entrusted her letter to two friends who were making a break for England in a small boat. They didn't make it and were captured at sea. When they were thoroughly searched before being jailed, Jopie's letter was found. The Germans then traced it to Jopie's school. Here the Head Mistress recognised her distinctive handwriting and sent for her from her classroom. She was arrested: "I was lucky being taken by German Naval Marines as they allowed me to go home first to pick up clothes. Then off to a jail nicknamed the 'Orange Hotel.' For a nineteen year old school girl, the days events were terrifying. She could hear people being taken from the cells and never returning. "There were screams all the time from victims in the serious interrogation unit."

Eventually Jopie was charged with 'no specific crime' and the court handed down a mandatory three month jail sentence. Because she had already served nearly this time awaiting trial she was released.

"I was obviously finished with school and so became a florist. A friend introduced me to a member of the 'Scouts of the Underground' group 'Albrecht.' I joined this sabotage group and my main job was to report on troop movements. Later on in 1945, the convoys of trailers carrying V1 and V2 rockets passed through the town to launch sites behind Heemstede. Of course spying was 'Verboten': The Gestapo caught many of us and they were usually executed. A few were sent to special camps in Germany. The result was just the same."

"Our family were fortunate avoiding many of the food shortages that occurred throughout Holland late in the war. My father had a large vegetable garden, he fished and eeled in the canals, and so we got enough food to be able to help other families."

By 1945 Jack 't Hart was instructing at an OTU in England and as such didn't fly in the 'manna' supply operation shortly before VE Day to provide desperately needed food to the Dutch people.

But with the liberation of Holland Jack was ordered by the Dutch Authorities to join a combined military group to re-establish control in Holland. They travelled across from England in a tank landing ship full of supplies and on landing Jack quickly found Jopie.

Jack and Jopie were married on 14 January 1947 while Jack was still serving in the Dutch Air Force and the wedding breakfast was supplied by another 'manna' air lift this time courtesy of the RNAF.

"The war in occupied Holland was horrid, not so much the fighting but the severe shortages of all basics, not just food. That's why when Jack had finally completed his 10 years service (as the RNAF required) we wanted to get away from all this in case it ever happened again so we emigrated to New Zealand.

– Jopie 't Hart

ABOVE: Jopie pictured at the florist where she worked after her release from prison

ABOVE: Smiles all around at Enslunde Holland. J t'Hart with pipe after re-mustering as a RNAF F/L based at Twente. This photograph was taken prior to a town parade in August 1945

ABOVE: Jopie and Jack at home 2006

Kiwis Do Fly

Sister Sunshine

Injured aircrew were very well looked after in hospital, be it taking care of injuries, fitting new limbs or undergoing burns treatment. For many hospital was a place to be safe, to unwind and to try to become normal again.

Friendships between airmen and nurses were naturally common and a surprising number resulted in marriage.

On 13 March 1945, prior to an Op (his 36th), Flying Officer Bill Simpson in a light hearted moment set off a flare pistol. The flare's phosphorous burst in his face. Bill was blinded and his moustache was burnt off. "I can never forget the smell of burning hair."

After local treatment Bill was transferred to Halton's Burns Unit where a certain night sister (Dulcie Anness) gave his eyes regular bathing. Bill was still blinded and the treatment continued for two weeks.

As related in 'Wednesday Bomber Boys,' one morning 'Sister Sunshine' was putting in eye drops when Bill started to see. "I think I'll marry you", "Get away with you, Bill Simpson" she said.

Marry her Bill did, on June 9, 1945. He wasn't alone in bringing an English Rose home to New Zealand.

– *Bill Simpson*

BELOW: **Bill in June 1945. The powder burns have been retouched from the photo.**

BELOW: Dulcie Anness – 'Sister Sunshine'

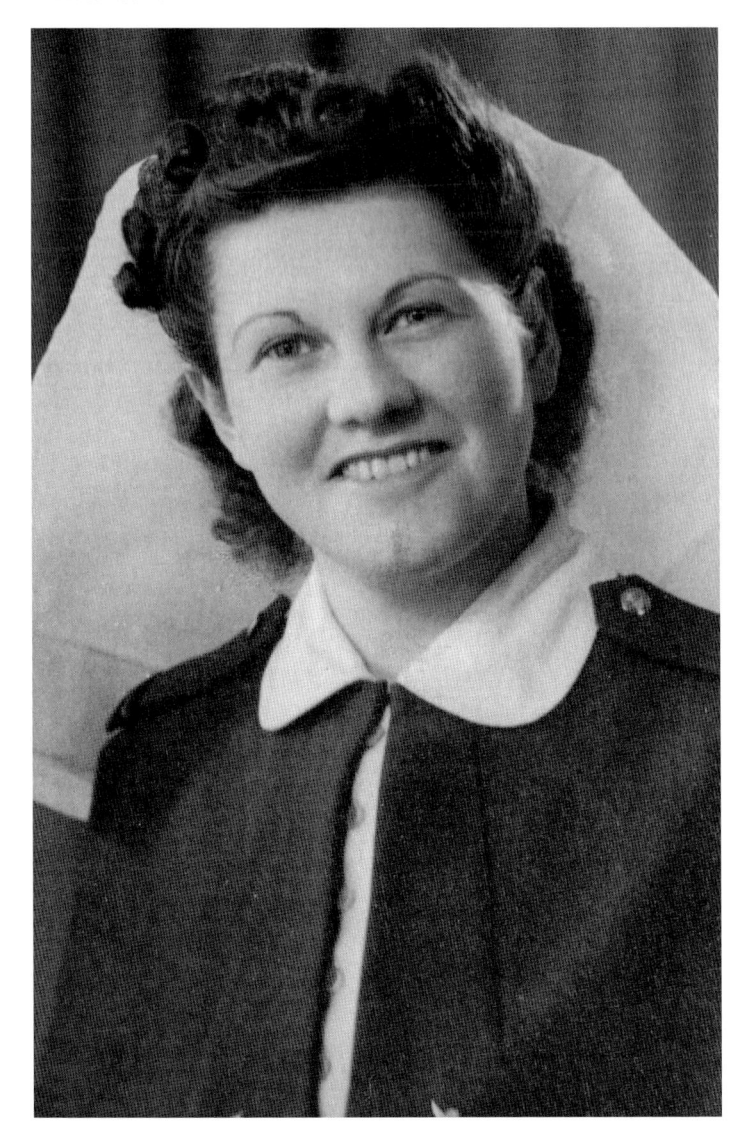

Chapter 16 – The Other Half

Blitz Nurse, Once a Kiwi

ORDEAL BY NIGHT

RAID ON LONDON

WHOLE STREETS IN FLAMES

AUCKLAND GIRL'S COURAGE

The story of London's epic battle against fire and explosion when the German raiders attempted to burn the city on the night of December 29 is graphically described by a New Zealander, Mr. R I. Johnstone, in a letter to Mr. R. J. Wink, of Mount Eden. Mr. Johnstone, who was previously in the Justice Department, is training with the New Zealand naval forces in England. Londoners, he says, are grimly determined that someone is going to pay for their sufferings.

"When the show started," he writes, "I was in the New Zealand Forces' Club in Trafalgar Square. We had just finished tea when there was a terrific explosion which seemed to be right above us. Windows gave and dishes broke and when we put our heads out of the door we saw that a high explosive bomb of heavy calibre had landed in the street just outside. There was a gaping crater and a gas main which had been hit was burning merrily.

Patrolling the Streets

'The police sent us back to the basement but as I was going down I met a girl heading for the door. She stopped me and said she had to go out. She was very perturbed (although she tried hard to disguise the fact) and asked me to go out with her. Her name is Anne Davidson and she hails from Auckland; she is a special air raid duty nurse.

"I put my tin hat on, slung my gas mask over my shoulder, grabbed her arm and went out. High explosives were still coming down and the showers of incendiaries were just starting. The din, most of it barrage, was terrific.

"From seven o'clock that night till seven o'clock next morning Anne and I patrolled the streets and saw London burn. It was like a huge torch. At 11 o'clock we were on Waterloo Bridge in the middle of a flaming circle. It was as clear as day and the heat quite made one forget it was a mid-winter night. I saw things that night I shall never forget but which I simply cannot record on paper. We walked down streets both sides of which were a mass of flames and saw a passenger bus caught by a high explosive and hurled 50 yards."

Fighters Engage Enemy

Mr. Johnstone says the fierceness of the fire proved to be the undoing of the attackers. Toward midnight the sky was so bright that fighter aeroplanes were able to go up and drive the raiders off. He and Miss Davidson were in Fleet Street when this occurred and they could plainly hear the Spitfires doing their job overhead.

"That night I saw bravery," Mr. Johnstone proceeds. "The London firemen and A.R.P. squads were magnificent. In the thick of the fires, with bombs raining down in thousands around them, they struggled and sweated with grins of defiance on their blackened faces. Miss Davidson was grand. We saw horrible sights—sights which would probably unnerve most girls of her age and never once did she flinch."

ABOVE: Sergeant Jim Dermody and his wife to be, Doreen Davidson

LEFT: An account printed in New Zealand newspapers in March 1941

Doreen Davidson was born in New Zealand but was only four when she was orphaned. Her parents were recent English immigrants and as she had no other New Zealand family this very young girl travelled back, half way around the world, to be with her nearest relative, an aunt.

In 1939 Doreen training as a nurse and joined the London Ambulance Service as the Blitz commenced. Jim Dermody arrived in UK in November 1940 and like many other Kiwis undergoing OTU training used his mid course leave to 'go up to London' even though London was still being bombed.

The NZ Forces Club in Charing Cross was always the first place to visit, catching up with friends, news and mail.

"That's where I first met Doreen, even though she was now a Londoner, accent and all, the NZ Forces Club was a magnet to her. She undertook a lot during the Blitz and saw such awful things. Like us, she was at real risk of being killed."

"We got on really well, well enough for me to ask her to become my wife. By then I had finished my first tour and was instructing at 12 OTU near Chipping Warden. We were married at Aston Le Walls, at the far end of Chipping's main runway."

"Once I received permission to live off station, Doreen and I moved into a little place at Banbury. I went to 'work' at the OTU while Doreen became a barmaid at Stratford upon Avon."

"With rationing so tight (we both had cards) I would eat at the OTU mess and we would pool our cards to get extra supplies. I'd eat any time, any place."

"In November 1943 when I was posted to 75 (NZ) Squadron at Newmarket, Doreen came with me. Being a nurse there were plenty of jobs

Kiwis Do Fly

available nearby. However life is full of surprises and after a lengthy sick period we were in for a shock when I was diagnosed with TB and spent months in hospital. Having my Doreen nearby helped so much with my recovery."

By November 1944 Jim's illness qualified him for repatriation and, they were soon on their way back to New Zealand.

– Jim Dermody

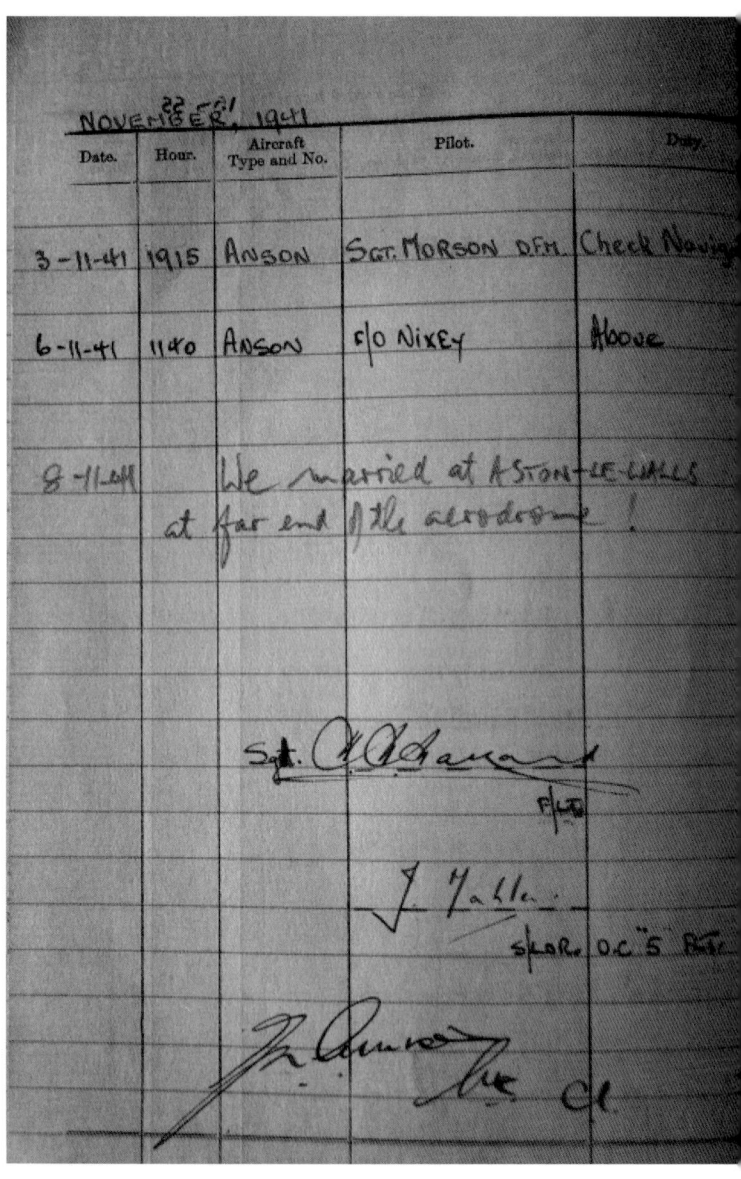

ABOVE: A unique entry in a log book, a wedding listed as an Op!

LEFT: Wedding Party with wartime restrictions:

Left to right: Jim Dermody, Mrs D Dermody, best man Lionel Knight (from Jim's crew) and Lionel's fiancé

Chapter 16 – The Other Half

War Bride

"Once my tour as a navigator on 622 Squadron had been completed, I was promoted to Warrant Officer and posted back to 11 OTU at Westcott, where I had come from just a few months previously."

In December 1944, three flying crews were selected to transfer to Transport Command at Stoney Cross and Des Andrewes became navigator for one of them. "242 Squadron were without any aircraft and everyone became a bit grumpy with the weather and no flying. A group of Aussie pilots were posted up to Stoney Cross from the Brighton Transit Centre where they'd been awaiting repatriation. Things got a bit hot, especially when a bunch of ex-OTU Wellingtons were delivered and one of them had been on operations since 1942 and worn out."

"Two of my crew mates drank at a pub at Lyndhurst and spotted a couple of girls – come on down and meet them, one's a matron. I thought matrons were forty year old biddies, but my word this matron was blonde, a year younger than me, and looked after a children's evacuee hostel. What a blind date! Joyce Winter was her name, and we got on pretty well. With my Commanding Officer's permission we were married in April 1945. There wasn't a lot of flying from Stoney Cross until the new Stirlings arrived, so I moved into the hostel annex, where we set up home."

"The Squadron eventually moved to nearby Merryfield and began eight-day long supply flights to Karachi. Joyce who was now pregnant with our first son, moved back home to her parents. This entailed quite a bit of train travel for me on visits and even though there wasn't much flying, the midday-Saturday to evening Sunday passes weren't quite long enough. So as a newly commissioned Flying Officer I awarded myself extended leave to Monday evenings. My mates in the Squadron would sign in for me on the Monday morning. Gradually I found a Thursday evening to Tuesday leave even better. In between times I spent as little time in the Mess as possible so the other officers wouldn't really notice when I was absent."

"During the early part of 1946 I was put down for the Karachi run, but declined as I might miss my repatriation notice. The third time, our Navigation Leader, Wally, said he'd not seen my face for a while (it had been two weeks) and he knew all about the signatures in the chitty book. "Better show yourself a bit or otherwise I will get it in the neck!" So off to Karachi I went in York MW232."

"In July 1946 our son was born and we were still waiting to go home and start a new life, when a telegram arrived from New Zealand Headquarters that an assisted passage for Joyce and my new son was available, I couldn't reply quick enough."

"The SS Lang's Bay brought us into Wellington in September 1946, almost four years since I had left for Canada."

"My final task was to transport my new English wife and son the length of the North Island to the remote township of Kohukohu on the Hokianga harbour and home."

NB: Des Andrewes's service had been longer than expected because a flights notice to him, and two other New Zealanders who were about to be married, wasn't seen until after it had expired. The notice was for married Kiwis with war brides to apply for immediate repatriation. The Adjutant said "bad luck, why not sign up for another six months and a cushy job?" Being the

– Des Andrewes

RIGHT: Wedding Day – April 1945

Left to Right:

Ted Featherstonehaugh (Des's school mate, also a navigator in 622 Squadron), Mary Winter (Joyce's sister), Des Andrewes, Joyce Winter, Ma Winter, Harry Winter (a WWI veteran, serving as an RAF Railway Transport Officer)

Chapter 17

Long Service

While over 2,000 New Zealand volunteers lost their lives serving with RAF Bomber Command the survivors continued to serve, throughout the war, only a few being repatriated due to injuries, illness or as reserved occupations.

Two tours (up to sixty operations in heavy bombers, or 100 in Mosquitos) were considered enough for the survivors to be posted to Headquarters or Training Commands.

Amongst the pre-1939 war course entrants a number served through until 1946, seven long years, while others joining later applied for and often secured post-war commissions in both the RAF and RNZAF.

Chapter 17 – Long Service

In Command – A Wingco

In 1942 Flight Lieutenant Jack Shorthouse was a flying instructor at 32 OTU (Patricia Bay, Vancouver Canada) but was suddenly recalled to England to rejoin active service with Bomber Command. "I had a quick transit. On 22 October I landed my last Anson in Canada and on 29 December was flying an Anson (N9945) from Saltby in England at 14 OTU on continuation training."

A posting to 1660 HCU (Swinderby) followed, firstly training on Manchesters then Lancasters. "Our passing-out test was to be part of the main force raid on Essen (Operation Wayover). In ED433 we dropped 12 lb incendiaries in canisters and a 4,000 pounder, a lot more than I dropped in all my Ops in Fairey Battles."

"The crew and I were posted to 44 (Rhodesia) Squadron at Waddington and a few days later I was promoted to Squadron Leader in command of 'B' flight. I had twelve crews to look after and we soon found that 44's Lancasters were rigged differently to any I'd flown before; they were a bit of a challenge. Late 1943 was a hectic time for the Squadron and Bomber Command but I was very fortunate

ABOVE: Wing Commander 189 Squadron

ABOVE: One year's losses on 44 Squadron, (April 1943 – April 1944) 30 aircraft. The October Raid over Berlin was particularly severe

ABOVE LEFT: September 1943, operations on 44 (Rhodesia) Squadron

LEFT: Jack's New Year Eve 1943 almost interrupted by German flack over Berlin. Carrying a very mixed bomb load Sqn Ldr Shorthouse brought JA684 back with "hydraulics shot away and the port inner on fire"

215

ABOVE: Operations as OC 189 Squadron December 1944

ABOVE & BELOW: 44 Squadron Lancasters KM-B (L7578) and KM-Q

that Mary (my Canadian wife) was finally able to come over to join me."

"Operations continued at such a pace that I finished my tour of 30 Ops with a dodgy trip to Berlin on 29 December 1943 in JA684."

Jack spent the next ten months at Bomber Command training Stations, with the instruction to 'lift their standards a bit.' First as Chief Flying Instructor at 5 LFS Syeston where the pass-out quota for pilots was down, "then, at 1623 hours 12 February 1944, I was told to get down to 1661 HCU at Winthorpe as CFI to sort them out. Then on to 1668 HCU at Bottesford where the quality of flying instruction was also poor."

"I was keen to get back onto operations and at the end of October 1944 I was promoted – Wing Commander J S Shorthouse DFC: I was just 24. With the promotion came more responsibility and I was detailed to commission a new Squadron (189) and set up a Station at Bardney. We got onto it pretty smartly."

"The Squadron was operational within two days and my first Op was to France (in PB745, CA-Q)."

"As Commanding Officer there were a lot of demands on my time just to keep the Squadron and Station running but I flew as many raids as possible. My last was on April 25 1945 in RF216 (CA-K) to Tonsberg in Norway."

"With VE Day, even though the war was over, my pre-war short service commission with the RAF meant I still had time to serve before being demobbed and I was transferred to Transport Command where multi-engine heavy ratings were very much needed. It meant flying the Liberator V, firstly at 1332 HCU at Riccall for type conversion then on 53 Squadron at Gransden Lodge. We were kept busy on trooping flights around the Middle East in early 1946 with the Squadron running a regular service through Italy, Egypt and Libya. It operated much as a scheduled airline and freight service."

"Eventually my release came through late in April 1946 and bringing KN756 back from Castel Bonito was my last RAF flight."

"These long trooping flights on 53 Squadron were later to prove very valuable when I applied for a civilian airline pilot's job."

– *Jack Shorthouse*

Chapter 17 – Long Service

RIGHT: Wing Commander Jack Shorthouse commissioning 189 Squadron with Secretary of Air

April 1945   189 SQUADRON   RAF FULBECK

W/Cdr J S Shorthouse introducing his crew to
Sir Archibald Sinclair, Secretary of State for Air.

l-r: F/Lt W Booth; P/O H R Pitcher; F/Lt R Elliott;
     F/Lt D J Barratt; F/O J Cornhill; F/O K Howard.

LEFT: Jack's Crew: Left to Right:
Standing – (P/O H R Pitcher (RG), F/L R Elliot (M/UG),
(P/O) K Howard (F/E), (F/O) J Cornhill (B/A)
Seated – (F/L) D Barrett (W/OP), JS, (F/L) B Asson (Nav)

ABOVE: Jack Shorthouse (centre) on 53 Squadron at Lydda, Palestine in March 1946. Final sortie via Bari (Italy) and Upwood.
Other crew members: Left to Right:
W/O Spriggins (F/E), W/O Ablett (2nd Pilot),
F/L Moore (Nav), P/O Gay (W/OP)

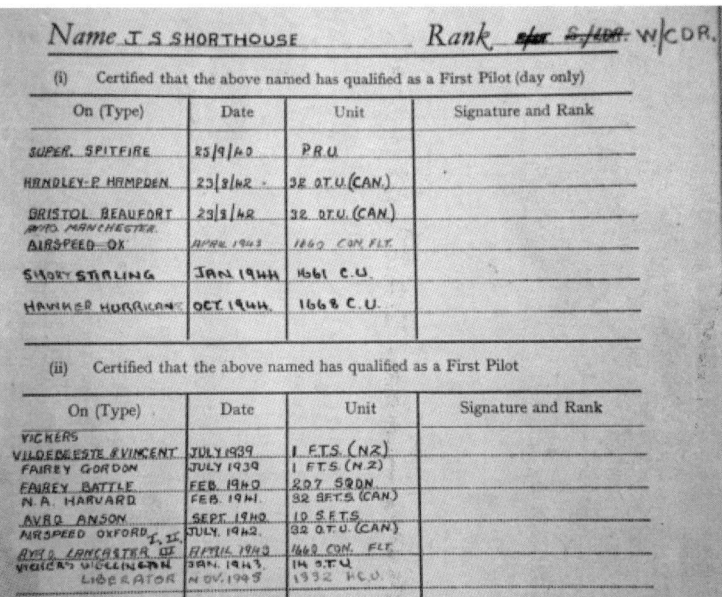

LEFT: First pilot qualifications on sixteen types, Vildebeeste to Liberator

Kiwis Do Fly

One Year, Two Tours

When Robin Craw completed his twin-engine conversion course on Oxfords in September 1942, he would have been surprised to learn that within two years he would be back on the family farm in Canterbury having completed two tours of operations.

Five months after the Twin Engine Conversion Course at Wigram, Robin was again flying Oxfords, this time with the AFU at Shawbury. By mid 1943 Bomber Command losses were very high and the demand for replacements (especially pilots) incessant. After a spell at 1521 BATU, Wymeswold, for Beam Approach Training, Pilot Officer Craw moved onto Wellingtons at 11 OTU (Oakley). Such was the pace of training he took Stirling N3760 (1657 HCU) on a solo on October 9 1943.

With his new crew, he was posted to 199 Squadron at Lakenheath. Robin did the traditional sprog trip as second pilot to Pilot Officer Lumsdale in EX-P on a run to Berlin. On December 20th Robin carried out his first Op as Captain. "This trip was a bit of a problem as we lost a motor and needed to hold on with three until the target! Welcome to Operations."

"199 Squadron (although of 8 Group) did quite a few special drops supplying the French Underground, our crew doing three in January 1944. Our two longest trips were in March down to the Spanish border, my log showing 9 hours 15 and 8 hours 25 minute runs."

"We finished 22 Ops on Stirling's without any real problems and our last on 10 April 1944 was remembered by all the crew for the huge electrical storm we encountered. It was spectacular."

Robin normally could have expected leave and then perhaps a spell instructing at an OTU, but just thirteen days after his last Operation with 199 Squadron he had been posted to Warboys for Pathfinder Force training.

"Four days later (on April 27 1944) I had converted onto Lancasters and flown my first solo on type. Things didn't let up at all and on May Day I flew as second dickie on 7 Squadron based at that time at Oakington."

"Our crew's first full trip was to Montdidier, a railway centre north of Paris. We were classified as BBS, supporters of the Master Bomber and flew circuits around the target until we were called to run in to drop flares or bombs."

"The Wizernes raid on July 5th was remembered by all the crew as we had a thousand pounder hang up in the bomb bay and a Ju88 night fighter gave us plenty of attention. We caught fire and had to make use of the big emergency airfield at Woodbridge in Suffolk."

"The pace of operations didn't let up at all after D-Day, they really increased so my 50th and last Operation came up on August 18 with a run to Bremen. I had done a tour in just six weeks."

"In all I'd completed 714 hours, 225 of them at night."

A notice came through on the 31st August that I was to be repatriated to New Zealand pending Pacific service.

"My father was unwell so I was released to run our family's farm. With so many servicemen overseas the New Zealand Government were concerned about food and grain production (much of which went to the UK). Looking back, seventy two Ops in nine and a bit months now seems a bit pushed but I don't remember it that way."

– Robin Craw

ABOVE: Where it all started. First solo 1942

ABOVE: Robin's crew.

Left to Right: Robin Craw (pilot), Ron Johnson (Nav), Ron Smith (W/Op), Gordon Gibson (B/A), Jack Owen (F/E), Bert Fox (M/UG), Bob Harpur (RG)

Chapter 17 – Long Service

LEFT: 199 Squadron lined up ready for a station parade and visit by the Duke of Gloucester Lakenheath 1943

RIGHT: The last Stirling Op, April 1944 on EX-N

LEFT: The usual dispersal of Stirlings at Lakenheath

Two Tours

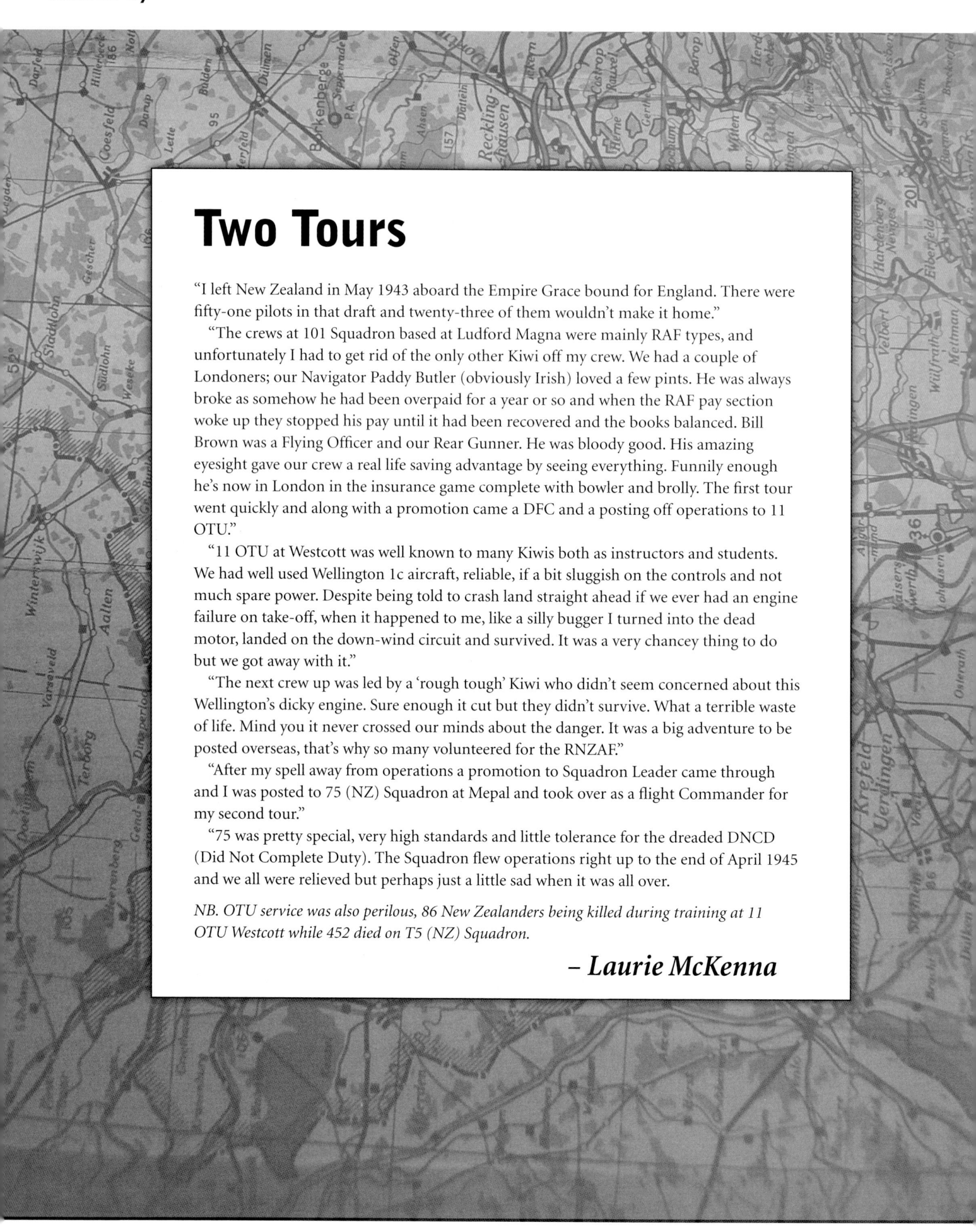

"I left New Zealand in May 1943 aboard the Empire Grace bound for England. There were fifty-one pilots in that draft and twenty-three of them wouldn't make it home."

"The crews at 101 Squadron based at Ludford Magna were mainly RAF types, and unfortunately I had to get rid of the only other Kiwi off my crew. We had a couple of Londoners; our Navigator Paddy Butler (obviously Irish) loved a few pints. He was always broke as somehow he had been overpaid for a year or so and when the RAF pay section woke up they stopped his pay until it had been recovered and the books balanced. Bill Brown was a Flying Officer and our Rear Gunner. He was bloody good. His amazing eyesight gave our crew a real life saving advantage by seeing everything. Funnily enough he's now in London in the insurance game complete with bowler and brolly. The first tour went quickly and along with a promotion came a DFC and a posting off operations to 11 OTU."

"11 OTU at Westcott was well known to many Kiwis both as instructors and students. We had well used Wellington 1c aircraft, reliable, if a bit sluggish on the controls and not much spare power. Despite being told to crash land straight ahead if we ever had an engine failure on take-off, when it happened to me, like a silly bugger I turned into the dead motor, landed on the down-wind circuit and survived. It was a very chancey thing to do but we got away with it."

"The next crew up was led by a 'rough tough' Kiwi who didn't seem concerned about this Wellington's dicky engine. Sure enough it cut but they didn't survive. What a terrible waste of life. Mind you it never crossed our minds about the danger. It was a big adventure to be posted overseas, that's why so many volunteered for the RNZAF."

"After my spell away from operations a promotion to Squadron Leader came through and I was posted to 75 (NZ) Squadron at Mepal and took over as a flight Commander for my second tour."

"75 was pretty special, very high standards and little tolerance for the dreaded DNCD (Did Not Complete Duty). The Squadron flew operations right up to the end of April 1945 and we all were relieved but perhaps just a little sad when it was all over.

NB. OTU service was also perilous, 86 New Zealanders being killed during training at 11 OTU Westcott while 452 died on T5 (NZ) Squadron.

– Laurie McKenna

Chapter 17 – Long Service

Pathfinder

Having been evacuated from Singapore in 1942, Flying Officer Keith Boles returned home to New Zealand without one hour flown in combat.

The staff at RNZAF Headquarters decided another run through basic training would help Keith fill in time. "I was really brassed off with this so I volunteered to be OC of a batch of 99 LACs being sent to Canada for training away from the action, Singapore all over again!"

"We left on the 'Uruguay' in April 1942 and docked in San Fransisco three weeks later where the LACs destined for observer training moved onto Canada."

"I was now a 'free' man and keen as ever continued my voyage to England and eventually to 15 AFU in Yorkshire for continuation training, and then to an FIwS."

"For the next two years I seemed to be sidelined although I became a Beam Approach instructor to future bomber pilots, I still hadn't flown on one operation."

"Finally in 1944 after reminding the Liaison Officer at HQ that I was a NZ volunteer, I was quickly posted to the Mosquito Training Unit and then on to 109 Squadron (Pathfinder Force) at Little Staughton. Obviously, all that steady on beam flying made me suitable material for Oboe operations. With my navigator we put in some pretty good runs with tight marking on a number of targets. In March 1945 I received my 'Scraper' (made up to Squadron Leader) one of several in 'A' flight."

"Marking targets using Oboe demanded very accurate flying. The accuracy of the marking was verified even before you landed. My tour of 52 operations was completed without drama and I was then posted to an OTU and finally onto transports. I returned to New Zealand briefly before coming back to England and de-mobbing.

– *Keith Boles*

ABOVE: April 1942 and contingent 121 parade before the Governor General Sir Cecil Newall before embarking in Auckland. Future aircrew are sporting their white 'under training' caps flashes. Keith Boles is looking at the camera

ABOVE: At Acaster Malbis (Yorkshire) 30 July 1942 No. 15 (Pilot) Advanced Flying Unit. Keith Boles is bottom right

221

Kiwis Do Fly

RIGHT: Target marking over Leipzig/Englesdorf Marshalling Yards on 10 April 1945. The white marker sits squarely over the yards with a train beside. 'Error 10 yards'

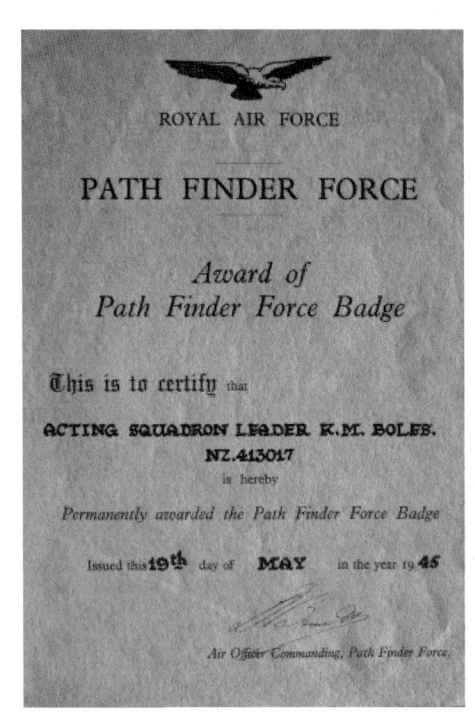

ABOVE: Acting Squadron Leader Boles Pathfinder Badge Certificate signed by the AOC AVM Bennet

ABOVE: Squadron Leader Boles with his 'A' flight air and ground crew posed in front of the solid-nosed Oboe Mosquito B XVI HS-C showing at least 50 operations. This photograph shows the number of crew, both air and ground, required to maintain one flight operational

Chapter 17 – Long Service

RIGHT: Close up of PFF Operations Board for 4 April 1945 Squadron Leader Boles 109 Sq. Oboe equipped Mosquito B XVI (HS – H) marking Lenna (Prague) T/O 2027 and landing back at Little Staughton 0040 after marking at 2240

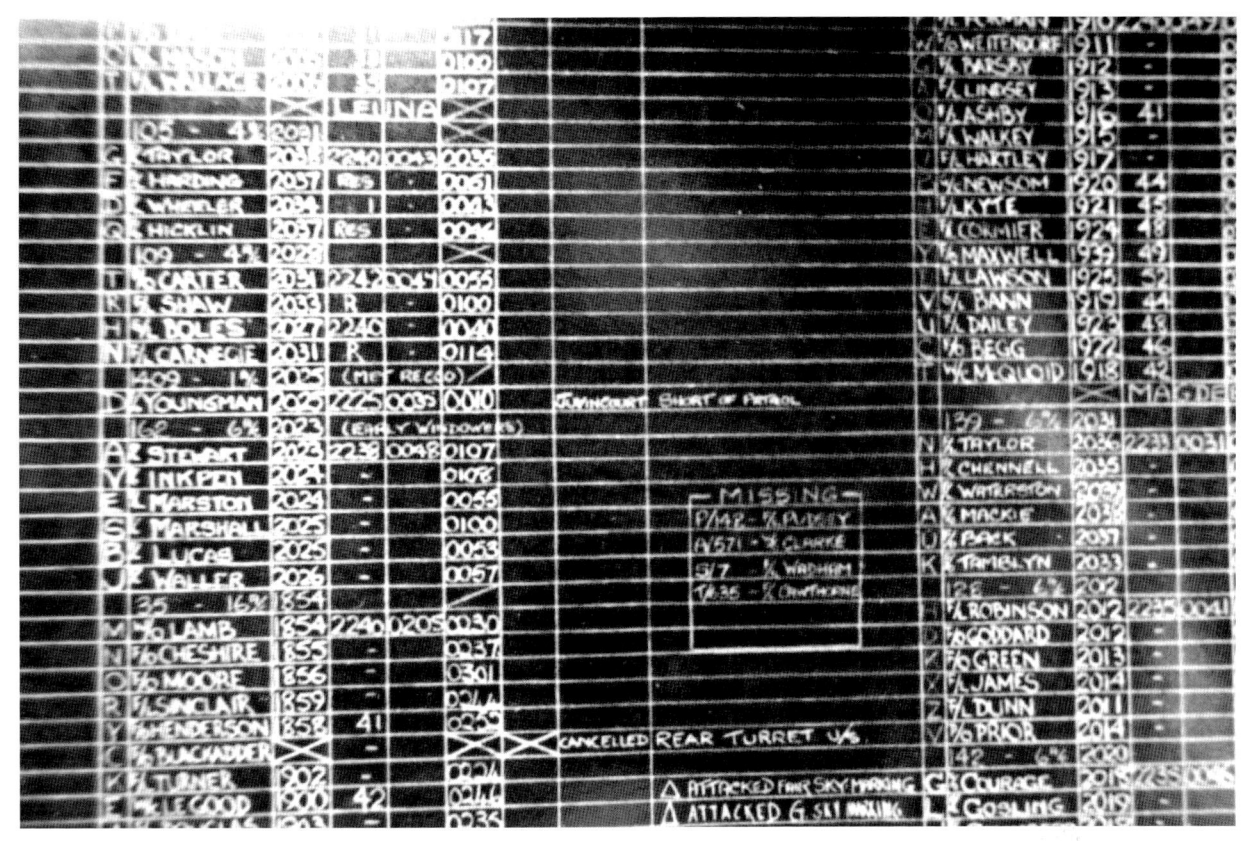

BELOW: Future PFF Navigators on a specialised course at 1655 MTU (RAF Warboys) before posting to OBOE or LNSF Squadrons. Jeff Watkins DFC (5th from left, front) crewed up with Keith Boles on 109 Sq.

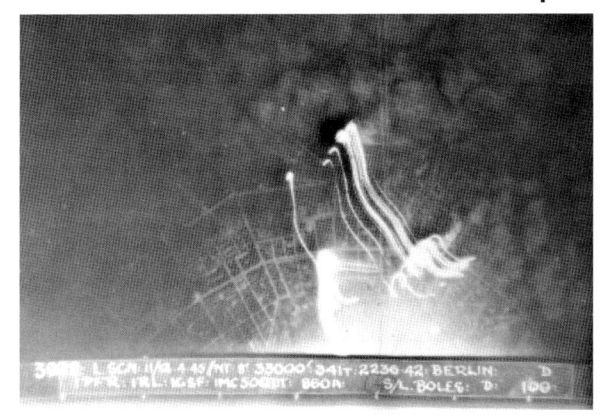

ABOVE: Oboe marking over Berlin 2236 hours 11 April 1945. The release point was now in range of Oboe transmitting units based in Germany, the 33,000 ft altitude flown was dictated by the line of contact needed for the intersecting beams. Two search light beams can be traced back and converging in the target area

RIGHT: VE Day. The complete 109 Squadron. Squadron strength totalling 165 (including WAAFs) Keith Boles is seated above the second WAAF on the right. One Mosquito appears to be ML931

223

Kiwis Do Fly

617 Squadron – The Cheshire Era

"After enlisting in the RNZAF I was advised that I was acceptable as a gunner but not as a pilot unless I completed a correspondence course in mathematics. It took me a year and a steep learning curve to come to grips with algebra, logarithms and trigonometry needed to meet RNZAF standards. It seemed double Dutch but in the end I was accepted for pilot training and reported to the ITW at Levin on July 5th 1941."

Once Les had passed out from initial flying training he was posted to Canada and the Cessna Cranes of No 4 SFTS. Six months later with his new crew they flew a first operation from 29 OTU, taking their Wellington to Dusseldorf. After converting to Lancasters the crew were posted to 97 Squadron and flew operations until / volunteering for duties with the new 617 Squadron and the planned Dams raid.

"Following the Dams raid, active operations got underway again in July 1943 on specific long distance targets in Italy, landing at Blida, Algeria. During this period our Lancasters were fitted with SAB MKIIA bomb sights, we trained at dropping practice bombs from 20,000 feet."

"In November 1943, the Squadron had another change of direction with the arrival of our new Commanding Officer, Leonard Cheshire. He quickly gained my respect both as a man and a leader. He was humble, self effacing, quietly spoken and a droll sense of humour. Although intense by nature, he never ordered or demanded anything, but gave his orders as simple requests. He constantly thought of ways of improving target marking and bombing methods so that the Squadron became highly efficient at destroying individual targets while minimising injuries to the French."

"In February I was promoted to Squadron Leader and Commander of 'B' Flight, while on March 24 the Squadron itself was enlarged to three flights. Dave Shannon and Joe McCarthy took over 'A' and 'C' flights so we had an Englishman as Commanding Officer, and an Australian, a New Zealander and an American leading the flights. As original 617 people we became known as the 'old firm'."

"Like all RAF Bomber Command Squadrons, the lead up to D-Day created plenty of work over France. On April 20th we raided marshalling yards in Paris and Woodhall Spa's Base Commander came along with me "to have a good look!" On the way home I offered Air Commodore Satterly the pilots seat. Obviously he hadn't flown for a while as he wandered off course. It wasn't long before my navigator's Scottish voice came over the intercom, "please stick to the course, pilot!" At that I poked my head around into the nav. compartment and thumbed in the pilot's direction. Jock put his hands over his eyes in horror."

"When there was little improvement in the Air Commodore's flying I advised him to stay on 270°. That was the only time I had the opportunity to give a much more senior officer an order."

"After a period of low level marking with Lancasters, Cheshire persuaded AOC 5 Group that Mosquitos were more suited to that role and 617 took four on charge. Cheshire and three others, including fellow Kiwi, Terry Kearns, flew the Mossies while I became Lancaster Leader."

RIGHT: 617 Squadron post D-Day is busy raiding transport targets and E-Boat pens to reduce German response to the Normandy landings. Les munro's 'personal' Lancaster LM482 was lost on the Kembs Dam raid on 9 October, 1944

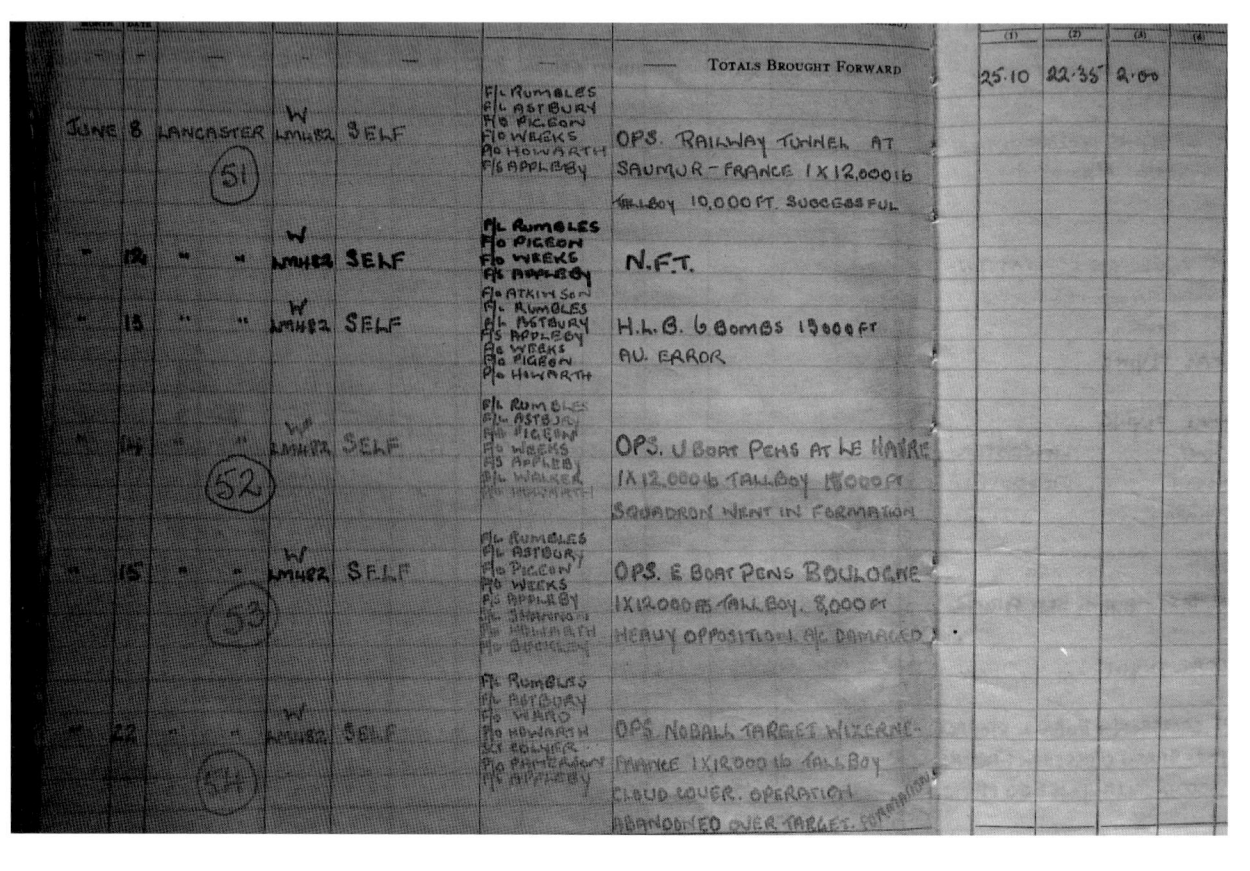

Chapter 17 – Long Service

"On 22 April 1944 Cochrane decided to apply 617 methods to 5 Group as a whole, 97 (my old Squadron) and 83 Squadron both flying Lancasters and 627 Mosquito Squadron was seconded from No 8 PFF Group to gain experience in the marking and bombing methods 617 had developed. The first target was Brunswick. As Bombing leader, I acted as liaison between Cheshire in charge of the marking force and the Lancaster force above. As a major trial for 5 Group it was not successful. The weather was bad, the flares dropped by some of the PFF aircraft were well off target meaning that the low level markers had difficulty seeing the right target, but the major problem was radio."

"There was heavy radio communication interference during the track into Brunswick as one aircraft had left its transmitter on. Their crew chatter was broadcasting to all and sundry as well as blocking the VHF channel. By a process of elimination and listening to what was being said, we found that the culprit was a PFF aircraft. I asked Percy Pigeon (my Wireless Operator) to send a radio message to all PFF aircraft (using the code assigned to them) ordering them to check their transmitters. The effect was immediate. Silence!! But it had already affected transmissions from Cheshire to the other markers and myself."

"My log book reads, "Failed to back up markers, not visible in time. Bombed at 18,000 feet. Attack not successful"."

"Two nights later a similar attack on Munich was highly successful and caused more damage to the city than all previous attacks. Of note that shortly after leaving the city and with the sky still bathed in the light of the fires, I saw the silhouette of a Wellington bomber a couple of thousand feet above us flying in the opposite direction. On reporting this at debriefing we were advised that the Germans had several Wellingtons which they used as decoy aircraft to infiltrate our streams and attack our bombers."

"From mid-June we began a series of daylight operations the first being a high level attack on U-Boat and E-Boat pens at Le Havre. For take-off we lined up on the beginning of the runway and the adjoining perimeter track with each aircraft commencing its take-off run before the preceding aircraft had left the runway. This enabled the Squadron to form up fairly quickly, until we had all 22 Lancasters flying in one single formation. We were all carrying Tallboys and bombed Cheshire's markers from 18,000 feet. That's 220,000 lb of high explosive in one place at one time!"

"A similar Operation on the E-Boat Pens of Boulogne was carried out the next day, again facing heavy flak but we were later told that these two operations had destroyed 133 E-Boats eliminating a major threat to the Normandy armada."

"The 12,000 lb Tallboy became 617's weapon of choice and there followed a series of high level daylight attacks on V2 sites.

The Operation against a Noball target at Mimoyecques on 6 July was to be my last operational flight. Two days later AVM Sir Ralph Cochrane, AOC 5 Group decreed that Leonard Cheshire, Dave Shannon, Joe McCarthy and I would all cease operations. He would brook no argument. I have always looked back with considerable pride as being a part of 617 Squadrons Cheshire era, Leonard being awarded the Victoria Cross for his outstanding efforts."

"I had flown 58 operations without a spell but I was still disappointed that I finished just two trips short of a milestone 60."

"Sir Ralph Cochrane had driven down to Woodhall Spa to give us the news and advised that he wanted me to take over command of 1690 Bomber Defence Training Flight based at Scampton. A desk job at HQ wasn't an option."

"1690 BDTF flew Hurricane fighters and carried out simulated attacks on the Group's Lancasters to give the pilots and gunners practice. Gradually the units replacements came from Bomber Command and Cochrane requested the flight place greater emphasis on night interceptions. So here I was faced with converting from flying four engine Lancasters to single engine Hurricanes. One circuit in a Harvard and my conversion was complete."

"From Scampton I flew three familiarization flights in the Hurricane, some two and a half hours, before engaging in my first fighter affiliation practice, a Lancaster from 617 Squadron! Following some night flying practice and additional daylight F/A exercises I flew my first night affiliation. I never really enjoyed these, perhaps a fear that I wouldn't break off soon enough. However in the year I flew with 1690 BDTF there were no near misses except my first."

"Practising night interceptions in a single seater required co-operation with the aircraft to be attacked. They would join the circuit over our aerodrome with all lights on, I would form up, lights out and the exercise began. Once complete it was lights back on and the Lancaster would navigate me back to base."

"Following the now lit up Lancaster back to Scampton I decided to try a barrell roll. Once upside down I forgot all my aerobatic training in Tiger Moths and pulled back on the stick instead of pushing it forward. Into a steep dive the Hurricane went. Pulling up, the Lancaster was by then miles away and it was a sheepish Les Munro bomber pilot that followed it back to base.

"1690 BDTF was home for just over a year and I clocked up 204 hours on Hurricanes."

"By August 1945 I had been released from 1690 and was awaiting a posting to Transport Command when the Japanese surrendered. An immediate repatriation to home was approved and off on the SS Andes I went."

Les Munro was discharged on 6 February 1946 and following fifteen years working on Government schemes to rehabilitate servicemen onto farms, became a farmer himself in 1961. Farming and local politics have occupied him ever since.

– Les Munro

Chapter 18

Thanks for Coming

While the great majority of aircrew just gritted their teeth and carried on, a few got the shakes, some were shell-shocked or just cracked up. If the station doctor didn't pick up these conditions and take the crewman off flying duties, they faced the horrific charge of Lack of Moral Fibre (LMF). Stripped of rank and hustled off the station, these poor souls were not discharged but were to be found in the most menial of tasks. Still with their battle ribbons intact (as they were conferred by the King), many with AFC, DFC and DSO awards became ACH GD (cleaners). Crewmen who were really 'bonkers' stood a better chance of being stood down on medical grounds and returned to civilian life. It's said that the US military were much better at spotting at risk servicemen and instituted some form of treatment, but not the British.

Even the battle wounded were often cast aside into holding camps. Harry Furner, a Mid Upper Gunner was blinded in one eye defending his Lancaster and its crew. He was posted to Eastchurch after his release from hospital in 1944. "Here we were second class servicemen. Given poor food, the only fuel came from the camp huts we tore down. Parades were casual and the Camp Commanding Officer called them 'absolutely optional.' Certainly an attitude we weren't used to."

Eastchurch was a crummy place to end the war – the only entertainment was watching the weeks collection of pregnant WAAFs being sent away up to London on the 'Blunderbus'. A year after Harry's fight with a Bf110 night fighter he received a discharge into civilian life.

New Zealanders seemed to fare better than the British. After recovering from their wounds, if a suitable posting could not be found, they were repatriated home. Yet even here they faced a dilemma in adjusting back to civilian life. Still yearning for the team spirit, adventure and danger found in RAF life they found it lacking in their new civilian lives. The large responsibilities they happily accepted as 20 year old airmen in running a crew or a flight of thirty men they found on returning home these responsiblities were the preserve of older peace-timers. Quite untouched by the war they were reluctant to delegate to these very capable 'youngsters'. And the last thing these civvies wanted to hear was, "I remember over the Ruhr." No wonder they formed small groups and found the RSA clubs a home away from home. Over a beer they could at least talk to others with the same experiences and outlook.

One quoted, "All I want my Country to remember is that I fought for honour and our safe land and now just give me a fair go."

Chapter 18 – Thanks for Coming

Goodbye

As the European war drew to a close, Bomber Pilots in particular looked to the future and perhaps 'staying in' the RAF. They wanted to continue their flying careers even though they knew it meant loss of rank they had attained during 'wartime service only'. But many were told bluntly "don't bother re-applying, the peace time RAF is for the British!" An attitude rather reminiscent of infamous WWI Generals happy to use colonial cannon fodder only as long as it was needed, and then disregard them with little credit.

While the more 'glamorous' Fighter Command saw many Kiwis (especially the Aces), continue to serve and attain high rank in the post-war RAF, Bomber Command was destined to have little support in the immediate post-war period. The treatment of their Commander, Air Chief Marshal Harris and the British Labour Government's refusal to issue a Bomber Command medal (when all other Commands received them) upset the veterans of this bloody campaign and the snub continues to rankle even to this day.

However with post-war shortages of pilots and the imminent Cold War, the RAF again turned to New Zealand and significant numbers signed up for short service and later permanent commissions. Wing Commander Bill Simpson QSO DFC flew with, and later commanded, 90 (Signals) Group, while Squadron Leader John Buckley went onto Photo Reconnaissance with 683 Squadron eventually mapping much of East Africa. Wing Commander Dick Broadbent, DFC, stayed on in Bomber Command eventually served on the Headquarters staff of the V-Bomber Force.

Kiwis Do Fly

What's Next

The majority of RAF Bomber Command pilots returning home to New Zealand hoped for aviation jobs. The opportunities were slim. Union Airways (soon to be incorporated into the National Airways Corporation) and the Australian, British and New Zealand owned British Pacific Airways (later TEAL) had few vacancies. Many flying jobs were picked up by RNZAF Pacific veterans. The lucky ones like Roy Montrowe DFC with 42 Ops on Wellingtons in the desert and 50 on Pathfinder Mosquitos in Europe, secured a junior pilot job in a 90 mph Dominie with NAC.

Wing Commander, Jack Shorthouse DFC was offered a job as second-pilot on Short S 30 Flying Boats. "The Captain was an ex-RNZAF Catalina pilot of all things. I looked back at being Chief Flying Instructor (at Bottesford) and a Station Commander in charge of two thousand airmen and twenty-four aircraft, and here was someone next to me, in Command with no real Ops, nor much night flying. What did I do? I swallowed my pride and accepted the offer."

"I've no regrets but at 55 with 21,500 hours and finally flying decent jet airliners I was retired under the compulsory companys rules."

Of course most didn't return to flying. John Tarbuck (Lancaster skipper) went back to Nestlé, George Hitchcock took advantage of a Serviceman's Scholarship Scheme to study medicine while yet others went building, farming or became company reps. Asked now about their wartime service, a glint comes to their eyes, "I'd do it all again!"

RIGHT: Captain Jack Shorthouse, Air New Zealand international pilot with 21,000 hours up on retirement and qualified to fly twenty-four different aircraft

Chapter 18 – Thanks for Coming

Around the World

After VE Day, Keith Boles was scheduled to be demobbed but took six months rehabilitation leave in the UK. A spell in RAF Halton hospital delayed his repatriation yet again. "Anyhow I was offered a post on VIP Lancastrians as second dickey. My higher ranked Captain, only had experience on Dakotas. He'd never flown with four Merlins before and no matter how much I suggested how he should get the revs, airspeed and trim right he couldn't, so we just squashed along instead of flying."

"We then embarked on what ended up being an early round the world flight. Using a VIP Lancastrian we flew New Zealand's Minister of Finance, Walter Nash, back home via USA and the Pacific. Once we had delivered our human cargo we flew back through the East to Malta where I spent a weeks compulsory break with gyppo tummy. When I recovered, it was back to Bassingbourne."

"With the Lancastrians sold, I was posted to a Ferry Flight (this was now 1946), our first task being to deliver nine Airspeed Oxfords to the reforming Danish Air Force."

"This we did and settled into an ex-Luftwaffe station. However, we then seemed to drop off the radar and HQ overlooked any return arrangements."

"So for two great weeks, thirty of us enjoyed Danish hospitality before we reminded the Air Attache and were sent for."

"At the time the RNZAF was purchasing a large number of Mosquitos (75) for post-war re-equipment and I was in the right place to accept a ferry pilot position. I was allocated an FB VI to bring back to RNZAF base Ohakea. The aircraft were overhauled at an RAF MU, then we left Pershore, across France, the Middle and Far East to Singapore. A hop to Darwin then down to Sydney's Bankstown. The final 1,200 mile leg to RNZAF Ohakea often turned into a race with wagers and some substantial dividends being paid. I was only glad to have put the 72 hour ferry trip behind me although (and I wasn't to know it then), once I'd shut its Merlins down, I was never to fly again except as a passenger."

– Keith

ABOVE: The Lancastrian at RCAF Rockcliffe (outside Ottawa) July 12 1946. Deputy Prime Minister Walter Nash (light suit centre) with Government officials and RCAF representatives. The Lancastrian carried a crew of four, seconded to the King's Flight. F/L Keith Boles fifth from right

ABOVE: Mosquito FB VI NZ 2325, YC–A of 75 squadron. This aircraft (ex RAF TE 913) was ferried to New Zealand in 1947 and after service was stored at RNZAF Woodbourne before being sold and broken up. Many of the 75 Mosquitos delivered were never used

An Early End

"After serving on 12 OTU at Chipping Warden as a Navigating Instructor I was tour-expired and married." Jim Dermody became 'unexpired' and underwent training at 1651 HCU (Waterbeach) before being posted to 75 (NZ) Squadron and its Stirlings at RAF Mepal in November 1943.

"Our crews' aircraft was BK695, a pleasant thing to fly in and our re-introduction to Operations was a leaflet drop on the 26th to the Frisian Islands."

"Leaflets were often taken along and varied from the mild to the chilling. We weren't in any doubt what those on the ground copped when we dropped high explosive instead."

"By Christmas I wasn't myself and was so unwell by January 1944 that my Op on the 14th was the last in my log book. The next two Ops I didn't have the energy to even write them up. I was lucky that my wife Doreen was a nurse and made me to see Mepal's Medical Officer."

"I'd always been lean but was shocked to learn I'd lost two stone! I was even more shocked, perhaps shattered when the diagnosis was TB. Remember, in those days there was no treatment, no antibiotics and the outlook was grim."

RIGHT: RAF Hospital Ely's recovery home where Jim Dermody spent six months

"Off to Ely Hospital I went, checked again by two doctors this time, but with the same diagnosis. That was the end of flying the only 'cure' being bed rest, good food and fresh air!"

"Doreen moved close to Ely, where I was to spend the next six months gradually recovering. We were finally repatriated home in November 1944 funnily enough with 75 (NZ) Squadron's flight commander Squadron leader Dick Broadbent, who had finished his two tours."

"Two relapses nearly put an end to any post-war service, but my Air Force days were certainly over and back to the Tax Office I went."

– Jim Dermody

75 (NZ) Squadron turnout November 1943

Chapter 18 – Thanks for Coming

Welcome Home – The Andes Boys

As thousands of New Zealand servicemen were repatriated after VE Day, their sole thought was of demobilisation and return to civilian life. Even though the war with Japan continued, most expected a lengthy leave and perhaps a call up in 1946.

Amongst the ships carrying Australian and New Zealand veterans home was the cruise liner 'Andes'. A large, fast ship, it reached Australia from Southhampton in record time. With New Zealand just 1,200 miles away across the Tasman, all were hopeful of disembarking two days later. But this was late October and there was a public holiday, Labour Day, on the Monday. The waterside workers (notorious Commies) refused to work that weekend so the Andes trickled across the Tasman to Lyttleton then Wellington on the Tuesday.

"We'd already heard of some of the antics of these bedroom warriors going on strike before. Apparently the US Navy at times had to use its own Marine soldiers to load cargo for the Solomon Islands campaign. To say the Andes boys were annoyed was an enormous understatement, there was nearly a riot aboard ship."

"Once we'd finally pulled alongside, the few wharfies were pelted with eggs and garbage (and worse). When the Defence Minister (Hon. F Jones) tried to board, he and his staff received the same."

"By the time we disembarked the wharfies had vanished, just as well, as they would have been in very serious trouble."

"Some of those aboard had been away overseas for years and to those in 'reserved occupations' to have holidays was just too much to bear. It was a bitter memory of what should have been a great arrival."

"This memory stayed with me post-war and when during 1951 (in the midst of the Korean War) the wharfies again went on strike, I was one of the first to volunteer as a strike breaker. They called us scabs, we were war veterans and had faced worse than these softies. Rather than the sedition charges they eventually faced I'd have had them up for treason."

ABOVE & BELOW: The SS Andes at Portsmouth, packed with Australian and New Zealand Air Force crews

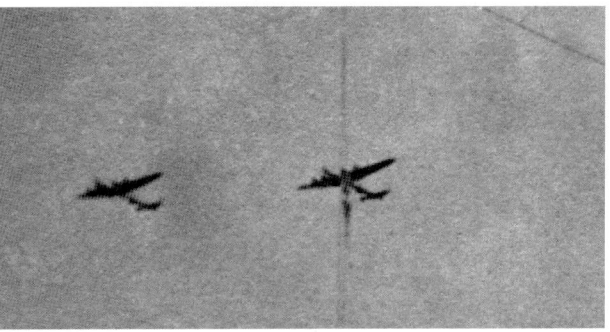

RIGHT: A pair of new 75 (NZ) Squadron Lincolns flying from Spilsbury farewell the boys

ABOVE: Not the welcome expected. The RNZAF band showered with coins eventually took refuge in the wharf cargo sheds

RIGHT: A mid-ocean concert on a record Southampton to Melbourne run

231

Chapter 19

Back Into The Blue

After VE day, aircrew repatriated home from Europe were retained in RNZAF service pending further duties against the Japanese, but with the atomic bombs being dropped and the subsequent Japanese surrender, demobbing was accelerated. Newly arrived home aircrew were sent on extended leave which lasted most of 1945. With release papers in hand, many had had enough of the service and returned to post-war jobs, John Tarbuck (a Lancaster pilot) back to Nestlé, Des Andrewes (a navigator on 622) back to the families rural store, and even fighter ace Jim Sheddan went back to the bush and farm contracting. In anticipation of yet another war being possible, discharged aircrew, especially pilots were retained on the reserve list for another twenty years.

"But many of us had the flying bug bad and we wanted to fly for civil airlines." "Even with a log book full of hours on night operations in high performance aircraft I had to grit my teeth and fly as a junior officer in a pre-war de Havilland Rapide at all of 90 knots. The skippers seemed to have been picked from the Pacific theatre boys who flew long daylight runs on the fringe of the war. Perhaps they thought us real operational types weren't to be trusted flying straight and level as we might have thrown in the odd corkscrew manoeuvre to liven up the day!"

That these decorated war veterans were second choices to the emerging New Zealand airlines such as Union, NAC and PCAP airlines still rankles even today.

Chapter 19 – Back Into The Blue

Back Wearing Blue

In 1947 the RAF found itself desperately short of aircrew, despite having demobbed thousands just two years before. There was a particular need for, experienced Mosquito pilots. The RAF wanted over one hundred.

The RNZAF could help little as it had just purchased 75 ex-RAF Mosquito FB VI's and would have its own difficulties training sufficient crews.

The RAF advertised in New Zealand papers and opened a recruiting office at the British High Commission. Of those attracted were then Flight Lieutenant Bill Simpson DFC (later Wing Commander) and his fellow Mosquito pilot and mate, John Buckley. Bill had been instructing at the Tauranga Aero Club and being back in Tiger Moths, while pleasant, didn't provide much of a challenge.

Bill had flown operations on 109 Squadron's Oboe Mosquitos while John had served with 627 Squadron part of 5 Group's Special Operations Force. Both pilots were accepted and Bill Simpson recalls, "I enjoyed being back in the RAF and enjoyed the flying immensely. As an ex-Oboe man, I was drafted into a unit of 90 Signals Group."

"We covered the length and breadth of Britain on Signals work and GSE radar checks. Eventually flying came to an end and off to the Air Ministry I went to be part of the Hercules buying team and the Belfast controversy. The latter were not needed but politics got in the way."

"As part of this evaluation of the Hercules, I spent time with the USAF Military Air Transport Service and a highlight was landing a USAF Starlifter at Auckland's Mangere airport when it opened as Auckland International." Bill Simpson retired from the RAF in 1970 and is now President of the New Zealand Bomber Command Association.

Unlike Bill Simpson, John Buckley had been just cruising along after being demobbed. John, ever the fatalist, accepted whatever happened. There was no choice between continuing his trade apprentiship and flying again.

"I took up a Short Services Commission as a Flight Lieutenant on 109 Squadron (Bill's old Squadron) which was now at Coningsby and using the B 35 mark of Mossie for low level attack. However, before too long, I was posted on to Photo Recce work with 540 Squadron at Benson. Perhaps somebody had seen the cine film taken from my aircraft on the raid on Oslo's Gestapo HQ in 1944!"

"I had been appointed as a Flight Commander on 540 Squadron which had been given the task of an aerial survey of Turkey and the Suez Canal Zone. However the hot climate played havoc with the aircraft's wooden structure."

The Squadron had been expected to carry on with surveys of East Africa but with the serviceability problems, 540 Squadron was relieved by 683 flying Lancasters 50. John, a long time Mossie pilot, converted onto 'heavies'."

"The flying was great and the social life very active, and this period was the most fullfilling I spent in the RAF, but like all good things it came to an end when I posted myself to a desk job in Whitehall. Even though I enjoyed my role as a Squadron Leader commanding ATC Units throughout England, I felt that the Air Force was really about flying, and without it it held little attraction and I retired in 1960."

– John Buckley

ABOVE: 683 Squadron Habbinaya Iraq, AOC inspection of the six PR Mosquitos and six PR Lancasters 1953. John as Flight Commander welcomes 'the boss'

LEFT: Tropical No 5's for the Mess Ball Niarobi 1953 – John is third from left

Kiwis Do Fly

Pacific Blue

Jack Shorthouse completed his short service commission as a decorated Wing Commander. "I had been a Station Commander with 2,000 people under my command, but on joining NAC I was introduced to 'the finer points of flying' by the airline instructor who had less hours than me, very few in four engined aircraft, and had never been in combat. But I swallowed my pride and said "right Skipper!"

Jack's perseverance did win through and his Captaincy arrived at the time when the new TEAL (Tasman Empire Airways Limited) had purchased Short Solents and were conducting proving flights across the South Pacific to Tahiti.

"I loved this part of the world and this unique service was named the Coral Route. It was a magical time when air travel was an expensive luxury. We would stop over in Aitutaki Lagoon in the Cook Islands and while the Solent was being refuelled, the passengers enjoyed a barbecue lunch and a swim in the lagoon. The route we surveyed was leisurely, with quite short flights."

THE CORAL ROUTE

Mechanics Bay (Auckland) to Lauthala Bay, Fiji	1159 Nautical Miles
Lauthala Bay to Satapuala, Samoa	612
Satapuala to Aitutaki, Cook Islands	763
Aitutaki to Papeete, Tahiti	589
and the return:	
Papeete – Bora Bora (French Polynesia)	139
Bora Bora – Aitutaki	461
Aitutaki – Satapuala	
and so on back to Auckland via Fiji.	

Jack grew to love the Solent. The room in the cockpit was amazing, very comfortable. In fact all the crew had room and a comfort equivalent to the passengers. Built by Shorts (who had produced the Stirling and Sunderland), the pilot's seat in all three aircraft was always fondly remembered.

Jack went on to become a Senior Captain, flying progressively more modern aircraft as they came into service. First the DC6, then Lockeed Electras, DC8s, DC10s "they were cracker aircraft" and finally onto the Boeing 747.

When Jack retired at Air New Zealand's mandatory age of 55 in March 1975, he had accumulated 21,500 hours. "If I'd been an American I would still be flying at 70!"

"The 1950's were a glamorous time to be flying. We still had a full crew: pilot, co-pilot, navigator, wireless op and flight engineer. Only the gunners were missing."

– Jack Shorthouse

ABOVE: Cockpit

ABOVE, BELOW AND BOTTOM RIGHT: Inside TEAL's Solent ZK-AMO (now on display at MOTAT, Auckland) shows how well the crew were catered for

On the Coral Route in Tahiti

ABOVE: Engineer's Panel  **RIGHT:** Radio Table

Chapter 19 – Back Into The Blue

ABOVE: On the Coral Route in Tahiti

ABOVE: Jack's favourite jet, the DC10 "the first airliner with inertial navigation and bags of power"

ABOVE: Checking the Electras legs!

ABOVE: At retirement

ABOVE: The late Jack Shorthouse at home 2007

Kiwis Do Fly

Again

"During my service career I'd become conditioned to accept things as they came along and wasn't fussed if things weren't all they'd been promised."

"Like the others, I'd joined up because of loyalty to New Zealand, but also for the chance for travel and adventure. I had really preferred one of the ground trades such as electrical, which would have set me up after the war, but when I applied for the trades (unlike everyone else who wanted to be a pilot) I was told they were full! What's available? I'm happy with anything, the only vacancies are for pilots I was told so off to flying training I went. It was a good introduction to the mysterious way of the Air Force."

"On 627 Squadron, the Commanding Officer was a pretty hard man, not just on me but everyone. Because I could take his ranting I think that upset him. To get even, I'm sure he put me on more than my share of dodgy do's the Squadron undertook."

"Like many others after demobbing, I was at a bit of a loose end and when the chance of re-mustering with the RAF on a short service commission, I thought why not? So back onto Mossies on 540 (PR) Squadron and eventually to the East African survey using Lancasters. It was a great time, with no fuss. I got a good run in the post-war RAF as Kiwis seemed to get away with things which otherwise would be frowned on."

"Eventually I did less and less flying and more 'admin.' One afternoon when I was left in charge of the office, an Air Ministry signal came through requesting a bod to be recommended for what was a very nice appointment. Not being too impressed with my current 'job' I duly completed the signal and back it went. My Commanding Officer was stunned two weeks later when my self-appointed posting came through."

– *John Buckley*

RIGHT: LANCASTER: Not for the social use of! Having flown TW916 (a 683 Squadron PR Lancaster) up to Eastleigh to attend a Saturday night function. John is told by the CO (in civvies) Group Captain Ian Lawson that he should return whence he came! 27 July 1952.

Chapter 19 – Back Into The Blue

Nuclear Deterrent

Following tours on Wellingtons in 40 Squadron and Stirlings with 75 (NZ) Squadron, Dick Broadbent (Wing Commander DFC MiD), left 75's Base at Mepal to attend Staff College in March 1944.

"As I was two tour expired the Air Ministry put me into a group of thirty officers studying the utilisation of resources at RAF bases. Although it sounds dry and dusty we uncovered some remarkable statistics, especially with vast stocks of spares not being shared by Groups or even amongst Stations.

The level of non-operational staff in some establishments also gave cause for concern. Eventually my departure date for New Zealand was confirmed, and I arrived home for Christmas 1944, and a posting to RNZAF Headquarters."

Like many, Dick was dissatisfied with post-war opportunities and rejoined the RAF. "Bomber Command was now converting to jet power, and it was an exciting time to be a pilot. The Cold War ensured a continuing supply of funding."

"I was fortunate to be involved in this activity and enjoyed many career highlights along the way and as a New Zealander I was often brought into special events. On one such occasion in 1954 I had the honour to be given a part in the ceremonies in Athens which were connected with the unveiling of the Commonwealth War Memorial. Appropriately enough this was to be unveiled on Anzac Day. I was in command of the RAF guard of honour, and, besides the RAF contingent, there were guards of honour from the Navy and the Army, and each was accompanied by its own full-strength band. The whole British contingent was got together in Malta some three weeks before the ceremony for training. We went from Malta to Athens on the aircraft carrier HMS Theseus and trained each day on the flight deck during the passage."

ABOVE: Aboard HMS Theseus bound for Athens, 1954

"Once in Greece we all trained again for several days, in company with large detachments of the Greek forces and their bands. The training was carried out on a large plain several miles from Athens and we were hosted by the Greek Forces living in their tents, barracks and eating their food, sometimes most unpleasant!"

"We were informed that the arrangements for the ceremony itself, which was to be performed by the King of Greece, were in the hands of a Greek Army Brigadier, but we never saw this gentleman. We were not allowed into the city, nor did we have a rehearsal of the parade itself."

"On the grand day we marched several miles to the square where the ceremony was to take place. We were all dressed in winter uniforms, unluckily, as it was a boiling hot day. I think about a thousand troops formed up in this small square, which was about the size of a rugby pitch. It was quite a solemn occasion with a large assembly of dignitaries from all over the Commonwealth and representatives of the Allies and the British Forces and members of various Royal Houses."

"Once we had all settled down, the Brigadier in charge of the ceremony appeared on the rostrum by the memorial and began giving his orders to the parade. Unfortunately, he spoke in Greek, and it was at this point things began to go wrong. None of the British forces could follow his instructions and somehow or other, all the guards of honour came to the 'Present arms' position before the official speeches began and stood like this for something like fifteen minutes before the actual unveiling was attempted."

"After a while men began to faint, and a fair bit of grumbling started amongst the British parties. Immediately alongside my RAF lot was the Army guard made up of members of the 51st Scottish Highlanders. The Highlanders have the highest reputation for toughness in action, but I can assure you they were not so tough that day. Some forty-two of them from their hundred strong guard of honour 'bit the dust.' The RAF and the Navy fared somewhat better. I am not sure about the Navy, but my RAF had only lost thirty-six at the conclusion of the ceremony."

"After speeches, the King of Greece came to the fore to unveil the War Memorial, which I think was a figure or group of figures on top of a column, the whole being draped with flags of the various nations. I say: "I think it was a group of figures," because we never did see the

Kiwis Do Fly

memorial, as the harder His Majesty pulled, the more stubbornly the drapes seemed to hold on. At last, after pulling from out in front, from the left, then the right, the poor Royal person gave up in disgust and walked away. All the Forces were still at 'Present arms.' There was a lot of confusion, with First Aid parties scrambling around, taking off the fainted personnel and kicking their rifles into the gutters."

"The subsequent march-past and saluting a veiled War Memorial are beyond my memory. However, there was some recompense. We were informed the next day that the Greek Army Brigadier had been reduced to the rank of Captain."

Dick was appointed to Flying Control and Flying Instructor as the first of the V-Bombers, the Vickers Valiant, was introduced to service. "I was with 138 Squadron in 1955, then moved to 48 Squadron a year later, then finally onto 7 Squadron in September 1960." With unexpected fatigue problems the Valiants were retired and scrapped. By September 1962 they were all gone and I moved to 139 and then 101 Squadron with the replacement Handley Page Victors. "Once I became OC Ops at RAF Wittering there was less and less chance to fly, but I had put a few hours up in the Valiant, nice to fly, you could drift up to 50,000 feet as fuel burnt off; a bit higher than my old Stirling!"

Spending more and more time grounded, Dick's last flight as Captain was in an Anson (TX 223) on May 30th 1963. "By then I was stationed at Bomber Command HQ at High Wycombe as one of two Air Tactical Officers responsible for V-bomber operations, response and target selection, but my lips are sealed about that job!"

– Dick Broadbent

ABOVE TOP: Briefing meeting with General Eisenhower at Staff College, 1944 – Dick Broadbent in the rear centre

ABOVE: Inspection of ATC Cadets as OC RAF Wittering

RIGHT: Helping the New Zealand Dairy Board and food rationing

Chapter 19 – Back Into The Blue

Op No. 15 with a 60 Year Gap

On 17 July 2004, Harry arrived at the Canadian Warplane Heritage Museum at Hamilton, Ontario to receive a birthday present.

Having just turned 80, Harry was at the museum to take a flight in one of only two Avro Lancasters still flying. It was 60 years and 23 days since he had last flown Operationally in a Lancaster. As a mid upper gunner he and the rear gunner were badly injured by an attacking Luftwaffe fighter. Blinded in one eye from perspex splinters, Harry hadn't flown in a military aircraft since.

With briefing over, it was out to the Lancaster to be seated in the rear of the fuselage just forward of the main door. Small windows allowed the passengers to view the proceedings from the pre-flight checks, engine start-up to just after take-off.

Harry was naturally apprehensive given his last Op, but thanks to the Crew Chief Randy Straughan it was arranged to give Harry the wireless operators seat up front for take-off. The four Rolls Royce Merlin engines were started and the aircraft taxied out to the main runway. Pre-flight checks completed, the Lancaster surged forward with a deafening roar and took off heading east towards Niagara Falls, the destination for the flight.

After take-off, an okay was given to move about the aircraft and the four passengers aboard were able to take in the views from the mid-upper turret, wireless operator's windows and astrodome and also the cockpit.

Following the waters edge along Lake Ontario the Lancaster travelled at around 2,000 feet, excellent views of the countryside to starboard and pleasure craft out on the lake to port.

Heading inland the Lancaster arrived over Niagara Falls and

ABOVE: Easy to exit when there's no flak or movement

ABOVE: Harry Furner (centre with dark sweater) and his son Phil (left) with the crew of KB 726

proceeded to circle the falls. Then headed back to Hamilton this time on a more inland route and on arriving back performed a customary low flyby of the museum complex.

Harry had also brought along his wartime Air Gunner's log book to which this flight was duly added and signed off by the pilot. Talking with some of the Lancasters ground staff, Harry was asked what he thought of having had a flight in the Lancaster again all these years later. He remarked that "60 years ago I'd never have thought I would fly in a Lancaster at the age of 80, its been a wonderful experience, especially with no one shooting at us!"

ABOVE: Harry with movie producer Peter Jackson in 2007 during research for the re-make of 'The Dam Busters' movie

– Harry Furner

Chapter 20

Casualties of War

RAF Bomber Command's 389,800 operations and 1,000,000 tons of bombs dropped during WWII cost 55,500 men and 9,000 aircraft in action. A further 1,560 men and women died while working as ground crew.

At the beginning of WWII, bombing was the only way in which the British could effectively wage war on Germany. Until 1942, bombing was limited to specific military targets and avoided deliberately bombing urban areas. After 1942, more widespread 'area' bombing was introduced which targeted main industrial areas and in some cases urban areas. The idea was to not only to destroy the German war industry but also to demoralise the German population.

Many saw area bombing as a justified response to the Blitz. The German bombing of London and many other major British cities in 1940 and 1941 killed 43,000 British civilians. However, late-war bomber attacks on German cities such as Dresden are now considered to be very contentious. In this raid the Nazi authorities claimed 250,000 killed and called it an atrocity yet the confirmed figure is actually 25,000. For the Germans, the bomber offensive meant they had to maintain defences against attack and continually rebuild damaged roads, railways, supply systems and buildings, diverting resources away from waging war.

At a German High Command Conference in 1944 Field Marshal Erwin Rommel said to Hitler you must stop the bombers or we cannot win, we shall go on losing another city every night. History shows he was right.

Sixty years later we can clearly see what RAF Bomber Command achieved, but we cannot put ourselves in the position of the decision-makers of that time. The men who flew for Bomber Command had no say in the political decision making or the formulation of strategy. They simply did a difficult, dangerous, cold, lonely and always thankless job to the best of their abilities, to end the war as soon as possible.

Chapter 20 – Casualties of War

Counting the Butcher's Bill

'Kiwis Do Fly' is about the life of over 6,000 volunteers and not so much about the daily blood and guts of death. Yet they did die horrible deaths in their hundreds. The losses of New Zealanders in RAF Bomber Command total some 2,265 from latest research: An horrific death rate. When added to those who became POW's or were injured, our airmen faced a casualty rate of over 35%, something not experienced since trench warfare in WWI.

Each airman was highly trained and skilled. It had taken perhaps two years to prepare them for their first Operation in action, only to be killed, if not on their first, but before their thirtieth Operation. A dreadful waste, yet there was no acceptable alternative.

Errol Martyn's 'For Your Tomorrows' shows – New Zealand losses in RAF Bomber Command during the bad days of 1943:

Week 1	Monday 2 August 1943	12 killed
Week 2	Monday 9 August 1943	9 killed
Week 3	Monday 16 August 1943	6 killed
Week 4	Monday 23 August 1943	14 killed
Week 5	Monday 30 August 1943	33 (16 from 75 (NZ) Sqn)
Week 6	Monday 1 September 1943	11 killed

Eighty-five killed in just five weeks. Today, a loss rate like this would be politically unacceptable, yet one third of New Zealand's total WWII casualties came from aircrew losses and were tolerated by both the politicians and the public. Victory was such a relief.

However, it has become 'fashionable' amongst some to question RAF Bomber Command's integrity. Certainly in 1945, UK's new Labour Government took immediate steps to distance itself from the bombing, yet it was the very same people who had authorised the attacks and determined priorities. It was conveniently forgotten that Bomber Command provided the only offensive weapon against Nazi Germany for five long years, and it was still needed even after D-Day to clear the way for Allied Armies and to 'suck General Montgomery over the Rhine!' Simply put, the war would not have been won without extensive bombing of industrial, rail and civilian concentrations. However non-PC it may seem today, wars are fought to be won, not lost, and casualties amongst civilians will always be large unless future conflict is undertaken in an arena between groups of brave politicians.

New Zealand Casualties of War:

Year	War	Casualties
1895	Boer War	230
1914–19	WWI	18,166 (Gallipoli 2,721, Somme 3,200, Messines 5,300) (NZ Population 1.2 million)
1939–45	WWII	12,050 (NZ Population 1.6 million)
1950–54	Korea	35
1960–64	Malaysia	15
1964–76	Vietnam	37
2000–01	E Timor	4

World War II: Killed in Action:

Service	Number	Details
Army	7,277	(6,235 Desert/Italy)
Navy & Merchant Marine	674	(170 Mediterranean)
Air Force	1,829	RAF Bomber Command
	467	RAF Fighter Command
	270	RAF Coastal Command
	86	RAF Training Command
	367	Middle East Air Force
	102	Far East Air Force
	330	Pacific Theatre
	436	New Zealand
	81	Canada
	156	Fleet Air Arm
	4,099	

From GG Page (2001)

Kiwis Do Fly

Chapter 21

A Memorial

With the complete restoration of a display Lancaster at Sir Keith Park Memorial Airfield (MOTAT Auckland), RAF Bomber Command (NZ) Association established a dedicated Remembrance area and developed displays including a full scale Ops Room.

During 2006 – 2009 the Association founded a memorial fund to produce a permanent bronze work to honour aircrew who died in action over Europe.

Support came from Corporate and Charitable Trusts, with many donations from ex-aircrew themselves, both throughout New Zealand and overseas.

The memorial was designed and built by Richard Taylor of Weta Workshops and depicts a crew after a long operation over enemy territory.

On March 1, 2009 in the Auckland War Memorial Hall of Memories, the memorial was dedicated. An RNZAF Colour Party stood guard while the memorial was unveiled by Chief of Air Force AVM G Lintott CNZO and NZ BCA President WJ Simpson QSO, DFC (W/C RAF Rtd).

RIGHT: The NZBCA memorial unveiled by Chief of Airforce AVM Lintott CNZO and Association President WJ Simpson QSO, DFC. Leading the prayer is Reverend Jack Ward, himself a veteran, serving as a navigator on 75 (NZ) Squadron

ABOVE: Some of the 120 veterans who attended the Dedication and Remembrance service

242

Epilogue

"In time of war, men strive and men die for the protection of their country and their loved ones and for the ideals in which they believe. No sacrifice is too great and no ordeal too bitter to deter the tide of human effort towards victory."

"Indeed, in the agony and squalor of war, man has reached his true greatness but it is only when peace comes that there exist the conditions in which the ideals for which we fought can be achieved."

"We are the same men and women who fought beside those who died. We are made of the same stuff which achieved greatness in time of war. Therefore, in peace, let us think and act as aggressively as we did in war, so that we may achieve freedom, fair play, decency and integrity, internationally and personally – which the dead of two wars so nobly earned."

AVM Don Bennett – Pathfinder Force

Afterword

"Bomber Command played an ever growing part in all our war plans and eventually made a decisive contribution to victory."

"The Casablanca directive issued to both British and American Bomber Commands on February 4, 1943 gave them their task in the following terms."

"Your primary objective will be the progressive destruction and dislocation of the German military, industrial and economic system and the undermining of the morale of the German people to the point where their capacity for armed resistance is fatally weakened."

"But it would be wrong to end without paying our tribute of respect and admiration to the officers and men who fought and died in this fearful battle of the air, the like of which had never before known. The moral tests to which the crew of a bomber were subjected reached the extreme limits of human valour and sacrifices. Here chance was carried to its most extreme and violent above all else."

"They never flinched or failed. It is to their devotion that in no small measure we owe our victory. Let us give them our salute."

Sir Winston Churchill

From: The Second World War – Cassell & Co, 1952

Appendix 1

Flying Badges Worn by RNZAF Aircrew Serving in the RAF

PILOT FLYING BADGE: All pilots were trained and graduated within the Royal New Zealand Air Force training scheme. They were then posted to home, to the Pacific or European theatres, or to Canada for further training

OBSERVER BADGE: Also known as the Flying 'A' hole. It was replaced by bomb aimer, navigator and air gunner badges mid 1942

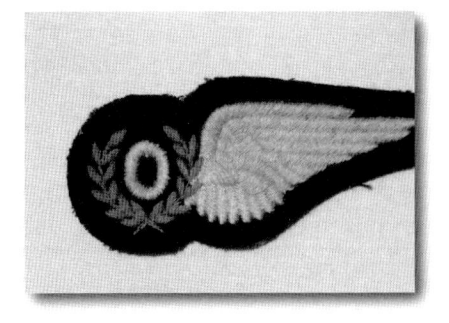

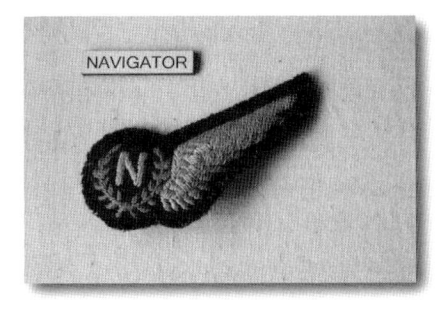

NAVIGATOR BADGE: Awarded on completion of the training course either under the Empire Training Scheme in Canada or in New Zealand

SIGNALLER BADGE: Introduced for specialist radio/radar operators

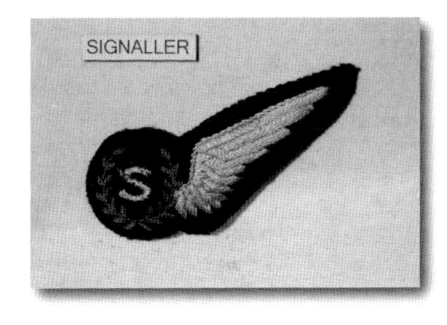

BOMB AIMER BADGE: The third new badge following redefinition of the original RAF Observers role

AIR GUNNER BADGE: Both mid upper and rear gunners wore this badge

FLIGHT ENGINEER BADGE: Most flight engineers allocated to Bomber Squadrons were English and trained at the RAF Technical Training Schools. They would join their aircrew at HCU

Appendix 2

The RNZAF at War

The RNZAF traces its history back over eighty-five years to when the New Zealand Aviation Corps was formed as part of the Army. Consisting of just two officers and two airmen, a reserve of 72 ex WWI pilots were recruited and in June 1923, this group became the NZ Air Force, an arm of the Territorial Forces. Equipment was drawn from WWI Imperial gift stocks, that had been supplied in 1919 to encourage Commonwealth countries to establish their own flying corps. It included Bristol Fighters and Avro 504K biplanes.

During 1936, in response to International concerns, The Honourable Wing Commander Ralph Cochrane was loaned by the RAF to report to the NZ Government on the feasibility of establishing a real Air Force. At the time the NZ Air Force could muster just twenty officers and 107 air crew and were still using WWI equipment.

A year later after Cochrane's report was accepted, he was appointed as the first Chief of Air Staff. The New Zealand Air Force by then had expanded to operate twenty nine aircraft, including twelve Vickers Vildebeestes (listed as a bomber force) with two Gloster Grebe fighters to protect them.

By September 1939 the RNZAF had ordered thirty Vickers Wellingtons which were ready to be ferried out to New Zealand from the UK. In addition numbers of Vincents, Gordons and Baffins were being delivered from RAF stocks. Following the declaration of war against Germany, the New Zealand Government made the Wellingtons and their crews available to the RAF. They would become 75 (NZ) Squadron and serve until the end of the war in Europe.

At home, despite service numbers increasing to 10,500 by the end of 1941, venerable 1920's design aircraft continued to provide the country with its only air defence until in late 1942 when deliveries of US produced Hudsons and Kittyhawks began arriving.

The wartime RNZAF had two key functions, the first being its 1939 commitment to the Empire Air Training Scheme. New Zealand's annual quota was:

Pilots: 880 fully trained and 520 for further training in Canada.

Aircrew: 546 Observers and 936 air gunners for final training in Canada.

The second function was the training, equipping and maintenance of twenty seven combat Squadrons in the South Pacific as first line defence against the possible invasion by Japanese and to fight alongside US forces.

Europe

No 75 (NZ) Bomber Squadron was formed on April 1 1940 at Feltwell. Some five hundred New Zealand air crew were already serving throughout the RAF and as newly trained reinforcements arrived they were posted to RAF Bomber, Fighter and Coastal Commands.

In 1941 the second NZ Squadron was formed, No 485 flying Spitfires that had been purchased by public subscription in New Zealand. Five further New Zealand Squadrons followed.

NO.	FORMED	COMMAND	LAST OPERATIONS	EQUIPPED WITH
75	April 1940	Bomber	24/4/45	Lancaster
485	March 1941	Fighter (then 2nd TAF)	7/5/45	Spitfire
486	March 1942	Fighter (then 2nd TAF)	4/5/45	Tempest
487	August 1942	Bomber	2/5/45	Mosquito
488	June 1942	Fighter (Singapore 1941)	25/5/45	NF Mosquito
489	August 1941	Coastal	21/5/45	Beaufighter
490	March 1943	Coastal (West Africa)	6/5/45	Sunderland

By war's-end in 1945 almost 11,000 New Zealanders had served with the RAF, 3,285 being killed and 548 taken prisoner of war, a casualty rate in excess of 34%. The majority (over 2,000) were from RAF Bomber Command.

Pacific

With Australia as a forward base, US troops and material staged through New Zealand and from 1942 US aircraft, spares and petrol allowed the RNZAF to expand rapidly. Following the battles of the Coral Sea and Guadalcanal, the RNZAF began to take an increasing part in the SW Pacific front.

Twenty-seven combat Squadrons were raised and maintained at eleven bases in Tonga, Fiji, the New Hebrides and Solomon Islands.

BASES:

Lauthula Bay (Suva) Fiji	Flying Boat
Nausori (Fiji)	Anti-ship Reconnaissance
Nandi (Fiji)	Anti-ship Reconnaissance
Tonga	Anti-ship Reconnaissance
Norfolk Island	Staging Post from NZ to New Hebrides
Espiritu Santo (New Hebrides)	Base Depot
Piva (Solomon Islands)	Bomber and Fighter Base
Guadalcanal (Solomon Islands)	Bomber and Fighter Base
Emirau (Solomon Islands)	Bomber and Fighter Base
Green Island	Bomber and Fighter Base
Los Negros	Bomber and Fighter Base

FLYING UNITS:

Bomber	Number 1–4 Squadrons	Lockheed Hudsons & Venturas
	Number 8 and 9 Squadrons	Lockheed Hudsons & Venturas
Fighter	Number 14–26 Squadrons	Kittyhawks then Corsairs
Flying Boat	Number 5 & 6 Squadrons	PBY Catalinas
Dive Bomber	Number 25 Squadron	Douglas Dauntless
Torpedo Bomber	Number 30 & 31 Squadrons	TBF Avenger
Transport	Number 40 & 41 Squadrons	Lodestar, C-47 Dakota

Supporting these Squadrons were twelve Maintenance/Servicing Units, three Base Workshops, eleven radar stations and several airfield construction units.

By March 1944 these units mustered 5,309 aircrew, while the RNZAFs total strength reached 41,595.

New Zealand

The training schemes developed during the early 1940s required a huge support organization which grew from 3668 personnel in 1940 to about 29,000 in 1944. Along with the demands from the Army and Navy for servicemen plus the requirements made by the War Work Scheme, who were building and servicing facilities for the US Armed Forces, 70% of New Zealand men became directly involved in the war effort. The manpower shortage reached such acute levels during 1944 that Army Units were seconded for urgent agricultural harvesting.

New Zealand was behind only Britain and Russia in its manpower commitment to the war.

Aircraft

New Zealanders serving in RAF Squadrons were operated standard RAF bombers, fighters and patrol aircraft, almost all being of UK manufacture.

In New Zealand the de Havilland factory at Rongotai (Wellington) manufactured Tiger Moths and Oxfords for training while all combat aircraft were supplied from the USA under Lend Lease.

From 1942, almost 1,000 combat aircraft passed into RNZAF ownership, supplemented by over 60 transport and communication types. Two hundred Harvards were also supplied for training, a number of which are still flying as warbirds 60 years after arriving in New Zealand.

The detailed breakdown of US supplied aircraft was: –

TYPE	SERIAL	TOTAL
Lockhead Hudson III	NZ2001–2094	94
Lockhead Ventura (RB-34 models)	NZ4501–4639	139
Curtiss P-40 (E, K, M, N Models)	NZ3001–3293	293
Corsair (F4U)	NZ5201–5486	286
Corsair (F4U)	NZ5501–5577	77
Corsair (FG-1)	NZ5601–5661	61
Consolidated Catalina (PBY-5A)	NZ4001–4022	22
Consolidated Catalina (PB-2B)	NZ4023–4056	34
Douglas Dauntless (SBD)	NZ5001–5068	68
Grumman Avenger (TBF)	NZ2501–2548	47
Douglas Dakota (C-47A&B)	NZ3516–3558	
	NZ3501–3506	42
Lockhead Lodestar (C-60A)	NZ3507–3515	9
NA Harvard (II and III)	NZ901–1102	212

At war's-end, transport types were passed to existing domestic airlines and during 1946 these airlines were amalgamated into a nationalised domestic carrier, National Airways Corporation.

Front-line types (Hudsons, Venturas, Kittyhawks and Corsairs) were progressively scrapped at Rukuhia, the last being melted down in a final clean up during 1964.

The RNZAF retained Catalinas for its South Pacific patrol work, some C-47s for transport and its Harvards for training, while new combat aircraft were once again drawn from RAF stocks or ordered directly from UK manufacturers.

Appendix 2

ABOVE: Early equipment Blackburn Baffin NZ161 at Wigram

ABOVE: P-40E (NZ3113) 14 Squadron, Henderson Field, Guadalcanal 1942

ABOVE: The first Lend Lease Hudsons (from RAF orders) on Coastal Patrol still retaining their standard RAF markings and camouflage – NZ2001 nearest

ABOVE: F4U – ID Corsair, NZ5218 'Kiwi Corsair' (USMC)

ABOVE: Lockheed RB-34 Ventura (NZ4513), No. 2 Squadron Torokina 1944

ABOVE: NZ4055 PB2B Catalina 5 Squadron RNZAF

Appendix 3

RNZAF Aircrew Training Scheme

Following WWI, numbers of New Zealanders were accepted for direct entry into the RAF and by 1939 some 500 were serving officers. With the formal establishment of the RNZAF in 1937 equipment and training schemes were established and a Civil Reserve formed.

To accelerate the initial supply of pilots to the RAF, local aero clubs were contracted for flying training and the graduate pilots drafted into the war course scheme. Those on the first schemes reached England during 1940 in time for the Battle of France, Battle of Britain and the first bombing raids on Germany, 1650 New Zealanders being with the RAF by early 1940.

Once the Empire Air Training Scheme had been organised the RNZAF had the task of providing 2,900 aircrew to the RAF each year.

Pilots undertook a 30 week course in New Zealand before being posted, while Observers/Navigators and Air Gunners completed six weeks of basic instruction before completing their specialist sixteen week courses in Canada.

Unlike other Commonwealth aircrew, RNZAF personal operated under the RAF scheme of tours (30 operations in Bomber Command) before 'resting' as instructors at Operational Training Units (OTU) and then returning to operations. This meant that the RNZAF were unable to rely upon trained crew being rotated back to the Pacific theatre. It also meant that instructors had to be trained and only at New Zealand based OTUs could operational and combat experience be shared. Engineering staff were trained and retained for New Zealand and Pacific service. As a result, RNZAF crews in Europe and even New Zealand Squadrons relied upon British Flight Engineers.

All RNZAF aircrew were volunteers and if selected, undertook a six week initial training course. Wing Commander W J Simpson recalls, "There was no guarantee that you would complete the course and you could be switched to another aircrew category at any time." It could be quite arbitrary, an increased demand for gunners in Europe could well see observers being transferred into that section. Tom Whyte, failing a Tiger Moth check flight at EFTS Ashburton, became a rear gunner in 101 Squadrons Lancasters, while Jim Sheddon, selected as a gunner because of poor maths, had a great eye and ended the war as a pilot commanding 486 Squadron on Spitfires with seven and a half kills.

The RNZAF Initial Training Wing (ITW) was originally established at Rongotai (Wellington) and moved through several sites during the war, firstly Wereroa (Levin), then Rotorua and finally Camp Delta in Blenheim.

Those training as Observers (Navigators) or Wireless Operator/Gunners were screened, and those selected for Europe were shipped to Canada for 12 – 16 weeks specialist training. Having passed this phase with perhaps just 100 hours airtime these aircrew crossed the Atlantic to the RAF reception Centres (Brighton or Bournemouth), before being drafted to AFU then OTU. Eventually, depending on demand, the airmen were posted to an operational Squadron.

Those volunteers 'lucky' enough to be selected as pilots were sent on to an Elementary Flying Training Schools course of six weeks. The RNZAF operated four EFTS, Taieri (Otago), Bell Block (New Plymouth), later moved to Ashburton (Canterbury), Harewood (Christchurch) and Whenuapai (Auckland).

Trainee pilots were expected to fly solo within ten hours, the CFI check flights being well remembered by all those who failed and were remustered. Some were given a reprieve of a few more hours training.

Another memory of veterans was there being no ceremonial parade for presentation of the coveted flying badge or 'wings.' Such was the urgency of wartime training, the flying test and examination results were just posted on the notice board and personnel had to draw their flying badges from the stores and sew them on themselves!

Following a brief leave, the trainee pilots were screened into multi-engine (bombers/transport) or single engine (fighters). The sixteen week Flying Training Schools courses were operated from Wigram (Multi-engine), Ohakea (multi and single engine) or Woodbourne (Specialised Instructor Training).

Service flying was the key role of the FTS where new pilots flew exercises in navigation, bombing and gunnery. Others were posted to RNZAF Hobsonville where the mysteries of flying boats and marine handling were taught. Most of these nautical types moved onto Pacific based Catalina Squadrons while a few were destined for 490 Squadron in West Africa on Sunderlands.

With perhaps 13 to 14 hours total flying time and promoted to Sergeant, the selection board drafted the graduates to RNZAF Pacific Group or to the RAF in England. There, more training was spent with AFU flights before posting to OTUs.

Many found themselves in 'Operational Squadrons' within a year of commencing training and with perhaps just 250 hours of flying experience. They needed to learn very quickly to have any hope of surviving a tour of thirty operations in RAF Bomber Command.

To support the huge training scheme operating from six RNZAF stations, various civilian aircraft were initially impressed into service, from Avro Avians (NZ542) to Wacos and Porterfields (NZ598). A selection of pre-war military aircraft also soldiered on including Fairey Gordons, Blackburn Baffins and Vickers Vildebeestes.

These venerable types were gradually replaced

as locally assembled de Havilland Tiger Moths and Airspeed Oxfords came into service while some 200 Harvards (NZ901-1102) were supplied from USA for advanced training.

The schools output continued throughout the war but in mid 1944 the Empire Air Training Scheme began to reduce intakes as an end of the European war became apparent. The last troopships taking RNZAF crew to Europe were the SS General Howze which left on 6 July 1944 taking 179 air crew to Canada while the Empire Grace left for Liverpool on 8 August 1944 carrying 46 radar mechanics.

In Britain by May 1945 aircrew centres still held RNZAF personnel awaiting final training and Operational postings. New pilots were being posted to the Fleet Air Arm for carrier operations against the Japanese, but the large deployment of RNZAF personnel for the European war was over. During WWII over 12,000 aircrew sailed from New Zealand for Europe, and over 3700 were killed on active service, a 30% casualty rate.

RNZAF AIRCREW SCHEME

All aircrew:	Initial Training Wing (ITW)	Rongotai 1939	4–6 weeks (Pilots)
		Levin 1940	
		Rotorua 1941	Air Gunners, Observers (12 weeks) then to Canada
		Delta 1943	Pilots to EFTS
Pilots:	Elementary Flying Training School (EFTS)	No 1 Taieri	
		No 2 Bell Block later Ashburton	6–8 weeks on Tiger Moths
		No 3 Harewood	
		No 4 Whenuapai	
	Service Flying Training School (SFTS)	No 1 Wigram	(Multi-engine) 16 weeks
		No 2 Woodbourne	(Instructors)
		No 3 Ohakea	(Single-engine)
		To UK (RAF) or Pacific (RNZAF)	

LEFT: The Hinemoa Hotel Rotorua, home to many at ITW. Lectures took place in the halls, shops and large sheds

RIGHT: ITW Delta 1944. Tom Whyte (L) sporting the white aircrew volunteer flash in his forage cap. Tom became a Lancaster rear gunner on 101 Squadron RAF

LEFT: ITW Camp Delta, John Barton learning to march in 1943. On 21 March 1944 he sailed for Canada and navigators training and a year later he was posted to an operational Squadron (101) in time for VE Day

ABOVE: The Delta Memorial plaque

RIGHT: Multi-engined training on Oxfords for those destined for bombers (NZ1260, 1261)

LEFT: For fighter pilots, hours on Harvards (NZ1098)

LEFT: Course 19 (pilots). ITW Levin July 1941 Bill Simpson on the right with John Rothwell next to him

RIGHT: Every pilot's favourite moment, in this case Robin Craw after his first Tiger Moth solo at Harewood EFTS. Multi-Engine Oxford solo at Wigram FTS

LEFT: Presentation of the coveted Flying Badge

RIGHT: Passing out Parade, 135 hours completed and 580 over Europe to come
(R Craw)

Appendix 4

NX665 New Zealand's Lancaster

The memorial Lancaster on display at the Museum of Transport and Technology's aviation collection is a late model B VII that has been restored to wartime Mk III configuration.

This aircraft was built by Austin Motors as NX665 and was delivered to the RAF in June 1945. The aircraft remained in store at 38 MU Llandow in Wales until 1952 when it was one of 54 that were rebuilt to MR standards and sold to the French for service in L'Aeronavale. The modifications included the removal of the Martin mid-upper turret. Its replacement would later cause major problems during the aircrafts restoration to wartime standard.

NX665 was serialled WU 13 (Western Union 13) and served in France for a decade until being transferred to Morocco where it continued to serve in the maritime reconnaisance role.

In 1961 WU 13 returned to Le Bourget for overhaul and a year later along with WU 21 (NX664) it was transferred to Escadrille 9S in Noumea, New Caledonia. One of their four Lancasters visited RNZAF base Whenuapai shortly afterwards and was noted by Bob McGarry, then serving as a fitter. Following discussions with Mr M Sterling (a founding member of the newly formed Museum of Transport and Technology (MOTAT), a letter was sent to the French Authorities requesting that one of the surviving aircraft be donated when its operational life was over.

In March 1964 WU 13 again visited Whenuapai and the French Government offered the aircraft to the people of New Zealand, in return for flying the delivery crew back to Noumea! The offer was accepted and WU 13 was finally presented by the French Charge d'Affairs at a ceremony on April 15 1964.

The following day the Lancaster flew on display around towns in the upper North Island and on landing NX665 was finally retired from service.

WU 13 was dismantled, transported to the new MOTAT site, and re-assembled by RNZAF fitters, going on display as a feature of the fledgling museum.

A Lancaster maintenance group was formed by ex 101 Squadron Navigator John Barton and this group, athough older and now reduced in numbers, have continued maintenance on the aircraft for over forty years.

In 1986, with the formation of the NZ Bomber Command Association under President Bill Simpson a strong partnership was formed between the Association with its fund raising abilities, and the restoration group. The 'Save the Lancaster' project resulted in a specially built pad and hangar at the adjacent Sir Keith Park Memorial Airfield (now MOTAT 2) and by February 1988 NX665 was under cover.

After two decades of work and many thousands of hours by volunteers and veterans the aircraft is fully restored and complete, in correct 1944 camouflage and markings. The starboard side is painted as ND752 AA–O of 75 (NZ) Squadron while the port side is PB 457 SR–V of 101 Squadron.

Adjacent to the aircraft are a series of exhibits containing photographs and artifacts of New Zealand airmen who served in RAF Bomber Command.

ABOVE: WU 13 arrives – last flight over Auckland, April 16 1964

ND752, AA–O, 75 (NZ) Squadron

One of 600 Mk IIIs ordered from AV Roe (Chadderton) and delivered to RAF Bomber Command between December 1943 and May 1944 fitted with Rolls Royce Merlin 38 engines.

ND752 was delivered to 75 (NZ) Squadron in March 1944, it is known to have completed an operation against Duisburg on 21 May 1944.

The aircraft took off from RAF Mepal, Cambridgeshire, and was reported missing on 21 July 1944 on a raid to the oil refinery target at Hamburg.

At 0140 hours it was reported as having crashed at Udenhout (near Tilburg), Holland, the airframe having logged 199 flying hours by then.

The crew for that operation were as follows;

PO H Burt	RNZAF	Pilot	Killed	26 Operations
F/S V Connell	RAAF			
W/O H Coedy	RCAF			
W/O G Gillan	RNZAF	W/Op	Killed	26 Operations
Sgt V Cornish	RAF		Killed	
Sgt F Carter	RAF		Killed	
Sgt G Levy	RAF		Killed	

Five of the crew baled out after the aircraft had been hit by flak on the way home over Holland. The Lancaster was too low by the time Pilot Officer Burt and Sergeant Carter jumped and their chutes failed to open. F/S Connell and Warrant Officer Coedy were captured and became POW's. PO Burt and Sergeant Carter are buried in the Gilzerbaan General Cemetary at Tilburg. On the same raid 75 (NZ) Squadron lost a further five aircraft with twenty New Zealand crewmen being killed. A further four New Zealanders were killed on the same raid, flying LM181 of 514 Squadron. A costly raid taking the lives of 24 Kiwi aircrew.

PB457 SR–V, 101 Squadron

One of 800 ordered from AV Roe (Chadderton) in April 1943 as a Mk III with Rolls Royce Merlin 38 engines.

PB457 was delivered to 101 Squadron at Ludford Magna in August 1944, it was equipped with ABC (Airborne Cigar) radio counter measures equipment.

The aircraft is known to have completed operations to:

Stettin 29/30 August 1944
Essen 25 October 1944 (daylight)
Merseburg 06/07 December 1944
Nuremburg 02/03 January 1945

The aircraft caught fire in a hangar at Ludford Magna on 03-02-45 while undergoing a 75-hour inspection and was destroyed. No injuries to personnel were noted.

Note: The fate of PB457 has been incorrectly recorded in previous publications with Lancaster PA237 which for a time also wore the codes SR–V while at 101 Squadron and was lost on a raid to Pforzheim on 24 February 1945.

Some information has been provided by Larry Wright of Canada (a Lancaster and Manchester Historian).

ABOVE: Occupying the perimeter RNZAF Whenuapai, April 20 1964

ABOVE: September 9 1987. A permanent home at MOTAT at last

ABOVE: May 9 1997 and the mid-upper turret is finally fitted. Note the wooden framework of the tracking guide coaming. From Left: John Tarbuck, Alan Wiltshire and Ken Boult – showing satisfaction after a frustrating period of engineering design

ABOVE: 1999 and part of the bomb load is reconstructed by the team
Left to right: Doug McDonald, Lance Young, Murray Rolfe, Des Hall, Doug Taylor, Eric Jones

ABOVE & LEFT: complete and fully restored

Location of Selected RAF Airfields and Bases

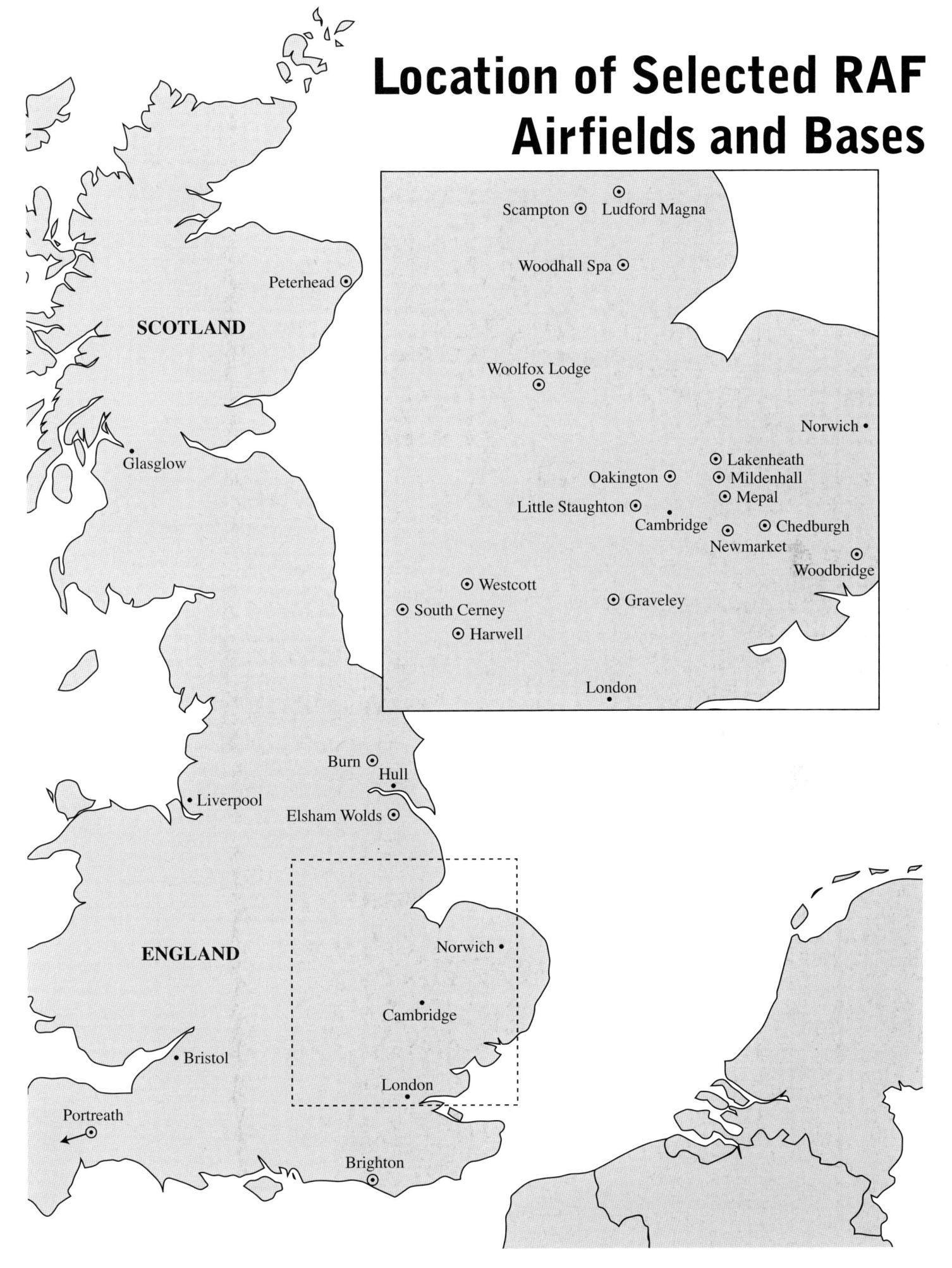

Kiwis Do Fly

Location of Selected RAF Bomber Command Targets

Bibliography

Print:

Title	Author	Publisher	Year
A Brief History of the RNZAF	Anon	RNZAF	
Action Stations Vol 1-8	Various Authors	Patrick Stephens Ltd	1979
Avro Lancaster	H. Holmes	Airlife	2002
Barnes Wallis's Bombs	S. Flower	Tempus	2002
Beam Bombers	M. Cumming	Sutton	1998
Bomber Command	R. Overy	Harper Collins	1997
Bombs	S. Flower	Tempus	2002
Bombs on Target	R. Mayhill	Patrick Stephens	1991
British Military Aircraft Serials	B. Robertson	Patrick Stephens	1979
By Such Deeds	C. Hanson	Volplane Press	2001
De Havilland Mosquito	R. Caruana	Warpaint	
Flying Into Hell	M. Rolfe	Grubb Street	2004
For Your Tomorrow Vol 1–3	E. Martyn	Volplane Press	1998
History of the Delta Military Camp	D Inkster	B.P.	1984
Lancaster Target	J. Currie	Goodhall	1977
Lancaster	M. Garbett, B. Goulding	PRC	1991
Lancaster at War	M. Garbett, B. Goulding	Ian Allen	1971
Lancaster NX 665	M. Sterling & J. Duncan	MOTAT	1992
Mosquito	E. Bishop	Airlife	1959
Mosquito Survivors	S. Howe	Aston	1986
Mosquito Squadrons of the RAF	C. Bowyer	Ian Allen	1984
New Zealander's with the Royal Air Force V II	H.L. Thompson	NZG Printer	1956
Night After Night	M. Lambert	Collins	2005
Pathfinders At War	C. Bowyer	Ian Allen	1977
RAF Bomber Airfields	J. Falconer	Ian Allen	1992
Squadrons of the Royal Air Force	J. Halley	Air Britain	1985
Tempest Pilot	J. Sheddon	Grub Street	1993
The Avro Lancaster	F.K. Mason	Aston	1989
The Berlin Raids	M. Middlebrook	Viking	1998
The Bombers	N. Longmate	Hutchinson	1983
The Dam Busters	P. Brickhill	Pan Books Ltd	1954
The Second World War	Sir Winston Churchill	Cassell & Co.	1952
Ton Up Lancs	N. Franks	Grubb St	2005
Wednesday Bomber Boys	P.J. Wheeler	MOTAT	2005
Wings Over Waipapakauri	O. Ramsey	Private	2007

Websites: The following sites contain aircraft, squadron and aircrew details.

www.worldwar2exraf.co.uk	Squadron, personnel and airfield details
www.evidenceincamera.co.uk	PR photos of UK and Europe
www.lostbombers.co.uk	Loss records of aircraft and aircrew
www.iwm.org.uk	Imperial War Museum
www.rafa.org.uk	RAF Association
www.Lancaster-archive.com	Lancaster details
www.nationalarchives.gov.uk	Records
www.cwgc.org	Commonwealth War Graves
www.kiwiaircraftimages.com	NZ Lancaster walk through
www.rafbombercommand.com	RAF official site
www.cambridgeairforce.org.nz	RNZAF Station Histories
www.627 Squadron.co.uk	Squadron site
www.associations.rafinfo.org.uk	Association register
For Airfield Sites	Google Earth
For Information	Google the keyword

Kiwis Do Fly

Glossary

AA	Anti-aircraft artillery, also called 'ack ack' and flak
AC	Aircraftsman
A/C (a/c)	Aircraft
ACH	Aircraft Hand.
AFC	The Air Force Cross, an award to an officer for meritorious flying not in the face of the enemy
AFS	Advanced Flying School
AFU	Advanced Flying (training) Unit
A/G (AG)	Air Gunner
AOC	Air Officer Commanding
ASR	Air Sea Rescue
ATC	Air Training Corps, also Air Traffic Control
AVM	Air Vice Marshal
AWOL	Absent without leave. A very serious offence in the military
B/A	Bomb aimer
Backer up	Pathfinder Force reserve target flare marking aircraft, used if the Primary Marker was off target or if his flare went out
'Bar Peter'	Individual aircraft were often called by their code letters according to the phonetic alphabet. If there were two 'Peters' on a squadron, one might have a line ('bar') under or over the letter to distinguish them. Alternatively, a small '2' might be appended, as with John Tarbuck's Lancaster ME830, UM-M2 'Mother Two' of 626 Squadron
BAT	Beam Approach Training
BATF	Beam Approach Training Flight
BATU	BAT Unit, where pilots were trained to descend to a low altitude in relative safety by listening to radio signals, in order to land in bad weather
BCATP	British Commonwealth Air Training Plan. Set up in 1939, this programme produced about 140 000 qualified aircrew for the Allied air Forces during WWII. Of these, just over seven thousand were New Zealanders
BDTF	Bomber Defence Training Flight. See Fighter Affiliation
Bleepers	Avoidance repeaters fitted to barrage balloons, detectable by the a/c W/Op
Cat E	Aircraft written off
Cat 5	Aircraft written off (the later abbreviation, still in use)
CdeG	Croix de Guerre or 'War Cross'. A French (and Belgian) honour, which can be bestowed upon foreign combatants whose heroism benefits France
CFI	Chief Flying Instructor. The pilot in a training unit responsible for flying standards, second in seniority only to the Officer Commanding
Chance Light	A powerful horizontal searchlight beside the touchdown point illuminating the landing area. A very substantial obstacle for a landing aircraft to hit
Cookie	A 4000lb blast bomb
Corkscrew	A violent manoeuvre to avoid fighter attack. A form of barrel roll with crossed controls, it was very unpleasant for the crew, and could cause the aircraft to break up. It was practised during fighter affiliation sorties
Corp	Corporal. Informal, but not derogatory
CSE	The Central Signals Establishment of the RAF, formed post-war at Watton
DCO	A log book entry showing 'Duty Carried Out' – a successful sortie. See DNCO
Dead Reckoning	Finding position in flight using airspeed, forecast wind and time alone without being able to use a visual fix, sextant, or any radio aids. Strictly 'ded' from 'deduced', but usually written 'dead'.
DFC	Distinguished Flying Cross, awarded to officer ranks for meritorious operational flying
DFM	Distinguished Flying Medal, awarded to NCO crew, as above
DNCO	'Duty Not Carried Out' – see DCO above. Even with good reasons, a DNCO was frowned upon. Sometimes DNCD – 'Did not complete duty'
DSO	Distinguished Service Order, an award to officers considered above the DFC and usually bestowed for leadership and skill as opposed to skill alone
Dumbo	American term for an air-sea rescue aircraft
E-Boat	Allied name for the German Schnellboot or S-Boot, their Motor Torpedo Boats
EFTS	Elementary Flying Training School
Elsan	Trade name of the chemical toilet carried in large aircraft. Since, however, crew members could rarely leave their posts in flight without endangering everyone, it often went unused even in extremis
ETA	Estimated time of arrival

F/A	Fighter Affiliation. RAF Fighters, often flown by bomber pilots on 'rest tours', would carry out dummy attacks on bombers so the latter's crew could practice the all important teamwork and manoeuvres to escape		enlarged Tallboy
		Group	Force of Squadrons and Stations, eg 5 Group, 8 Group
		HC	High Capacity, a type of bomb with a light case and a greater proportion of explosive. The GP or 'General Purpose' was an 'ordinary' bomb
F/E	Flight Engineer		
F/Lt	Flight Lieutenant		
F/O	Flying Officer	HCU	Heavy (bomber) Conversion Unit
F/Sgt	Flight Sergeant	HE	High Explosive
FIDO	Fog Dispersal System. This relied on lines of petrol burners alongside the runways of just seventeen selected UK airfields to warm the air and disperse fog. It used huge amounts of valuable petrol, created very turbulent air over the runway and was a serious fire hazard if the aircraft left the runway. For these reasons, it was selectively used but saved many aircraft and aircrew.	H2S	A ground mapping radar system especially useful where a shoreline or big river gave a clear image. Tragically, an intact set fell into German hands very early on, and they soon devised a way to home night fighters onto its transmissions. The origin of the designation H2S was never recorded
		IFF	Identification Friend or Foe. Radio signal transmitted by aircraft to prevent attack by Allied forces, to prevent so called 'Friendly fire'.
Flak	Anti-aircraft artillery		
'Flaming onions'	Tracer rounds, visible in daylight		
Form 700	The technical log for an individual aircraft. All problems would be entered by the aircrew, all rectification and routine servicing by the groundcrew.	IO	Intelligence Officer. He both briefed and debriefed aircrew, a two-way process
		ITW	Initial Training Wing
		Jankers	Slang for punishment duties – cleaning the toilets, for example
Gardening	Mine Laying. The mines themselves were called 'vegetables'		
		"Joe"	An agent. See SOE
G/C	Group Captain		
GCI	Ground Control Interception, i.e. radar guiding a fighter onto a bomber	LAC	Leading Aircraftsman
		Lend-Lease	The system by which America (starting well before Pearl Harbour) supplied huge amounts of equipment to the Allies at no cost. Post-war, everything had to be returned or scrapped
Gee	A radio navigation system relying on ground stations, and therefore of limited range (related to height)		
Gee-H (or G-H)	A radio bombing system, more on the lines of Oboe than Gee, able to handle up to eighty aircraft at a time, compared to just a handful with Oboe	LFS	Lancaster Finishing School. As Lancasters were regarded as the best heavy bomber by Air Chief Marshal Harris, as few as possible were used for training, that being mainly done with Halifaxes. Pilots destined for Lancasters then had just a handful of hours on the type to complete their training
Gen	Slang for useful information		
Geodetic	A form of structure consisting of light metal girders notched together at right angles, devised by Barnes Wallis. It was very effective, but only used in his designs for Vickers.		
		LG	Airfields in the desert (Landing Grounds) were numbered, eg LG 237 rather than named
'George'	The semi-official name of the early auto-pilot fitted to RAF Bombers during WWII	LNSF	The all-Mosquito Light Night Strike Force
Goldfish Club	Membership was achieved by ditching on Operations – and surviving	M/UG	Mid Upper Gunner
		Main Force	Collective term for the Heavy Bombers of Bomber Command, excluding PFF, LNSF etc
GP	See HC		
Grand Slam	22000lb bomb filled with Torpex, designed by Barnes Wallis, carried only by modified Lancasters of 617 Squadron. In effect, an	'Manna drops'	Sorties to drop food to the starving Dutch as the war was about to end. The Germans agreed to hold their fire, and not to appropriate the

	food. The aircraft flew with guns armed, but the truce held. Many lives were saved by what must have been the most satisfying operations of all. The USAAF did the same, under the prosaic name of 'Operation Chowhound'.	OTU	Operational Training Unit
		Parramatta	Target marker laid by radar. See 'Wanganui'
		PBY	Designation for the Catalina flying boat/amphibian
Maquis	French Resistance movement	Peri track	Perimeter track. Most airfields, even those with grass runways, had a paved track around the edge of the landing area. When not in use by aircraft, it was used by any vehicle, unlike the runways
Master Bomber	A very experienced pilot who assessed the target marking and directed the Main Force aircraft by radio as to which target indicators to aim at. Having to circle over the target was a perilous task. A deputy was in the same danger, there ready to take over if the Master bomber was shot down		
		PFF	Pathfinder Force
		P/O	Pilot Officer
		POW	Prisoner of War
		Primary Marker	The first aircraft to attempt marking of a target. If inaccurate, 'Backer-ups' would try, often with a different colour marker, and the Master Bomber would then direct the Main Force as he saw fit
MiD	Mentioned in Dispatches, a distinction that confers a medal ribbon		
MoTaT (MOTAT)	The Museum of Transport and Technology, Auckland, New Zealand		
		PRU	Photo Reconnaissance Unit
MTU	Mosquito Training Unit. Officially named the Mosquito Conversion Unit, and based at RAF Marham, it was usually called the training unit	Q Code	Since morse code was used for communication, a list of common questions was made up using just 'Q' plus two more letters for brevity. The two letters often related to the information requested
MU	Maintenance Unit. MUs stored and converted aircraft, and did major repairs, but most maintenance was done on the operational bases by the squadron groundcrew		
		QDM	What direction are you? (Question – Direction Magnetic?)
NAAFI	Navy, Army and Air Force Institute, which provided the RAF with additional catering	QFE	What is the barometric pressure (with which to set the altimeter) at your airfield? (Question – Field Elevation?)
Nav	Navigator		
Newhaven	Target marker dropped visually. See 'Wanganui'	QSO	Queen's Service Order, a New Zealand honour for civilian work.
NCO	Non-Commissioned Officer		
(O)AFU	Advanced Flying Unit for Observers	R/T	Radio telephony for air to air and air to ground communication
Oboe	Radio bomb aiming system, where an aircraft is flown very accurately along a curved circumferential beam and drops a marker on receipt of a signal from the transmitting station. Extremely accurate but range was limited by the curvature of the Earth, and only a handful of aircraft could use the system at one time		
		RAF	Royal Air Force
		RAAF	Royal Australian Air Force
		RCAF	Royal Canadian Air Force
		RG (R/G)	Rear Gunner
		Rodded	A bomb with a rod extending forward to cause detonation at ground level rather than below, for blast effect
OC	Officer Commanding		
Op	Standard slang for an 'Operation', a flight over enemy territory. Bomber Command usually demanded thirty Operations before a person completed a Tour, and was 'rested' in a training role for six months. A second Tour of twenty Ops followed, very rarely a third after another 'rest'. Thirty Ops may not seem a lot, but with casualty rates of nearly 50% averaged over the whole of the War, and far higher in the mid-war years, those surviving even their first Tour were few indeed.	RNAF	Royal Netherlands Air Force
		RNZAF	Royal New Zealand Air Force
		SABS	Stabilising Automatic Bomb Sight, used first by 617 Squadron in late 1943. The Mk XIV bomb sight (introduced in 1942) was used by other Units
		Sarge	Sergeant. Informal but not derogatory
		SEAC	South East Asia Command, the RAF Command involved with the Japanese war

Second Tactical Air Force	In mid-war, Fighter Command was split into two organisations, the ADGB and 2TAF. The former (Air Defence, Great Britain) defended the Country, the latter was a mobile expeditionary force that moved to the Continent after D-Day
SOE	The Special Operations Executive that organised and trained Agents ("Joes") to operate behind enemy lines in both Europe and the Far East. It was tasked by Churchill to "Set Europe alight"
Sortie	Any productive flight, training or operational, not necessarily over enemy territory. Fighter pilots tended to call operational flights sorties, not 'Ops'
Sprog	Slang for an inexperienced person. Not usually derogatory
SFTS	Service (as opposed to civilian) Flying Training School
SP	Service Police. Not a popular group, but they had a thankless task. Also 'Snoops'
Sqn Ldr	Squadron Leader, also S/Ldr, S/L
Sqn	Squadron
Tallboy	12000lb Bomb, designed by Barnes Wallis, carried only by Lancasters of 9 and 617 Squadrons
TI	Target Indicator flare
Tiger Force	With the end of war in Europe, Bomber Command re-organised to send a substantial force to the Far East. With Japan's surrender, they were recalled
Tour	See 'Op'
U-boat	German Submarine, from the German 'U-boot' (Unterseeboot or 'Under sea boat') and anglicised
Upkeep	Barnes Wallis's 'bouncing bomb' (officially a revolving mine) used by 617 Squadron on the Dams raid
U/S	Unserviceable
USAAF	United States Army Air Force. Only in 1947 was the fully independent USAF formed
U/T, u/t	Under Training
VC	The Victoria Cross, the highest award for bravery in the Commonwealth Forces. That Fighter Command received just one VC (during the Battle of Britain) to Bomber Command's 17 (plus four more to bomber crewmen not in Bomber Command per se) says nothing about their relative capacity for bravery but everything about what Bomber Command crews were called upon to do most nights
VE Day	Victory in Europe day – May 8th 1945
'Vegetable'	A sea mine, laid on a 'gardening' sortie
VHF	Very High Frequency Radio, allowing short range communication only. Long range communication was by morse radio-telephony
Vichy French	French forces loyal to the government in France 1940 - 1944, and not the Free French Forces fighting alongside the Allies
VJ Day	15th August 1945, the day of the Japanese surrender
Volkssturm	German equivalent of the Home Guard, of troops unfit for the front line
V-1	The German Flying Bomb, or 'Doodlebug', correctly the Fieseler Fi 156
V-2	The German ballistic missile, against which there was no defence
WAAF	Womans Auxiliary Air Force, or a member of
Wanganui	A form of target marker. The PFF used three main types of marker for the Main Force to aim at. Markers laid visually on the target were called 'Newhaven', those laid on the ground in poor visibility using H2S radar were called 'Parramatta' whilst sky marking parachute flares drifting over targets obscured by cloud were called 'Wanganui'. The British, Australian and New Zealand place names were the birth places of three of Air Vice Marshal Bennett's PFF staff, and reflected the cosmopolitan nature of the PFF (And the RAF)
W/C	Wing Commander
W/O	Warrant Officer
W/Op	Wireless operator
Wimpey	Affectionate nickname for the Vickers Wellington, from 'J Wellington Wimpey', a cartoon character of the era
Window	Radar reflecting foil strips, to confuse the Enemy
Wingman	The smallest tactical formation for day fighters was two aircraft. The leader manoeuvred and attacked as he wished whilst his wingman protected him. The Luftwaffe introduced this tactic, the RAF following when their 'vic' of three aircraft was proven far less effective

Kiwis Do Fly

Index

This index does not include aircraft types.
Contributors are referenced on page 14.

Ablett W/O (Pilot) 217
Acthim, Sgt J (RAAF) 157
Aldridge, Don 115
Allard Baron Antonine 25
Anderson, Cyril (Pilot) 76
Anderson, Sgt (Pilot) 81
'Andes' 176, 25, 231
Andrews Sqn Ldr F RNZAF 33
Anness, Dulcie 210
Ansell, Flt Sgt (RAAF) 157
'Aorangi' 172
Appleby, Frank (F/E) 131, 195
Asquith, Sgt (M/UG) 86

Baigent, Wg Cdr Cyril 139
Balmanno, Flt Sgt D (RAAF) 157
Barlow, Sgt Roy (Pilot) 165
Barrett, Flt Lt DJ (W/Op) 217
Barron, Wg Cdr Fraser DSO* DFC DFM 170, 184, 204
Baxter, John 192
Beatley, Bill (Pilot) 179
Beswick, F (Pilot, RNZAF) 168
Bennett, AVM DCT 86, 173, 183, 222, 243
Biggar, Jock 152
Biggs, Ken (Pilot) 179
Bismark 32
Bithell, Frank (W/Op) 52
Blance F/O Ian (Pilot) 142, 147, 152
Blackburn, W/O Blackie 175
Blaus, F/S (Nav, RNZAF) 129
Boag, F/S (B/A, RNZAF) 129
Booth, W Flt Lt 217
Bothy, F/O (RAAF) 43
Boucher, Flt Lt (Pilot, RNZAF) 181
Bournemouth 38, 202
Box, Sgt DFM (R/G) 172
Bridges Sgt Alan DFM (W/Op) 57, 86,
Brighton PRC 39, 47, 51, 96, 136, 140, 141, 213
Brook, Peter (W/Op) 87
Brown, F/O Bill (R/G) 63, 220
Brown, R (Pilot) 179
Brownie (Pilot) 52

Buck, P/O P (Pilot) 162
Burberry Gordon (M/UG) 43
Burke, Tommy (Pilot) 179
Butler, Bob (R/G) 83, 84
Butler, Jimmy (Pilot) 179
Butler, Paddy (Nav, RAF) 63, 220

Cadd Flt Sgt (Nav) 52
Cairns, Flt Sgt W, RNZAF (W/Op) 205
Campbell (Pilot) RCAF 67
Cardwell, Frank (Nav) 75
Carter, Sgt D (F/E) 205, 254
Carter, Harry 180
Castagnola (Pilot) 126
Catell Sgt Jim 35
Chalmers, Flt Sgt Jock (B/A) 137, 138
Checketts, Sqn Ldr Johny 59
Cheshire, Gp Capt GL VC (Pilot) 75, 132, 224
Churchill Sir Winston 11, 244
Clarkson, Flt Lt Dickie (Nav) 184, 185, 186
Clay, Jimmy (B/A) 131
Clements Doug (Pilot) 40
Climo, Fred (W/Op) 142, 152
Cochrane AVM Sir Ralph 21, 34, 225, 246
Coddington R 28, 29
Cook, Gordon (W/Op) 127
Cook Sgt Terry (Pilot) 56
Cooney, Sgt E 26, 29
Copley LAC 23
Cornhill, F/O J (B/A) 217
Coster, F/O (Pilot, RNZAF) 129, 130
Cotterill Sgt 23, 25
Craighead, John (A/G) 191, 192
Crete 28
Crosbie, Flt Lt (Nav) 120
Cunningham, Bob (Pilot) 179
Curry, Wg Cdr 192

Dalcolm, B DFC (Pilot, RNZAF) 167
Dalgleish Bill (B/A) 57, 85, 86
'Darvel' 50

Davidson, Doreen 211
Dawkins, Burt (F/E) 87
Dean Peter (W/Op) 43
Diack, Jimmy (Pilot) 179
Dobbin, Flt Lt (Pilot) 175
Dogwood, Wg Cdr 174, 175
Dray, A DFC (Pilot) RNZAF 168
Dumbo Missions 46, 47, 181
Dunkley, F/S (Nav) 69

Ebbett Fg Off 21
Elliot, Flt Lt R (MU/G) 217
'Empire Grace' 220
Emslie, Colin (Nav) 133
Evans, Flt Sgt Ian 138

Fabian, P/O Jack (Nav) 162
Farley, Neville (R/G) 78, 111
Farnell, Fitz (W/Op) 191, 192
Featherstonehaugh, Ted, RNZAF (Nav) 213
Fish, Basil (Nav) 75, 127
Fox, Bert (M/UG) 123, 170, 200, 218
Foxcroft, F/O DFC (Pilot) 190
French Resistance 153 – 156
Freyberg Lt Gen BC, VC 26, 88
Furner, Phil 239
Futter, K (F/E) 43

Gale, F/O KW (Nav) RAAF 190
Gay, P/O (W/O) 217
Gibson, Gordon (B/A) 123, 170, 200, 218
Gibson, Wg Cdr Guy VC 58, 76, 192
Giles, Paddy 152
Gilson, Sgt KE (Nav) 157
Gorden, Doug 115
Gould, Sgt (R/G) 116
Greenough, Flt Sgt Claude (Nav) 137, 138
Grei g, Colin (Nav) 142, 152
Groundcrew 57, 64, 167

Hackman F/O (Pilot) 52
Haden, Andy DFC (Pilot, Nav, B/A) 202

Hall, Wg Cdr Bingham 86
Hall, Charlie DFC (Pilot) 175
Hall, W/O Jock 41
Halliwell W 13
Hamilton, Charles (F/E) 191, 192
Hampton, Len (Pilot) 124
Hancock, Flt Sgt (Nav) 184
Harpur, Bob (R/G) 123, 170, 200, 218
Harris, ACM Sir Arthur 227
Harris, F/O Brian DFC (Nav) 190, 191, 192
Hart, Alan 97
Hartman (Medical Officer) 179
Hassell, Cyril DFC* (Nav) 181, 188
Hawkins, Percy 84
Hayward, Sqn Ldr Guy (A/G) 162
Haywood, Wg Cdr 174, 175
Heald, Flt Sgt S RNZAF (B/A) 205
Heath, P/O (Cameraman) 120, 121
Hebbard Colin 'Lofty' (B/A) 21, 75, 127, 128, 129
Hendrickson, Sgt Ivan 35
Hendry Jim (RNZAF) 47
Hendry, F/O V (B/A) 134
Herrold, Tony (Nav, RNZAF) 97
Hiam G 13,
Hillford, Les (B/A) 87
Hitchcock, G 124
Hodgom Sqn Ldr 25
Holden, Bob (Pilot/BA) 83, 84
Holloway, Stan (Pilot) 83, 84
Howard, F/O K (F/E) 217
Howarth, Bill (M/UG) 131
Howells, F/O (M/UG) 134
Howlett, Flt Lt (Pilot) 179
Hughes, Harry (Nav) 106, 107
Hunt, Sgt J (F/E) 134
Hyde, Bill (F/E) 142, 144 – 150, 152

Isaacson, Flt Lt PS (Pilot) RAAF 169

264

Iveson, Sqn Ldr Tony (Pilot) 126

Jenkins, Frank (A/G) 142, 152
Jillians, Sgt F (W/Op) 134
Johnson, Ron (Nav) 123, 170, 200, 218
Joll, Sqn Ldr J RNZAF 33
Jones, P/O Dudley Charles (Nav) 49, 57
Jones, F (The Hon, Defence Min) 231
Jones, Stan (R/G) 33
Jones, WJ (R/G) 130
Jones, Flt Sgt DFC 86
Jordan, Sir WJ ('Bill'), KCMG (NZ High Commissioner) 35, 36, 192
Joy, Bill (R/G) 87

Kearns, Terry (Pilot) RNZAF 224
Kilminster, Jim (F/E) 57, 85, 86
King George VI 2, 86
King, Tom (Nav) 124
Kitson Flt Lt (Pilot) 179
Knight, Lionel (F/G) 83, 84, 212
Knilans Lt N USAAF 21

Lambell, Norman (R/G) 127
'Langs Bay' 213
Langston P (MU/G) 57
Law, Bobby (Pilot) 179
Lawson, Gp Capt Ian 236
Lawton, Sgt (Nav) 172
Leeming, J (F/E) 41
Light Night Strike Force 36, 38, 164, 166, 183, 184
Lintott, AVM G CNZO (CAS, RNZAF) 242
Lockhart, Wg Cdr DSO DFC 184, 187
Long, Johny (Pilot) 179
Lumsdale, P/O (Pilot) 218

MacMullen, Sqn Ldr (Pilot) 179
MacQueen (Pilot) 179
McCarthy Flt Lt Joe (Pilot) 76, 224
McGinson Sqn Ldr (Pilot) 59
McGreal, JT, DFC (Pilot) RNZAF 168
McIvor, F/E 33

McKenzie J (B/A) 43
McTaggert Sgt 52
Maaker, Mac (B/A) 142
Mackley, F/O Bill 164
Maher, Johnny (R/G) 136
Malta 26, 27, 28
'Maltan' 75
Maltby, Flt Lt Dave (Pilot) 76
Maquis 143 – 151
  'Maurice' 144 – 148
  'Hugo' 145 – 147
  'Emile' 147 – 149
Marks, Vernon (R/G) 124
'Mariposa' 51
Marsden, Geoff (Pilot) 77, 111
Martin, F/O Phil (Pilot) 127
Martindale, Sqn Ldr (Pilot) 43
Maryan, Ron (A/G) 97
Matheson, Archie DFM (Nav) 188
Matthews Taffy (F/E) 40
'Mauritana' 141
Max, Wg Cdr R 33
Mears, Sgt L 26, 29
Megginson, Sqn Ldr (Pilot) 81
Millar, Dusty (Pilot) 208
Moen Eric 34
Montgomery, Field Marshal BL, KG, GCB, DSO 123, 133
Moore, Flt Lt (Nav) 217
Morgan, Perenara 'Pere' 37, 38, 167
Munro Sgt (W/Op) 52
Murphy V (R/G) 41

Nash, Walter (Dep PM) 229
New Zealand Bomber Command Association 13, 233, 242
New Zealand Forces Club 38, 89, 95, 98, 211
Newton, Wg Cdr (OC 75 Sqn) 136
Nicholas T (W/op) 41
Norman Jack (B/A) RCAF 56

Oboe 38, 101, 119, 122, 167, 194, 221, 222, 223
'Orcades' 50
Osborne Sgt 52
Outram, Eric (Pilot) 208
Owen, Jack (F/E) RCAF 123, 170, 199, 200, 218

Palmer, Sqn Ldr RAM (Bob) VC DFC (Pilot) 101
Parrott Frank (R/G) 40
Pathfinder Force 47, 57, 79, 118, 123, 142, 166, 168, 199, 204, 222, 223, 225
Pawsey John (M/UG) 56
Peachey Harry (W/Op) 56
Pigeon, Percy (W/Op) 76, 131, 195, 225
Pitcher, HR P/O (R/G) 217
'Popsey' (Pilot, RAAF) 64
Porter, Sgt 28
POWs 43, 47, 53, 57, 138, 140, 147, 156
Prebble F 13
'President Grant' 37
Prior, Flt Lt Dickie (Pilot) 175

'Queen Elizabeth' 49
RAF Airfields:
  Abingdon 183
  Acaster Malbis 221
  Alness 52
  Bottesford 208, 216
  Bardney 208, 216
  Bari, Italy 67
  Bassingbourne 35, 36, 229
  Benson 23
  Binbrook 24, 73, 190, 207
  Blyton 191, 192
  Bridlington 110, 111
  Brindisi 175
  Bourn 166
  Burn 77, 79, 91, 99, 111
  Castel Benito, Italy 216
  Castle Camps 61
  Castle Combe 108, 136
  Chedburgh 40, 136
  Chipping Warden 136, 211, 230
  Church Lawford 38
  Cocos Islands 169, 196
  Coningsby 110, 113, 192, 233
  Dalcross 151, 152
  Dallachy 38
  Downham Market 124, 166
  Dunholme Lodge 208
  Eastchurch 226
  East Kirkby 97, 163
  Echimines, France 24
  Elsham Wolds 57
  Elvington 70, 79, 99
  Feltwell 136, 246

Finningly 190
Fiskerton 51
Gilze, Holland 61
Grangemouth 178
Gransden Lodge 166, 216
Gravely 78, 106, 107, 166, 184, 185
Grimsby/Waltham 56
Habbinaya, Iraq 233
Harlaxton 19
Harwell 26, 44
Helwan, Egypt 31, 44
Heston 25, 207
High Ercall 157
Hixon 49
Holme on Spalding Moor 191
Honington (USAAF/RAF) 33
Kabrit, Egypt 28, 29
Kinloss 164
La Sabala, N Africa 179
Lakenheath 168, 204, 219
Lindholme 48, 56,191
Linton on Ouse 164
Little Rissington 94
Little Staughton 101, 105, 118, 119, 122, 166, 167, 221, 223
Llandwrog 42
Lossiemouth 76
Ludford Magna 63, 75, 81, 130, 165, 167, 220
Luqa, Malta 27
Lydda, Palestine 217
Mepal 42, 43, 64, 81, 92, 108, 133, 136, 138, 152, 173, 176, 205, 220, 231, 237
Merryfield 213
Mildenhall 87, 92, 196, 202
Millom 202
Milltown 129
Melsbroek, Belgium 203
Newmarket Heath 33, 35, 83, 84, 162, 168, 176, 211
North Killingholme 43
Oakington 2, 123, 166, 170, 192, 200, 204, 218
Oakley 95, 218
Odiham 111
Ossington 38, 167
Penrhos 110
Peterhead 120, 178, 179
Portreath 27, 28, 138
Riccall 216
Rosieres, France 203

Kiwis Do Fly

St Athan 52, 64
Salbani, India 53
Saltby 215
Scampton 76
Seletar (Singapore) 50
Shawbury 218
Silverstone 22
Skaebrae 179
Skellingthorpe 2, 82, 102, 153
South Cerney 38, 49, 67, 95
Snaith 111
Spilsbury 43, 176, 231
Spitalgate 19
Stoney Cross 213
Stradishall 33, 204
Swinderby 22, 215
Syreston 208, 216
Tarrant Rushton 67
Tengah (Singapore) 50
Ternhill 25
Tuddenham 170
Twinwood Farm 19, 103
Upwood 49, 85, 86, 166
Volkel, Holland 21
Waddington 70, 215
Waltham/Grimsby 56
Warboys 47, 118, 191, 192, 204, 218
Waterbeach 230
Watton 60
Westcott 40, 51, 92, 94, 97, 142, 164, 202, 213, 220
Whitchurch 157
Wickenby 66, 190, 191
Wing 140
Winthorpe 208, 216
Woodbridge 57, 85, 86, 91, 204, 218
Woodhall Spa 22, 58, 64, 75, 76, 120, 127, 129, 190, 192, 224, 225
Woolfox Lodge 51
Wratting Common 19, 42
Wymewold 218
Wyton 32, 109, 166, 173
RAF Landing Grounds, North Africa:
  LG 106 26, 3, 166
  LG 109 31
  LG 224 28, 163
  LG 237 27, 28, 30, 31
RAF Groups:
  1 Group 51

5 Group 22, 34, 76, 120, 192, 224, 225, 233
8 (PFF) Group 167, 191, 218, 225
205 Group 26, 106, 163, 164, 166
RCAF Bases:
  Calgary 207
  Manitoba 40
  Medicine Hat 49
  Moose Jaw 25, 49, 178, 179, 207, 208
  Rockcliffe 229
  Uplands 178
  Vancouver Island 207, 215
RNZAF 20, 32, 33, 34, 46
RNZAF Bases:
  Ashburton 22
  Bell Block 42
  Burnham 141
  Camp Delta 112
  Fiji 202
  Green Island, Solomons 181
  Harewood 183
  Henderson, Guadalcanal 180, 181
  Levin 37, 50, 181, 224
  Milton 42
  Nadi, Fiji 46
  Ohakea 37, 141, 169, 180, 181
  Rongotai 34, 37
  Rotorua 42, 136, 141
  Taieri 37, 136
  Torokina 181, 182
  Whenuapai 37
  Wigram 19, 22, 34, 61, 204, 218
  Woodbourne 183, 229
RNZAF Units:
  2 FTS 183
  5(GR) Squadron 46
  6 Squadron 14, 46, 47
  14 Squadron 182
  15 Squadron 180, 181, 182
  75 Squadron 229
  Aerodrome Construction Unit 50
Rankin, Percy (W/Op) 83
Reekie, Sgt J 26, 29
Relph, A (Pilot) RNZAF 168
Richmond, Hector (B/A) RNZAF 97
Roberts F/O 43

Robertson, Eddie (Pilot) RNZAF 97
Robson, Sgt G (R/G) 134
Rogers, Sgt G 162
Rolls, Harry (W/Op) 79
Rommel, Field Marshal E 26, 29, 106
Roseman, N (Pilot) RNZAF 168
Ross, Nicky (Pilot) 195
Ross, Flt Lt (Pilot) 174
Rothwell Sqn Ldr G, RAF 33
Rothwell, Johnny 37, 38
Rudkin Sgt (W/Op) 52
Rumbles, Jack (Nav) 131
Russell, Harry (B/A) 171
Russell, F/O Wynn (Pilot) 134, 173

Sarill, Bob (Pilot) 179
Sarsky G (B/A) 40
Satterly, Air Cdr HV (Pilot) 224
Saunderson, John 184, 186, 188
Sayer, Flt Lt (Pilot) 130
Second Tactical Air Force 20, 203
Seldon S (R/G) 57, 86
Shannon, Sqn Ldr Dave (Pilot) 224
Sheddan Flt Sgt Alex 20, 178
Shephard Jerry RNZAF (Nav) 40
Sherman George RNZAF (Mu/G) 40
Smith, Ian (Pilot) 179
Smith, Phil (A/G) 97
Smith, Ron (W/Op) 123, 170, 200, 218
Smith, Sgt (W/Op) 116
Snout F 19
Solin, Don (Pilot) 175
Soulsby, P/O G 26, 29, 194
Speacely, F/O Chuck (B/A) 124
Speer A 12
Spencer, Oscar (B/A) 142, 147, 152
Spriggins, W/O (F/E) 217
Squadrons of the RAF:
  7 (PFF) Sqn 2, 14, 123, 166, 170, 184, 204, 218, 238
  9 Sqn 68, 127
  10 Sqn 163

12 Sqn 14, 23-25, 190, 191, 207
15 Sqn 14, 59, 81, 170, 202
25 Sqn 61
34 Sqn 50
35 (Madras Presidency, PFF) Sqn 13, 14, 69, 77, 88, 166, 185, 187
40 Sqn 14, 32
43 Sqn 179
44 (Rhodesia) Sqn 14, 215, 216
48 Sqn 238
50 Sqn 2, 14, 82, 153
51 Sqn 13, 14, 111
53 Sqn 216, 217
57 Sqn 13, 14, 97, 163
58 Sqn 164
61 Sqn 13, 14
75 (New Zealand) Sqn 13, 14, 33, 42, 43, 59, 64, 81, 108, 133, 134, 136, 138, 139, 141, 142, 152, 162, 168, 170, 173, 176, 205, 211, 220, 230, 231, 233, 237, 242, 246
77 Sqn 14, 173, 183- 185
83 Sqn 225
90 Sqn 14, 19, 103, 170
97 Sqn 14, 76, 131, 224, 225
98 Sqn 14
99 Sqn 14, 35, 83
100 Sqn 14, 46, 56, 196
101 Sqn 10, 14, 59, 63, 73, 90, 124, 165, 167, 191, 220, 238
103 Sqn 14, 49, 57
104 Sqn 28
105 Sqn 122, 166, 167
109 (PFF Oboe) Sqn 2, 13, 14, 38, 60, 99, 101, 105, 107, 118, 122, 166, 167, 194, 221, 223, 233
115 Sqn 115
128 Sqn 166
138 Sqn 238
139 (Jamaica, PFF) Sqn 85, 166, 173
183, 184, 238
142 Sqn 166
148 (SOE) Sqn 13, 14, 26-31, 40, 41, 67, 164, 175, 194

156 (PFF) Sqn 14, 49, 57, 85, 189, 191, 192
162 Sqn 166
163 Sqn 166
164 Sqn 178, 179
166 Sqn 20, 178
189 Sqn 14, 178, 208, 215–217
199 Sqn 14, 168, 204, 218, 219
202 Sqn 14, 52
207 Sqn 14, 23, 43, 165
218 Sqn 188
220 Sqn 163
231 Sqn 196
242 Sqn 213
253 Sqn 179, 180
298 Sqn 14, 67
306 (Polish) Sqn 127, 128
356 Sqn 14, 52, 53, 169
405 Sqn, RCAF 166
460 Sqn, RAAF 73
463 Sqn, RAAF 13, 14, 70, 88
485 (New Zealand) Sqn 14, 20, 115, 162, 246
486 (New Zealand) Sqn 14, 20, 21, 115, 178, 246
487 (New Zealand) Sqn 14, 202, 203, 246
488 (New Zealand) Sqn 61, 62, 246
489 (New Zealand) Sqn 246
490 (New Zealand) Sqn 47, 246, 250
514 Sqn 167
540 Sqn 233, 236
550 Sqn 14, 43
571 Sqn 166
576 Sqn 13, 14, 51
578 Sqn 13, 14, 111
582 (PFF) Sqn 99, 101, 166
600 Sqn 52
617 Sqn 2, 13, 14, 22, 58, 75, 76, 126, 127, 129 – 131, 192, 195, 224, 225
622 Sqn 2, 13, 14, 51, 97, 202, 213
624 (SOE) Sqn 13, 14, 40
626 Sqn 13, 14, 55, 66, 123
627 Sqn 14, 64, 91, 120, 121, 188- –192, 225, 233, 236

635 (PFF) Sqn 14, 46, 69, 166
683 Sqn 227, 236
692 (Fellowship of the Bellows) Sqn 13, 14, 60, 106, 107, 164, 167, 184, 185, 187, 188
Stafford D 12
Standing, F/S John (M/UG) 124
Stevenson, A (Pilot, RNZAF) 168
Stillwell, Ron (Pilot) 178
Struthers, Chook (Pilot) 87, 197, 198
Symons, P/O (W/Op) 162
Swaffield, Don DFC (Nav) 124
Swilt, Dennis (M/UG) 87

Tait, Wg Cdr JB DSO*** DFC 126
Tallboy 22, 126, 127, 129, 130, 224, 225
'Tamaroa' 35
Tarrant, Flt Lt (Int Off) 179
Taylor, Sgt TS 157
Taylor, P/O W 157
Theseus, HMS 236
Thompson, Flt Lt J 91
Thompson, F/O 162
Thousand Bomber Raids (Cologne, Essen, Bremen) 32, 33, 36
Tibby, Frank (W/Op) 97
Tilley, Frank (F/E) 127
Timms, Bob (Pilot) 179
Tizard Rt Hon R 13
Todd, Flt Lt DH, DFC (Pilot) 73
Towson, Titch 192
Trent, Gp Capt L, VC DFC 34
Trowhall, F/S Bill (F/E) 124

Units of the RAF, Squadrons excepted:
 CFS, Upavon 86
 1 PRU, Heston 25, 207
 9(O)AFU 110
 14 AFU 167
 15 AFU (Castle Combe) 108, 136
 3 LFS (Feltwell) 136
 5 LFS 22, 216
 10 OTU 13, 183

 11 OTU, (Westcott) 26, 40, 42, 44, 94, 97, 104, 142, 162, 164, 202, 213, 218, 220
 12 OTU 32, 33, 36, 108, 136, 137, 140, 211, 230
 14 OTU 215
 15 OTU, Harwell 42, 45, 51, 81, 95, 97
 17 OTU 22
 19 OTU 164
 24 OTU 173, 183
 25 OTU 190
 29 OTU 76, 224
 32 OTU 215
 45 (P)AFU 221
 51 OTU 61
 58 OTU 178
 12 AFU 19
 15 AFU 221
 2 SFTS 178
 4 SFTS 224
 31 EFTS 49
 32 S/EFTS 25, 178, 207, 208
 35 SFTS 207
 1332 HCU 216
 1409 Met Flight 166
 1521 BATU 218
 1536 BATU 19
 1651 HCU 42, 230
 1653 HCU, Chedburgh 40, 136
 1655 Mosquito Conversion Unit 167, 173, 183, 192, 221
 1656 HCU 48, 56, 191
 1657 HCU 33, 204, 218
 1660 HCU 22, 82, 215
 1661 HCU 216
 1662 HCU 191, 192
 1668 HCU 216
 1690 BDTF 225
 Night Fighter Flight 19

'Uruguay' 50, 221

Valander John (R/G) 43
Vale, Alex (Pilot) 179
'Vulcan' 152

Walker, F/O Arthur DFC (B/A) 75
Wallis, Sir Barnes Neville, CBE 58, 76, 195

Wanganui (flare) 33
Ward, Jack VC (Pilot) RNZAF 172
Ward Rev J (Nav) 13, 242
Ward G (B/A) 41
Ware, F/O E, RNZAF (Pilot) 205
Warwick, Sqn Ldr J DFC (Nav) 192
Watkins, Flt Lt Jeffery DFC* (Nav) 194, 223
Watson, Sgt (Nav) 114
Watson, Sgt (M/UG) 162
Watts, F/O (Pilot) 173
Weeks, Harvey (R/G) 131, 195
Wells, Wg Cdr EP DSO DFC ('Hawkeye') 162
Whalley, Sgt (F/G) 114
White, Flt Sgt J, RCAF (MU/G) 205
White, F/S Tommy (W/Op) 136
Widdowson Sqn Ldr DFC (Pilot) 172
Wigley, AG (Pilot) RNZAF 168
Wild Harry (Nav) 41, 175
Wilkin, John (Nav) 190, 191, 192
Wiltshire Alan 42, 255
Winter, Joyce 213
Wirepa, F/O George (B/A) 167
Woodhouse, Gp Capt 174
Wookey Jack (R/G) 56
Wright, Sgt R (R/G) 205

Yates, Sgt RB (F/E) 75
Young, David 'Wattie' 37, 38

Kiwis Do Fly